Desire Lines

The inscription of memory through architecture and heritage practice in cities and public spaces has acquired an unusual salience and topicality in contemporary South Africa. Attempts to alter the spatial and visual landscapes of the past have been accompanied by contests over relevance, meaning and the nature of what constitutes communities and their histories. The issue of heritage practice elicits daily debates and discussions about what the practice of defining, identifying and developing heritage sites involves and the problems that emanate from that process.

This collection investigates cities as sites of memory and desire (and of fear and forgetting); as contested spaces given to plays of power and privilege, identity and difference. How have the profound social and political transformations and the release of energies in South Africa post-1994 been written into its cities and public spaces?

Desire Lines: Space, Memory and Identity in the Postapartheid City addresses the innovative strategies that have emerged in the sphere of public culture in postapartheid South Africa. The case studies pay particular attention to how these strategies relate to contests over heritage practices in community museums, tourism and other memory projects. The book explores attempts to recast heritage in contemporary South Africa as well as the conditions of constraint under which newer cultural practices and representations have emerged.

This selection of papers draws together work by architects and planners, historians, archaeologists, social anthropologists and other scholars working in the fields of African Studies, Literary Studies, Heritage and Public Culture Studies and from the spatial disciplines. It offers insight into the debates that have reconfigured the shape of city spaces, and of heritage and public culture, while posing new questions in the direction of scholarship.

Noëleen Murray is an architect and lecturer in the Centre for African Studies at the University of Cape Town, SA.

Nick Shepherd is an archaeologist and senior lecturer in the Centre for African Studies at the University of Cape Town, SA.

Martin Hall is an historical archaeologist and professor. Currently he is Deputy Vice Chancellor, Academic Affairs, University of Cape Town, SA.

THE ARCHI*TEXT* SERIES
Edited by Thomas A. Markus and Anthony D. King

Architectural discourse has traditionally represented buildings as art objects or technical objects. Yet buildings are also social objects in that they are invested with social meaning and shape social relations. Recognising these assumptions, the Archi*text* series aims to bring together recent debates in social and cultural theory and the study and practice of architecture and urban design. Critical, comparative and interdisciplinary, the books in the series, by theorising architecture, bring the space of the built environment centrally into the social sciences and humanities, as well as bringing the theoretical insights of the latter into the discourses of architecture and urban design. Particular attention is paid to issues of gender, race, sexuality and the body, to questions of identity and place, to the cultural politics of representation and language, and to the global and postcolonial contexts in which these are addressed.

**Edited by Noëleen Murray,
Nick Shepherd and Martin Hall**

Desire Lines

Space, memory and identity in the
post-apartheid city

Routledge
Taylor & Francis Group

LONDON AND NEW YORK

First published 2007
by Routledge
2 Park Square, Milton Park, Abingdon, Oxon OX14 4RN

Simultaneously published in the USA and Canada
by Routledge
270 Madison Ave, New York, NY 10016

Routledge is an imprint of the Taylor & Francis Group, an informa business

2007 Selection and editorial matter: Noëleen Murray, Nick Shepherd and Martin Hall;
individual chapters: the contributors

Typeset in Frutiger by Wearset Ltd, Boldon, Tyne and Wear

Printed and bound in Great Britain by The Cromwell Press, Trowbridge, Wiltshire

British Library Cataloguing in Publication Data
A catalogue record for this book is available from the British Library

Library of Congress Cataloging in Publication Data
Desire lines : space, memory and identity in the post-apartheid city /
edited by Noëleen Murray, Nick Shepherd & Martin Hall.

    p. cm. — (The Architext series)
Includes bibliographical references and index. 1. Public spaces—Social aspects—South
Africa. 2. Memory—Social aspects—South Africa. 3. Architecture and society—South
Africa. 4. South Africa—Social conditions—1994– I. Murray, Noëleen, 1968- II. Shepherd,
Nick, 1967- III. Hall, Martin, 1952–
  NA9053.S6D465 2007
  720.1'030968—dc22
                                                                    2006100812

ISBN10: 0-415-70130-9 (hbk)
ISBN10: 0-415-70131-7 (pbk)
ISBN10: 0-203-79949-6 (ebk)

ISBN13: 978-0-415-70130-3 (hbk)
ISBN13: 978-0-415-70131-0 (pbk)
ISBN13: 978-0-203-79949-9 (ebk)

Contents

Contributors

Azeem Badroodien is on the staff of the UNSECO Centre for Comparative Education Research at the University of Nottingham (from Jan 2006). His main academic work focuses on how apartheid and geographical/social/identity issues impacted on the ways in which the lives of institutional (reformatory) boys were shaped, and how this can inform discussions on race.

Matthew Barac's current research at the Cambridge University Department of Architecture springs from practical experience on urban transformation projects in Cape Town. He is an architect, writer and teacher, and in 2004 he and photographer David Southwood won the International Bauhaus Award.

Pia Bombardella is a graduate anthropology student. Previously she has been a researcher for RESUNACT (from which the paper for this edition emerged), a researcher and co-ordinator of a project relating to women's health in southern Africa, and an associate in the Department of Social Anthropology at the University of Cape Town. She is presently lecturing in Social Anthropology in the School of Social and Government Studies at North-West University.

Lindsay Jill Bremner is Honorary Professorial Research Fellow at the University of the Witwatersrand School of Arts. In 2002, while Professor of Architecture at Wits, she won the Bessie Head Non-Fiction Fellowship Award for five essays written for the title *Contemporary Johannesburg: Cultures, Spaces, Identities*. Her book *Johannesburg, One City Colliding Worlds*, was published in 2004. She will shortly be taking up the position of Chair of Architecture at Temple University in Philadelphia.

Christian Ernsten is a graduate African Public Culture student. His research focus is heritage management in Cape Town in relation to the institutional memory of the city's past. He finished a Masters in History at the University of Groningen, specialising in the culture and politics of civil society building in former Yugoslavia.

Harry Garuba teaches at the Centre for African Studies, University of Cape Town, and has a joint appointment with the English Department. His research interests include African Literature, Postcolonial Theory and Criticism, African Modernities and Intellectuals/Intellectual Traditions of African Nationalist Writing.

Martin Hall is Deputy Vice Chancellor of the University of Cape Town. He is an historical archaeologist who has written on the origins of the Zulu Kingdom, the archaeology of colonialism in comparative perspective and contemporary uses of heritage. He is past president of the World Archaeological Congress and Professor of Historical Archaeology at the University of Cape Town.

Tobias Hecht is a freelance editor and writer with a PhD in social anthropology from Cambridge. His most recent book is entitled *After Life: An Ethnographic Novel*. His other books include the ethnography *At Home in the Street: Street Children of Northeast Brazil*, which won the Margaret Mead Award. His short story 'La Sexta Columna' won second prize in the 2005 *Hucha de Oro*, Spain's most important contest for short fiction. His current work is on depression.

Premesh Lalu is Associate Professor in the Department of History and heads the Programme on the Study of the Humanities in Africa (PSHA) at the University of the Western Cape. His articles have appeared in *Current Writing*, *History and Theory*, *South African Historical Journal*, *Journal of Higher Education in Africa and Innovation*. He is currently preparing a manuscript *In the Event of History: On the Postcolonial Critique of Apartheid* based on his University of Minnesota doctoral dissertation.

David Lurie is a self-taught photographer who began working full time on documentary projects in 1995, following the publication of his book *Life in the Liberated Zone* (1994). He has exhibited on South Africa in Newcastle upon Tyne and Los Angeles. He received the World Understanding Award at the 61st Annual Pictures of the Year International Competition for the book from which the images featured here are taken. His latest book, *Images of Table Mountain*, was published in June 2006.

John Matshikiza was born in Johannesburg, lived in exile for 32 years, and currently resides once again in his native city. He is a writer, actor and director, and has been writing a provocative column, WITH THE LID OFF, for the *Mail and Guardian* for the last seven years.

Lynn Meskell is Professor of Social and Cultural Anthropology at Stanford University, California, and Honorary Professor at the University of the Witwatersrand. She is founding editor of the *Journal of Social Archaeology*. Her most recent books include *Object Worlds in Ancient Egypt* (2004), *Embedding Ethics* (2005) and *Archaeolologies of Materiality* (2005).

Noëleen Murray is an architect and academic based in the Centre for African Studies at the University of Cape Town. She has lectured and published variously in architecture and in African Studies, Heritage Studies and in Public Culture Studies. Her research interests include postcolonial approaches to architectural history and theory, critiques of disciplinary formations and modernity and spatial theory.

Njabulo S. Ndebele is Vice Chancellor of the University of Cape Town, and has held office in a range of public organisations including that of Chair of the South African Universities Vice-Chancellors' Association (SAUVCA), executive board member of the Association of African Universities, board member and Chair of IDASA, trustee of the Nelson Mandela Foundation, Lovelife and the Mandela-Rhodes Trust. He is an award-winning writer. His publications include *Fools and Other Stories*, *Rediscovery of the Ordinary* and, more recently, *The Cry of Winnie Mandela*.

Ciraj Rassool is Associate Professor of History and Acting Co-Director of the Centre for Humanities Research at the University of the Western Cape, where he also teaches Museum and Heritage Studies. He has written widely in the fields of Museum and Heritage Studies, Visual History and Resistance Historiography. He is a trustee of the District Six Museum.

Steven Robins is an Associate Professor in the Department of Sociology and Social Anthropology at the University of Stellenbosch. His research interests include land, memory and identity, citizenship and governance, and social movements. The editor of *Limits to Liberation: Citizenship, Governance and Culture after Apartheid*, he is currently writing a book on post-apartheid social movements.

Nick Shepherd is Senior Lecturer in the Centre for African Studies at the University of Cape Town, where he convenes a postgraduate programme in Public Culture in Africa. In 2004 he was a Mandela Fellow at Harvard University. He is a member of the executive committee of the World Archeological Congress, and has published widely on archaeology and society in Africa.

David Southwood is a freelance photographer who contributes to a range of publications from *The Architectural Record* to *Adbusters*. His work is in national collections and he recently won the Bauhaus Award with Matthew Barac. His current work is concerned with the representation of everyday life.

Abdulkader I. Tayob is a Professor in the Department of Religious Studies at UCT and until mid-2006 occupied the ISIM Chair at Radboud University Nijmegen, the Netherlands, where he directed a research programme on contemporary Islamic identity and public life. His research interests include understanding the modern intellectual history of Islam, and Islam in public life in Africa since decolonisation.

Vanessa Watson is a Professor in the City and Regional Planning programme in the School of Architecture, Planning and Geomatics at the University of Cape Town. She researches and publishes in the areas of planning theory, with a particular interest in multiple modernities and power.

Leslie Witz is a member of the History Department at the University of the Western Cape and is also Acting Co-Director of the Centre for Humanities

Research. His research centres around how different histories are created and represented in the public domain through memorials, museums and festivals and tourism. He is the project leader of Project on Public Pasts. His book, *Apartheid's Festival: Contesting South Africa's National Pasts* was published in 2003.

The **Research Unit for the Archaeology of Cape Town** (RESUNACT) is a collaborative project focusing on the archaeology of colonialism.

The **Project on Public Pasts** (PoPP) is a National Research Foundation-funded project based in the History Department at the University of the Western Cape. It broadly considers the various ways that public inscriptions of and upon the landscape of the past, often grouped together under the broad rubric of heritage, are a means of producing history. Specifically it analyses and maps the meanings that are produced in different cultural and historical sites in the Eastern and Western Cape, the genealogy of these historical productions and visitor and community responses.

Acknowledgements

One of the pleasures of coming to the end of a long project is that it allows one formally to thank the many people who have helped along the way. The book *Desire Lines* began life as a series of workshops jointly convened by the Project on Public Pasts and the Research Project on the Archaeology of Cape Town. First and foremost, thanks are due to our colleagues in the Project on Public Pasts, many of whose papers appear here: Premesh Lalu, Ciraj Rassool and Leslie Witz. The conventions of editorship single out an individual or a small group of individuals; properly speaking this has been a collaborative project involving a bigger circle of people than appear on the masthead.

In the second place we would like to thank Jill Weintroub for her exemplary editorial assistance and general guidance. Additional thanks are due to the National Research Foundation of South Africa for financial assistance; to our colleagues in the Centre for African Studies, Brenda Cooper and Harry Garuba; to Eva Franzidis and Charmaine McBride for practical support; and to Caroline Mallinder and Georgina Johnson of Routledge for their professionalism and patience.

We haven't included a dedication page in this volume. Finally, thanks are due to each of our partners for doing the heavy lifting which makes possible the light work of intellectual engagement.

Introduction

Space, Memory and Identity in the Post-apartheid City

Nick Shepherd and Noëleen Murray

desire line (di.ZYR lyn) n. An informal path that pedestrians prefer to take to get from one location to another rather than using a sidewalk or other official route.

This collection of essays examines the fertile, contested and surprising intersection between notions of space, memory and identity in the post-apartheid city. Our approach has been to view cities as sites of memory and desire (and also sites of fear and forgetting); as contested spaces given to plays of power and privilege, identity and difference; as palimpsests of historical experience, in which underlying strata disconcertingly erupt into those above; and as lived spaces in the everyday performance of urban life. As the title and unifying theme for this work we have taken the suggestive notion of 'desire lines', a term from planning used to describe those well-worn ribbons of earth that you see cutting across a patch of grass, often with pavements nearby. In the words of John La Plante, the chief traffic engineer for T.Y. Lin International, an engineering firm, desire lines 'indicate yearning' (Brown 2003). We use the notion of desire lines in a more general way to indicate the space between the planned and the providential, the engineered and the 'lived', and between official projects of capture and containment and the popular energies which subvert, bypass, supersede and evade them. In particular we have found this conceptualisation useful in looking at South Africa because here, as in many other colonial contexts, modernist planning coincided with forms of racialised population control. Desire lines, often crudely drawn onto city layouts in red ink, became the modus operandi for government-led segregationist practices.

Accordingly, the collection focuses on the interplay between forms of urban practice and resistance to these practices, between material realities and public processes at play in the post-apartheid city, and between mainstream and marginalised conceptions of space. Our argument throughout is that it is above all in the making and unmaking of its urban spaces that one can chart the development of new and emergent public cultures in post-apartheid South Africa. The collection addresses the strategies that have emerged in the spheres of public space in post-apartheid South Africa, especially as these relate to contests over identity, heritage, memory and community projects. Some initial questions are: How have the profound social and political transformations and the release of energies in South Africa post-1994 been written into its cities? How have popular projects of memory, identity and restitution been manifested in the making and unmaking of its urban spaces? What new public spheres – and new publics – have emerged in the course of a decade of democratic governance?

A key feature of this collection is its multidisciplinary nature, with contributions from architects, planners, historians, anthropologists, geographers, literary critics and archaeologists. It offers insight into the debates that are reconfiguring the shape of buildings, cities, heritage projects and expressions of public culture while posing new questions about the directions of disciplinary scholarship. At the same time it takes its place within both local and global debates and traditions of scholarship in urban studies. As a way of situating our work in relation to these debates and traditions, this introduction takes the following form. First we review those 'tropes of space' through which the South African landscape has been figured and refigured. Then we examine some recent projects and works which form points of departure for our own approach.

TROPES OF SPACE: FIGURING THE SOUTH AFRICAN LANDSCAPE

The figuring of the South African landscape in the historical imaginary has traditionally taken colonial settlement as its starting point for formal discussions of the 'history of architecture'. Typical scholarship, even by established academics such as Ronald Lewcock and others, refers to colonial contexts in which there are significant pre-existing built contexts and those in which there are not, positioning South Africa in the latter category and thereby situating the beginning of the study of the built environment firmly within the colonial period (Lewcock 1988). Questions of the pre-existing, indigenous settlement patterns and built structures (however temporary) have been studied and considered under the label of 'vernacular architecture' or through the ethnographic lenses of disciplines such as anthropology and archaeology. In so doing the study of the built environment of South Africa has been divided into what Amos Rapoport calls studies of 'high style and the vernacular' (1992).

This, we suggest, is the first 'trope' of South African space-making, the idea of the 'primitive', 'indigenous' or 'vernacular' which as a concept is perpetuated in the contemporary context in the form of 'modern vernacular' (Rapoport 1969: 2–3). New objects (and by implication subjects) of study, much like their traditional predecessors, include shack dwellings and informal settlements understood as 'the direct and unself-conscious translation into physical form of a culture, its needs and values – as well as the desires, dreams and passions of a people' (Rapoport 1969: 2). In this understanding, space has been studied as part of a broader colonial knowledge system based on racialised categorisation systems of the so-called 'Western tradition'. It is against these ideas of space that papers by Robins and Lurie, Barac and Southwood, and Witz, have been produced to problematise the space of the township (a trope to be discussed later). Architecture in South Africa that falls into these categorisations includes so-called 'ethnic' architectures (those of the Zulu, Xhosa, Sotho, Ndebele and so on), as well as the 'folk' architecture of the early Dutch settlers at the Cape in the seventeenth and eighteenth centuries.

The next trope of South African architecture is the well-known 'Cape Dutch architecture' which, although often confused with the 'folk' architecture discussed above, is the 'high' architecture produced in the period of Dutch colonisation after 1652, when the Cape was occupied as a refreshment station by the Dutch East India Company and became more settled. Recognisable for their strong references to Dutch metropolitan built forms, with whitewashed gables and laid out in H-, T-, or L-shaped plans, these buildings in Cape Town and on farm estates represented substantial societal capital (Hall 1994). The Cape Dutch style gained international attention and recognition by scholars of architecture in the metropolitan world as the only merit-worthy building type in South Africa, and formed the basis for the stylistic revivals of the late nineteenth century by architect Herbert Baker and others. The Cape Dutch is an important historical trope as it has come to signify not only the period of Dutch rule at the Cape (1652–1795), but was later (under apartheid) considered the most authentic form of South African architectural heritage. In this way recovery of Cape Dutch architecture became synonymous with conservation practice as well as nationalist Afrikaner history.[1] Significantly, the best critique of the operations of power and style in the Dutch period relating to architecture have been written by historical archaeologists (and not architectural historians), and in particular by Martin Hall.[2] It is this presence that Hall and Bombardella respond to in their chapter exploring the interlinking concepts of heritage and experience in the postmodern spaces of contemporary Cape Town.

Following this is a trope that we have called Empire, spanning the period in which the British occupied and systematically colonised the Cape. In this period, much as in other British colonies, South Africa experienced the emergence of cities and architectures that connected it to the British Empire, whereby ideas and styles (as well as actual building materials) were imported from metropolitan England and overlaid on the local context. In almost every town and city there are remnants of this. Alongside the buildings, botanical gardens and landscaped parks laid out by the British, there are a plethora of monuments and memorials to great individuals of the time, statues of monarchs such as Victoria, dockland names, street and building names, archival and bibliographic collections, Anglican church schools, mission institutions, and many more. Local literary scholar Peter Merrington, writing about the time of Union in 1910, has described what he terms the 'imperial heritage paradigm' which invokes this period of memorialisation and wealth through increasing industrialisation and the lucrative development of mining capital alongside mass labour exploitation and racial polarisation (Merrington 1997).

Perhaps the most famous spatial collaboration at this time was that between industrialist and Cape parliamentarian Cecil John Rhodes and architect Herbert Baker, producing spatial schema and architecture on a grand scale and relating the Cape to other projects of the British Empire such as Edwin Lutyens's work in India. Aspiring to domination of the African continent, the partnership envisioned imperial power along the Cape to Cairo axis. Remnants of this trope remain manifest in the post-apartheid city not only through buildings but through the strong institutionalising effects of Empire. In this collection the work of Garuba and Badroodien explore two such institutional spaces which bear histories of marginalisation as penal spaces – Robben Island and the Ottery School of Industries. These exist alongside the now sometimes shabby memorials to great achievements and monuments of the period of British rule in South Africa, but have seldom been the subject of in-depth study from a socio-spatial perspective.

The period after the Union of South Africa in 1910 embodied the beginning of the tropes of nationalism and apartheid that had far-reaching effects on our landscape and society. All the chapters in this book respond in some way to these through considerations of social processes such as forced removals (Rassool, and Shepherd and Ernsten on the legacies of forced removals in Cape Town) or through the inscription of Afrikaner nationalism on the land (Meskell on the Voortrekker Monument), as the period that saw the emergence of modern architecture and urban planning. By way of example, in 1910 Herbert Baker was commissioned to design the new Union Buildings and in his notes on his concept for the baroque-inspired plan, with two symmetrical wings placed on top of a hill in the countryside outside Pretoria, he described the meanings of the space he envisaged as symbolic of the '[bringing together] … of the two races in South Africa, Boer and Brit'.[3] This comment, a note quickly scribbled, embodies the growing blindness and arrogance of white South Africans to the majority black population, which characterised the apartheid period, from the election of the Nationalist Party in 1948 to its demise in 1994, when the African National Congress under Nelson Mandela took power.

Around 1910, under the influence of prominent public figures such as Jan Smuts, there was a rising interest in 'heritage', and in the declaration of monuments by the Commission for the Preservation of Natural and Historical Monuments, Relics and Antiques (Van Riet Lowe and Malan 1949). These monuments comprised prehistoric sites as well as colonial buildings, battle sites and some natural phenomena, and were designated under the guidance of archaeologists and architects who conducted surveys of 'Old Cape Homes and prehistoric art sites' (Van Riet Lowe and Malan 1949: 6–7). Suddenly, heritage was part of a national project, and as A.J. Stals, then Minister of Education, mentioned in support of the commission's work: 'We have every reason to believe that the inspiration of our cultural origins will continue to sustain us in our efforts to build a united, happy and God-fearing nation' (quoted in Van Riet Lowe and Malan 1949: 6–7). Subsequently, heritage preservation became a key component of Afrikaner cultural rightist nationalism. Shifts occurred in line with this so that by

1972 the list of monuments in South Africa included mainly buildings and a (limited) number of sites that represented this nationalist history (Oberholster 1972). Large-scale pageants and memorial events were arranged to commemorate the centennial of the arrival of Dutch settler Jan van Riebeeck, and the Great Trek (of Afrikaners into the interior of the country) was re-enacted in a centennial 'trek' in 1938. Historian Leslie Witz writes that 'taking place at the height of the apartheid era, the [Van Riebeeck] festival was viewed by many as an opportunity for the government to promote its nationalist, separatist agenda in grand fashion' (Witz 2003). Chapters in this book explore the relationship between history and heritage in the post-apartheid period through projects for new museums. In addition, with the transition to democracy (and in reaction to nationalist histories of the past), contests have emerged over heritage and identity, most bitterly fought over questions of burial and marginalisation (as explored here by Tayob, Lalu, and Shepherd and Ernsten).

Statutory apartheid had far-reaching implications for the shaping of South African space and, while not exceptional (many other countries around the world have been formed by racialised legislation and colonial policies of white supremacists), it took form in particular ways in South Africa. There is an extensive body of scholarship spanning the fields of geography, political studies, planning and historical studies that traces the development of the apartheid city and analyses the ways in which apartheid segregation was made material through spatial planning. For the purposes of the works contained in this book, apartheid is viewed not only as a spatial phenomenon, but rather through asking questions about location, space and place that are interrogated as intersecting and interwoven systems of the administration of people, space, power and control, and through the experiences of apartheid subjects. One of the key features of the apartheid period, architecturally speaking, was the appropriation of the forms of international modernism to signify the modernity of the apartheid state. In this respect South Africa resembles a number of colonial and former colonial contexts. For example, in a passage on 'Heritage and National Identity in the Post-Colonial World', Thomas Markus and Deborah Cameron (2002) draw on the work of Abidin Kusno (2000) to describe a trajectory of styles in another former Dutch possession, Indonesia. Early attempts to create an 'Indies architecture' as a synthesis of Dutch and Indonesian characteristics were replaced in the post-independence period by a reliance on international modernist forms as a mark of modernisation and development. More recently, there has been a move to post-modern, high-tech architectural forms, which celebrate science and technology as ways forward (Markus and Cameron 2002; Kusno 2000).

Because of the close correlation between apartheid legislation and town planning, post-apartheid space in South Africa remains very affected by the patterns of organisation and the forms of the apartheid city. According to Bremner,

> it was the countless instruments of control and humiliation (racially discriminatory laws, administration boards, commissions of inquiry, town planning schemes, health regulations,

pass books, spot fines, location permits, police raids, removal vans, bulldozers) and sites of regulation and surveillance (registration offices, health clinics, post offices, recruitment bureaus, hostels, servant rooms, police cells, court rooms, park benches, beer halls) that delineated South African society during the apartheid years and produced its characteristic landscapes.

(2005: 123)

In this 'landscape of apartheid' there were a number of key categories of space that were created by apartheid planning that still characterise the apartheid city, and are particular to South African city space. Apartheid spatial planners used international models of modern town planning approaches to segregate space. This resulted in the division of both national and city space. Through the spatial enforcement of key pieces of legislation such as the Group Areas Act of 1950, the state envisaged a nation in which people's movement was administered and in which the minority white population controlled both town and country spaces. On a national scale, farmlands and agricultural towns were declared white group areas, pushing the remainder of the population into specially designated 'native' reserves called Bantustans, or into 'townships' which were established as dormitory ghettos on the edges of urban areas. 'White space' included city centres, suburbs, game reserves, farms, beaches and mountains, and black subjects of apartheid only entered these spaces temporarily as labourers, and had to carry identification documents to certify their right to enter.

Through forced removals, the clearing of 'black spots', policies of influx control, the migrant labour system, the Immorality Act, and other devices of population control, the apartheid state managed a complex system of spatially conceived law enforcement. 'White spaces' and 'black spaces' remained separate through devices such as empty tracts of land – 'buffer zones' between areas declared for different racial groups. Education was separate and inferior for black people through policies of 'Bantu education', and spaces of resistance and racial coexistence such as inner city areas of Sophiatown or District Six, as well as rural sites of settlement at mission stations and schools, were systematically destroyed. In their place the most significant trope of space to emerge and grow was the space of the 'township', and it is this primary dichotomy within the post-apartheid city (between city, suburb and township) that characterises lines of wealth and poverty, access to resources, forms of exclusion, crime and violence, and many other aspects of life.

Writing about Johannesburg, the architect Fanuel Motsepe suggests that with the opening up of our cities, the city is becoming more like the township rather than the other way around. He theorises this as a 'township metropolis':

a formerly racially divided city undergoes a constant process of appropriation in relation to both material possession (the growth of the black middle class) and to the imaginary boundaries that every Johannesburg resident, black and white, now experiences. Those formerly excluded now feel they have every right to share such an urban space and, through their material and imaginary occupation of this city, they form links with even larger worlds. Increasingly the styles, needs, and struggles of the township occupy the centre of the city itself, whether through the interpretation of built space or the emergence of cosmopolitan fashion and music styles – kwaito and loxion culture for example.

(in Mbembe and Nuttall 2005: 197)

Following from this is our last trope, that of the multicultural ideal of the post-apartheid 'One Nation', discursively framed in the democratic moment of transformation in 1994 through the multicultural ideology of the 'Rainbow Nation'. The Rainbow Nation ideal was promoted in every possible medium, from television to billboard advertisements, and through tourist images, new school curricula and even on T-shirts suggesting a society post-race in which South Africans could find, as the African National Congress slogan had it, 'a home for all'. However, as many of the authors in this collection highlight, real 'life in the ever divided landscape of South African cities still continues to be constitutive of hybridities of real, everyday, "lived" experience and essentialised mythologies' (Murray 2006: 4). Concepts of home as explored by literary scholar and author Njabulo Ndebele in the final chapter of this book, exist in stark contrast to this ideal as new faultlines develop in South African society and in postmodern global culture. South Africa post-apartheid is as much plagued by figures such as the migrant refugee who is subject to xenophobia, as it is a site for the productive renegotiation of personal and national identities.

More than ten years after the transition to democracy in 1994, we argue that the built landscape of South Africa is, on the one hand, still significantly formed by the historical processes and power plays which continue to underpin the concepts and methods used in current spatial practices, as well as being profoundly affected by social changes and new social formations. Heritage practice finds realisation in this political, physical and social landscape that is hybrid as well as diverse, a space in which multiple publics exist and compete for resources and opportunities. In addition, the historically established built landscapes, in our cities, townships, towns, farmlands and rural 'homeland' spaces are merging as South African society is opened up to globalising forces in which the tensions of wealth and poverty create an ever-increasing division between the rich and poor, between migrants and citizens, between men and women, and between the spaces that one comes to occupy by virtue of one's mobility or otherwise. It is in this 'jamming' together of previously distinct social categories post-apartheid and their associated distinctly formed spaces that the spatial disciplines and specifically the practice of heritage finds itself in a postmodern world confronted with a whole new set of challenges.

At the same time, the period post-1994 has been an unexpectedly productive one for architects in South Africa. Bremner reflects on the scope and role that architectural projects have played in the reconfiguring of national memory and the recasting of heritage practice in the post-apartheid period:

State-sponsored competitions, new government policies, globalisation, tourism, new modes of urban competitiveness, the collisions and confusions of urban restructuring: these have all located architecture at the heart of the project to re-imagine our [South

African] national identity, and presented it with unparalleled opportunities to re-imagine itself – what it is, how it operates, what it builds and how it looks.

(2000: 98)

This is not to deny that the spatial disciplines, specifically architecture, have been inextricably tied into projects of national memory and identity historically, but that:

> The transition to democracy has been unexpectedly good to South African architects and South African architecture, hardly known for its contribution to pre-1994 liberation politics. But many questions about architecture's broader responsibilities to reshape and rebuild our society, and itself, remain unaddressed and unanswered.

(2000: 98)

At the same time a number of recent works and projects have set out to address these questions. These form points of departure for the contributions to this volume, and it is to these that we now turn.

THE AFRICAN METROPOLIS?

A first point of departure is the recent challenge aimed at local traditions of urban studies in South Africa by Achille Mbembe and Sarah Nuttall (Mbembe and Nuttall 2004). Writing in a special edition of the journal *Public Culture* focused on 'Johannesburg: The elusive metropolis', they describe a body of work dominated by functionalist and instrumentalist accounts, that treat the city as 'a problem to be solved' (p. 358). This includes post-apartheid studies, most of which fall within an urban development paradigm, and which are 'more con-cerned with whether the city is changing along vectors of institutional gover-nance, deracialisation of service provision and local politics than with citiness as such' (p. 358). What gets lost is the sense in which 'the city always also operates as a site of fantasy, desire and imagination' (pp. 355–6). 'Indeed' they write, citing the work of Ash Amin and Nigel Thrift (2002),

> a city is not simply a string of infrastructures, technologies, and legal entities, however networked they are. It also comprises actual people. Images and architectural forms, footprints and memories; the city is a place of manifold rhythms, a world of sounds, private freedom, pleasures, and sensations.

(p. 360)

Part of this is a more general problem of scholarship and representation relating to Africa as a whole. Relegated to the twin provinces of anthropology and devel-opment studies, both of which constitute 'sciences of alterity and difference', the starting point for many studies of Africa has been 'the unconscious belief that particular modes of describing reality are appropriate to "modern" societies, on the one hand, and to non-literate, underdeveloped, and "residual" worlds on the other hand' (p. 350). They write:

As far as the nature of theory and the nature of Africa are concerned, functionalism and instrumentalism have always been the order of the day. At no time have the analytical and normative strands of functionalist, neoliberal, and Marxist political economy been eclipsed by cultural studies, postcolonial studies, or postmodern criticism. As the African predicament becomes ever more complex, the manifestations of the crisis are to be found in a loss of the virtues of curiosity and astonishment at what the (African) world might be.

(Mbembe and Nuttall 2004: 350)

As to how one prises open such discourses to allow for 'curiosity and astonishment' – more particularly, to recover a sense of lived experience and 'citiness' – Mbembe and Nuttall make a number of recommendations. The first is to focus on the inherently contradictory, unfinished nature of cities, their tendency to evade and embarrass dominant ideas and schemas. Citing John Rajchman (2000), they write that 'rationally planned or not, the city is better understood in terms of the manner in which it deals with its *fuites* (leaks)' (2004: 354). Elsewhere they write of the 'unfinished city' in which

conceptions of race are being reinterrogated and remade in myriad ways; and in which cosmopolitanism resides, flourishes, or lies dormant... thrust by the force of circumstances into a conversation between the past and the future, between Africa and the world.

(p. 366)

The second is to pay attention to the 'imbrication of city and township'. Rather than an emphasis on marginality, where the 'township is both of the city and not of the city', attention should be directed to 'township dwellers' practices and imaginations of citiness or the place of the township in the making of the city's many identities' (p. 357). A third strategy is to penetrate beneath the surface of the city, to an underneath world of hidden histories and concealed labour: 'beneath the visible landscape and surface of the metropolis, its objects and social relations, are concealed or embedded other orders of visibility, other scripts that are not reducible to the built form, the house façade, or simply the street experience of the metaphorical figure of the *flaneur*' (pp. 363–4). With Johannesburg in mind, a city 'born out of a ruthless, extractive, mining economy', they suggest that the characteristic urban figure one encounters is that of the migrant worker. It is the migrant – rather than the *flaneur* – who functions as both 'the paradoxical cultural figure of African modernity', and 'the one who is both beneath the city and outside its orders of visibility' (p. 364).

Finally, and more generally, they write:

One of the more potent ways of disrupting or 'jamming' the dominant imaginings of Africa is therefore to concern ourselves anew with space and with discontinuities, to revisit our topographical imagination .... In the attempt to overturn predominant readings of Africa, we need to identify sites within the continent, entry and exit points not usually dwelt upon in research and public discourse, that defamiliarize commonsense readings of Africa.

(Mbembe and Nuttall 2004: 352)

New entry points, cultural 'jamming', leakages, the world beneath, the figure of the migrant, the unfinished city, the salience of imagination and desire: all of these imply the possibility of more open readings, as well as providing potentially productive methodological points of departure. At the same time, they serve to articulate local scholarship with global debates and contemporary directions in urban studies.[4] However, to understand the local roots of this concern, one needs to go further back to a body of work and a set of events which are arguably not sufficiently appreciated by Mbembe and Nuttall in making their polemic, and which resulted in the most important South African architectural publication of the 1990s.

ARCHITECTURE, APARTHEID AND AFTER

The book and exhibition blank_Architecture, apartheid and after (1998) had their origins in a project initiated by the Netherlands Architecture Institute (NAi), as part of a year-long focus on 'South African Seasons'. It was initially conceived as a research project and 'exposition' of South African architecture which aimed to 'begin a description of the built landscape of South Africa still undergoing a tremendous socio-political upheaval and transformation from the tyrannies of the past' (DeKler 1997). The Cornell University-trained architect, Hilton Judin, was appointed to curate the exhibition. He employed a team of like-minded researchers from around South Africa, mostly young practitioners with a more broadly framed interest in the spatial disciplines.

At an early stage it was decided that a simple exposition of architects and their work was an inadequate way to describe the complexities of the making of South African space. Furthermore, it was agreed that buildings displayed out of context were 'a meaningless architectural self-indulgence' in the context of framing such a review project (Murray 2005). Important questions were posed around the relation between architecture, colonialism and apartheid in South Africa. As an alternative way in, a set of themes or 'positions' were identified, including: 'Invasions', 'Violence', 'International Tendency', 'Fortification' and 'Promised Land'. As well as functioning as a thematic 'map' or structuring device for the book, these provided researchers and contributors with a starting point to begin to reposition their thinking about the city.

On 16 December 1998 – the Day of Reconciliation in South Africa – the blank_ exhibition was opened in Rotterdam in a glitzy affair that was ceremonially attended by the Queen of the Netherlands. Among the invited guests who had contributed to the project were researchers, curators, exhibition designers, architects, planners, photographers, sound artists, journalists, academics, literary scholars and filmmakers. A point of significance was the number of contributing practitioners whose connection to architecture was more tangential: David Gold-blatt, Santu Mofokeng, Ferial Haffajee, Philip Millar, Nina Cohen, Zwelethu Mthethwa, Greg Marinovich and Melinda Silverman. In his opening address the writer and critic Njabulo Ndebele said: '[We] should begin what is perhaps the most important South African dialogue since the national dialogue that led to the writing of the constitution. This is the dialogue about writing the land' (Ndebele 1998).

The design of the *blank_* exhibition was striking. Set in the main exhibition space of the ultramodern NAi building, it turned around a visual conceit which sought to invert the associations of light, from the colonial trope of light in a dark continent, to light which is cruel, implacable, unforgiving. Twelve hundred vertical fluorescent tubes were suspended from the ceiling. Spectators picked their way over a false floor covered with lumpy recycled car tyre matting ('made by women in rural KwaZulu-Natal from tyres originally imported from Europe', as the critic Tony Morphet (1999: 4) noted at the time). The exhibition material itself was contained in 200 laminated perspex panels, suspended between floor and ceiling, with larger objects dotted around the exhibition space. Particular efforts were made to secure and display the actual archival material: photo-graphs, drawings, maps and plans, a huge granite bust of Hendrik Verwoerd – master of whiteness – set in the dim entrance tunnel. According to Judin (1997), '[t]here are no shadows here. It is all light. White blinding light. More light in here than any could have anticipated. As if we are only moving out of light into more light. White everywhere.'

The book *blank_Architecture, apartheid and after* (Judin and Vladislavic 1998), itself a 'seminal' moment in South African architectural studies (Fisher 2004), is an interesting hybrid of photographic essays, reflective 'think pieces' and academic papers. Key contributions include Melinda Silverman's exploration of architect Gawie Fagan's early work for Volkskas Bank ('"Ons bou vir die bank": Nationalism, Architecture and Volkskas Bank'); David Bunn's detailed unpacking of inspirited meaning in 'Whited Sepulchres: On the Reluctance of Monuments'; and Santu Mofokeng's photographic essay, 'Appropriated Spaces'. Widely hailed in architectural and interdisciplinary circles internationally, the *blank_* project was poorly received or ignored at home. A millennium review published by the South African Institute of Architects, *Architecture 2000*, para-phrases Gus Gerneke, a retired professor of architecture from Pretoria University, in describing the version of South African architecture presented by the *blank_* project as 'ponderous. Deadly serious. Imbued with politics and sinister motives.' Gerneke goes on to question 'the absence of apolitical work, and work by frivol-ous architects, [as well as the absence of work by] idealists who designed … merely to produce good architecture' (Prinsloo *et al.* 2000).

With hindsight, such comments tell us more about the state of South African architecture after apartheid, than they do about the object at hand. The notion of architects as apolitical idealists who labour in the enclosed contexts of disciplinary practice 'merely to produce good architecture' remains a powerfully attractive disciplinary narrative, in architecture as elsewhere. In fact, the *blank_* project was both ambitious and well ahead of its time. On the one hand, it insisted on situating South African architecture in the prevailing contexts of colonialism and apartheid. On the other hand, it sought to shift the focus away from built structures as the iconic 'objects' of architectural debate, to issues of culture and identity, and the social and political contexts in which buildings are made and used. This necessarily involved opening architectural debate to broader debates in the spatial disciplines and beyond. It also involved addressing the messy field of engagement by professionals in the spatial disciplines during the apartheid and colonial periods, and the complexities of practice at the margins.

As a first 'thinking through' of the problematics of 'architecture, apartheid and after', *blank_* remains relevant, and elements of its methodology, its energy and its optimism have formed part of our own approach. At the same time, the lukewarm reception of *blank_* within South Africa remains emblematic of a broader reluctance to engage critically with the relation between disciplinary practices and apartheid, a reluctance which remains as entrenched at the time of writing as it was in 1998.

PUBLIC AND HIDDEN HISTORIES

Our third point of departure is two Cape Town-based research projects in which each of the editors of this volume has been involved, the Project on Public Pasts, and the Research Project on the Archaeology of Cape Town. Both projects attempt to address the problematics of disciplinary practice after apartheid – one within history, the other within archaeology – and both offer new ways of thinking about cities, their contested memories and their layered pasts. The Project on Public Pasts (PoPP), based in the History Department at the University of the Western Cape, came about in response to developments in the discipline post-1990. On the one hand, these saw the increasing involvement of historians in the public sphere, assisting government commissioners, land claimants, museum curators, the South African National Parks, the South African Heritage Resources Agency and different structures in the tourist industry. On the other hand, a developing critique on the part of some academic historians saw engaging in such work – loosely grouped under the rubric of 'heritage' – as compromising the integrity of the discipline.

PoPP was conceived as a response to the latter position. According to PoPP convenor Leslie Witz (2002), 'Heritage is a complex, varied and disputatious field and it is precisely because of the possibilities of contestation in the public domain that academics need to engage with this field.' He continues:

> We are concerned to investigate how the visualisation of pastness generates, in different ways and on several fronts, precisely what a history is about. To take heritage seriously is to look at ways in which it can open debates around the representation of pasts and consider the different ways that pastness is framed and claimed as history in its own right.
>
> (Witz 2002)

PoPP projects have been concerned with emergent discourses of memoriali-sation and commemoration (in the case of the Truth and Reconciliation Commis-sion, the centenary of the South African War and the 350th anniversary of Dutch occupation of the Cape). They have focused on cultural sites and landscapes, included contested sites of burial and re-interment; and they have interrogated new tourist practices, particularly in the areas of cultural and heritage tourism. A particular point of focus has been work with community museums, and PoPP has been involved in the development of the Lwandle Migrant Labour Museum in the Western Cape, and the South End Community Museum in Port Elizabeth, as well as ongoing work with the District Six Museum. PoPP exhibitions include *Y350? Old Memorials in New Times* (debating the continued presence of colonial memorials), *Townships, Moments and Memories* (exhibited at the Sivuyile Tourism Centre in Guguletu) and *Memorials beyond Apartheid*. If there is a uni-fying theme in the work of PoPP, then it is an interest in 'public inscriptions of and upon the landscapes of the past', and the manner in which these become a means of generating history.

The Research Unit for the Archaeology of Cape Town (RESUNACT) was based at the University of Cape Town between 1995 and 2001. It aimed to carry out research in the archaeology of Cape Town, concentrating on the nineteenth century, and to make the results of this research publicly accessible. RESUNACT projects included a public archaeology programme working with local schools, the publication of a quarterly newsletter called *Cape Town Underground*, running an archaeological laboratory in the District Six Museum and a number of excavations (at the site of the first Dutch colonial fort on Cape Town's Parade, and at a number of sites in District Six). Conceived in response to the isolationism of academic archaeology under apartheid, RESUNACT was concerned to open archaeological procedures and methodologies to public scrutiny, and to demon-strate the potential of archaeology in contributing to projects of public history and memory.

Taken together, these two research projects underline a number of themes and approaches which have been useful to us in thinking through our own prac-tice. The first is an interest in issues of memory and identity, particularly as these are rooted in city sites and landscapes, and in the processes of public history and memorialisation which have sought to disinter, rework and reinstate them in the post-apartheid period. The second is in underlining the significance of institutions of public culture, particularly community museums, as points of focus in refigur-ing the city. The third is the potentiality of new methodologies, in particular an engagement with the 'underneath' world of hidden histories and occluded experience. In the case of Johannesburg, the occasion for penetrating this world is the goldmine. In the case of Cape Town, a colonial city which is itself a palimpsest of successive occupations, this encounter is effected through the archaeological excavation, but also through the oral history interview. The repeti-tion and cross-cutting of wall footings and occupation horizons, the layered strata, the remains of the dead themselves, add a further dimension to our understanding of the city as an accumulation of surface features, to include notions of succession and decay.

And if the emblematic figure of African modernity in Johannesburg is the migrant worker, a figure that moves from the margins to the underground world of the mine, then in the case of Cape Town, with its history of (limited) racial cohabitation and subsequent segregation through apartheid, the emblematic urban figure is the victim of forced removal. The experience of forced removal has emerged as a key event in shaping communities of memory in the post-apartheid period, just as it has been central to public negotiations around heritage, identity and the transformation of urban spaces. The figure of the forcibly removed forms a kind of absent presence at the centre of contemporary discourses of the city, just as s/he haunts post-apartheid urban imaginaries. In this significant sense the unfinished business of the post-apartheid city, its lines of yearning and desire, are etched deep in living memory, form a supervening grid through which the city is experienced, and erupt into the present to define the limits and possibilities of urban transformation.

*

In their different ways the contributions to this volume are attempts to depart from the established lines of disciplinary practices, and to map alternative approaches to the city. Steven Robins and David Lurie have collaborated before in the production of a photographic essay on life in Cape Town's urban periphery. In 'Planning Fictions', Robins examines the micro-politics of housing and urban renewal in the coloured working-class neighbourhood of Manenberg near Cape Town. He shows how housing interventions are often deeply embedded in a discourse of development that seeks to create good governance and virtuous consumer-citizens out of the raw material of bricks, mortar and 'unruly masses'. Noëleen Murray's chapter focuses on the way in which modern architecture intersects with apartheid modernity, and explores continuities in the making of architectural space in the post-apartheid period. She surveys developments from the early avant-garde of the 1930s to contemporary modernisms; and from the internationalism of copied ideas to forms that claim inspiration from Africa.

Drawing on recently completed anthropological research in Cape Town, Vanessa Watson describes the limitations of planning discourse in accounting for notions of 'deep difference' and 'conflicting rationalities'. She writes that what is required

> is a better understanding of the interface between political interventions on the one hand, and the nature of responses by people who are targets of such interventions, as they adjust their everyday lives to embrace, reject or hybridise the technical and managerial systems which continually attempt to create order and predictability in urban environments.

The transition to democracy in South Africa has produced a new genre of buildings, heritage sites and memorials around the country which constitute an evolving cartography of sites devoted to apartheid memory and narrative. They are new kinds of cultural institutions, some public, some private, some site-specific, some at a physical distance from the events they commemorate, but all evoking new kinds of public consciousness and new kinds of public encounters. Lindsay Bremner's chapter examines the Apartheid Museum in Johannesburg, reflecting on the way in which it negotiates processes of memory formation, on the role of museums and memorials in the project of nation-building, and on the role of buildings as repositories for collective memory, replacing living memory with its institutionalised forms. In 'Picturing Cape Town' we reproduce the work of three young photographers who took part in a project in November 1996 looking for 'fresh eyes' on a newly democratised city. Ten years later their images evoke a new set of meanings, their own lines of nostalgia and desire.

Ciraj Rassool's chapter focuses on the District Six Museum in central Cape Town, a community-based initiative which provides a space in which critical per-spectives on the past, on notions of race and identity, and on heritage and museum practice are debated and displayed. In his account, 'the District Six Museum has created a space of reflection, annunciation and memorial that insists on the possibility of self-representation in South African public culture'. Harry Garuba gives an account of visits to the new national museum on Robben Island. He asks how hegemonic discourses of the anti-apartheid struggle and the role of Robben Island intersect with the discursive economy of the heritage industry and global tourism on the one hand; and on the other, how the per-sonal lives and subjectivities of the ex-political prisoner tour guides emerge in their narratives and memories of their time spent on the island.

Focusing on the Ottery School of Industries on the Cape Flats, Azeem Badroodien examines social institutions as sites of memory and identity, but also as occasions to problematise discourses of modernity and rationality, and notions of welfarism as applied by the apartheid state. Lynn Meskell draws on the notion of 'double temporality' to interpret the proliferation of museums and monu-ments in post-apartheid South Africa. A series of sites in and near Johannesburg – the Hector Pieterson and Apartheid Museums and the Voortrekker Monument – are examined as spaces in which South Africans find themselves acknowledg-ing, reconciling and re-crafting specific histories and pasts for present purposes.

A number of chapters are concerned with burial sites as points of focus in negotiating the legacies of the past, and contemporary notions of development and heritage management. In Abdulkader Tayob's chapter, public discussions and debate around a disputed gravesite in Cape Town, popularly conceived as a Muslim burial ground, provide an opportunity to reflect on the meanings of historical significance, modes of evidence, and the ramifications of heritage man-agement in post-apartheid society. In 'Leaving the City', Premesh Lalu uses accounts of commemorative practices surrounding the graves of Xhosa patri-archs in the Eastern Cape to open up questions concerning contemporary dis-courses of development, and the erasure of subaltern histories. Nick Shepherd and Christian Ernsten follow the events around the contested exhumation of an early colonial burial site in Green Point, a district of Cape Town. Lining up archaeologists, human biologists and city managers on the one hand, against community activists and traditional and spiritual leaders on the other, these events provide a compelling instance of the playing out of competing notions of culture, identity and memory in post-apartheid society. They also provide 'points of fracture' through which to glimpse post-apartheid urban imaginaries.

The final set of papers reflect on what might be termed the paradoxical openness of the post-apartheid city: on the one hand, the existence of profoundly new opportunities; on the other hand, the perpetuation of past discourses and entrenched inequalities. Matthew Barac's interest is in 'transit spaces', those spaces which are at the same time sites of change, set to deliver 'freedom's promise', and sites of the accommodations and conflicts of everyday life. He writes: 'It is within a reciprocal exchange between the township's improvised places and the imaginary metropolitan spaces promised by freedom that the key to a meaningful urban future is to be found.' Taken from a cherry-picker hoist, David Southwood's photographs seek to subvert the genre, being less interested in surveillance and control than in seeking out sites of potentiality and transformation, and emergent desire lines.

Martin Hall and Pia Bombardella explore the space of the 'experiential, consumer economy' emerging in new shopping malls and casino complexes. Embodying contrasts between wealth and poverty, and frequently evoking heritage in their pitch for the attention of the consumer, these malls and casinos establish their own traceries of promise and desire. Leslie Witz describes the manner in which the township tour, a characteristic post-apartheid touristic genre, incorporates heritage sites and museums to present a repackaged and recoded tourist image of Cape Town as 'the Mother City of Africa'. While the city centre is figured as a space of progress and civilisation, the surrounding townships are packaged as 'living museums', characterising an essential Africa.

Author and critic Njabulo Ndebele provides a set of 'public reflections' on space, memory and identity, as a way of marking ten years of democracy in South Africa. John Matshikiza contributes a regular column to the *Mail & Guardian* newspaper, itself a post-apartheid institution. Witty, thoughtful, keyed-in to contemporary trends and developments, in many respects his is *the* voice of post-apartheid society (or at least, of society as we might want it to be). Finally, Martin Hall writes an afterword in which he reflects on the historical embeddedness of desire lines in the social construction of space and time, closing with a pair of improbable images: Rem Koolhaas in the President's helicopter, aloft over a smouldering Lagos, and the melancholy fate of the Khoi woman 'Eva'/ Krotoa, the 'woman between'.

REFERENCES

Amin, A. and Thrift, N. (2002) *Cities: Reimagining the Urban*, Polity: Cambridge.

Bremner, L. (2000) 'Re-imagining Architecture for Democracy', in I. Low, J. Sandler and

S. Hugo-Hamman (eds) (2000) *Space and Transformation 10 Years of Democracy*, the Digest of South African Architecture 2004/2005, Cape Town: Picasso Publishers: 98–9.

—— (2005) 'Border/Skin', in M. Sorkin (ed.) *Against the Wall, Israel's Barrier to Peace*, New York: New Press: 122–37.

Brown, P. L. (2003) 'Whose Sidewalk Is It, Anyway?', *New York Times*, 5 January.

DeKler, A. (1997) *South African Seasons, March 1997–March 1998*, Rotterdam: Netherlands Architecture Institute.

Fisher, R. (2004) *Architecture South Africa, Journal of the South African Institute of Architects*: 101–2.

Hall, M. (1994) 'The Secret Lives of Houses: Women and Gables in the Eighteenth-Century Cape', *Social Dynamics* 20 (1): 1–48.

Judin, H. (1997) *blank_Architecture, apartheid and after*, unpublished exhibition proposal for the Netherlands Architecture Institute (NAi).

Judin, H. and Vladislavic, I. (1998) *blank_Architecture, apartheid and after*, Cape Town and Rotterdam: David Phillip and NAi.

Kusno, A. (2000) *Behind the Postcolonial: Architecture, Urban Space and Political Culture in Indonesia*, London and New York: Routledge.

Lewcock, R. (1988) 'Models and Typology in European Colonial Architecture', *SA Architect*: 33–6.

Low, I., Sandler, J. and Hugo-Hamman, S. (eds) (2000) *Space and Transformation 10 Years of Democracy*, the Digest of South African Architecture 2004/2005, Cape Town: Picasso Publishers.

Markus, T.A. and Cameron, D. (2002) *The Words between the Spaces: Buildings and Language*, London and New York: Routledge.

Mbembe, A and Nuttall, S. (2004) 'Writing the World from an African Metropolis', *Public Culture* 16 (3): 347–72.

—— (2005) 'A Blasé Attitude: A Response to Michael Watts', *Public Culture* 17 (1): 193–201.

Merrington, P. (1997) 'Heritage, Genealogy, and the Inventing of Union, South Africa, 1910', Africa Seminar, Centre for African Studies, University of Cape Town, 7 May.

Morphet, T. (1999) 'Divided Spaces', *Mail & Guardian* 8–14 January: 4.

Murray, N. (2005) 'Spaces of Discipline/Disciplines of Space: Modern Architecture and Uytenbogaardt's Dutch Reformed Church in Welkom, South Africa', Programme for Science Studies in the South Seminar, University of Cape Town.

—— (2006) 'Reframing the "Contemporary", Architecture and the Postcolony' in T. Deckler, A. Graupner and H. Rasmuss (eds) *Contemporary Architecture in a Landscape of Transition*, Cape Town: Double Storey: 4–8.

Ndebele, N. (1998) Unpublished opening address, *blank_Architecture, apartheid and after* exhibition, Netherlands Architecture Institute, Rotterdam, 16 December.

Oberholster, J.J. (1972) *The Historical Monuments of South Africa*, Cape Town: Rembrandt van Rijn Foundation for Culture.

Prinsloo, I., Van Wyk, L., De Beer, I. and Jacobs, H. (eds) (2000) *Architecture 2000: A Review of South African Architecture*, Cape Town: Picasso Headline Publishers.

Rajchman, J. (2000) *The Deleuze Connections*, Cambridge, MA: MIT Press.

Rapoport, A. (1969) *House, Form and Culture*, New Jersey: Prentice-Hall.

—— (1992) 'On Cultural Landscapes', *Traditional Dwellings and Settlements Review* 3 (2): 33–47.

Smith, D. (ed.) (1992) *The Apartheid City and Beyond: Urbanisation and Social Change in South Africa*, London and Johannesburg: Routledge and Wits University Press.

Van Riet Lowe, C. and Malan, B.D. (eds) (1949) *The Monuments of South Africa*, Johannesburg: State Information Office.

Watts, M. (2005) 'Baudelaire over Berea, Simmel over Sandton?' *Public Culture* 17 (1): 181–92.

Witz, L (2002) Research report: Project on Public Pasts (PoPP) for the National Research Foundation, www.uwc.ac.za/arts/history/researchindex.htm#POPP.

—— (2003) *Apartheid's Festival, Contesting South Africa's National Pasts*, Bloomington and Indianapolis: Indiana University Press.

Part I

Planning Fictions

Chapter 1: Planning Fictions

The Limits of Spatial Engineering and Governance in a Cape Flats Ghetto

Steven Robins

When a tornado swept through Manenberg, a working-class, coloured community on the Cape Flats in 1999, a senior city official told reporters that this was a Godsend; it was divine intervention. Manenberg had for many years been the nerve centre of Cape Town's gang and drug underworld, and the destruction of a number of three-storey flats in Manenberg was seen as an opportunity to raze these buildings and rebuild the area from ground zero. It was widely believed that Manenberg's rental flats had become gang strongholds, and by building freestanding, low-income houses and introducing individual home ownership, it would be possible to rebuild Manenberg as a virtuous community of responsible property owners. Not only would this undermine de facto gang control over access to a significant section of the City of Cape Town's (CCT) rental stock, but the 'rent-to-buy' housing scheme would reduce residents' dependency on a paternalistic local state. However, the scheme encountered violent resistance from former backyard shack-dwellers and unemployed residents who were excluded from participating in this housing programme. In addition, many back-yarders were violently opposed to the fact that outsiders from various parts of Cape Town qualified for homes as part of the programme. Following the destruction of property at the construction site, the CCT successfully sought a court interdict preventing a group of community activists from approaching the building site.

The developments after the Manenberg tornado raise a number of questions: Why did this 'progressive' CCT housing and tornado rehabilitation programme find itself in direct conflict with the so-called beneficiaries? How did city planners and officials come to believe that individual home ownership could dramatically transform the social fabric of this working-class neighbourhood characterised by exceptionally high levels of unemployment, crime, gangsterism and violence? What kinds of utopian visions animated such faith in modernist socio-spatial engineering? And, finally, what is it about modern states that seems to result in the endless recycling of these planning fictions?

STATES OF SURVEILLANCE AND FICTIONS OF CONTROL?

James Scott's influential book, *Seeing Like a State* (1998), attempts to understand statecraft as a process of rendering populations 'legible'. Scott argues that this has been achieved through a series of disparate state practices of surveillance and control including sedentarisation, the creation of permanent names, the establishment of cadastral surveys and population registers, the invention of freehold tenure, the standardisation of language and legal discourse, the design of cities and the organisation of transportation. These practices have functioned 'as attempts at legibility and simplification':

> Much of early statecraft seemed similarly devoted to rationalizing and standardizing what was a social hieroglyph into a legible and administratively more convenient format. The social simplifications thus introduced not only permitted a more finely tuned system of taxation and conscription but also greatly enhanced state capacity. They made possible quite discriminating interventions of every kind, such as public-health, political surveillance, and relief for the poor.
>
> (Scott 1998: 3)

Scott concludes that these state interventions tend to fail because they are designed and implemented as top-down, standardised packages that ignore the complexity of informal social processes. Nonetheless these state technologies of surveillance and control appear to have had some successes in the advanced capitalist countries of the North. It is less clear, however, to what degree these state technologies and practices have been effective in colonial and postcolonial countries in the developing world.

This question is taken up in Timothy Mitchell's *Colonizing Egypt* (1998). Mitchell draws on a Foucauldian analysis of the modern disciplinary state to investigate new forms of colonial state power based on the re-ordering of space and the surveillance and control of its occupants. According to Mitchell, the Panopticon and similar disciplinary institutions were developed and introduced, in many instances, not in France and England, but on the colonial frontiers of Europe, in places like Russia, India, North and South America, and Egypt. Nineteenth-century Cairo, for example, provided an excellent opportunity to establish a modern state based on the new methods of disciplinary powers including military reform, the supervision of hygiene and public health, compulsory schooling, agricultural reforms involving controls over movement, production and consumption, and the rebuilding of Cairo and other Egyptian towns and villages to create a system of regular, open streets that were conducive to surveillance and control (Mitchell 1998: x).[1]

James Scott, Tim Mitchell and Foucauldian analyses of development discourse more generally (see Escobar 1995; Ferguson 1990) tend to stress the omnipotence of state discourses and the docility of subject-citizens, who appear in these writings as passive victims of an all-encompassing modern state apparatus. The Manenberg case study, however, draws attention to problems with

Foucauldian analyses of disciplinary institutions and the surveillance state. Every-day life in 'unruly' places such as Manenberg draws attention to the limits of state power and control, for example, by highlighting the agency and resistance of citizens who are exposed to state interventions. In other words, these are any-thing but the docile subject-citizens assumed in much Foucaultian analysis.

The post-apartheid state has encountered countless problems in its attempts to 'reclaim the townships'. These problems include urban land inva-sions, high levels of crime and violence, and the non-payment of rental, rates and levies for water and electricity. One of the most serious problems faced by the state is how to deal with 'informal' and illegal activities that are increasingly sustained by a political economy of criminal syndicates and gangs involved in drug trafficking and other illegal activities. Working-class communities are no longer the romanticised spaces of heroic resistance to apartheid. Instead, many of these poor communities have become, from the perspective of the state, 'unruly' spaces of dysfunction and disorder.

Attempts by the CCT to re-establish governance in Manenberg were directed through a variety of interventions including the introduction of indi-vidual home ownership, 'oil spot' strategies of policing and crime prevention, and the 'hardening' and protection of public facilities. In other words, significant aspects of the city's intervention involved what Sally Merry (2001) refers to as 'spatial governmentality'. Starting from the premise that 'houses are much more than bricks and mortar', this chapter examines the micro-politics and develop-ment discourses of housing and urban renewal in Manenberg following the tornado that swept through the neighbourhood in 1999. It shows how housing interventions are often deeply embedded in ideological conceptions of 'develop-ment' that seek to create good governance and virtuous consumer-citizens out of the raw material of bricks, mortar and 'the unruly masses'.[2] It will become clear that, despite claims to the contrary, low-income housing and urban plan-ning in South Africa has always been ideologically charged, and planners, policy-makers, city managers and activists have engaged with urban development interventions in relation to politically charged questions of race, ethnicity, cit-izenship and governance.

Manenberg regularly features in the media as a space of 'social pathology' and dysfunctionality, a representation that is reproduced through almost daily violence and gang killings. It is also associated with the highly militaristic and hierarchical prison gangs such as the '28s' and '26s' that have in recent years transformed themselves into sophisticated corporate structures connected to multinational drug cartels and crime syndicates such as 'The Firm', the 'Hard Livings' and the 'Americans'. Drug trafficking, alcohol sales and distribution, gun-running, taxis and sex work are the major sources of revenue of this multibillion-dollar industry. With its extremely high levels of unemployment and poverty, Manenberg has become a ripe recruiting ground for the foot soldiers of the drug kingpins, the merchants and hitmen.

It was within this scenario that planners, policy-makers and senior managers identified Manenberg as one of Cape Town's six 'zones of poverty'[3] that required 'special treatment'. The devastation unleashed during the tornado provided a unique opportunity to intervene in the social fabric and spatial design of Manenberg. The city's Department of Community Development (Devcom) was responsible for the implementation of the tornado rebuild and urban regeneration programmes in Manenberg.[4] In line with statutory development frameworks, CCT defined its major tasks as: (1) to re-establish governance in a gang-ravaged part of Cape Town; (2) to bring marginalised citizens into the mainstream market economy; and (3) to create conditions conducive to citizen participation in everyday political life (Devcom director Ahmedi Vawda, personal correspondence; see Chipkin 2005).

One of Devcom's key strategies was to use individual ownership of low-income houses as a means towards rebuilding moral and political community and breaking the stranglehold of gangs that controlled many council rental flats ('courts'). A key element in this strategy was to replace rental housing with individual home ownership. Council flats were perceived to reproduce the conditions of welfare dependency that contributed towards the disintegration of the nuclear family, which was deemed responsible for systemic social problems in Manenberg. Devcom's argument was that the Manenberg community was 'dysfunctional' because family units tended towards disintegration and were therefore unable to socialise youth into adulthood (see Chipkin 2005; Salo 2005). Devcom's task, then, was to create the conditions for 'proper' governance and citizenship in what was deemed to be a 'dysfunctional' community.[5]

City strategists assumed that it would be possible to re-establish governance and improve the neighbourhood through a combination of individual home ownership and urban spatial design innovations. For instance, one of the problems identified with Manenberg's flats was that gangsters had open access through the courtyards. Barriers were subsequently built around existing courtyards and new houses in order to limit access to outsiders. It will be shown that the planners' over-emphasis on physical form and spatial design did not take into account the structural dimensions of the political economy of gang violence. Neither was this spatial design approach able to counter the socio-cultural dimensions of gang culture by addressing the 'distinctive milieus for social interaction from which individual [gang members] derive their values, expectations, habits and states of consciousness' (Harvey 1985: 118).[6]

City managers and planners believed that home ownership and spatial design alone could make a significant contribution towards re-establishing governance in Manenberg. The scheme that was introduced, however, was challenged by community activists, poorer residents, illegal sub-tenants and backyard shack-dwellers who were initially excluded from the scheme.[7] The liberal individualist conception of the 'consumer-citizen' (or 'citizen-customer') clashed with deeply embedded community structures, neighbourhood and gang networks, and communal solidarities of residents, especially within poorer sections of the community. Community activists claimed that the city was undermining community interests and 'community consciousness'. The city council's attempt to create a 'new citizen identity' through home ownership was bound to encounter obstacles given the political economy of gangs, drug trafficking and everyday violence in Manenberg.[8]

THE STRUCTURAL DIMENSIONS OF GANG VIOLENCE AND 'DYSFUNCTIONAL' COMMUNITIES

In terms of CCT thinking, home ownership would facilitate the creation of a secondary housing market and the improvement of the built environment, thereby acting as a catalyst for urban regeneration programmes. It was believed that housing development could contribute towards improving the built environment and the social fabric and moral economy of Manenberg. The city's scheme sought to establish a secondary housing market that would kickstart a cycle of upward mobility through the creation and expansion of poor people's investment in their asset base. This would in turn stimulate the local economy and increase the rates base (*Community Development Report* 2000). In other words, along with safety and security projects and economic development programmes, housing would become a key catalyst for a systemic programme of urban regeneration.

The Manenberg Disaster Committee (MDC), a civic organisation that emerged in response to the 1999 tornado, challenged the city council's housing scheme by claiming that it ran counter to community interests. It appeared that the city council's senior managers and planners did not properly understand the political and economic structures that reproduced poverty, crime, violence and 'dysfunctional' patterns of behaviour associated with places like Manenberg. Council management failed to understand and acknowledge the structural and institutional obstacles to attempts to re-establish governance and incorporate 'the poor' into the market economy.

For decades, the city council has been dominated by engineers and planning technocrats for whom the provision of basic services (water, electricity and refuse collection), rather than community development, has been seen to be its core business. This technicist perspective failed to appreciate the social and political implications of Cape Town's drug economy, gang violence and unemployment for governance and service delivery. As a result, the council was unwilling and unable to address the impact of growing unemployment resulting from shifts from a traditional manufacturing economy to a service sector economy focusing on tourism, the film industry, and IT and financial services.[9]

Instead of addressing the implications of these job losses, CCT senior management and the private sector celebrated the fact that, in the first ten months of 2001, R7-billion had been poured into huge building projects in central Cape Town (*Sunday Times* 11 November 2001). This fitted in with private sector and council fantasies of establishing Cape Town as a globally competitive service economy replete with international convention centres and five-star hotels, business and recreation centres and mega-shopping mall developments. None of these developments, however, are likely to provide significant numbers of jobs to people living in Manenberg or other working-class Cape Flats townships.

The formal economy is thus increasingly unable to provide employment to poorly educated and unskilled residents of neighbourhoods such as Manenberg. By contrast, opportunities do seem to exist for those willing and able to particip-ate in the violent economies of drug trafficking, protection, extortion, crime, sex work and the taxi industry. While most gang members in Manenberg are young men who spend their days fighting over women, masculine pride and reputa-tions for toughness, their activities are tied to the recruitment of dealers and merchants into massive drug operations based in other parts of the city, for instance Green Point and Sea Point. In addition to these very real economic opportunities, the lure and glamour of gang culture is fuelled by urban mytholo-gies surrounding notoriously wealthy and powerful 'Hard Livings' gangsters such as the Staggie brothers. Notwithstanding attempts by the council to re-establish governance and spatial governmentality through the creation of safe public spaces, these initiatives continue to be undermined by this political economy of crime, violence and unemployment.

A (POST) DREAMSCAPE AT THE CAPE OF STORMS

Cape Town's city managers and planners imagine their city's future as a globally competitive city with advanced IT and financial service sectors, and a booming tourism industry with world-class hotels and convention centres, a Californian dreamscape at the tip of Africa. Although the 'Californianisation' of Cape Town is indeed taking place, it seems to be replicating itself less as Africa's Silicon Valley than as a fortress city of gated communities (Caldeira 1996, 2000), featur-ing 'zero-tolerance' policing, community policing strategies (for example, neigh-bourhood watches, commandos and vigilante groups), private security companies, automated surveillance cameras, barbed-wire fencing and vicious guard dogs on one side of the divide and urban ghettos of racialised poverty and violence on the other (Davis 1990; Nederveen Pieterse 2000). After apartheid, the 'black townships' of Cape Town have become even more segregated and disconnected from the white middle-class parts of the city. In a context of rising levels of crime and violence, the townships are perceived by middle-class subur-ban residents to be even more dangerous and 'unruly' than they were under apartheid.

Despite concerted city-wide planning initiatives aimed at desegregating the apartheid city, the everyday socio-spatial legacies of apartheid continue to be reproduced: middle-class Capetonians seldom venture near 'the townships' and fears of 'black crime' continue to fuel a booming security industry and fortified architecture of fear in the leafy middle-class suburbs and shopping malls (Davis 1990). While the media and the middle classes regard the unacceptably high levels of crime and violence as an indication of a severe crisis of governance, there is a loud silence on the role of neo-liberal policies in reproducing the conditions of poverty and unemployment that sustain these violent economies. With the limited state resources available for policing, like so many cities in the North, the policing of middle-class residential and business districts is being outsourced to private security companies, resulting in new forms of spatial governance (Merry 2001; Robins 2000).

This crisis in governance is particularly evident in South African cities, where the social order is built upon a combination of systems of punishment, discipline and security (Merry 2001). In Cape Town, the micro-management of urban space is most successful in the historically white, middle-class parts of some South African cities. Here spatial governance usually involves a range of exclusionary practices, including the exclusion of 'offensive behaviour' and people, usually the poor and homeless, who look dangerous or disorderly. In the absence of resources for surveillance cameras and private security beyond the fortified walls of middle-class suburbs and shopping malls, the state continues to struggle to re-establish governance in 'unruly townships'.

The state's sanctioning of community policing structures has largely been a response to the government's recognition that it does not have the capacity and resources to deal with the massive explosion of criminal and gang activities in South African cities (Steinberg 2001; Comaroff and Comaroff 1999).[10] This shift to community policing can be seen as a form of 'outsourcing' of policing functions by a neo-liberal state unable to address crime on its own. It also draws attention to the state's acknowledgement of the need to reclaim governance in poor communities.

The example of Manenberg suggests that communities with weak governance structures and poor policing capabilities can become a nightmare in which citizens are terrorised by warlords, shack-lords and gangsters. For instance, in May 2002, the Cape Teachers' Professional Association made a passionate plea to Members of Parliament to address the violence and gangsterism affecting schooling on the Cape Flats: 'There is a war going on. The government does not run places like Manenberg, the gangsters do,' Chris Cox, spokesperson for the association told Parliament's education portfolio committee (*Cape Argus* 15 May 2002). Several preachers, Imams and teachers who were supposed to accompany the association members to Parliament and make presentations withdrew at the last minute, citing fear and intimidation by gangsters. It was precisely such a scenario that plagued the city's urban renewal programmes. Residents told of the physical dangers involved in having to navigate competing gang territories to access trains, taxis and facilities such as schools, the clinic, the library or housing office. The clinic had to be relocated to a classroom in a Manenberg school because it was situated in the middle of a gang battlefield. The attempt to secure council facilities and create safe public spaces proved to be more difficult than was initially anticipated. Before proceeding to a detailed discussion of these governance issues, however, it is necessary to situate Manenberg within the broader socio-spatial order of the apartheid city.

'FORTRESS LA' AT THE TIP OF AFRICA? SPATIAL GOVERNANCE AFTER APARTHEID

The race and class divide between Cape Town's historically white inner-city and southern suburbs on the one side, and the black and coloured townships on the other, remains firmly intact in the new South Africa. By removing black and coloured residents from multiracial working-class inner-city neighbourhoods such as District Six in the 1960s and 1970s, and relocating entire communities to out-lying Cape Flats townships such as Manenberg and Gugulethu, apartheid planners created the racialised grids of the apartheid city. The relocation of communities to council flats on the Cape Flats represented a first wave of modernist social engineering. These housing interventions drew on Le Corbusier's visionary manifestos. While these housing schemes were an integral part of apartheid segregationist planning, recent housing development schemes discussed below have been 'progressive' interventions aimed at reforming the social and spatial fabric of fragmented and 'dysfunctional' communities shattered by unemployment, violence and the devastating legacies of the forced removals of the 1960s and 1970s.

The template of the 'postmodern', post-apartheid city could seamlessly settle upon the spatial order produced by this earlier wave of apartheid social engineering. In recent years, the historically white, middle-class parts of contemporary Cape Town have witnessed a massive expansion of gentrification, mega-developments, heritage and tourist sites, and spectacles of consumption such as the Victoria and Alfred Waterfront, the GrandWest Casino development, and the Cavendish Square, Tygervalley and Century City mega-shopping mall-cum-recreation centres. These relatively new spaces of capital investment contrast starkly with the poverty and desolation of the racially segregated townships of the Cape Flats. The racialised geographies of post-apartheid Cape Town reproduce the spatial logic of capital under apartheid despite the dramatic political reforms of the 1990s. The black and coloured working classes remain trapped in places of extreme poverty located at a considerable distance from middle-class (mostly white) centres of commerce, tourism and consumption. This socio-spatial divide is reproduced through investment strategies that tend to steer clear of the Cape Flats ghettos. A multimillion-rand surveillance and security sector ensures that middle-class neighbourhoods and shopping malls are defended against what is perceived to be a dangerous underclass 'other'.

In this contemporary scenario of class warfare and the 'militarisation of everyday life', public space is destroyed in order to insulate, spatially and socially, the middle classes from undesirable 'others'. For instance, in new mega-structures and super-malls, street frontage is designed in ways that consciously exclude the underclasses and street persons, and hawkers, strollers and street people are often evicted from shopping malls by private security guards always on the lookout for non-consumers who might disrupt public consumption. Meanwhile, those who live in South Africa's urban ghettos find themselves socially and spatially imprisoned in repressive and bloody war zones where their security and safety can no longer be guaranteed by a state financially hamstrung by cutbacks brought about by neo-liberal fiscal austerity measures. Given this privatisation of the policing of public places, it is only the wealthy who are able to afford the services of private security firms while the poor remain easy targets of gang and criminal violence.

While the 'city state' claims that it is committed to undoing and dismantling the racialised grids of the apartheid city, national and global capital undermines these plans by continuing to flow to middle-class parts of the city. What this means is that the coloured and black working classes and the unemployed continue to be confined to under-resourced spaces of poverty and violence that are at great distances from the fortified, middle-class spaces of consumption, recreation, tourism and business. These processes are reinforced by a state that is unwilling or unable to intervene in land markets, thereby reproducing apartheid planning practices that locate low-income black housing development at the southwest periphery of the city where land is cheapest. The following section discusses spatial governance and planning in the making and unmaking of the apartheid city.

SPATIAL GOVERNANCE, THE PLANNER'S FETISH?

Manenberg was established as a 'coloured township' following the 1960s and 1970s Groups Areas Act forced removals from District Six and other white parts of Cape Town. The design of coloured, working-class townships such as Manenberg was based on Ebenezer Howard's 'Garden City' model, with blocks of flats, terraced and semi-detached houses, and a standardised architecture (Pinnock 1984). Situated 15 kilometres from Cape Town's city centre, Manenberg is spatially isolated from adjacent townships by means of highways, main roads, railway lines, green belts and buffer strips (Jensen and Turner 1996: 83–5; Le Grange and Robins 1997). These socio-spatial legacies continue to have a profound influence on the shape of Cape Town after apartheid.

The story of Manenberg shows how housing interventions are often deeply embedded in ideological conceptions of 'development' that seek to create good governance and virtuous consumer-citizens out of the raw material of bricks, mortar and 'the unruly masses'. Despite claims to the contrary, low-income housing and urban planning in South Africa has always been ideologically charged, and planners, policy-makers, city managers and activists have engaged with urban development interventions in relation to politically charged questions of race, ethnicity, citizenship and governance.

HOUSING CITIZENS IN THE CAPE OF STORMS

Council flats were perceived to reproduce the conditions of welfare dependency that contributed towards the disintegration of the nuclear family, which was deemed responsible for systemic social problems in Manenberg. Devcom's argument was that the Manenberg community was 'dysfunctional' because family units tended towards disintegration and were therefore unable to socialise youth into adulthood (see Chipkin 2005; Salo 2005). In other words, Devcom's task was to create the conditions for 'proper' governance and citizenship in what was deemed to be a 'dysfunctional' community.

Cape Town's ANC-dominated City Council attempted to re-establish governance as a necessary condition for citizen participation in public life in Manenberg. However, rather than resorting to a conventional policing solution to Manenberg's governance crisis and social problems, Devcom sought to address these problems by creating the conditions for the participation of marginalised citizens and poor communities in the mainstream economy and public domain. This objective was to be achieved through a variety of interventions in Manenberg, including ensuring safer access to facilities such as libraries, clinics and the housing office. Devcom director Ahmedi Vawda argued that large numbers of Manenberg residents were involved in daily interactions with council officials in the clinics, libraries and housing offices, and that these interactions were crucial for re-establishing governance. Yet, during 1998 gang violence in Manenberg had resulted in the closing down of all council facilities for extended periods. This ongoing situation of gang violence and disruption undermined council developmental initiatives.

The devastation of the August 1999 tornado had left hundreds homeless, and gang violence was on the increase. By November 2000, seven Manenberg children had died in the crossfire as a result of gang shootouts in the area. In addition, as a result of many years of unrelenting gang shootings and violence in Manenberg, council staff at libraries, clinics and housing offices were suffering from acute forms of psychological trauma and stress disorders. A City of Cape Town *Community Development Report* (3 February 1998) stated that 'there is a potential collapse of service provision in libraries, child care, health and housing in Manenberg, [and] gang violence is having a direct impact on service delivery'. The report went on to call for 'urgent attention and a course of action to physically protect staff and ensure emergency support is available'. This resulted in the 'hardening' of the library, clinic and housing office buildings at the cost of hundreds of thousands of rands. Meanwhile, many council staff who were receiving trauma counselling were unable to cope with the extraordinarily high levels of stress and violence in Manenberg. Despite the fortification of council buildings, in early 2000, the housing office and clinic, which were situated in the nerve centre of 'Hard Livings' territory, were relocated to a safer site. The relocation in turn led to accusations from residents and NGO and CBO representatives that the council was more concerned about its buildings and its staff, who were virtually all non-residents of Manenberg, than about ordinary residents who had to face these harsh conditions of violence on a daily basis.

Devcom's Ahmedi Vawda envisaged the provision and upgrading of community facilities such as libraries, community centres and computer laboratories as a central component of a strategy aimed at diverting youth from the dangerous streets to the safety of learning environments. This was perceived by Vawda to be in line with Cape Town's urban development strategy aimed at preparing youth to enter the new information economy with its growth sectors in IT and financial services. However, violence in Manenberg presented serious obstacles to this strategy of promoting the growth of knowledge industries.

Given this context of daily gang violence, it is perhaps not surprising that Manenberg came to be represented in the media and policy documents as a place of 'social pathologies', 'dysfunctionality', violence and trauma. What is less evident is how and why senior city managers came to conceptualise individual home ownership and the creation of a secondary housing market as the panacea for these problems of social order and governance. It is clear, however, that many Manenberg residents were themselves calling for the ANC-led city council to intervene more directly in eradicating gang activities, creating housing opportunities and improving the physical environment.[11]

Given the extraordinary levels of violence in Manenberg, and the council's responsibilities to protect its staff as well as ordinary citizens, the city was clearly obligated to intervene in order to 're-establish governance'. Devcom's 'hardening' of council buildings and the use of housing delivery to re-establish governance failed, however, to adequately take into account the structural dimensions of a political economy of drugs and gang violence. So what kind of state and state intervention would have been necessary to re-establish governance in Manenberg?

CONCLUSION

In this chapter, I have argued that attempts by city authorities to re-establish governance in Manenberg failed because of the inability of the state to address growing unemployment in an urban environment characterised by a thriving drug and gang economy involving sex work, crime, protection syndicates and a booming taxi industry associated with violence and gang control over transportation routes. This failure to re-establish governance occurred despite concerted efforts by city planners and officials to spatially engineer the built environment through the establishment of individual home ownership housing schemes and the 'hardening' and protection of key government buildings such as clinics.

The contestation between the state and gangs over the control of space in Manenberg is part of a broader process in terms of which current investment strategies and urban development schemes have avoided poor parts of Cape Town, thereby reproducing the socio-spatial inequalities of the apartheid city. Despite the many well-intentioned interventions by city authorities, the socio-spatial logic of the apartheid city persists. Investors and businesses continue to gravitate towards the well-policed, historically white, middle spaces of the city These parts of Cape Town have indeed been incorporated into a representation of Cape Town as a globally competitive, multicultural city driven by the tourism industry and the IT and financial service sectors. There are, however, at least two other sides to Cape Town. The one side is the 'fortress city' of middle-class neighbourhoods characterised by gated communities, neighbourhood watches, vigilantes, private security companies, surveillance cameras, high walls and barbed-wire fences. On the other side are the urban ghettos of the Cape Flats characterised by racialised poverty, crime and violence.

Post-apartheid Cape Town remains a deeply divided city, with middle-class enclaves fortified against townships that are perceived as dangerous 'no-go zones'. It is within this highly polarised urban landscape that spatial governmentality has become such contested terrain. New forms of spatially organised crime control that characterise contemporary Cape Town include a proliferation of gated communities, and numerous initiatives aimed at creating prostitution- and crime-free zones through the use of closed circuit television cameras and 'zero-tolerance policing'. Even graffiti artists have found themselves the targets of this new urban warfare against 'grime'. As Merry (2001: 16) points out, 'these are all examples of new regulatory mechanisms that target spaces rather than persons [and that] exclude offensive behaviour rather than attempting to correct or reform offenders'. The urban renewal programme introduced in Manenberg following the destruction caused by the tornado in 1999, represented such an attempt to regulate space through architectural design, individual home ownership and security devices. These initiatives were meant to complement modern disciplinary penalisation but were vastly different in their logic and technologies (Merry 2001). The Manenberg case study suggests that this attempt at spatial governmentality has failed to dislodge the deeply embedded gang structures and activities that have been fuelled by the shift of the Western Cape economy from traditional manufacturing to a service- and tourist-driven economy. This troubling account from the Cape of Storms is yet another global warning about the rough weather that awaits city planners and officials who uncritically embrace utopian modernist visions, whether they be Le Corbusier's 'Garden Cities', Devcom's individual home ownership dreamscape of suburban bliss, or the urban manager's cybervisions of a globally competitive, IT-driven, Silicon-Valley economy at the tip of Africa.

REFERENCES

Argus (2001) 18 August, p. 2.

Caldeira, T. (1996) 'Building Up Walls. The New Pattern of Segregation in Sao Paulo', *International Social Science Journal* 48(1): 55–65.

—— (2000) *City of Walls: Crime, Segregation, and Citizenship in Sao Paulo,* Berkeley: University of California Press.

Chipkin, I. (2005) '"Functional" and "Dysfunctional" Communities: The Making of Ethical Citizens', in S. Robins (ed.) *Limits to Liberation: Citizenship and Governance after Apartheid,* Oxford: James Currey Publishers.

Comaroff, J.L. and Comaroff, J. (eds) (1999) *Civil Society and the Political Imagination in Africa: Critical Perspectives,* Chicago, IL: University of Chicago Press.

Community Development Report, Urban Regeneration 2000, City of Cape Town, 24 October.

—— (1998) City of Cape Town, 3 February.

Davis, M. (1990) *City of Quartz: Excavating the Future of Los Angeles*, London: Verso.

Escobar, A. (1995) *Encountering Development: The Making and Unmaking of the Third World*, Princeton, NJ: Princeton University Press.

Ferguson, J. (1990) *The Anti Politics Machine: 'Development', Depoliticization and Bureaucratic State Power in Lesotho,* Cambridge: Cambridge University Press and Cape Town: David Philip.

Harvey, D. (1985) *The Urbanization of Capital*, Oxford: Basil Blackwell.

Jensen, S. and Turner, S. (1996) 'A Place Called Heideveld: Identites and Strategies among the Coloureds in Cape Town, South Africa', Research report no. 112, Department of Geography and International Development Studies, Roskilde University, Denmark.

Le Grange, L. and Robins, S. (1997) *The Wetton–Landsdowne Road Corridor Area: The Identification of Culturally Significant Places and Opportunities*, South Africa: s.n.

Merry, S.E. (1981) *Urban Danger: Life in a Neighbourhood of Strangers*, Philadelphia, PA: Temple University Press.

—— (2001) 'Spatial Governmentality and the New Urban Social Order: Controlling Gender Violence through Laws, *American Anthropologist* 103: 16–29.

Mitchell, T. (1998) *Colonizing Egypt*, New York: Cambridge University Press.

Nederveen Pieterse, J. (2000) *Global Futures: Shaping Globalization*, London and New York: Zed Books.

Pinnock, D. (1984) *The Brotherhoods: Street Gangs and State Control in Cape Town*, Cape Town: David Philip.

Robins, S. (2000) 'City Sites: Multicultural Planning and the Post-apartheid City', in S. Nuttall and C.A. Michael (eds) *Senses of Cultures: South African Culture Studies*, Cape Town: Oxford University Press.

Salo, E. (2005) 'Race Laws, Gendered Tactics: On Becoming Respectable Mothers during the Apartheid Era', in S. Robins (ed.) *Limits to Liberation: Citizenship and Governance after Apartheid*, Oxford: James Currey Publishers.

Scott, J. (1998) *Seeing Like a State: How Certain Schemes to Improve the Human Condition Have Failed*, New Haven, CT: Yale University Press.

Steinberg, J. (2001) *Crime Wave: The South African Underworld and Its Foes*, Johannesburg: Witwatersrand University Press.

Sunday Times (2001) 11 November.

Chapter 2: 'Manenberg Avenue is Where it's Happening'

Images by David Lurie[1]

Manenberg housing was built in the 1960s according to the fashion for neighbourhood unit planning and in part response to the forced removals from inner-city areas such as District Six. Photographer David Lurie's ten images from Manenberg Avenue form a detailed study of life in one of Cape Town's poorest parts. They present perhaps one 'point of view' from the main drag in the modernist planned dormitory ghetto of Manenberg.

These images were also informed by another 'point of view'. In 2000 the photographer approached anthropologist Steven Robins and asked to read some of his work on Manenberg. Lurie read two papers, 'At the Limits of Spatial Governmentality: A Message from the Tip of Africa', and 'City Sites: Multicultural Planning and the Post-apartheid City' (Robins 2000, 2002), after which he began his photographic project. What emerges when viewing the final pictures (of which those included here form a select part), are questions about the interrelationship between these two ways of seeing space in the post-apartheid city.

On one level, the images might present 'a counter-narrative … to the dominant image of the desirable world class city' (Jeppie 2004: 17), a position that lays claim to the possibilities of the critical nature of photography which is informed by scholarly work. On another level, there is something profoundly disturbing about the ways in which the images have entered spaces of display in art galleries and been published in expensive coffee-table books, and questions about voyeurism, and the objectification of poor subjects, seem inevitable (Sassen 2005: 1).

How then does one begin to think about the ways in which spaces in the post-apartheid city are being viewed? How does a photographer find himself drawn to practising his art in a place such as Manenberg? What has informed his eye? Through which theoretical and critical lenses is he doing this 'looking'? Or can it simply be put down to a form of brave artistic voyeurism into what historian Shamil Jeppie terms 'the dangerous, the unspeakable, in the post-apartheid city' (Jeppie 2004:17)?

From the low-down perspective of the street in Figure 2.1, where the harsh

Figure 2.1

Figure 2.2

Figure 2.3

Figure 2.4

Figure 2.5

Figure 2.6

Figure 2.7

Figure 2.8

Figure 2.9

Figure 2.10

and barren linearity of the street and the housing blocks are only disrupted by the figures of children playing beside the road, to the super-close-up shot of the bicycle-rider wearing Levi 515 denim jeans and a gunbelt (Figure 2.7), or the lone child playing on a jungle gym in a playground surrounded by shacks (Figure 2.4), the lines of planned intention in the city are evident against the lives of the people who inhabit the space. As in much of Lurie's recent work, the images are juxtaposed against the distant view of Table Mountain, which is somehow out of reach, a symbol of the unattainable on the horizon.

The placement of the ten images (Figures 2.1 to 2.10) presented here is deliberate. In reading Steven Robins's new work with these images in mind, a sense of the tensions between academic critique and photography as a work of art simultaneously come to the fore.

There are many questions. What happens when a photographer and an anthropologist enter into an academic conversation through the exchange of work? Is the photographic image a document that testifies to patterns of ongoing violence in the city? Can the photographer achieve a photographic distance or does the act of looking underline a power relation? Can images narrate spaces or does photography inevitably romanticise its subjects? Is this perhaps the power of the photographic image – to create a sense of discomfort? Or is photography of this sort the ultimate act of authorising modernism? By freezing the image in time, does its meaning become fixed in the act of wishing to reveal the inner world of a place that itself exists on the fringes and margins of space in the 'New South Africa'?

Perhaps more simply, what are the lines of 'sight' and 'desire' that under-pin a photographic project such as David Lurie's *Cape Town Fringe, Manenberg*

Avenue is where it's Happening? How does life on the urban 'fringe' circulate and enter the elite spaces of artistic consumption? What does this mean about ways in which the city is viewed and who is doing the looking? And how do these images contribute to a 'visual library of the urban spaces of South Africa' (Jeppie, 2004: 17)?

REFERENCES

Jeppie, M.S. (2004) 'Cape Town Fringe Introduction', in D. Lurie (ed.) *Cape Town Fringe, Manenberg Avenue is where it's Happening*, Cape Town: Double Storey.

Lurie, D. (ed.) (2004) *Cape Town Fringe, Manenberg Avenue is where it's Happening,* Cape Town: Double Storey.

Robins, S. (2000) 'City Sites: Multicultural Planning and the Post-apartheid City', in S. Nuttall and C.A. Michaels (eds) *Senses of Cultures: South African Culture Studies*, Oxford: Oxford University Press.

Robins, S. (2002) 'At the Limits of Spatial Governmentality: A Message from the Tip of Africa', *Third World Quarterly* 23.

Sassen, R. (2005) *David Lurie's Manenberg Avenue is where it's happening,* Artthrob Reviews at www.artthrob.co.za/05jan/reviews/lurie.html, 08.09.2005.

Chapter 3: Remaking modernism

South African Architecture In and Out of Time

Noëleen Murray

Modern architecture arrived in South Africa as early as 1925 and as in many other places in the world, a small group of faithful followers of the International Style began making buildings according to the principles outlined by its proponents (Herbert 1975: 1).[1] Since then architecture in South Africa has more or less followed the trends of architectural style and fashion internationally (Cooke 2006a: 3).

Although contemporary architectural practice has since taken on a less strict adherence to the principles of high modernism that characterised the work of the early modern movement, for the most part architects working locally are producing work that remains rooted in internationalist 'discourses' of design (Herbert 1975; Markus and Cameron 2002).

Contemporary architecture in South Africa post-apartheid is arguably much like work anywhere else in the world where, in postmodern ways, styles, trends and influences are juxtaposed and coexist in cities that are increasingly hybrid and disjointed from their modernist and colonial masterplans (Murray 2006: 8). Yet at the same time there are moments in the making of buildings in which the translations of received forms and practices take on local characteristics – where place-making and identity-making intersect through a search by architects for a uniquely 'South African architecture'.

Within this contemporary reality city spaces have also become sites for the 'playing out' of the politics of identity. Almost everywhere you go new buildings and developments are being labelled, styled and marketed with a distinctive identity. Very often this identity appears arbitrary with labels such as 'Cape Vernacular', 'Tuscan', 'Moroccan', 'French Provençal' or 'Italian Renaissance' becoming commonplace on billboards advertising everything from new housing developments in townships to suburban malls and inner-city redevelopment projects. At the same time, there have been many serious-minded attempts to recast space post-apartheid with projects which have been set out to address inhibiting aspects of the apartheid city and to change the identity of places with histories of exclusion, violence or segregation. These include projects such as new museum initiatives and urban designs for new public spaces.

South Africa is an interesting place to begin examining the nature of the transference and reception of modern architectural ideas – a place where the project of modernity was made material through the application of modernist planning ideas in the service of the apartheid state and as a means to implement segregationist legislation such as the Group Areas Act. My interest in modernism is twofold. It lies first in the persistent presence of modernism (or 'new' modernism as it is often called) in South African urban space with its diversity of manifestations and applications post-apartheid, and second, in the attention this draws to the politicised nature of South African space, space in which modernist design has been deployed variously as a form of asserting spatialised racial control, or in the service of Afrikaner, and more recently African, cultural identity. Modernism has also been part of the project of industrialisation and the language of modernity has been (and continues to be) used in the promotion of a technologically advanced state (Fisher *et al.* 2003: 68).

This chapter is positioned in the precarious emergent space of new architectural debate internationally whereby architectural scholarship is beginning to take on the issues that have been discussed in the humanities over the past 20 years through cultural studies and more recently in the debates by authors working in the field of public culture against more established forms of architectural writing historically. In Africa and particularly in southern Africa I suggest this position is emergent for a number of reasons. First, because of the vexing presence of colonial contexts which can only really be considered through a reading of the relations of power, race, interdependent global economies and exchange. Second, because of the established knowledge fields enabled by interdisciplinary scholarship in fields of study in postcolonial studies, heritage studies, gender studies and the like, architectural materialism can no longer be simply viewed through the conventions of aesthetic appreciation and as abstract form-making. Lastly, through my own personal experiences working firstly within an architectural department before moving into the humanities, where the need to problematise the operations of space and place have challenged me to explore the underlying processes of design and building more carefully.

Consequently, this chapter explores ten 'moments' of architectural design in order to investigate ways in which this internationalism has been translated and mutated in the making of buildings in South Africa since 1930. Rather than attempting a comprehensive presentation of the history of South African architectural modernism, I have chosen ten forms of practice which typify sets of ideas represented more broadly in the 'canon' of buildings designed by architects in this country. Each moment explores questions of spatial identity and modernity. Each moment represents work completed by architects recognised for their excellence in design. Some reflect a localising or contextualising trend in the search for African and South African identity, while others are more confidently products of global ideas. The moments take in work produced in the heroic period of modernism between the 1920s and 1950s, as well as others in which modernism has been re-imagined, reinvented and remade over time. I argue that, as an underlying ethos, modernity and the ideas and principles of international modernism can be seen to operate as a more or less continuous form of practice over time.

The ten moments are presented as sets of keywords representing special relationships between forms of practice and interpretations of these forms. They are Avant-garde/modern, Afrikaner/apartheid, African/ethnic, community/public, Cape regional/vernacular, Africa/modern, heritage/memory, international/global, township/freedom and exhibition/review.

RETHINKING MODERNISM

Architectural modernism has necessarily become viewed as only one part of the global projects of modernity, and critiques thereof need to be positioned in relation to the processes characterised by modernity more broadly – those of increased industrialisation, imperialism, colonialism, racial exclusion and societal ordering. If we accept, after the theoretical insights of Foucault and Lefebvre, or the postcolonial critiques of Appadurai, Mbembe and others, that current disciplinary thought formations and knowledge constructions about space are limited (contained even) by the epistemologies of modernity, how then do we begin to think through, in very practical ways, the possibilities for re-positioning spatial practices within a context such as Africa, or more specifically South Africa (Mbembe 2001; Appadurai 1996; Lefebvre 1991; Foucault 1976)? How do we deal with the histories of marginality, discursively inscribed through the twin 'gazes' of developmental discourses and spatial ethnography (Mbembe and Nuttall 2004)? Where do these fit into the consumerism of global capitalism? How does practice respond to the needs of different publics? How do we re-imagine the concrete in a postmodern, globalising world of hyperreality? Can we see 'contemporary' architecture in any way that is detached from the project of modernity (Murray 2006: 4)?

In making an argument about architectural modernism as a more or less continuous practice over time, modern architecture in South Africa necessarily has to be understood within a continuous relationship with the history and theory of the Western tradition emanating from the metropolitan centres of Europe and the Americas. By posing a relation – with all the associated complexities – between centre and margins and interrogating conceptions of modernism and modernity within the complex relationship between metropolitan ideas of space and the circulation of these ideas to colonial contexts, it becomes possible to situate an argument about colonial modernism in a dialectical relation between these two interrelated sites of modernist expression (Herwitz 1998).

Therefore, as Daniel Herwitz has argued, it follows that modernism in the South African context can only really be understood in terms of its relation to the metropolitan centres of Europe and America. He argues that the first form of modernism emanates from the centre – where modernism – in art and architecture – arose in the context of spirited 'cultures' of modernism. In contrast, the second form exists at the margins where modernist art and architecture developed along significantly different lines (Herwitz 1998).

> If modernism originates in the first instance out of a specific form of urban life, then what does this mean to originate elsewhere, where that form of life is largely absent or minimal? In South Africa for example?
>
> (Herwitz 1998: 406)

This raises questions about studies of the margins and specifically of the architecture that it produces. It follows that the transference of metropolitan modernist ideals cannot be seen to have circulated in any simplistic manner. If modernism emerged according to distinct modalities of a specific 'form of urban life', what does this mean for another site in which modernism is produced (Herwitz 1998)? One take on this argument – from the perspective of the centre – would be that it is impossible for anything authentic or new to be produced outside of this site of production. This reinforces notions of the margins as remote, detached and inferior sites of production, condemned to 'receiving' ideas from the centre which are then applied in an uncritical manner. The space of the margins, in this conception, is 'stagnant and incapable of the invention of anything as urbane as modernism'. Another angle on this argument might resist the notion that the space of the margins is one of backwardness, simply caught in a time-lapse waiting to receive 'secondhand ideas from the centre' (Herwitz 1998).

These two positions are echoed by South African architect Hannah le Roux, who suggests two ways of 'revisioning modernist architecture in Africa' produced during the 1920s and 1950s. Le Roux frames two visions for modern architecture in Africa:

> Vision 1:
> The project of modern architecture is a failure in Africa. The buildings are shells, void of any aesthetic qualities that are respected by their tenants, and impossible to maintain.
>
> Vision 2
> The buildings are, on the other hand, highly lively and animated settings, replete with sounds, social relations and multiple functions. In this vision they are preferable to the sterile modernisms of Western institutions that are the backdrop to everyday lives characterised by monotony, order and cleanliness.
>
> (Le Roux 2005: 52)

These two points of view seem to suggest that the contemporary reality lies somewhere between the simple binaries of the centre and margins – where the emergence and production of modernism at the margins exists in the context of a continuous dependency on the colonial centre or its postcolonial successor. In order for modernism to assert a new dimension, it has to endure this dependency and be satisfied with simply converting 'received forms' for its own purposes (Herwitz 1998). In the broadest sense, as Herwitz argues further, in the case of South African architecture this cultural and stylistic intermingling has yet to take place. Countering this view is Julian Cooke, editor of *Architecture South Africa*, who optimistically argues that instead of being 'absorbed in the global common denominator', South African architects are beginning to make a real contribution (Cooke 2006a: 3).

REMAKING MODERNISM

In narrating the making and remaking of architectural space in the post-apartheid city, where it is accepted that new forms coexist and compete with their predecessors within cities, possibly the greatest challenge to the discipline of architecture is to begin to find ways to 'think through', 'narrate' and write about architecture and urban design that will enable a general critical and theoretical understanding of the process behind the making of buildings and the workings of architects as authors of spaces. Inevitably this requires a broader set of theoretical readings and the need to apply these theories to the materiality of architecture. As I have argued elsewhere, conventional forms of writing within the discipline are strangely dominant and persist as an internal disciplinary 'language' of sorts. This language is governed by a discourse of aesthetic appreciation and description, hagiography, self-promotion and post-rationalisation (Murray 2006: 4).

Architectural critic Greig Crysler has argued that notions of the city have changed radically over the last half-century through the processes of globalisation. Crysler argues that we can no longer talk of cities as 'bounded domains', but instead need to think of interconnected urban networks. '[T]he categories of nation, city, architecture and building cannot be understood as separate entities: they exist as simultaneous and overlapping conditions' (Crysler 2003: 1).

This supports the interpretation of architecture as – 'a trace of international networks and flows of investment' (Le Roux 2005: 43), or, as in Le Roux's paraphrasing Anthony King's argument, a reflection of 'the intertwinement of colonialism with global trade and investment [which] has shaped linkages and connections within the spatial logic of the metropolitan/peripheral relationship' (King cited in Le Roux 2005: 44). Consequently, if urban contexts are now subject to these overlapping conditions, it follows then that the spatial disciplines are being challenged to respond in ways that are increasingly interdisciplinary. Crysler continues:

> Given that disciplines such as architecture, planning, geography and urban studies continue, for the most part, to be organised around professional training and research that is linked to specific scales of analysis, how should theory be transformed to meet the challenges of the globally interdependent conditions in the twenty-first century metropolis?
>
> (Crysler 2003: 1–2)

In answering this question he suggests that changes are needed not just within disciplines and between them, but that there is a need for the examination of how and why disciplines are constituted as discourses. In a similar vein, Mbembe and Nuttall offer a similar new reading of what they term 'the African Metropolis'. Writing in response to Michael Watts's critique of the special edition of the journal *Public Culture*, they assert:

> 'Johannesburg – The Elusive Metropolis' was deliberately conceived as an invitation to browse through the city, its debris, its hypermodern structures, its plans and its leakages, if necessary by way of vignettes, snapshots, scenes, sights, voices, and where need be, fragmentary accounts …. Far from closing the city to interpretation or presenting it as an 'asylum', the various contributions taken together are testimony to a volatile and highly creative process of city transformation. Indeed motion is what we wanted to capture, while at the same time exploring the splintering quality of the metropolitan experience itself.
>
> (Mbembe and Nuttall 2005: 199)

TEN MOMENTS OF MODERNISM

1 Avant-garde/modern

One of the associations most often made with the modern movement in architecture is that of the avant-garde. In this way architectural creation of early avant-garde modernist buildings became synonymous with small groups of architects working with the style and forms of international modernist practice as only one manifestation of global modernity in the early twentieth century. South Africa is no exception where architects belonging to what is now known as the Transvaal Group of modern architects aligned themselves with the radical social and political ideals of the modern movement internationally and began to reproduce its forms (Herbert 1975: 3). From seminal early works such as houses by Martienssen and Stern by the practice Martienssen, Fassler and Cooke in the early 1930s through to projects such as the radical leftist student scheme entitled 'Native Housing' by Connell, Irvine-Smith, Jonas, Kantorowich and Wepener in 1939, modern architecture and planning became the spatial language for the visioning of political allegiances to socialist ideals (Connell *et al.* 1939; Herbert 1975; Japha 1985).

The heady days of this avant-garde idealism began to dissipate by the 1940s, with only a few architects remaining faithful to the goals and visions promised by European modernism (Herbert 1975: 3).

> Within a decade [1930s] South Africa was swept from the backwaters of architectural provincialism into the mainstream of the International Style …. Then almost inevitably the flow [of modernist ideas] broadened. As the movement widened, its intensity and impetus diminished …. for a further period of growth.
>
> (Herbert 1975: 1)

Figure 3.1
Avant-garde/modern:
Tree House, Cape Town,
1999.

From this point on, ideas about modern architecture moved beyond the small group centred on Wits University in the then Transvaal. In other centres such as Pretoria, Cape Town and Bloemfontein, modernism became adopted and the style was entrenched across the political spectrum. The enticing forms and visions of the International Style remained as an important reminder of the 'new' and fashionable, especially in cities such as Johannesburg where metropolitan modernity was gaining popularity (Chipkin 1993).

Inevitably for architects, as stylistic modernism became more mainstream, the political associations became less self-consciously applied when designing buildings, although some of the disciplinary mystique and purism has remained. If the notion of the avant-garde represents the moment of reception of modernist ideas into South Africa, then the notion of the 'modern' can be traced as a thread through to contemporary award-winning projects such as the one by architects Anya and Macio van der Merwe-Miszewski (Figure 3.1). Working with ideas of pure form and adhering to the modernist ethics of honesty to materials, structure, and of 'form following function', works such as this can be seen as part of international flows of ideas, capital and investment, part of a continuous

Figure 3.2
Afrikaner/apartheid: Taal
Monument, Paarl, c.1960.

international conversation about modernity. Whether consciously applied as precedent or not by its architects, 'Tree House' bears reference to other famous modernist icons such as the Eames House, House Chareau or to work by modernist masters such as Alvar Aalto and Mies van der Rohe. At the same time, it makes its own iconic vision-statement, with the tree metaphor reflecting the context of its site on the slopes of Table Mountain in elite suburban Cape Town.

2 Afrikaner/apartheid

The second moment marks how modernism became 'domesticated' as the style of choice for use in the latter part of the twentieth century in the service of Afrikaner nationalism. This is possibly the crudest application of modernist design ideas and forms from the city scale down to individual buildings. Many international styles and variations of modernism were emulated in the project of asserting nationalist spatial identity. From the art deco style of Gerard Moerdyk's design for the Voortekker Monument, to the Corbusian planning for Cape Town's Foreshore reclamation project; from the fluid forms and expressionism of the Taal Monument (Figure 3.2), to the brutalism of the Pretoria State Theatre and Strydom Monument; and from the regionalist modernism of Fagan's Volkskas Bank buildings to the Kahnian modernism of the Rand Afrikaans University, modern architecture became the style and visual language of the apartheid period.

Thus modernism became the means by which Afrikaner advancement could make its mark on cities, distinguishing itself from the British imperial styles of Victorian and others (Silverman 1998: 129). Simultaneously, apartheid modernity was reinforced by the establishment of new institutions and new systems of racialised power. In this line, much has been written about the apartheid city and the manipulation of urban planning to suit the segregationist ideals of the apartheid state, while less has been said about the particularities of the ways in which internationalist models of building were mutated to suit the programme of keeping racially different groups of people apart on a daily basis.

Many apartheid modernist buildings distinguished themselves from their international counterparts in quirky ways: with separate entrances for 'blacks' and 'whites' in all municipal and state buildings; in the provision of 'native living quarters' in houses and blocks of flats in 'white' Group Areas; or on the urban scale in the creation of the space of the 'township' (dormitory ghettos near cities and towns) with special buildings such as migrant labour hostels, beer halls, pass offices and the like.

The powerful and longlasting effects of this planning and architecture are only just beginning to be realised. At the time of writing, over ten years into democracy, the determining effects of these forms of building and planning still very much affect the daily lives of South Africans. Ironically, South African space remains divided, contested and profoundly affected by these historical manifestations of city-making that 'act back' in the present.

3 African/ethnic

The third moment explores the relationship between ideas of Africa and notions of ethnicity within the spatial disciplines. Possibly the 'hottest' debate in local architectural circles over the last ten years has been around the quest and desire to inscribe buildings with African identity. The 'heat' in these debates, I believe, has come from an awkwardness around the articulation of race in the spatial disciplines (Neuhleni 2000: 69). From debates in the university studios to experiments on the ground, the African moment in the discipline has historically been an ethnographic one. With the emergence of significant numbers of black students and practitioners from the late 1980s onwards, the debate has shifted towards questions of curricula, 'standards' and access to the spatial professions. These have yet to be clearly articulated or reflected on, and the spatial disciplines still lack an adequately enabling language of critique (Neuhleni 2000: 90).

A second aspect of this 'moment' is a more historical one. Ethnographic studies of African architecture abound, where traditional dwellings and settlement forms have been studied, classified, drawn and documented. Working much like colonial anthropologists in 'the field' and in the academy, these architects have collated extensive and significant records of traditional ways of living. These studies rely on many of the characteristics of colonial scholarship, such as tribal classification and rural geographies. Key works include Peter Rich's study of the Ndebele, Barry Bierman's studies of the Zulu 'indlu' (beehive hut), Franco Frescura's work on traditional forms of mission architecture and many others. In these instances, notions of 'tradition' operate as 'an antithetical discourse [that]

Figure 3.3
African/ethnic: House
Rich, Johannesburg,
1978.

maintains the opposition between a developing urban and undeveloped rural' (Judin and Vladislavić 1998: 30). Tradition has also had an ethnic association, whereby architects have used their knowledge of traditional settlements in acts of stylistic translation into new architectures as a form of stylistic postmodernism. Peter Rich's own house in suburban Johannesburg uses Ndebele-inspired wall motifs and colours (Figure 3.3).

A third aspect is that of the influence of African art on modern art and architecture, which is known to have inspired metropolitan modernism. South African architecture is no exception to the global trend. From as early as the 1930s in Johannesburg and Pretoria modern architecture has been influenced by African settlement forms, art and culture. Examples include Norman Eaton's House Greenwood (1930) in which he created an 'African village' for the servant's quarters, and Pancho Gueddes's eclectic modernist architecture, painting and sculpture (1960s to 1990s) through to contemporary schemes for bushveld lodges such as Singita Lebombo in the Kruger Park by OMM Designs (Cooke 2006b: 11).

4 Community / public

The fourth moment explores what is probably one of the most misused terms under apartheid in South Africa – the word 'community', which became synonymous with socially enforced understandings of racial 'groups'. For instance, the government Department of 'Community Development' was the institution through which the Group Areas Act was enforced and which carried out forced removals and the like. In a series of keywords presented at the beginning of the volume *blank_Architecture, apartheid and after* (Judin and Vladislavić 1998), one idea of 'community' is explored:

> Who exactly is the community in South Africa? Are there not more complex social arrangements as well as conflicting interest groups that must be accounted for? How are these different groups to make up a community? Why is this 'community' always seen to be black and never white? There was a tradition of constructing 'community buildings' in the black areas. These buildings are easy to recognize: they have brightly coloured curvilinear forms. This style was never pursued in municipal buildings or any other government structures in white areas, where there were of course no 'communities' to be accommodated. White public buildings were imagined, designed and built differently, with what must have been other criteria and intentions.
>
> (Judin and Vladislavić 1998: 20)

Notions of the community architect and planner are positioned somewhere between these two poles. On one level, practitioners who were opposed to the apartheid status quo undertook work in township spaces as an act of resistance during the struggle against apartheid. Practices and groups such as Planact in Johannesburg and the Development Action Group in Cape Town took risks through intervening in disputes and aiding development, particularly in the 1980s. On another level, community architects and planners by virtue of their outsider status, also bought into a series of at best misguided and at worst patronising, ideas about African space-making and practices. These are the crudely translated curvilinear forms and bright colours to which Judin and Vladislavić allude. Figure 3.4 illustrates work by Cape Town-based community architect Carin Smuts.

Another idea of community is one which is exerted from within, such as in the case of the District Six Museum which claims to be a 'community museum', where the idea of community is used to resist notions of conventional heritage practice and museum-making. In the case of the District Six Museum, the idea of community is an enabling and powerful one, which allows for the stories and memories of ex-residents of the infamous site of forced removal to be told in more or less unmediated ways (Prosalendis and Rassool 2001; see also Rassool, this volume).

Ironically, post-1994 many misconceptions still exist, and are perpetuated by the homogenising tendencies of multiculturalism and the imaginaries of the 'new' South Africa and the 'rainbow nation'. Instead of 'new solutions' to 'urban problems' being solved by space-making practices in a liberated country, now more than ever, issues of land and the city, of memory and identity, access and control, race and gender, are being contested as confident new publics emerge and lay claim to rights and access to land and resources. Almost daily, newspapers carry reports about land invasions and new removals, from buildings that have been illegally occupied, to disputes over cultural or religious rights and burial sites (see Tayob; and Shepherd and Ernsten, both this volume).

5 Cape regional/vernacular
I suggested earlier that questions of African identity and indigeneity have been surprisingly absent within the spatial disciplines, and that these have been under-

Figure 3.4
Community/public:
Ulwazi Youth Centre,
Langa, 1990.

stood through a type of 'ethnic' categorisation. Similarly, there has been little coming to terms with the naming of practices and 'movements' within South African architectural practice. The fifth moment aims to shift attention geographically from Johannesburg and Pretoria in the north to Cape Town in the south to examine stylistic dimensions of this categorisation and in particular the naming of 'Cape' architecture as a specific, (superior even) regional typology of building.

While the impetus of the ideals of the International Style took root in Johannesburg in the 1920s and 1930s, architects in the Cape remained more conservative and provincial (Herbert 1975: 1). Modernism only really became the mode of design under the new appointment in the 1940s of Englishman Professor Thornton-White at the University of Cape Town (Fisher *et al.* 2003: 71). Instead of aspiring to the international scene alone, architects drew inspiration from the local colonial architecture of the Cape Dutch – an architecture of white-washed walls and thatched roofs set in spectacular mountainous settings – which became a regionalist source of inspiration for modernism. Very soon there were a number of architects working in this regionalist modernist way, including Revel Fox, Gabriel Fagan and later many others.

House Wilson by Revel Fox (Figure 3.5) is an example of this regionalist modernism. Drawing on traditional architectural elements such as the white walls, expressive chimneys, barn forms, as well as using local climatic devices such as small window openings with shutters for shade, and orientated in the landscape to afford views of mountains and farmlands (yet remaining decidedly modern stylistically) this architecture soon gained popularity among designers as a way to reconcile modernist ideas with the historical traditions of building in the Cape.[2]

This regionalist trend was essentially a romantic traditionalism, which also began to appear in the Cape through ideas about urban design. Under pre-eminent practitioner Roelof Uytenbogaardt a language of space-making emerged, which fused the romantic traditionalism of Italy (where many local students continue to go for postgraduate studies) with that of the Cape winelands. Using concepts and precedents such as axial ordering in the landscape, along

Figure 3.5
Cape regional/vernacular:
House Wilson, Worcester,
c.1958.

with spatial and built hierarchies and the delineation of walled 'werf' spaces, a local language has developed.

Allied to this appreciation of the local 'Cape' architecture is the work of a group of lay enthusiasts who under James Walton established the Vernacular Architecture Society in South Africa. In keeping with the aims and practices of the parent Vernacular Architecture Society in Britain, the group began raising awareness of 'vanishing' settler or 'folk' architecture from the eighteenth century onwards. Studies of traditional settlements have also been the main research product of academics at the University of Cape Town and others whose work in surveying and documenting Cape architecture has been extensive. These works are taxonomies (Foucault 1976), the best known being those by Ronald Lewcock, Hans Fransen and Mary Cook, Vivienne and Derek Japha, John Rennie and others.[3]

Ironically, this fascination with the vernacular (the dictionary definition of which is 'native, belonging to the country of one's birth') has never been questioned or critiqued, and both these practices continue into the present. Architects are still searching for ways to give modern buildings local identity. Examples of this mode of architectural expression range from the Hout Bay Library by Uytenbogaardt and Rozendal, to new interventions on wine farms by Kruger Roos and Van der Merwe Miszewski Architects and others.[4] Similarly, as South Africa opens up to new development and globalising forces, the impetus to save vanishing local 'traditions' of building has persisted and the romantic regionalist approach has continued almost uninterrupted.[5]

6 Africa/modern

The sixth moment examines South Africa's place in contemporary Africa. One of the defining moments of the political transition in South Africa post-1994 has been the establishment of new democratic mechanisms such as the Truth and Reconciliation Commission (TRC), and the new constitution. These have seen South Africa become a key player in international peace processes. Therefore, the architectural competition for the design of the Constitutional Court complex (Figure 3.6), sited in the precinct of Johannesburg's 'Old Fort', a colonial prison in Hillbrow, attracted attention from local and international architects alike.

The winners of the competition, Durban-based OMM Design Workshop and Urban Solutions (DWUS), conscious of the potential power of inverting a previously penal space into a space of freedom, set out to make a building that is inspired by Africa but simultaneously modern. In describing his design approach, architect Andrew Makin drew a clear distinction between the court buildings and Johannesburg's widely fêted post-apartheid African mall: 'The idea of the court is not to make it like Melrose Arch' (cited in O'Toole 2004/5: 97). The result is a series of modern forms with African-inspired texture and adornment, and metaphoric use of elements such as the 'great African staircase'. Lindsay Bremner highlights important distinctions in the design elements of the new building:

Figure 3.6
Africa/modern: the
Constitutional Court of
South Africa,
Johannesburg 1998.

No building is more significant ... than the recently completed Constitutional Court
building .... Bold, decorative, invoking our multiple pasts in a powerful symbol of an
open, transparent judiciary, this building stands in stark contrast to the other highest
court ... the Appeal Court in Bloemfontein, whose closed façade and formal axial composition represents all that the new court has displaced.

(Bremner 2004/5: 98)

Countering this view, art critic Sean O'Toole is more circumspect, warning of the
untested idealism which the design reflects (O'Toole 2004/5: 97). However,
much like new work emerging in fashion, music, dance and art, architecture
such as this plays with identity in interesting new ways. Culture is viewed as
hybrid and fluid rather than fixed, where ideas and stereotypes about culture and
race in Africa are being played with and used as ways of renegotiating identity,
as South African cities are reframed as 'critical sites for the remixing and
reassembling of ... identities' (Nuttall 2004: 431).

7 Heritage/memory
Moment number seven seeks to reflect interplays between new forms of public
culture and the ways in which heritage and memory are being mobilised in the
remaking of 'nation'. Freedom Park in Pretoria is a state-sanctioned 'legacy
project' (Figure 3.7). Here the ANC-led government has set aside resources for
the transformation of arguably one of the most politically charged Afrikaner cultural spaces in the country, the land surrounding and including the Voortrekker

Figure 3.7
Heritage/memory:
Freedom Park, Pretoria,
2004.

(Afrikaner Settler) Monument (see Meskell, this volume). Through this project, linked to nation-building initiatives, notions of Afrikaner nationalism are being replaced with ideas of African tradition and indigeneity. Elements of the Freedom Park project include a garden landscape in which traditional healers can grow medicinal herbs, and a new museum and archive which aims to house 'tangible' as well as 'intangible' heritage (NHRA (National Heritage Resources Act) 1999).

Bold and large in scale, the Freedom Park initiative is one of a plethora of new heritage projects to be undertaken post-apartheid. New museums that narrate stories of the struggle against apartheid are emerging around the country, and architects (along with historians) are key players in the visioning of these new spaces. Aside from being lucrative commissions for architects, these projects have received significant state funding to institutionalise and establish new histories of struggle. In so doing architects have inadvertently become agents in the re-imagining and representation of history (Bremner 2004/5: 98 and this volume).

In some cases new museums have been conceptualised as architectural projects first and foremost, with high-profile architectural competitions being advertised for their design.[6] Concurrently many of these museums have been challenged to rethink notions of their collections and have relied on oral sources to present collective memory as a way of addressing 'silences' in the formal archives (Hamilton *et al.* 2002). From the Robben Island Museum in Cape Town to the Apartheid and Hector Pieterson Museums in Gauteng to the Mandela Museum in Qunu, Eastern Cape, and the Red Location Apartheid Museum in the Nelson Mandela Metropole (previously Port Elizabeth), these new museums have relied on up-to-date modern architectures and exhibition design for their displays. In many instances they tell similar stories about the struggle against apartheid, triumph over these struggles, and about freedom. Through the rewriting and rescripting of space post-apartheid, these museums and their architectures are part of the assertion of a new national identity (Witz 2005).

8 International/global

Moment number eight is probably the most stable and continuous form of architectural practice that seeks engagement and legitimacy internationally, exemplified by the central atrium in the interior of MMA Architects' new South African Embassy in Berlin (Figure 3.8). Sophisticated and modern, the building marks South Africa's confident return to international diplomacy. The architecture is a restrained modernism which sits comfortably in a setting such as Berlin, where modern architecture is juxtaposed against the historical architecture of the old European city.

Here the use of modernist architecture (significantly designed by two of South Africa's leading black architects) is seen as signalling South Africa's

Figure 3.8
International/global: the
South African Embassy,
Berlin, c.1999.

independence.[7] Through the use of a modernist language of architecture, the building is somehow released from the imperialist neo-classical associations of, for example, Herbert Baker's South Africa House in London. While the architecture is confidently and understatedly metropolitan, free of the heavily African iconography and adornment of the neo-classical approach, African identity is subtly inserted through the placement of the baobab sculpture in the central atrium space (Makeka 2006).

This internationalism can also be seen through the roles architects and planners have played as key image-makers in South Africa's attempts to re-enter global events. Architects have, for example, been commissioned to build pilot projects such as sports halls to bolster bids to the Olympic Games or other international sporting events. These buildings are incongruous in their presence in the contemporary city set amid shack lands in poor areas such as Khayelitsha.[8] Similarly, in the present revisioning of architecture where memory, space and identity are part of the post-apartheid urban imaginary, new global forms of public space are developing in the postmodern malls of South African cities.

The space of the 'experiential economy', exemplified by mall spaces which are virtually indistinguishable from those in other parts of the world (Hall and Bombardella, this volume), makes for an interplay between these market-driven spaces of cultural fantasy production and the urban reality of cities marked by the spatial practices of the apartheid state. These postmodern spaces exist in stark contrast to their modernist predecessors and contemporary modernist-inspired visions of the city. Perhaps, most ironically, the global moment in architecture is linked to the flows of international capital and operates in direct contradiction with current pressures and issues of development.[9]

9 Township/freedom

Moment number nine looks at the interplay between the restrictive space of the township and the space of freedom. Local debates about public space and the city have revealed a slippage between different perceptions around 'township' space in South Africa post-apartheid.[10] What has emerged is the need to examine, to historicise and to reflect on the categories and terms used to describe the city, and in particular, the use of the term 'township'. On the one hand architects, planners and others in the spatial disciplines use the term to describe a 'category' or 'typology' of spatial design. Townships, in this conception, are seen in stable material terms. Increasingly, however, simply understanding the formal spaces created by apartheid modernist practices, laid out and built according to a set of visibly recognisable spatial ordering devices, is not enough basis for critical engagement with the social issues of space and place (Murray 2004: 2).

In contrast to this understanding, perceptions of township spaces by publics who have experienced 'townships' firsthand describe a broader, more complex set of experiences of space. The experience of the township post-apartheid inevitably responds to these different perceptions of space

(Mbembe and Nuttall 2004). The space of the townships as a so-called 'free space' also exists against its opposite in the post-apartheid city where in suburbia, spaces of fear and control are reflected in high walls, electric fencing, security patrols and gated communities (Markus and Cameron 2002: 115–19; Lewis 1998: 84–91).

Concurrently the developmental discourses of the township as a space of underdevelopment, in need of upliftment and somehow peopled with an uncritical citizenry persists. People's needs and aspirations have been easily ignored by local authorities who have continued (assisted by architects and urban designers) in a self-assured policy of spatial intervention.[11] Forms and images of township architecture have to a large extent remained pervasive, despite the presence of resistive, critical and imaginative publics.

This is not to say that township space has not been re-imagined and transformed in interesting ways. Iconic apartheid spaces like single-male hostel compounds in places like Langa and Lwandle near Cape Town, for example, have been successfully converted into family units.[12] Urban renewal projects and service upgrading have seen the quality of urban infrastructure improve. Some special places are even being restored such as the project for the San Souci cinema by Lindsay Bremner, and 26°10′ South Architects for the Vuyani Dance Company in Kliptown near Johannesburg (Steenkamp *et al.* 2006: 42):

> The San Souci was a community cinema [in Kliptown] in which many famous South African musicians, including Miriam Makeba, performed during the apartheid era. It fell into disrepair and was plundered by people looking for building materials and burnt down in 1995. In 2002, a large number of interviews showed that, even in its ruined state, it remained an important place in the memories of local people; therefore the decision was made to reconstruct it as a venue for education, recreation and as a 'living archive'.
>
> (Steenkamp *et al.* 2006: 42)

The township is also significantly the site of new museum initiatives from the large-scale, state-funded projects of nation-building, such as the Hector Pieterson Museum in Kliptown (Figure 3.9) through to small-scale, self-initiated projects such as the Lwandle Migrant Labour Museum near Somerset West, the first township-based museum in the Western Cape (Mgijima and Buthelezi 2001). Concepts of township are represented through different discourses of freedom. In the Apartheid Museum in Gauteng the visitor experiences the grand narratives of apartheid through being given a racial classification at the door which influences his or her journey through the museum. In local museum spaces such as at Lwandle, the history of the township is told through the local experience of the migrant labourer. Visitors are taken through the township to visit Hostel 33 (a preserved hostel) and to experience the township firsthand (Mgijima and Buthelezi 2001: 5).

Figure 3.9
Township/freedom: The
Hector Pieterson
Museum, 2003.

10 Exhibition/review

The last moment is concerned with the portrayal of architectural practice. I have referred elsewhere to 'writing', 'building' and 'exhibition' as 'intersecting forms of practice' that comprise the activity of the architectural discipline in South Africa (Murray 2006: 6). However, it is difficult to ignore that as primary activity, the spatial disciplines and in particular architecture are focused on the practice of building.

Many of the ways in which architects think and write about the discipline are influenced by this focus. From the early publications in the *South African Architectural Record* and in *Zero Hour* by Rex Martienssen and colleagues in the 1930s, to the latest publication from the San Paulo Biennale in 2005, writing, reflection and exhibitions about architecture have centred on the showcasing of work by individuals. This biographic mode is a standard international convention for exhibitions, and for architectural 'monographs' which are the accepted genre for publishing the life work of architects. Largely uncritical and hagiographic, these forms of reflection and review persist without interrogation by either the profession or the academies.

Two contemporary architectural projects undertaken in South Africa in the last ten years are worth exploring to illustrate this argument. The first, initiated in 1997 by the Netherlands Architecture Institute (NAi), culminated in the exhibition *blank_Architecture, apartheid and after*, and the publication of the same name (Judin and Vladislavić 1998). This was an ambitious interdisciplinary project that sought to interrogate the making of the South African landscape in all its complexity. The second, undertaken by the South African Institute of Architects and entitled *Architecture 2000*, was envisaged as a millennium review authored by professionals, and structured chronologically around the notion of a timeline (Prinsloo *et al.* 2000).

Both projects set out an agenda based on the idea of assessment and reflection, and attempt to reflect an overview of the development of the spatial disciplines in South Africa, but they differ in important ways. The first is methodological. Whereas the *blank_* project reviewed architecture in relation to apartheid, which necessitated making a conceptual break with conventional forms of scholarship within the discipline, the *Architecture 2000* project works more or less within the conventions of architectural production in the field. The second relates to the foci of the work. While the *Architecture 2000* publication considers the building as the central 'object' of practice, the *blank_* project seeks to interrogate architectural debate and to situate this within the broader debates in the spatial disciplines and beyond. In positioning themselves in these ways, the two publications reveal fundamentally different approaches. The starting point of

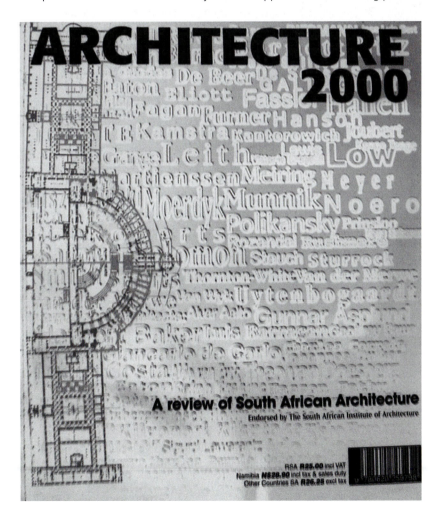

Figure 3.10
Exhibition/review:
Architecture 2000: A Review of South African Architecture.

*blank_* required engagement across a series of literatures, both within the spatial disciplines and in broader interdisciplinary studies, and in particular, in finding the relationship between debates around apartheid and broader critiques of modernity. As a commentary of the state of debates in the discipline, the process of reviewing implied finding a position from which to reflect on the complexities of disciplinary engagement and knowledge production. By way of contrast, the *Architecture 2000* project focused in detail on architects, their built work and some writings. Its cover is made up of a collage of architects' names presented in a 'relief' graphic (Figure 3.10).

The desires of the authors and collaborators on these projects (in both cases numerous) sought to achieve similar aims – those of review and display of a body of work from South Africa. Together, both projects represent the most comprehensive attempt to date at gathering and collating material about South African architecture. Given the strong focus on practice and building in architecture, the production of these texts is doubly important as little scholarly work has been produced since 1994. The *blank_* project stands as a project of critique, revealing the messy field of engagement by professionals in the spatial disciplines during the apartheid and colonial period. It offers no 'solutions', no 'answers', but rather leaves the viewer/reader with a sense of the overwhelming complexities of practice at the margins. The *Architecture 2000* publication on the other hand is a valuable record – attempting a comprehensive history of South African architecture – in the manner of many revisionist historical projects. Significantly, it showcases the achievements of architects and presents a temporal history revealing the scope and range of work produced by individuals, who – during the apartheid years – were outside of the international field of vision and the publication draws attention to this work.

REFERENCES

Appadurai, A. (1996) *Modernity at Large: Cultural Dimensions of Globalisation*, Minneapolis: University of Minnesota Press.

Bremner, Lindsay (2004/5) 'Re-imagining Architecture for Democracy' in I. Low, J. Sandler and S. Hugo-Hamman (eds) *Space and Transformation 10 Years of Democracy*, Digest of South African Architecture, Cape Town: Picasso Headline: 98–9.

Chipkin, C. (1993) *Johannesburg Style: Architecture and Society, 1880s–1960s*, Cape Town: David Philip.

Connell, P.H., Irvine-Smith, C., Jonas, K., Kantorowich, R. and Wepener, F.J. (1939) *Native Housing – A Collective Thesis*, Johannesburg: Witwatersrand University Press.

Cooke, J. (2006a) 'Joining the World', *Architecture South Africa* March–April: 3.

—— (2006b) 'Singita Lebombo', *Architecture South Africa* March–April: 10–13.

Crysler, C.G. (2003) *Writing Spaces: Discourses of Architecture, Urbanism and the Built Environment, 1960–2000*, London: Routledge.

Deckler, T., Graupner, A. and Rasmus, H. (2006) *Contemporary South African Architecture in a Landscape of Transition*, Cape Town: Double Storey.

Fisher, R., Le Roux, H., Murray, N. and Sanders, P. (2003) 'The Modern Movement Architecture of Four South African Cities', *do co .mo.mo Journal* 28, March: 68–76.

Foucault, M. (1976) *The Archaeology of Knowledge*, New York: Harper and Row.

Hamilton, C. *et al.* (2002) *Refiguring the Archive*, Cape Town: David Philip.

Herbert, G. (1975) *Martienssen and the International Style: The Modern Movement in South African Architecture*, Cape Town: A.A. Balkema.

Herwitz, D. (1998) 'Modernism at the Margins' in H. Judin and I. Vladislavić (eds) *blank_Architecture, apartheid and after*, Rotterdam: NAi: 404–21.

Japha, D. (1985) 'The Social Programme of the South African Modern Movement in South Africa', Africa Seminar paper, Center for African Studies, University of Cape Town.

Judin, H. and I. Vladislavić (1998) (eds) *blank_Architecture, apartheid and after*, Rotterdam: NAi.

Le Roux, H. (2005) 'Foreign Parts', keynote address, *Modern Architecture in East Africa around Independence*, published conference proceedings: 43–52.

Lefebvre, H. (1991) *The Production of Space*, trans. D. Nicholson-Smith, Oxford: Blackwell.

Lewis, M. (1998) 'Armed Responses' in H. Judin and I. Vladislavić (eds) *blank_ Architecture, apartheid and after*, Rotterdam: NAi: 84–91.

Lokko, L.N.N. (ed.) (2000) *White Papers, Black Marks: Architecture, Race, Culture*, London: Athlone Press.

Low, I., Sandler, J. and Hugo-Hamman, S. (eds) (2000) *Space and Transformation 10 Years of Democracy*, Digest of South African Architecture 2004/5, Cape Town: Picasso Headline.

Makeka, M. (2006) *Architecture and an African Aesthetic*, Presentation Cities Reading Group, Cape Town: Isandla Institute, April.

Markus, T. and Cameron, D. (2002) *The Words between the Spaces, Buildings and Language*, London: Routledge.

Mbembe, A. (2001) *On the Postcolony*, Berkeley: University of California Press.

Mbembe, A. and Nuttall, S. (2004) 'Writing the World from an African Metropolis', *Public Culture* 16 (3): 347–72.

—— (2005) 'A Blasé Attitude: A Response to Michael Watts', *Public Culture* 17 (1): 193–201.

Mgijima, B. and Buthelezi, V. (2001) 'Mapping Museum–Community Relations in Lwandle', *Mapping Alternatives – Debating New Heritage Practices in South Africa*, conference paper, Centre for African Studies, University of Cape Town: 1–12.

Murray, N. (2004) 'Modernism, Marginality and Apartheid: Architecture, Planning an Urban Design in South Africa', Africa Seminar paper, Centre for African Studies and the Graduate School in the Humanities, University of Cape Town, September: 1–9.

—— (2006) 'Reframing the "Contemporary", Architecture and the Postcolony', in T. Deckler, A. Graupner and H. Rasmus (eds) *Contemporary South African Architecture in a Landscape of Transition*, Cape Town: Double Storey: 4–8.

Neluheni, M. (2000) 'Aparthied Urban Development' in L.N.N. Lokko (ed.) *White Papers, Black Marks: Architecture, Race, Culture*, London: Athlone Press: 66–91.

Nuttall, S. (2004) 'Stylising the Self: The Y generation in Rosebank, Johannesburg', *Public Culture* 16 (3).

O'Toole, S. (2004/5) 'The Splintered Metropolis' in I. Low, J. Sandler and S. Hugo-Hamman

(eds) *Space and Transformation 10 Years of Democracy*, Digest of South African Architecture, Cape Town: Picasso: 94–7.

Prinsloo, I., Van Wyk, L., De Beer, I. and Jacobs, H. (eds) (2000) *Architecture 2000: A
Review of South African Architecture*, Cape Town: Picasso Headline.

Prosalendis, S. and Rassool, C. (eds) (2001) *Recalling Community in Cape Town: Creating
and Curating the District Six Museum*, Cape Town: District Six Museum.

Silverman, M. (1998) '"Ons bou vir die Bank:" Nationalism, architecture and Volkskas
Bank', in H. Judin and I. Vladislavić (eds) *blank_Architecture, apartheid and after*, Rotterdam: NAi: 128–43.

South Africa Government, National Heritage Resources Act (NHRA) 1999.

Steenkamp, A., Raman, P.G and Cooke, J. (2006) 'Project Awards – Biennial Awards',
Architecture South Africa March/April: 40–4.

Witz, L. (2005) 'Perspectives on Collecting and Exhibiting for New and Diverse Audiences',
unpublished conference paper, History Department/Center for Humanities
Research/African Program in Museum and Heritage Studies, University of the Western
Cape: 1–17.

Chapter 4: Engaging with Difference

Understanding the Limits of Multiculturalism in Planning in the South African Context

Vanessa Watson

In some recently completed anthropological research,[1] Ngxabi (2003) relates how her Xhosa-speaking informants consistently refer to their Cape Town dwellings as *indlu* (a house) which is different from *ikhaya* (a home, usually to be found in the Eastern Cape). The term *indlu* has traditionally been used to refer to individual structures in a homestead which accommodate some members of the family (perhaps a wife and her children), but only together do the structures constitute *ikhaya* or *umzi* (a home). The term *ikhaya*, Ngxabi argues, suggests connectedness and it is a place where such connections can be made concrete through rituals which allow communication with deceased family members. *Ikhaya* is the place of graves, and this makes it sacred, giving the place power over the living. It is the place where rites of passage best take place, because here the child, becoming an adult, can be introduced to her ancestors who will then watch over her. It is the place where a child's umbilical cord is buried (it is dug into the wall of the great house of the home of the baby's father) and through this a strong connection is made between the soil of that place and the living human being. To be buried at this place is then a vital reconnection with home and with family members who have passed on.

The term *indlu*, by contrast, originally suggests separation within a family, but is also used to refer to formal urban dwellings because they serve to physically separate people from kin and from ancestors (Ngxabi 2003). The sense of separation from ancestors is attributed to the lack of yard space around urban dwellings, the difficulty of configuring the use of this space, and urban controls over space use. Contact with ancestors occurs primarily through the keeping of cattle and many rituals are based in the cattle byre. Without these, connection with deceased kin is difficult and an *indlu* cannot be considered *ikhaya*.

The unsatisfactory nature of urban dwellings is reflected again by Ngxabi's respondents in the term they use to refer to Cape Town: *esilungweni* (place of the white peoples' ways). One respondent (Ngxabi 2003: 53) describes the city as a place of *impangelo* (working for a wage, derived from the word *ukuphanga*, meaning to eat as fast as you can so that you can get more than others eating from the same plate). This conveys a sense of competition between people engendered by engagement in the urban economy, and is described as a form of moral degradation as it erodes values of reciprocity and mutual help. Thus Ngxabi's respondents see both living in the city and in urban dwellings as contributing to a process of individualisation which is at odds with the communal nature of Xhosa culture.

Interestingly, not all urban dwellings are viewed in the same light. Dwellings in informal settlements are seen as approximating more closely a rural setting, and here Ngxabi found people who were attempting to keep cattle and to practise adapted forms of ritual in their cattle byres. Some of these households expressed strong resistance to moving to the new Reconstruction and Development Programme (RDP)[2] houses in the nearby area of Crossroads (the scheme had been named *Veza*, meaning 'show foot' – suggesting that when a big man sleeps in these small houses, his feet will protrude outside), as the move implied a severance of communal ties: with extended family members who could not fit into the tiny houses, with neighbours with whom reciprocal relations would be broken, and with ancestors with whom there could no longer be communication in the absence of space for even downscaled rituals. This gradual social isolation under conditions of economic marginality can be devastating for a household.

In terms of both normative frameworks and substantive content, planning (as a factor in city building and city management) has long had universalising tendencies. Forces such as colonialism, modernism and, more recently, globalisation, have had the effect of diffusing planning ideas and practices across the globe. The vehicles for this diffusion have included consultants, donor and development agencies, and globetrotting academics, but perhaps just as often they have been 'local' agencies seeking a quick solution through a cut-and-paste from a 'best practices' website.

PLANNING SOLUTIONS

A growing volume of literature documents the spread of spatial concepts and urban forms: garden cities, green belts, new towns and, more recently, waterfronts, mega-malls, and new urbanist 'villages', have found their way into almost every city in the world, creating high levels of physical homogeneity. Cape Town has all of these. In policy terms as well, international agencies such as the World Bank have been highly influential in spreading particular approaches to developing countries, and the low-income housing policy adopted by the South African government in 1994 was one such international model. Just as important, but more subtle, however, are the range of planning assumptions which underpin these physical forms and interventions. These are assumptions about the kinds of planning solutions which 'fit' particular social or economic needs, assumptions about the nature of households and how they survive economically, assumptions about culture and cultural expression, and assumptions about the kinds of processes (consensus-seeking or otherwise) through which planning issues can be resolved. It is in these arenas that universalising tendencies have been particularly strong, and have related to the assumed nature of the society with which planners interface.

The particular concept of society which, usually implicitly, shapes thinking and action in planning has been strongly shaped by post-Enlightenment and Western traditions. These ideas have shaped a dominant rationality which in turn sets standards of 'normality' regarding proper living environments, the proper conduct of citizens, the way in which individuals relate to society, notions of the public good, and so on. The notion of what is a proper living environment becomes stark in the context of developing countries where so often informal or shack settlements are regarded as unacceptable and in need of replacement by formal housing projects, as in the case of Ngxabi's story above. Extending the grid of formalised and regulated development over what is often termed the 'unruly' (or unrule-able) city shapes the planning effort in many cities of the developing world.

In this chapter, I argue that in many respects we are confronted by a situation of conflicting rationalities: on the one hand, the rationality of the technical infrastructural and managerial systems which are used to order urban environments, and on the other, the rationalities of those who are attempting to survive, materially and culturally, in what are often regarded as alien places. From the perspective of urban planning theory, there has been a recent shift towards accepting, and responding to, the realities of social difference and multiculturalism, and yet planning still finds itself trapped by the liberal philosophical foundations which shape its thinking. The next sections consider how planning thought has attempted to respond to these realities and how these attempts have reached their limitations.

ACHIEVING 'PROPER COMMUNITIES'

It is first necessary to examine the thinking that underlies the notion of a 'proper' community and proper housing in the South African context because it is these ideas which informed the state-initiated, physical project of house-building in the Crossroads area in Cape Town (the building of *indlu* or RDP houses). The sources for these ideas of a 'proper' community lie, in part, in South African government policy documents and, in part, in broader theories of development and planning.

The notion that poor people should be provided, by the state, with formal housing structures in planned and serviced areas forms the cornerstone of current South African national housing policy. In many areas, including that of Crossroads, this has been interpreted to mean that informal structures do not constitute acceptable housing, and must be replaced. The desire on the part of governments almost everywhere to formalise informal, irregular or illegal settlement has a long history, with its origins, as described by James Scott (1998: 4), lying in the early emergence of modern statecraft and its subsequent development into 'high-modernist ideology' aimed at 'the rational design of social order commensurate with the scientific understanding of natural laws'. These imperatives, in the first instance, shaped government action in Western-ised societies but were applied as well, often with missionary zeal, in colonial and postcolonial territories where development and modernisation came to mean the same thing. Ideals underlying this ideology have always been partly utopian (the creation of a better society and healthy, contented communities) but also partly bound up with the desire to administer, to control and to incorporate popula-tions into municipal finance systems.

Implicit in this ideology are the assumptions that occupants of informal structures (usually assumed to be small, stable, nuclear families) will accept the long-term, binding legal and financial obligations that accompany home owner-ship: adherence to various regulations regarding the use of the land and the conduct of the occupants (for example, respecting noise and health standards – with the keeping and slaughter of animals prohibited), and the payment of regular rates and service charges to the municipal authority. Also implicit is the assumption that shack-dwellers will be prepared to commit themselves to a particular piece of land or territory which they will come to regard as both their home (*ikhaya*) and as a marketable capital asset to be used for economic uplift-ment (the 'De Soto' thesis). Recent thinking on housing policy in the developing world (UN-Habitat 2002) ties the issue of shelter upgrade firmly to poverty reduc-tion and sustainable urbanisation, and argues particularly for the formalisation of tenure systems: the link between these remains somewhat unclear.

The post-apartheid commitment to meeting basic housing needs in South Africa was extended significantly in the policy documents and legislation which accompanied the transformation of local government. The White Paper on local government (Ministry for Provincial Affairs and Constitutional Development 1998) demands that municipalities become 'developmental' i.e. that they work with citizens and groups within communities to find sustainable ways of meeting social and material needs. The White Paper explains that this assumes the estab-lishment of democratic rule through elected councillors; that councillors should work with organs of civil society (seen as separate from the state); should foster community participation and (qualified)[3] consensus around development; and should work to build up 'social capital' to find local solutions to problems. What is involved in creating 'proper' communities is thus no longer a technical and managerial task, it is also a moral and political task (Chipkin 2003).

These ideas about state, citizenship and participation are not unique to South Africa: they are firmly rooted in current Western political and social theory, from which planning theory also takes its cue. Western traditions of liberal democracy, of which there are variations, influence much planning thought about individual rights and liberties, about ethical frameworks, and about plan-ning processes. Liberalism takes the individual as the basic unit of society, able to be conceptualised and defined independently of society, and in a normative sense holding a distance from society as an autonomous and self-determining being (Parekh 1993). Morality then, or the notion of the good, is not a socially or collectively imposed construct, but rather an aggregation of individual choices or preferences. Much land use policy, particularly in the US, has been driven by a utilitarian ethic which holds that the right decision is the one which creates the greatest aggregate level of social benefit, indicated by the price signals of a free-market economy in land. This view in turn sees land as an economic commodity, rather than (as in some other parts of the world) a communal resource with perhaps additional mystical or ancestral meanings. The British planning system, by contrast, has been far more accepting of a state interpretation of aggregated individual preferences, which sets the goals of amenity, convenience and efficiency as standards to define the best use of land (Campbell and Marshall 2002).

Planning theory, as well, has contributed to the conventional wisdom on the functioning of 'proper' communities, primarily through its ideas on decision-making processes in the context of urban and land development. Communicative action theory could be described as the current dominant approach in planning theory, although critiques of it have emerged (for example, see Tewdwr-Jones and Allmendinger 1998). In brief (Watson 2002), communicative action theory argues that planning decisions should be reached through collaborative processes involving all stakeholders, and conforming to particular rules which ensure that participation is fair, equal and empowering. Embedded in this approach are the assumptions that community divisions can be overcome and consensus reached on planning issues; that collaborative processes involving primarily civil society-based groups can act to put pressure on the state to act more responsibly; and that collaboration can provide a learning environment and build social capital within communities.[4] Significantly, however, as the Crossroads case shows, the splitting of extended families into individual, formal housing units is breaking social and family networks and probably doing a great deal to destroy social capital rather than to build it.

Certain planning theorists have attempted to move beyond the assumptions of universality contained in communicative action theory, which allows differences between actors to occur only at the level of speech or ideas, and which in turn can be overcome through the force of the better argument (Habermas 1984). Healey (1992: 152) acknowledges that communicating groups may operate within different 'systems of meaning', which means that 'we see things differently because words, phrases, expressions, objects, are interpreted differently according to our frame of reference'. The assumption that these differences can be overcome through debate in a consensus-seeking process remains, however.

Acknowledgement of diversity (and 'multiculturalism') is a central element in the work of Leonie Sandercock (1998a, 1998b, 2000). Her main point of departure is that citizenship is fragmented by identity, and that society is structured by culturally different groupings based on sexuality, ethnicity, gender or race. This diversity should be celebrated rather than repressed, and the claims of different groups need to be recognised and facilitated. It can be argued here that

Sandercock is not simply interested in recognising difference in procedural terms (in order to move towards a more homogeneous or equal society); she is interested in 'substantive difference', or affirming a society made up of different groups. This is promoting difference for its own sake. The difference with Sandercock's work is that she is concerned to build consensus between groups, which affirms and valorises difference rather than erases it, and which could take the form of resistance to the state. While this represents an important shift away from assumptions of universal citizenship, a belief that culturally different groups can reach consensus is present here as well.

These concepts and assumptions regarding the role and functioning of state, society and citizens thus define one set of rationalities which are usually at play and which would have informed the Crossroads housing project. They could be described as closely linked to ideas of modernity and progress shaped by a Western experience, as well as to normative ideas about state, citizenship and recognition of identity which have also largely emanated from that context. They help to define the notion of 'proper' citizens and communities which, at least at the level of rhetoric, drives the policies and actions of local authorities in South Africa and in other parts of Africa as well.

DEEP DIFFERENCE – CONFLICTING RATIONALITIES

Ngxabi's (2003) Crossroads story, which I am suggesting is far from unique in the cities of Africa, is telling us that a vast gap exists between the notion of 'proper' communities held by most planners and administrators (grounded in the rationality of Western modernity and development), and the rationality which informs the strategies and tactics of those who are attempting to survive, materially and culturally, in the harsh environment of Africa's cities.

The intention of the example above is not to romanticise cultural traditions, nor to suggest that they should be uncritically celebrated, as some positions on multiculturalism would have it. Communalist cultures can often disguise forms of discrimination. For example, Ferguson (in Ngxabi 2003: 70) noted that in Lesotho men keep cattle as a form of wealth as they are difficult for women to convert into cash. The Crossroads example does, however, provide evidence of the coexistence in South African cities of alternative rationalities or worldviews, which shape attitudes to land, its ownership and to the use of space, and which do not conform to what is considered proper by city managers and most built environment professionals. In fact, to some of Ngxabi's respondents, requirements linked to housing, tenure and space use in *esilungweni* were contributing to moral degradation and were directly undermining their own proper conduct.

The project, in Crossroads, of replacing informal shacks with formal structures in a planned and serviced township also reveals a significant failure to understand the survival strategies of those who live in the informal settlements. In resource-poor situations, marginalisation in all its forms requires that individuals operate within and through a dense web of personal networks, or sets of reciprocal relationships. The phenomenon of spatially 'stretched' households (Spiegel *et al.* 1996) and kinship networks which allows access to resources in varying urban, peri-urban and rural locations, as opportunity arises, has been well documented in Africa. Importantly, maintaining 'stretched' households or kinship networks produces frequent movement between urban and rural bases. Marginal economic and political opportunities, as they arise in different locales, require physical presence and hence movement. The population of Africa is highly mobile, ever shifting, ever searching for meager sources of survival; or alternatively moving to escape warfare, persecution or natural disaster. There may well be emotional ties to a piece of land somewhere – called, perhaps, home. But for many of the poor in urban areas, there may be little commitment to a particular place or territory, particularly under freehold tenure. Such commitment comes with economic progress, and with the ability to loosen relational ties and invest in land and structure rather than in maintaining social networks. Most urban projects assume commitment to a particular piece of land or territory and a continuity of presence, but it cannot be assumed that individuals or households will meet the requirements of 'proper' community members – investing in their land or home, contributing to rates and service charges, helping to build social capital and local democracy – when survival demands frequent movement.

Planning theories which attempt to recognise social difference and multi-culturalism represent an important advance. A multicultural approach would, in the Crossroads case above, directly draw attention to potential conflicts around the meaning and form of land and housing. But here again we have to be careful that the concept of identity which is embedded in the writings of largely Northern, developed world theorists, is appropriate to the local context.

The point has been repeatedly made that political struggles in Africa are far less like the identity/lifestyle politics which have become so visible in developed contexts and are far more likely to be reactive to material issues and the simple need for survival (Mohan 1997). This has led Mohan to argue that identity is not a useful starting point in understanding political struggles in Africa, or at least it may require a more complete understanding of the relations between materiality and identity. Authors highlight the extremely complex and fluid nature of identity in Africa. Social and economic collapse and turmoil leave many people with little sense of belonging (a process, some argue, which began with colonial penetration) or little idea of who represents them. One way out of this is to use identity in a highly opportunistic way:

> depending on the situation, sometimes religion, sometimes ethnicity may prove to be the determining factor in an individual's identity and behaviour. The organisational versatility of the orders that has made them the primary modes of organisation vis a vis the state lies in their capacity to adapt to this ambiguity, and even capitalise on it ....
>
> (Leonardo Villalon cited in O'Brien 1996: 63)

Thus identity in Africa is often a product of hybridisation, fusion and cultural innovation. It is frequently self-generated and self-constructed, sometimes with a renewed stress on ethnic identity or 'retribalisation', sometimes intertwined with global identities (De Boeck 1996). Currently, religious commitment offers many young people a way of escaping from social marginalisation, and O'Brien (1996: 64) comments that Christian missions are the biggest single industry in Africa today. Students are often in the vanguard of liberation movements, but their role is ambivalent, and may be related more closely to the desire to gain access to government jobs and membership of the ruling elite than to secure democracy. The political impulse of the crowd is above all economically motivated (O'Brien 1996).

Thus the recognition and celebration of identity, as advocated by Sandercock, needs to be thought about differently, given the continued focus of political struggles in Africa on material rather than lifestyle/identity politics. Nancy Fraser (2000) is concerned with identity politics more generally, but her arguments have relevance for operationalising this approach in African contexts. Her concerns are first, that demands for recognition are eclipsing demands for redistribution (in a context of growing economic disparity), and second, that the reification of cultural difference is encouraging separatism and intolerance. The results, she argues, are growing inequalities and a sanctioning of the violation of human rights. Identity politics displace struggles for redistribution in two ways. Some positions cast the roots of injustice at the level of discourse (for example, demeaning representations), rather than at the level of institutional significations and norms. This strips misrecognition of its social-structural underpinnings. Other positions, associated with cultural theory, assume that maldistribution is a secondary effect of misrecognition and that misrecognition should be considered prior to distributional issues. This appears to be Sandercock's position. Fraser (2000) argues that not only do these positions obscure the real roots of misrecognition, which lie in institutionalised value patterns, but that reification of identity creates a moral pressure for group conformity, obscuring intra-group struggles, such as that around gender.

These ideas suggest that local planners, who may be keen to foreground identity issues, need to proceed with great care. To the extent that they sideline distributional issues, they may exacerbate central problems of poverty and disparity. There is also the danger of failing to recognise that many expressions of identity are economically motivated and sometimes opportunistic. Assuming a primacy for identity may have economic consequences which are not entirely predictable or desirable.

Ngxabi's research in Crossroads is indicative of a clash of rationalities, or differences in worldview, which are so great that it is difficult to believe that any amount of discussion or conflict resolution could overcome the divide and achieve consensus: differences go far beyond speech-level misunderstandings or an unwillingness to see the others' point of view. There are also indications that assumptions about the role of identity in multicultural planning need to be treated cautiously so that we do not again make the mistake of imposing inappropriate conceptions of planning and development. Finally, the central assumption underlying housing projects in this context – that people will attach value to urban land as a marketable commodity – may hold for some, but clearly not for all.

RESPONDING TO CONFLICTING RATIONALITIES

Chabal and Deloz (1999) argue that it is a mistake to view Africa as a case of failed development; rather it is embracing modernity in a way which is highly particular to the economy and culture of the context. The result is a fusion of the institutions and practices of Western modernity with local ways of coping in a situation of rapid change and economic crisis. In similar vein, the post-development literature is now pointing to ways in which planning and development programmes are 'absorbed' selectively by target communities, and are mutated within local traditions and ways of doing things, giving rise to various combinations of what planners and urban managers regard as 'proper', and what communities might regard as more or less useful (see Arce and Long 2000). The term 'indigenous modernities' has been used to describe ways in which 'development packages are resisted, embraced, reshaped or accommodated depending on the specific content and context' (Robins 2003: 1). These writers are asking the question: how do people actually respond when confronted with attempts to impose particular forms of modernity; especially programmes which impose change in the use and control of territory, often accompanied by the destruction of social networks and forms of survival?

What we need to understand about modernity in the African context, Chabal and Deloz (1999: 148) argue, is that politics cannot be separated from the socio-cultural considerations which govern everyday life. There is constant and dynamic interpretation of the different spheres of human experience, from the political to the religious. What this gives rise to are ways of operating in relation to the state and economy that are different, but nonetheless highly rational. They can only be defined as irrational when an attempt is made to hold them up against models of Western modernity which claim a monopoly on rationality.

This in turn has implications for two important aspects of planning: the extent to which we continue to draw on universalised approaches to planning values (for example, holding to the idea that there is an undifferentiated 'public good' which should guide all development) or accept that values are highly 'situated' and context-dependent; and the extent to which we attempt to draw on 'local knowledge', which may give different understandings to expert knowledge.

On the question of values, it has been argued above that planners frequently operate within the framework of unified ethical positions such as utilitarianism, Rawlsian contract theory (Rawls 1971), Habermasian reasoning and consensus (Habermas 1984), or various forms of environmentalism. But a number of writers have attempted to probe the notion of universal ethics, and how we could regard the ethical frameworks of others, which may be different from our own. Some of these ideas have been inspired by a postmodern concern with the recognition of difference and by related feminist enquiry. Thus Haraway (1991: 191) proposes a doctrine of 'embodied objectivity' which involves 'seeing' from the perspective of the 'subjugated', not because people who are oppressed are 'innocent' but because 'in principle they are least likely to allow denial of the critical and interpretative core of all knowledge ... subjugated standpoints are preferred because they seem to promise more adequate, sustained, objective, transforming accounts of the world' (in Hall 2003). Within the planning field Campbell (2002) has argued that because planning problems are inherently 'situated' (and contested), we need to find an appropriate basis for ethical judgement in planning based on a relational understanding of society which recognises both difference and the common good. Planning should not, therefore, be about the imposition of fixed values, but rather about 'situated judgement with and for others ... in just institutions' (Campbell 2002: 282). Flyvbjerg (2001) draws on Foucault's concept of 'situational ethics', rejecting both a foundational and relativistic idea of norms, and accepting instead norms that are contextually grounded. This involves discovering the common view among a specific reference group to which the researchers refer.

On the issue of 'local knowledge', an important role for planners remains that of trying to gain a deeper knowledge of alternative rationalities, where these present themselves in the practical field. This in turn has the potential to uncover 'common ground' which is the precondition for understanding. There are linkages here to the recent work of Hajer and Wagenaar (2003: 22), who develop their ideas in recognition of a reality of conflicting values, where values cannot be seen apart from their context. Their idea of 'interpretive policy analysis' draws particularly on the need for an understanding of 'local knowledge' (Yanow 2003) which in turn is viewed from a cultural perspective, implying a focus on collectives (rather than individuals); their situated acts; related artifacts; the language used to engage them; their site-specific meanings; and the methods used to access them (Yanow 2003: 232–3). This work is calling for a fine-grained, situated, qualitative understanding of the everyday lives of ordinary people, to inform planning intervention. With this kind of understanding, even though it may well be partial, planners are better able to bridge the gap between conflicting rationalities in multicultural confrontations, as well as the interface between the conventional (and usually market-related) urban managerial, regulatory and technical systems and the daily lives of urban inhabitants.

There is a growing debate on the issue of 'local knowledge', which cannot be fully developed here, but which built environment professionals need to be aware of. Writers have questioned its incorporation into the modernist development paradigm, where a focus on 'indigenous technologies' has been seen as useful to the modernist project and largely about project feasibility. Hence writers such as Scott (1998) use the term 'practical knowledge' to emphasise its fluid, changing and contemporary nature; and 'endogenous knowledge' (Crossman and Devisch 2002: 99) meaning understanding determined by 'innate resources'. Both reject the implication of the term local knowledge to imply something necessarily small or local in scale. Both understand this knowledge to mean a great deal more than technical or traditional knowledge, but rather referring to a broader frame of concepts, values and discourses which comprise a particular worldview.

CONCLUSION

In this chapter, I have outlined the problems of universalism which have, for a long time, shaped the actions of those who intervene in the built environment. Liberalism, which has provided an overarching philosophy for planning thought, has itself always assumed universal relevance, and this in turn has inhibited a debate within the built environment professions regarding the implications of social difference. In the field of planning theory, there has been some important questioning of this universalism, and the position broadly termed 'multicultural-ism' recognises and affirms social difference and the role of identity.

I have argued, however, that multicultural planning has its limitations in contexts which are significantly different from those of the developed world, and in situations where differences go beyond simple misunderstandings of words and meanings and where they take on the nature of rationality conflicts. Thus assumptions of people's relationship to land, shelter and to the city, and assump-tions regarding the role and nature of identity and social networks, often do not hold in the cities of Africa, Cape Town included, and such differences often cannot be overcome through participatory or communicative processes, however well managed they may be.

What this requires, it is argued, is a better understanding of the 'interface' between policy interventions on the one hand, and the nature of responses by people who are targets of such interventions, as they adjust their everyday lives to embrace, reject or hybridise the technical and managerial systems which continually attempt to create order and predictability in urban environments. It is the kind of understanding of responses elicited by Ngxabi (2003) in her anthro-pological research which are extremely useful here. Along with this, it is sug-gested, we need to reframe some of the fundamental ideas regarding the nature of values in planning, and the extent to which we accept that they are shaped by particular contexts; and the role played by 'practical knowledge' as a basic infor-mant to intervention.

REFERENCES

Arce, A. and Long, N. (2000) (eds) *Anthropology, Development and Modernities*, London: Routledge.

Campbell, H. (2002) 'Planning: An Idea of Value', *Town Planning Review* 73 (3): 271–88.

Campbell, H. and Marshall, R. (2002) 'Utilitarianism's Bad Breath? A Re-evaluation of the Public Interest Justification for Planning', *Planning Theory* 1 (2): 163–87.

Chabal, P. and Deloz, J.P. (1999) *Africa Works: Disorder as Political Instrument*, International African Institute, Oxford: James Curry and Bloomington: Indiana University Press.

Chipkin, I. (2003) '"Functional" and "Dysfunctional" Communities: The Making of Ethical Citizens', *Journal of Southern African Studies* 29 (1): 63–82.

Crossman, P. and Devisch, R. (2002) 'Endogenous Knowledge in Anthropological Perspective', in C. Hoppers (ed.) *Indigenous Knowledge and the Integration of Knowledge Systems: Towards a Philosophy of Articulation*, Claremont (South Africa): New Africa Books.

De Boeck, F. (1996) 'Postcolonialism, Power and Identity: Local and Global Perspectives from Zaire', in R. Werbner and T. Ranger (eds) *Postcolonial Identities in Africa*, London: Zed Books.

Flyvbjerg, B. (2001) *Making Social Science Matter*, Cambridge: Cambridge University Press.

Fraser, N. (2000) 'Rethinking Recognition', *New Left Review* 3: 107–20.

Habermas, J. (1984) *The Theory of Communicative Action Vol. 1*, Boston, MA: Beacon Press.

Hajer, M. and Wagenaar, H. (eds) (2003) *Deliberative Policy Analysis: Understanding Governance in the Network Society*, Cambridge: Cambridge University Press.

Hall, M. (2003) *Situational Ethics and Engaged Practice: The Case of Archaeology in Africa*, paper presented at the Centre for African Studies, University of Cape Town.

Haraway, D. (1991) *Simians, Cyborgs and Women: The Reinvention of Nature*, London: Free Association Books.

Healey, P. (1992) 'Planning through Debate: The Communicative Turn in Planning Theory', *Town Planning Review* 63 (2): 143–62.

—— (1999) 'Institutional Analysis, Communicative Planning, and Shaping Places', *Journal of Planning Education and Research* 19: 111–21.

Ministry for Provincial Affairs and Constitutional Development (1998) *The White Paper on Local Government*, Pretoria: Government Printer.

Mohan, G. (1997) 'Developing Differences: Post-structuralism and Political Economy in Contemporary Development Studies', *Review of Radical Political Economy* 73: 311–28.

Ngxabi, N. (2003) 'Homes or Houses? Strategies of Home-making among Some AmaXhosa in the Western Cape', unpublished M.Phil thesis, University of Cape Town.

O'Brien, D. (1996) 'A Lost Generation? Youth Identity and State Decay in West Africa', in R. Werbner and T. Ranger (eds) *Postcolonial Identities in Africa*, London: Zed Books.

Parekh, B. (1993) 'The Cultural Particularity of Liberal Democracy', in D. Held (ed.) *Prospects for Democracy: North, South, East, West*, Cambridge: Polity Press and Oxford: Blackwell Publishers.

Rawls, J. (1971) *A Theory of Justice*, Cambridge, MA: Harvard University Press.

Robins, S. (2003) 'Whose Modernity? Indigenous Modernities and Land Claims after Apartheid', *Development and Change* 34 (2): 1–21.

Sandercock, L. (1998a) *Towards Cosmopolis: Planning for Multicultural Cities*, Chichester: John Wiley.

—— (1998b) 'The Death of Modernist Planning: Radical Praxis for a Postmodern Age', in M. Douglass and J. Friedmann (eds) *Cities for Citizens*, Chichester: John Wiley and Sons.

—— (2000) 'Negotiating Fear and Desire, the Future of Planning in Multicultural Societies', *Urban Forum* 11 (2): 201–10.

Scott, J. (1998) *Seeing Like a State,* New Haven and London: Yale University Press.

Spiegel, A., Watson, V. and Wilkinson, P. (1996) 'Domestic Diversity and Fluidity among Some African Households in Greater Cape Town', *Social Dynamics* 21 (2): 7–30.

Tewdwr-Jones, M. and Allmendinger, P. (1998) 'Deconstructing Communicative Rationality: A Critique of Habermasian Collaborative Planning', *Environment and Planning A* 30 (11): 1975–89.

UN-Habitat (2002) *Urban Development and Shelter Strategies Favouring the Urban Poor*, Nairobi: UN Governing Council of the United Nations Human Settlements Programme.

Watson, V. (2002) 'The Usefulness of Normative Planning Theories in the Context of Sub-Saharan Africa', *Planning Theory* 1 (1): 27–52.

—— (2004) 'Transforming the South African City: Issues of Culture', *Architecture SA* 8: Jan./Feb.

Yanow, D. (2003) 'Accessing Local Knowledge', in M. Hajer and H. Wagenaar (eds) *Deliberative Policy Analysis: Understanding Governance in the Network Society*, Cambridge: Cambridge University Press.

Chapter 5: Missing in Khayelitsha

Tobias Hecht

Before ushering me in, Nomsa put the big white bucket outside.

Holding her baby in one hand, she motioned then towards the interior of the cockeyed slant of wood, corrugated tin and heavy plastic sheeting that was her home, the only light streaming in through the open door. I made a mental list of everything I saw: two matching armchairs with clear plastic covers; an aluminum pot (dimpled, empty); a kerosene burner; a makeshift cabinet; some tatters of clothing in a slumping box; a portrait of Jesus; two single beds. Save young Nomsa and the baby, there was nothing else to include on the list.

One of the beds was Nomsa's. The other must have belonged to her mother who, not half a year ago, died at an age when other women might be setting eyes on their firstborn. Three generations in less than four decades. But now just two generations left and the baby wheezing the very strain of TB that, along with a lot of other illnesses, had accompanied the young grandmother to her skeletal, hairless, shattered end.

Sitting there, looking, wondering, counting, adding, subtracting, it seemed as if time and space were somehow off-kilter, the proportions all wrong. Put the tumbledown shack on wheels and onto the roads of southern California and it would be smaller than a Chevy Suburban. And the baby was impossibly diminutive for her twenty-one months. Jesus, for his part, about eye-level between the beds, hung askew and my presence was only one more piece of the misunderstanding. On my way to Nomsa's, a man had stumbled out of a shebeen only to halt in his tracks like a wind-up doll whose spring had suddenly lost all tension in the midst of a strange astonished gesture, eyes wide, mouth agape, frozen before the strange apparition of a white man in Khayelitsha.

What I was thinking was this: what is it like to watch your mother lose her hair, her flesh, her sight, her mind in a world that couldn't be twelve meters square and lacks a toilet? No one dies of that virus without a thousand episodes of diarrhoea. The sadness in Nomsa's eyes was more gaping than resignation.

I'd already visited the nearest municipal toilet. A five-minute walk through a gauntlet of tumble-down shacks, across a busy road, the stalls are at the long-distance minibus rank. This is where you come if you plan to ride one of those deathtraps the twelve or fourteen hours it takes to get to the Eastern Cape. Or if you live in the area and want to make use of a flush toilet. The thing is, none of the hundreds of nearby shacks have toilets either.

There is one redbrick building for the men, another for the women, six stalls each. Majola Kokoti, a man of about sixty with a nice hat and impenetrable eyes, stood outside, winding strips of toilet paper around his fingers, tearing each wad off the roll after about twenty sheets. If you pay the one rand he charges for entering the toilets, he gives you the paper for free. If you don't need it or can make do with less paper, whatever's left over is yours to keep.

I had mistakenly entered the women's side. There was no sign. A lady with an infant followed me in and, perhaps thinking I was some sort of municipal inspector, paid me no mind. But when she opened the first stall, from inside a man's drunken curses. She yelled at him – he was in the women's toilet, he must leave. He said he didn't care.

This is one way to relieve yourself. Come to the taxi rank, pay the one rand, get the paper from Mr Majola Kokoti. But at least three things must be kept in mind. First, the toilets are locked after sundown, so if it's dark there are no toilets anywhere remotely close. That means timing is of the essence. Second, if you're a woman you might find a drunken man in one of the stalls. So bring a stick or a friend, or several friends. Have a trusted man stand outside. Third, consider whether you can afford it.

Nomsa showed me her diploma from a one-week training where she'd learned everything you need to know to be a security guard. Only she hadn't found a job because the security firms won't hire you without matric and she'd gone only as far as seventh grade. Since the time her mother fell ill and lost her job as a char, Nomsa's sole source of income was a government grant for mothers of small children: R160 a month, about $25.

Back when Nomsa's mother was strong enough to walk to the toilet, a day with diarrhoea might have involved twelve trips. A dozen trips, a dozen rands: seven percent of Nomsa's monthly income. Imagine how much it would cost if a lawyer in Cleveland had to pay seven percent of his monthly take-home pay to cover the trips he made to the bathroom in a single day. Which is why alternatives must be found.

Nomsa's is the big white bucket she places outside whenever visitors arrive.

Part II

Sites of Memory and Identity

Chapter 6: Memory, Nation Building and the Post-apartheid City

The Apartheid Museum in Johannesburg

Lindsay Jill Bremner

On 27 April 1994, that which had structured every aspect of life in South Africa for 48 years – apartheid – passed officially into the realm of history. Statutory apartheid was over. What had until then been part of everyday life, now had to be recalled to be remembered.

This apparent rupture has produced, over the past ten years, a new genre of buildings, heritage sites and memorials around the country. The Robben Island and District Six Museums in Cape Town, the Museum of the Peoples' Struggle in Port Elizabeth, the Hector Pieterson Museum in Soweto, the Fort Museum in Johannesburg, the Cato Manor Museum in Durban, these and a growing number of others, constitute the evolving cartography of sites devoted to apartheid memory and narrative. They are new kinds of cultural institutions, some public, some private, some site-specific, some at a physical distance from the events they commemorate, but all evoking new kinds of public consciousness and new kinds of public encounters. They are containers of memory, both individual and collective, standing in for the historical practices known as apartheid, excavating the apartheid consciousness, and subjecting it to an exhibitionary gaze.

In so doing, these museums participate in two other projects. The first is the complex work of post-apartheid nation building. Post-apartheid museums have become sites in an extensive practice of nation building (as are the Truth and Reconciliation Commission, the new national anthem and flag, new public holidays, memorial services, autobiographical and biographical writings, television documentaries and dramatisations, and so on), where the idea of shared nationhood is being invented. Museum space is a synecdoche for this process of new memory work, where antagonistic, competing, conflicting, non-compatible histories are brought together and rewritten. These are not only sites of memorialisation, but also instruments for the invention of a new political identity, the post-apartheid nation. They reveal some of the themes, metaphors, and false presuppositions, errors and mythologisings that have been scripted into this narrative.

Second, during the last decade, the place of South Africa in the cartography of the global has been confirmed, as its diverse links to many places have been extended and as it has assembled an increasing diversity of trans-border social and economic relations (Figure 6.1). Our cities are now part of a new global space, which has brought new claims. In many ways, the city's spaces are being reconstituted by and in the image of new constituencies and producing new social and spatial morphologies. The city's economy is increasingly reliant on mobile users – tourists, international businesspeople and cross-border traders – politically unaccountable publics, who are leaving increasingly significant traces and making increasing demands on its infrastructures.

Memory infrastructures are undeniably affected by this, as they are seen as key instruments in the selling of South Africa to tourists and visitors. Apartheid memory has been incorporated into the rhetoric of tourism and national heritage, in which it competes with other spectacles of consumption (such as malls, casinos, game reserves, beaches and restaurants) for tourist dollars. It has contemporary value and social function, not only as container of memory and site of political invention, but also through successful participation in its own commodification. The implications of this for apartheid museums are significant – where they are sited, how they are imaged, how their memory narratives are constructed and how and to whom they are marketed.

In this chapter, I will interrogate one museum, the Apartheid Museum at Gold Reef City in Johannesburg, insofar as it offers the opportunity to reflect on how these three discourses of post-apartheid memory making are intertwined. I raise questions about the role of architecture as repository for collective memory, the function of architecture in replacing living memory with its institutional forms, the role of the museum in the project of nation building and on its func-

Figure 6.1
Global icon – Nelson
Mandela in the
Apartheid Museum.

tionality in a post-apartheid economy. This is underpinned by a number of key questions. What kind of memory has been shaped into built form in this building, and to what purpose? What processes of memory formation does it evidence? How does it negotiate memory – what memories, whose memories, what is remembered, what forgotten? How does the museum reproduce the notion of apartheid in the present and to what ends? And finally, what socio-political theories of the present emerge from this examination?

LANDSCAPE OF MEMORY

Two media critics who commented on the Apartheid Museum shortly after its opening in 2001, Charlotte Bauer and John Matshikiza, remarked on the powerful impact of the building on their emotions:

> The building's success as a memorial to suffering lies in the ability of its very structure to express and excite feelings.

(Bauer 2001: 24)

and

> The building is a well-designed prison, which fills one with claustrophobic panic on entering.

(Matshikiza 2001:19)

Buildings are material objects housing human activity and representations of, not only those activities, but also of social or material values conferred upon them by society. So, for instance, we recognise a certain building as a 'house', because its location, materials, spatial configuration and image represent 'house' to us, even if we have never been into it. Similarly, the material form of the house conveys information (or represents) to us certain things about the social or cultural or economic conditions under which it has been built. A classical façade to a contemporary house, for example, might represent wealth or conservatism, whereas a steel and glass box might represent 'architect-designed' or a high-tech hedonism. These meanings are associated with the building's form by social convention.[1]

In addition to these ordinary, everyday experiences and meanings associated with buildings, buildings and the spaces they make can be transformed into powerful poetic media when, through a variety of means – for example, how their spaces are organised, their combination of materials, the way light falls, the sequence of movement they structure – something else is brought 'into presence' (Norberg-Schultz 1983: 62). This might be a former experience or another place, it might be a particular emotion, it might be a dense collection of unspeakable, unconscious images all of which overlap in the experience being lived; in other words, when a 'two-foldness' or duplication of experience (Wollheim 1987: 46), which exceeds the logical distinctions of space and time occurs (Danto 1981). These experiences are based on individual, not collective histories.

The distinctive thing about the museum under discussion is that it not only presents a narrative of apartheid's history through a range of didactic media – photography, film, text, testimony and artifact – but that we also relive apartheid's numbing horror every time we move through it. In the Apartheid Museum, we 'dwell poetically' (Norberg-Schultz 1983: 67) in apartheid all over again.

The relationship between apartheid and imprisonment was a literal one. While it imprisoned thousands, often without trial, imprisonment also constituted the 'leading motif' (Matshikiza 2001: 19) of daily life under apartheid. A combination of restrictions and inhibitions, spatial distributions and temporal punctuations (normally associated with that of criminality and prison life) constructed detailed and precise tabulations of, and control over, the entire population. Daily rituals – where one walked, where one sat, where one ate, with whom one lived – were coded and infringements were criminalised. To live under apartheid was to be imprisoned in a colour-coded landscape.

The Apartheid Museum reconstructs these conditions, sometimes quite literally. Its enveloping windowless wall (stone packed in steel cages) and southwest corner lift shaft resembling a prison watchtower, make obvious connections to incarceration (Figure 6.2). Not knowing what this building is, one would probably guess it to be a prison. Township residents who drive past it every day call it 'Alcatraz'. On entry, one's ticket classifies one as black or white, re-enacting the discrimination practised in every social space and on entry into every public building under apartheid.

In other instances however, it does so by introducing recollection directly to the body of the museum-goer. After ascending the entrance ramp (Figure 6.3), and descending into the museum again, one feels 'claustrophobic panic' (Mat-

Figure 6.2
Southwest corner.

Figure 6.3
Entrance ramp.

shikiza 2001: 19). The gratuitous ascent and descent this involves invokes a sense of manipulation and control, of being distanced from the world around one and entering a secret, restricted realm where everything is unknown and unpredictable. The frosted glass and aluminium reception desk and electronic newsflash that face one on entry add to this feeling of alienation. They do not welcome. They are harsh, cold, mechanical and impersonal.

The building's interior utilises unrefined, hard, neutral materials – red brick, steel, raw concrete, and intentionally crude detailing. It is institutional, industrial and un-domestic. Its spaces are dungeon-like – dull, gray, sombre, devoid of natural light (Figure 6.4). The only spaces that are painted are the recreated solitary confinement cells, themselves bleak and sanitised. Natural lighting is kept to a minimum, often through openings located in positions that make it impossible to see out. The passage of time is obscured. Its acoustics are similarly deadened. Audio material is transmitted through overhead speakers that one has to stand directly beneath to hear. Outside of this space, sound is muted and multivalent – a dull, disturbing buzzing and bleeping permeates everywhere. The museum's exhibits are, for the most part, fixed to walls on purposely crude steel brackets or contained within steel cages (inspired by Palestinian artist Mona Hatoum) (Figure 6.5). These cages construct a maze of exhibits one moves around and through, claustrophobically en-caged in the exhibition oneself. The museum's three circular spaces – entry drum, 1980s' auditorium and TRC room – that one has to move around before entering, add to its maze-like qualities. They make one feel that there are unknown, hidden, impending knowledges within them; one enters with anxiety. Senses of alienation, dehumanisation, restriction and control prevail.

Figure 6.4
Interior exhibition space.

Figure 6.5
Steel cage exhibits.

Apartheid was not only an abstract political and administrative system. It was also one that worked on the human body as the prime object and target of its power (cf. Foucault 1977). It used a racialised body as the basis of social classification and political order. Legislation aimed at the disqualification of certain bodies from certain spaces. Bodies that failed to submit to its discipline were subjected to violent forms of humiliation, torture, mutilation and often death.[2]

The museum strongly expresses these conditions of violence and mutilation. It functions as a metaphoric body, damaged by apartheid. Its spaces are structured with elements that are named as parts of the body – a face brick and concrete 'spine' or 'backbone' (Rose 2001) structures its linear narrative. Figural spaces – the drum and smaller auditoria mentioned above – read as scattered organs, held together by the mucilage of movement. Its spaces, most noticeably the extraordinarily high-ceilinged ablution facilities, are intestinal, its maze-like routes visceral.

But this is not a whole, living body, held together in symmetrical arrangements and anthropomorphic hierarchy. Its skeletal structure has been fractured and reassembled (cf. Rossi 1981: 11, 12). Its skin is punctured, damaged and gaping. Its spaces modulate and twist, contort and bend, resembling the abnormal position a corpse assumes when it is carried (Figures 6.6 to 6.10).

Moving through this deformed, dead body, traversing its gaping wounds, stalking its fractured vertebrae, the viewer experiences the images of mutilation and death shown in many of the museum's films and photographs in a particularly disquieting way. The bodies of apartheid victims have been metaphorically

Figure 6.6
Elevation A.

Figure 6.7
Elevation B.

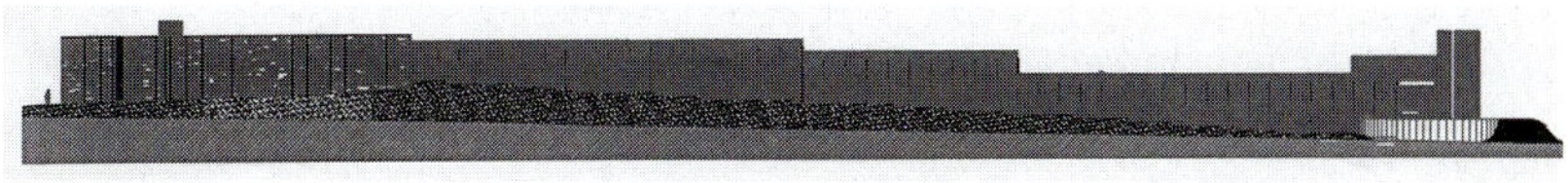

Figure 6.8
Elevation C.

Figure 6.9
Long section from arrival.

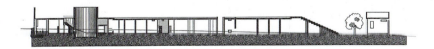

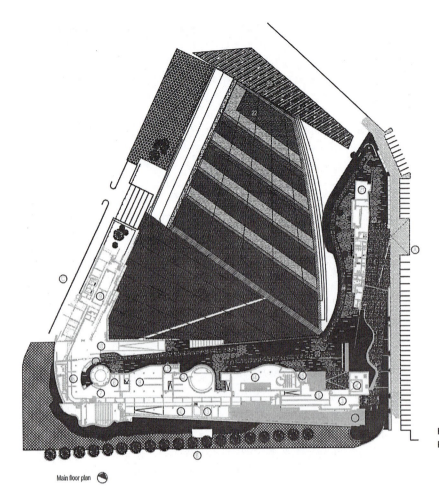

Main floor plan

Figure 6.10
Floor plan.

recalled. Once outside, there is no respite. Concrete paving slabs laid in charcoal gray pebbles make silent reference to the gravestones of apartheid's dead (Figure 6.11). Presentation and representation double up in an anguished and harrowing notation (cf. Blanchot 1986).

In his introduction to a section on Holocaust memorials in a recent issue of *Architectural Design*, Richard Patterson (2000) argues that what anchors social cohesion in the contemporary world is no longer the symbolic-mythic, but the traumatic-sublime. He draws on Slavoj Zizek's observation (Zizek 2000), that, since the Holocaust, there have not been human tragedies proper, but rather a horror so deep that it cannot be sublimated into tragic dignity. Whereas in the past, tragedy, as genre, served as model of social inclusion and responsibility (Ricoeur 1967), now it is only by being bound together as victims of shared or imagined trauma, of unspeakable events, through their memorialisation and eternalisation, that our humanity is affirmed.

While South African racism did not lead to killings on the scale of the Holocaust, it did (Appiah 1992) result in the judicial execution of more (mostly black)

Figure 6.11
External space.

people per head of population than most other countries, and to massive differences between the life-chances of white and black South Africans. It systematically disqualified, oppressed and exploited people who were not classified white, and used race as the basis for distinguishing between who was human and who was less than human, no evidence against which sufficed to alter that judgement. Apartheid distinguished on the basis of biology, reducing people to what Agamben (1998) calls 'bare life'.

It is therefore appropriate, on the basis of the degrees of human trauma they recall, to compare apartheid and Holocaust memory work. In the sense in which it impacts on the body, the Apartheid Museum functions similarly to Daniel Libeskind's extension to the Jewish Museum in Berlin (opened in 2002), 'a memorial destined to keep the wounds fresh' (Patterson 2000: 70). Here too, a world of disorientating street corners and artificial light cuts one off from the outside. Working with devices of disorientation, isolation and claustrophobia, Libeskind achieves a kind of subliminal horror in his building, 'subverting the "defensive re-ification" of the museum-goer's gaze' (Patterson 2000: 70). The Apartheid Museum succeeds in a similar transmission of the anguish, humiliation, and 'dreary horrors' of apartheid (Matshikiza 2001: 19).

INVENTING THE NATION

Every memory pertains to … a history that is constantly in motion.

(Mudimbe 1994: 143)

The term 'Apartheid Museum' implies that the multiple sets of institutional practices known as apartheid are sufficiently divorced from the now to be able to be remade in a museum and subjected to an exhibitionary gaze, and that, therefore, present institutional practice as 'post' or 'after' apartheid. To understand what this means, it is useful to draw on Anthony Appiah's discussion of the postmodern (Appiah 1992), in which he argues that 'postmodern' is after 'modern' in two distinct ways – 'consequentially' (or following on from) as well as 'after' (displacing or replacing). 'Post-apartheid', like 'postmodern', signals both a disentangling of ties, a rupture, as well as certain underlying continuities with the past. It is these relationships that museums working with apartheid memory negotiate.

The Apartheid Museum at Gold Reef City is different from other similar museums in South Africa (such as the Hector Pieterson Museum in Soweto, or the Museum of the Peoples' Struggle in Red Location, Port Elizabeth), in many respects, but pertinent here is that its siting does not mark any significant apartheid event or struggle. It has no specific locational or historical reference, neither is it associated with any particular community. It is a space in which memory floats in the realm of pure narrative.[3]

Museums are not neutral retrievals and collections of stored information about a dead past. They are rhetorical organisations of remembering and forgetting (Middleton and Edwards 1990). As rhetoric, they make certain claims about the past, to construct new memories for the future (Bartlett 1932). In this transmission, distortion and incompleteness is unavoidable (Hartman 1994). Every act of remembering includes a forgetting. Whenever history becomes memory and is institutionalised, certain choices are made, certain forgettings sanctioned, certain remembering disallowed. Institutionalised memory is inevitably partial memory, a formalised agreement between past and present. It is a site in which past, present and future forcibly intersect, enabling us, as individuals and societies, to construct and anchor our identities and envision our future.

Extending this idea, Ernst Renan (1882, in Appiah 1992) argues that group identity is always undergirded by selective remembering and forgetting. National identity and national heritage are invented through common memory and common tradition – a careful filtering of historical events into an official narrative as an homogenising legacy of values and experiences. 'The official constitution of a national history bequeaths us the nation', argues Appiah (1992: 94). It little matters that these entail false presuppositions, errors or inaccuracies. For 'invented histories, invented biologies, invented cultural affinities come with every identity; each is a kind of role that has to be scripted, structured by conventions of narrative' (Appiah 1992: 282).

Post-apartheid South Africa, like many postcolonial African states immediately after independence, was/is a 'state looking for a nation' (Appiah 1992: 262). Once the moment of cohesion against apartheid was over, the difficult task of constructing a new nation out of multiple and sometimes conflicting identities emerged.[4] The new nation had not only to accommodate former victims and perpetrators, but also to overcome the association of blackness with victimhood and of nationalism with negativity. The new South African state sought to construct itself as affirmative, as a truly communal event.

Apartheid was reinvented in the service of this project. In this context, again, a comparison with Holocaust memory-making, but this time in Israel (and, for that matter in the Holocaust Memorial Museum in Washington DC, though I will refer to this in another context later) is useful.

> Memorials to the Holocaust in Israel are more than a form of remembrance dedicated to its victims, for they are historically linked with the founding of the state. More explicitly than elsewhere, the function of the museum is … to keep the 'Holocaust alive' as part of the Israeli 'narrative'.
>
> (Patterson 2000: 76)

In Israel, like South Africa, traumatic memory is a fundamental part of national narrative-making. However, here the comparison ends. For in South Africa, the idea of the remembrance of the victims of apartheid is linked to and intersects with two other equally important national identity narratives. The first of these is that of resistance, defiance, struggle and triumph; a narrative of loss, heroism and celebration, in which national identity is packaged in terms of the resilience, resistance, vitality and creativity of apartheid's opponents. The second is a narrative of forgiveness and reconciliation, a necessarily publicly inscripted message of recuperation, around which the myth of post-apartheid as a unitary force (the so-called 'rainbow nation') is formed.

The Apartheid Museum participates in this project in a number of ways. Firstly, its narrative structure takes visitors on a didactic journey of apartheid's establishment, entrenchment and undoing. This begins with a film on the colonial origins of South African racism, followed by a route through the formation of the Union of South Africa in 1910, the rise of Afrikaner nationalism, the Sharpville massacre, the establishment of *uMkhonto we Sizwe* and the progressively intense struggles of the 1960s, 1970s and 1980s. It then juxtaposes two aspects of the moment of transition – the extreme violence that followed the unbanning of anti-apartheid liberation movements and negotiations taking place at the Congress for a Democratic South Africa (CODESA), and ends with the celebratory moment of the country's first democratic elections represented by the now iconic image of the jumbo jet flypast over the Union Buildings in Pretoria after the inauguration of President Mandela. Thereafter one passes through a room where a number of testimonies of well-known South Africans reflect on the meaning of freedom for them, and exits through a cubic space, where one is able to pick up a copy of the new South African Constitution, in the language of one's choice.

On the one hand, this narrative weaves one unheroically through the violations of apartheid. The section on the rise of Afrikaner nationalism and the reproduction of Ernest Cole's 1960s text, *House of Bondage*, is particularly memorable in this notation of domination. Alongside this is the heroic and reconciliatory vocabulary, culminating in giant images of Nelson Mandela's inauguration, Mandela and François Pienaar at the 1995 Rugby World Cup, and an enormous photograph of the members of the first democratic Parliament. This narrative is reinforced by the sequential topography of the museum's architecture, which

progresses from the blackness of the film auditorium, through sombre, underground exhibition corridors, into the naturally lit constitution cube (a geometric
figure associated with unity, Figure 6.12), and finally into the open where the
towering 'Pillars of the Constitution' triumphantly reorientate one in space after
one has traversed the maze-like museum interior (Figure 6.13).

In this respect, the museum invites comparisons with the narrative structure
of James Ingo Freed's US Holocaust Memorial Museum in Washington DC which,
similarly divorced from a Holocaust context, re-enacts Hitler's rise to power, the

Figure 6.12
Constitution cube.

Figure 6.13
Pillars of the constitution.

internment of victims in camps and ghettos, and their final liberation. Freed, like the architects of the Apartheid Museum, uses architecture (the face brick and metal of the gas chambers, the timber bridges of the Warsaw Ghetto), the manipulation of circulation (arbitrarily segregating individuals and groups upon entry), 'real' objects (barracks from Auschwitz, cattle cars, Nazi uniforms) to configure his narrative of Jewishness. Likewise, the Apartheid Museum uses an architecture of internment (rusting steel, stone walls), objects (makeshift guns retrieved from township wars, a police casspir (Figure 6.14), voting papers) and a parody of the Holocaust Museum's discriminatory entry sequence, to construct its narrative. Parallels are direct and unambiguous (Huyssen 1994).[5]

However, there are ways other than its depiction of the grand narrative of apartheid's demise in which the Apartheid Museum contributes to nation building. One of these is through the use of testimony already referred to. The simple gesture of recording and replaying South Africans from all walks of life 'speaking themselves' in the space of the museum, is one that (symbolically at least) helps in the constitution of the community of the nation.[6] Like the harrowing testimony heard by the Truth and Reconciliation Commission, speaking has proved to be a powerful vehicle of post-apartheid reconciliation. The other is the invitation the museum offers to examine intelligently the project of cultural representation, as it intersects with the project of nation building.

In postcolonial Africa, the idea of the nation is more than merely a consequence of the cultural hegemony of Europe and America who invented it. It has provided 'a way to articulate a resistance both to the material domination of

Figure 6.14
Police casspir.

the world empires and to the more nebulous threat to pre-colonial mores of thought represented by the Western project of cultural ascendancy' (Appiah 1992: 85). Ever since Herder, the most important philosopher of modern nationalism, the main instrument of nationality has been language (see, for example, Kohn 1967). In postcolonial Africa, this Herderian view produced on the one hand, a post-independence sentimental, nativist attachment to traditions (music, dance, dress, ritual and so on) as expression of the collective essence of a pristine traditional community (see Appiah 1992). It asserted an Afrocentric particularism against a Eurocentric universalism.[7] On the other hand, it promoted the 'turning' of colonial cultural instruments, in particular, language, 'from the projects of the metropole to the intellectual work of postcolonial cultural life' (Appiah 1992: 88). Here the use of colonial languages (English, French, Portuguese, Afrikaans) as modes for writing postcolonial subjectivities is particularly informative. ' "Here I am" Senghor once wrote, "trying to forget Europe" …. But for us to forget Europe is to suppress the conflicts that have shaped our identities, and since it is too late for us to escape each other, we might instead seek to turn to our advantage the mutual interdependencies history has thrust upon us' (Appiah 1992: 115). Postcolonial African indentity was seen as the outcome of the colonial encounter. It could only be built on the basis of both estrangement from, and mutual interpenetration of, indigenous tradition and insertions from the metropole.

Post-apartheid memorials and museums have been useful vehicles for the rehearsing of these debates. For instance, the first proposal for what became the Apartheid Museum was for a 'cultural village'. After numerous delays and recommissions, it was reconceptualised as a 'National Centre of Freedom and Negotiation', or a 'Peace Park', with the brief developed for the Apartheid Museum as its first phase. The identity of the museum was articulated in global terms. Its objective, coordinating architect Sydney Abramowitz has stated, was to design a museum to 'take its place in the family of great museums of the world' (Interview 2001). While its scope was global, its brief was developed in consultation with all 13 of the different cultural groupings in South Africa who were flown to Johannesburg and asked about their contribution to the new nation. Its architecture, however, adopts a neutral, international, modernist aesthetic, eschewing any reference to these traditions. If anything, it neutralises and naturalises its aesthetic via topography, into which architecture slips away and disappears (Figure 6.15).

In response to this, the Apartheid Museum in New Brighton, Port Elizabeth (recently renamed the Museum of the Peoples' Struggle) by Noero Wolff Architects adopts a site-specific approach and references steeped in metaphoric significance for the local urban community inculcate its architecture – a 'straightforward, slightly industrial aesthetic … a celebration of the ordinary materials the local people have scrounged over the years to keep out the rain … a nod to the railroad tracks' (Findley 2004: 29). The Museum of the Peoples' Struggle makes no attempt to construct a grand apartheid narrative, but rather houses 'different

Figure 6.15
The museum in its
landscape.

perspectives of the experience of apartheid' (Findley 2004: 31), telling the untold history of the people of the region. This is given architectural expression in 12 equally sized rooms called 'memory boxes' in which its multiple stories will unfold. Peter Rich, in his Mandela's Yard Museum in Alexandra township, Johannesburg, on the other hand, speaks about an architecture that 'culturally empowers' black South Africans. Rich mobilises an essentialising nativist rhetoric to derive a vocabulary of built form 'in harmony with indigenous cultures' (Manning 2004: 145), meaning, in his case, those of traditional Ndebele dwellings or of shack settlements.

These three examples indicate the intensity of the stories that architects are telling themselves as they grapple with the complexity of post-apartheid memory-making, their relationship to a conflictual and divided past and of architecture's role in it.

THE POST-APARTHEID CITY

In the introduction to Katherine Gibson and Sophie Watson's book, *Postmodern Spaces, Cities and Politics* (1995), they contrast and compare the pleasures of Benjamin's 'flaneur' and de Certeau's walker, with the contemporary experience of being 'seated in a tour bus speeding along a motorway with scenes of recognition and disarray flashing through the tinted glass' (Gibson and Watson 1995: 2). The detached disinterest of the stroller has given way to the disorientation and voyeurism of the tourist as the figure of contemporary urban experience and public life.

The story of the Apartheid Museum in Johannesburg cannot be divorced from this new logic. It was conceived of by brothers Solly and Abe Krok, the

Figure 6.16
The museum in its
context.

notorious purveyors of skin-lightening creams during the apartheid years, as part
of their bid to the Gauteng Gambling Board to secure a licence for the Gold Reef
City Casino. The museum is sited in a landscape otherwise devoted entirely to
fun – rollercoaster rides, slot machines, takeaway chicken, foot-long suckers,
dance spectaculars, a themed mining town (Figure 6.16). Its existence actually
has little to do with honouring apartheid's victims or reconfiguring its meanings,
but rather with securing a stake in a competitive gambling and tourist economy.
What more compelling way, than contributing to apartheid's recall, could one
find to sell a casino project to the provincial government's casino licensing
board?

The Apartheid Museum is testament, above all, to the 'social functionality
of culture itself' (Jameson 1988: 195). Apartheid has been reinvented as part of
the selling of the new South Africa to tourists and visitors. Packaged into spectacle and tourist dollars – the end of apartheid, 'Madiba magic', the 'miracle' of
the transition, the euphoria of the 1995 Rugby World Cup – has been recuper-
ated, or rather reconstituted, for new reasons. It has been incorporated into the
relentless logic of capital, what Simmel (1950) has called the 'culture of things',
or Appiah (after Marx) calls the 'money economy' (Appiah 1992: 234). The
underlying dynamic of cultural modernity means that, as history is transformed
into memory, it commodifies. As it does this, it is effectively depoliticised and
turned into a sign reading 'FOR SALE' (Harvey 1990; Appiah 1992). The museum
functions as one of the many new 'public theatres of late capitalism' (Mbembe
2004: 394) in the city, like the casino it mirrors, like Melrose Arch, Nelson
Mandela Square, the Neslon Mandela Bridge, or other new museums (the Hector

Pieterson Museum, the Walter Sisulu Square of Commemoration). It is a cavernous shopping mall for the selling of history.

This commodification has a number of implications. First, the building participates in its logic by circulating as a recognisable image of itself. It has been used frequently in television commercials, music videos and so forth, to brand products or personalities. It has become a brand itself, recently running its own marketing campaign in a 15-week series of full-page, colour advertisements in the *Mail & Guardian* newspaper (Figure 6.17). Its architecture, as with the Hector Pieterson Museum in Soweto, which was designed by the same architects, has come to stand in for the very idea of museum in a post-apartheid cultural economy – a globally recognisable architecture whose references are to the magazines and journals in which contemporary architecture circulates. This not only 'styles' apartheid memory in a particular way, it also associates it with the oeuvre of the building's designers. Apartheid memory 'belongs' in a sense to them more than it belongs to the collective.

Second, this genre of museum constructs new kinds of post-apartheid encounters. 'The museum seems designed for those who never really experienced the dehumanising repression of apartheid', suggests Lisa Findley (2004: 28). Its market is foreigners, tourists, white South Africans, or those black South

Figure 6.17
A full-page advert taken
from the museum's
15-week campaign in the
Mail & Guardian.

Africans who are young enough never to have experienced apartheid's discrimi-nations.[8] It constructs a voyeuristic spectacle, making apartheid visible and accessible to its clients in a sweeping grand narrative.[9] Most of the display in the museum is archival – film footage, photographs, already published texts. Very few material objects present the past. Apartheid is recalled at a distance, and pri-marily through recommissioned representational material. There are very few individual stories told. Where people tell their stories, bear witness to their apartheids, they tend to be its icons – Hendrik Verwoerd, Winnie Mandela, Man-gosuthu Buthelezi. Other more ordinary unknown people acquire iconic status, as their hyper-scaled presences tell their stories in the documentaries shown in the museum's viewing rooms. This effectively objectifies apartheid, thereby making it more easily consumable.

This is not, in my view, without value. For it should not be forgotten that apartheid was a crime against humanity and its recall should be accessible to these paying publics. While its mode of memory-making is theatrical and propa-gandistic, bringing together historical record and entertainment, it does bring a certain memory of apartheid's excesses into presence and keep them alive.

CONCLUSION

The Apartheid Museum in Johannesburg is a site where many of the contested themes and metaphors of post-apartheid cultural discourse are rehearsed. In it, apartheid history is rhetorically organised around the narratives of racism, dis-crimination, struggle and liberation pertinent to the current moment. These come together around tropes of rupture and disentanglement, which historicise apartheid, set it apart, and open the space for museological encounters with it – 'apartheid is where it belongs, in a museum', we are told in the newspaper advertisements for the museum.

In the triumphant though contested field of apartheid memory-making that emerges from this displacement, however, it is worth noting African scholar V.Y. Mudimbe's warning:

> Nevertheless, it is clear that evidence of the rupture, if indeed there was one, is not to be found in … new signs …. The body which lives or survives as the transcript of the meta-morphosis is still that which testifies to the break.
>
> (Mudimbe 1994: 135)

The problem with museological apartheid is that it obscures the fact that apartheid is not dead; that it is still written on the bodies of the many whose lives bear its traces – of those still subject to the entrenched racialised inequality persisting in South Africa today. It obscures the fact that apartheid is encountered daily on the city's streets, in its schools and hospitals, in its rape statistics, in the different life expectations of citizens, in the xenophobic attitudes of South Africans to foreigners in their country. Apartheid is far from over. It is premature to assign to it the status of 'dead history' and to encapsulate it as a museum piece.

REFERENCES

Agamben, G. (1998) *Homo Sacer: Sovereign Power and Bare Life*, trans. D. Heller Roazen, Stanford: Stanford University Press.

Appiah, A. (1992) *In My Father's House*, London: Methuen.

Bartlett, F.C. (1932) *Remembering*, London: Newbury Park.

Bauer, C. (2001) 'Speaking for Itself and for All of Us', *Sunday Times* 2 December: 24.

Benjamin, W. (1985) *One Way Street and Other Writings*, London: Pimlico.

Blanchot, M. (1986) *The Writing of the Disaster*, Lincoln: University of Nebraska Press.

Danto, A. (1981) *The Transfiguration of the Commonplace*, Cambridge, MA: Harvard University Press.

Findley, L. (2004) 'Red and Gold: Two Apartheid Museums and the Spatial Politics of Memory in "New" South Africa', *Architecture South Africa* July/Aug.: 26–32.

Foucault, M. (1977) *Discipline and Punish*, trans. A. Sheridan Smith, Harmondsworth: Penguin.

Gibson, K. and Watson, S. (1995) *Postmodern Spaces, Cities and Politics*, Oxford: Blackwell.

Hartman, G.H. (1994) 'Darkness Visible', in G.H. Hartman (ed.) *Holocaust Remembrance: The Shapes of Memory*, Oxford: Blackwell.

Harvey, D. (1990) *The Condition of Postmodernity*, Cambridge: Blackwell.

Huyssen, A. (1994) 'Monuments and Memory in a Post Modern Age', in J.E. Young (ed.) *The Art of Memory: Holocaust Memorials in History*, Munich: Prestel: 9–17.

Jameson, F. (1988) *The Ideologies of Theory: Essays 1971–1986*, vol. 2, Minneapolis: Minnesota University Press.

Kohn, H. (1967) *The Idea of Nationalism*, New York: Collier.

Manning, J. (2004) 'Rich Martins', in *Bartlett Works: Architecture Buildings Projects*, London: Bartlett School of Architecture, UCL.

Matshikiza, J. (2001) 'History in the Making', *Mail & Guardian*, 30 November–6 December: 19.

Mbembe, A. (2004) 'Aesthetics of Superfluidity', in *Public Culture* 16 (3): 373–406.

Middleton, D. and Edwards, D. (eds) (1990) *Collective Remembering*, New Delhi: Sage.

Mudimbe, V.Y. (1994) *The Idea of Africa*, Bloomington: Indiana University Press.

Norberg-Schultz, C. (1983) 'Heidegger's Thinking on Architecture', in *Perspecta* 20: 62–8.

Patterson, R. (2000) 'Introduction to the Holocaust Section', *Architectural Design* 70, 5 October.

Renan, E. (1882) 'Qu'est-ce qu'une nation', *Ouevres Completes*, vol. 1, Paris: Clamann-Levy: 887–906.

Ricoeur, P. (1967) *The Symbolism of Evil*, trans. E. Buchanan, Boston: Beacon.

Rose, J. (2001) Interview with the author.

Rossi, A. (1981) *A Scientific Autobiography*, trans. L. Venuti, Cambridge, MA: MIT Press.

Simmel, G. (1950) 'The Metropolis and Mental Life', in *The Sociology of George Simmel*, ed. and trans. K. Wolff, Glencoe, Ill: Free Press.

Wollheim, R. (1987) *Painting as an Art*, Princeton, NJ: Princeton University Press.

Zizek, S. (2000) *The Fragile Absolute*, London: Verso.

Chapter 7: Picturing Cape Town

Marwaan Manuel, Odidi Mfenyana, Nondumiso Ncisana

> What is a landmark? Is it a monument, a historic building, an ancient bridge, a mountain, a telephone pole? Or is it a sense of what every one of us feels when going back to places of our past, to our memories?
>
> (Miguel Angel Corzo, director, Getty Conservation Institute)

'Picture Cape Town' opened at the Castle of Good Hope Gallery in Cape Town in November 1996, and showed the work of ten young photographers, with little or no previous experience in the medium. Following the successful 'Picture LA' project, the Getty Conservation Institute sought fresh eyes on the city. Field director Gavin Younge describes the approach he took in choosing the photographers:

> I wrote to the principals of 159 high schools in the Cape Town area, explaining the project and asking them to recommend suitable candidates. I made it clear that I was looking for people between the ages of 10 and 18 years, from diverse backgrounds, who possessed an insight into their own communities or environments.

More than ten years on, the 72 photographs in the exhibition catalogue are themselves a landmark, a memory of the city in transition, legal segregation recently abolished, the first democratic elections a recent event, the ink still wet on the pages of South Africa's new constitution. A selection of the work of three of the contributors well captures the moment.

Marwaan Manuel was 16 when he took part in the 'Picture Cape Town' project, studying at Salt River High School and the Children's Arts Centre in District Six. He lived in the Cape Town suburb of Woodstock, where his mother provided a childcare service, and his father was a clerk at Groote Schuur Hospital.

Odidi Mfenyana, also 16 when he joined the project, is the son of a priest and lived in the rectory of the Holy Cross Church in Nyanga. He was attending school in Pinelands.

Nondumiso Ncisana, 14 when she joined the project, lived in Khayelitsha,

Figure 7.1
Cape Town on the walls
of Ashley Court.

Figure 7.2
A sausage-seller late at
night.

Figure 7.3
Washing lines, Lavender Hill.

Figure 7.4
Selling 'smilies'.

Figure 7.5
The broken umbrella.

Figure 7.6
Old and new together.

Figure 7.7
Richard and Patrick in
Nyanga.

Figure 7.8
Phumeza Dungulu ready
for school.

where her mother was the treasurer of a self-help project, and a domestic
worker. She travelled daily by train to the city centre, to attend the Cape Town
Commercial High School.

Zwelethu Mthethwa, part of the project team back in 1996 and today a
well-known photographer himself, sums up the experience:

The participants looked at Cape Town, the city in which they live, with critical eyes. They were challenged to question and explore their own feelings and ideas, their own preconceived ideas about 'other', and their relationships with one another and their environment.

REFERENCE

'Picture Cape Town: Landmarks of a New Generation' (1996) photographic exhibition at the Castle of Good Hope Gallery, November 1996, catalogue: Getty Conservation Institute and University of Cape Town: Cape Town.

Chapter 8: Memory and the Politics of History in the District Six Museum

Ciraj Rassool

Since the mid-1990s, when South Africa became a democracy, the country has been in the throes of addressing apartheid's legacy, as well as longer legacies of colonialism.[1] These efforts at reconstituting and reconfiguring a new society have occurred across a wide range of institutions and initiatives, some of which have been created by the resources of the state, while others have emerged out of the energies and imaginings of civil society. The Truth and Reconciliation Commission (TRC) was one such project, a product of political compromise, which attempted to establish 'the truth' of apartheid's gross violations of human rights, as well as to promote reconciliation of apartheid's 'victims' and 'perpetrators'. In the process of creating an 'official history' of apartheid, the TRC attempted to establish

> as complete a picture as possible of the nature, causes and extent of the gross human rights violations that were committed between 1 March 1960 and 6 December 1993, including the antecedents, circumstances, factors and contexts of such violations, as well as the perspectives of the victims and the motives and perspectives of the persons responsible for committing these violations.
>
> (*Truth and Reconciliation Commission of South Africa Final Report* 1998: vol. 1 ch. 4, par.31 (a))[2]

The TRC also saw that the creation of an electronic monument to apartheid's past, a grand spectacle through which South Africa's 'real history', live and visual, and seeking to recover the past, was anchored into homes, and public and private interior spaces in different corners of South Africa. In televised lessons of the past, broadcast to the nation, apartheid's hidden history was simultaneously revealed and revised as an essential 'building block' for the new nation.

In this chapter, I seek to understand how the resources of memory have been drawn upon in the imaginative reconstruction of South African society through the medium of cultural heritage. I begin an examination of the cultural workings of heritage, public history and identity formation under conditions of political transition in South Africa. I am concerned to understand the dominant discursive ways in which South Africans are being encouraged to consider, narrate and visualise their society and its past, as well as their own identities as individuals within it. The domains of heritage, cultural tourism and public history require serious examination, for it is here that attempts have been made to fashion the categories and images of the post-apartheid nation. It is also in this domain of historical production that important contests have been unfolding over the South African past. One of the most significant cultural institutions in which these contests over history and identity have been taking place is in the multifaceted space of the District Six Museum, an independent, community-based museum in Cape Town (Figure 8.1).

By the end of the 1990s, certain discourses had begun to crystallise as the chief modes of reading the 'nation', its people and its history. South Africa was being framed as a 'rainbow' or 'multicultural' nation, one characterised by 'diversity'. Having endured and survived the conflict and violence of apartheid and its predecessor racial systems, and having engaged in successive forms of resistance, South Africa's 'diverse' people, still characterised by separate and discrete ethnicities, had been placed on a path of achieving 'reconciliation' as the basis for the new 'rainbow nation'. The 'miracle' of the new South Africa and the demise of apartheid had been made possible by the 'wisdom' of heroic leaders, and especially by the 'special magic' of Nelson Mandela. In broad outline, these discursive contours – of a society of 'many cultures' and a history of 'great lives of resistance and reconciliation' – were emerging and taking shape in almost every sphere of heritage construction and public culture in South Africa, from television histories and cultural projects in the press, to the TRC and claims for land, from museums (new and old) and legacy projects, to new memorials and cultural tourism.

Figure 8.1
Ex-residents of District Six and land claimants fill the spaces of the District Six Museum in its early days.

And yet, it must be recognised that these dominant discursive forms were not uncontested. In significant cases, particularly in community museums and local cultural projects, certain initiatives had begun to push beyond these dominant narrations, contesting the constitutive elements of the nation, the cultural politics of tourism, as well as the signage systems and forms of memorialisation attached to urban and rural landscapes. So, while heritage projects continued to serve up new discourses of the heroic leader who delivered the nation from apartheid's evil, of the 'rainbow nation' where culture was being framed largely in primordial terms, and of reconciliation – South Africa's 'special offering' to the world, almost every sphere of heritage production was seeing complexity, controversy and contestation. This was especially the case in Cape Town in the District Six Museum.

CULTURAL TOURISM AND SOUTH AFRICAN HERITAGE

During the 1990s, tourism emerged as a system whose supposed economic and modernising benefits had the potential to trickle down to previously marginalised local communities. As community tourism became the buzzword of tourism's democratisation, a series of localised initiatives emerged to occupy the terrain of cultural tourism. These community initiatives ranged from ethnically packaged cultural villages (such as Shakaland in KwaZulu-Natal, Xhosaville in the Eastern Cape, Shangana in Mpumalanga and Lesedi near Johannesburg), to local craft initiatives among rural communities bordering national parks, urban township tours and action tours, which took visitors to sites of political struggle. In their varied attempts to present what they maintained was 'the other side', they tended to be directed along routes similar to those that South African tourism had traversed for a long time. In the tourist gaze, South Africans were being called upon to exhibit their 'unique and wonderful expression of life' and, through the camera, to be affirmed as 'the country's rainbow people' (SATOUR 1996).

Packaged as the recovery of a multicultural South Africa, culture and history were brought together into a timeless zone, a kaleidoscope of frozen ethnic stereotypes. A past–present relationship was established through the gaze on human culture scripted as traditional. But visits to the primitive in the diversity of South Africa were no longer cast as isolated encounters with 'natives in tribal setting'.[3] In the 1990s, they were being framed as encounters with living cultures arranged in ethnically based cultural villages, township tours and village craft projects, all jostling with each other to take their place as the authentic past of the nation's visual splendour. It was expected by emerging cultural and tourism policy frameworks that this living spectacle would take place on an extensive scale, and that each 'community' would participate in a grand national celebration by finding cultural expressions which had 'remained hidden from view' (SATOUR 1996).

The South African tourist spectacle of cultural stereotypes, many of which had been partially constructed in the colonial gaze and were now being re-imagined and repackaged, was not only directed at the international traveller. It was also directed at the 'rainbow people' and their constitution as nation. The visit to the cultural locality was presented as a way to know oneself and to learn about the other, and so become a nation. Acts of visiting, looking, taking in and learning in tourist contemplation and celebration were to be encouraged as part of the process of nation-making. And tourist agencies wanted to facilitate this outpouring of national feeling as part of tourism's 'reconstruction'. In the words of Paula Gumede of One City Tours in Cape Town, as she gave encouragement to tourist resorts to offer discounted rates to township tourists: 'We will enhance patriotism if we increase domestic tourism … because the more you know your country the more you love it' (*Saturday Business* 1996). The Minister of Defence, formerly chairperson of the National Council of Provinces and premier of the Free State, Mosiuoa 'Terror' Lekota, could visit the Basotho Cultural Village to find out about 'authentic Sotho lifestyles'; Zoliswa Sihlwayi, from Soweto, could go to Shakaland to become 'aware of his own culture'; and Xhosa-speaking schoolchildren could go to Xhosaville to 'learn their culture as part of community development' (Koch 1996: 5; *Cape Argus* 1995).

Tourist imaging was being made very real as land claims became based upon these re-imagined cultural identities (Land Claim Committee 1995; Rassool 1998).[4] The existence of communities and their boundaries became determined by their attraction to the tourist gaze, and their development became defined through the 'tourist centres' of the regional economy. In 'the thriving templates of tourism', new sets of homogeneous identities – permacultures – were being created and reinforced. This, in turn, became 'the community', its 'will' and 'needs', with 'folk life defined by the folk themselves', and where in the 1990s, Xhosaville was being run by a 'local entrepreneur' in conjunction with a leading organisation in the struggle against urban apartheid, the South African National Civic Organisation (Friedman 1996: 1, 3; Mayibuye Centre 1997: A2; *Cape Argus* 1995).

THE CENTRALISATION OF NATIONAL HERITAGE

But the discourse of many cultures was only one way in which South African heritage was being framed in the 1990s. A framework for memorialisation began to unfold which sought to construct forms of observance, remembrance and commemoration that would be a 'symbolic acknowledgement of our neglected, marginalised and distorted heritage'. New memorials and heritage sites began to emerge, new national museums began to take shape, and new national heritage trails were being planned. A Legacy Project was constituted by the cabinet within the Ministry of Arts, Culture, Science and Technology, and a draft 'portfolio of legacy projects' was released for discussion by the 'National Legacy Committee', an interdepartmental committee tasked with the establishment of 'new and diverse' memorials, museums and commemorations (Rassool 1997; National Monuments Council 1998; Mimeo 1999; Legacy Project Committee 1998).

The Legacy Project had been set up 'to approve and facilitate the setting up of new monuments, museums … plaques, outdoor artworks, history trails and other symbolic representations'. These would ensure that 'visible reminders' of the 'many aspects of our formerly neglected heritage' would be created. In addition, the committee sought to present 'a coherent set of principles' which would enable different initiatives to be 'harmonised' and ensure 'integrity, inclusiveness, balance and broad participation'. With wide distribution throughout South Africa, and with the focus on national symbols with 'provincial and local participation' encouraged, the proposed legacy projects would 'communicate a stimulating message of rich cultural diversity' (Legacy Project Committee 1998).

The central discursive feature of the programme of monumentalisation was the 'contribution' of leaders to 'our legacy of democracy'. Commemoration sites and plaques would honour 'great patriots' who 'achieved honour against tremendous odds'. Their homes and 'other significant sites associated with them' should be declared national monuments and 'special public ceremonies' should be held. A cenotaph 'for martyrs who fell in the armed struggle' and a cultural map of war graves were proposed. The life histories of 'literary ancestors', it was felt, could be celebrated through a programme of 'dedicating libraries'. In a broad-ranging proposal, a 'freedom park' was proposed which suggested the development of a 'dynamic multi-dimensional commemoration' aimed at telling the history of South Africa from precolonial times to the present. This project would 'commemorate all those who fell in the struggle for liberation' and at the same time, mark the 'celebration of the attainment of freedom and democracy'. It was envisaged that the project would be a symbolic expression of the themes of 'struggle, democracy and nation building', which would 'represent our past, present and future'. The components of the proposed 'freedom park' would incorporate, among others, a monument to victims of the struggle, a museum dedicated to the history of the freedom struggle, and an indigenous garden of reflection and meditation, possibly named after Albert Luthuli (Legacy Project Committee 1998).

But perhaps most significantly, it was recommended that a project called 'The Long Walk to Freedom: The Mandela Trail' be introduced. This initiative in tourism based on Mandela's well-established biography would connect 'many places of significance' associated with South Africa's first democratic president. Sites earmarked for inclusion were Mandela's Orlando West home, the location of his attorney's practice, the site of his incarceration during the treason trial in the 1950s, educational institutions such as Healdtown and Fort Hare. Additional sites proposed were Liliesleaf Farm in Rivonia, location of the High Command of uMkhonto we Sizwe in the 1960s, as well as the Grand Parade in Cape Town, where Mandela first spoke after his release in February 1990. An 'overarching, historical trail' of Mandela's 'life and times' would provide tourists with 'a portrait of the society in which he lived and struggled' and give a 'context to his steadfast vision of a non-racial society' (Legacy Project Committee 1998).[5]

In a statement released during 1998, the then Minister of Arts, Culture,

Science and Technology, Lionel Mtshali, announced that the cabinet had given its approval to a number of legacy projects to be launched during 1998 and 1999. Among these projects was a Nelson Mandela Museum to be established at Umtata in the Eastern Cape. This museum would house the many awards and gifts received by Mandela, and would endeavour 'to tell the story' of Mandela's life (Mtshali 1998). The Nelson Mandela Museum, 'named and themed after one of the greatest statesmen of our time', opened on 11 February 2000, the tenth anniversary of Nelson Mandela's release from imprisonment. This multi-site project was to be located in three centres, the renovated Bhunga Building in Umtata, at Mvezo and Qunu, and would comprise a 'conventional museum, a cultural village and a community centre' (Ngubane 2000).

In the course of making this museum display in the Bhunga Building, the objectives of the museum exhibition were outlined. These were to 'illustrate the life, the times, the philosophy and legacy' of Mandela within a local, national and international context. Nation-building and reconciliation would be articulated and promoted, while the exhibition would also provide an opportunity to 'consolidate our democracy by providing an understanding of the processes that led to it'. The life of Mandela would be a means to 'document the struggle for democracy and its context', and to 'trace cultural diversity and cultural mobility'. Extracts from *Long Walk to Freedom* complemented by photographs, press cuttings, pamphlets, posters and video footage would ensure that Mandela's 'thoughts and feelings' would be communicated 'in his own words'. Mandela's museum biography would be organised as history lessons for students and tourists, organised around five chronological modules. These would begin with Mandela's 'country childhood', while others would focus on his role in the liberation struggle before imprisonment, 'the dark years' of imprisonment, 'freedom' and 'democracy' (Nelson Mandela Museum Exhibition Committee).

A biographic character was thus being given to the cultural landscape, with the life of leaders becoming a central focus. Biography, conceived of in conventional ways, was confirmed as one of the chief modes of negotiating the past in the public domain, and was a central feature of stories of resistance and reconciliation, recovered as the basis of nation-building in the new South Africa. At the centre of all of this biographic activity, and reflected through a cluster of biographical projects, was the life of Nelson Mandela, whose 'long walk' came to symbolise the new nation's past (Rassool 1997). The Mandela Museum, the Mandela Trail and the Mandela Library at Constitution Hill in Gauteng – itself a legacy project – would join the Robben Island Museum, with its central feature Cell No. 5, in B Block, where Mandela had spent 17 years, in constituting a phalanx of public history projects at the apex of South Africa's heritage landscape. Together they would ensure that Mandela's 'walk to freedom' would remain the key trope for the nation's history narrated as the triumph of reconciliation.

HERITAGE CONTESTS AT THE DISTRICT SIX MUSEUM

Any attempt to understand the possibilities of a critical perspective on South African heritage and public history has to give attention to the multifaceted space of the District Six Museum in Cape Town.[6] The District Six Museum opened its doors in the old church of the Central Methodist Mission at 25A Buitenkant Street on 10 December 1994. Its opening exhibition was called *Streets: Retracing District Six.* Described as an 'archaeology of memory' (Morphet 1995), the museum was the culmination of years of planning, dreaming and imagining on the part of the District Six Museum Foundation. Emanating from the 'Hands Off District Six' campaign, the foundation was one of a range of organisations, institutions and cultural projects which had emerged between the 1970s and 1990s to preserve the memory of District Six. District Six, an area of inner-city Cape Town at the foot of the mountain, had seen the forced removal of 60,000 people from the heart of the city, and its material fabric razed to the ground, after it had been declared a 'white group area' in 1966.

Streets was to be open for only a couple of weeks. However, since that day in December 1994 when ex-District Sixer and then Minister of Justice, Dullah Omar opened the exhibition, the District Six Museum has not been able to close its doors. As funds were raised, the museum grew in complexity, both as an institution and in its museum work of collecting, exhibiting and educating. While the *Streets* exhibition was the core of its exhibitionary work for almost five years, a number of other exhibitions were mounted alongside it, expressing the museum's desire to tell more complex stories, to work with different mediums, to address specific audiences and even to go beyond the story of District Six itself. Among these additional exhibitions were *(Dis)playing the Game,* on the sporting and cultural heritage of Cape Town, *The Last Days of District Six: Photographs by Jan Greshoff,* a display of the architecture of the district before its bulldozing, *Buckingham Palace,* based on author Richard Rive's work, and aimed at school learners, and *Tramway Road*, about forced removals in Sea Point, near Cape Town, and attempts to rebuild that community.

At one level, the museum has been seen as a project about the histories of District Six, forced removals and the retrieval of memory as a resource of solidarity and reclamation. The museum speaks of itself as a 'community museum', whose work is addressed to a community who had been removed under apartheid. But in the face of a historiography which has tended to privilege District Six in the story of 'forced removals', the museum has also had to go further and address a general history of forced removals, narrated on a national scale. The museum's work suggests that it is this widespread experience of removals and social dislocation in South Africa that should rather be understood to be the source of a national history of South Africa. In its collections and curatorial work, the museum has sought to produce and generate, and to reflect upon such national histories through display and public education. At times this identification has intersected with the interests of the tourism industry, which requires a 'space of apartheid' for tourists to witness.

There have been different ways in which the story of the District Six Museum has been narrated. Institutional histories of committees and founders, and political histories of civic politics, agitation and mobilisation around the scarred landscape of the district have stood alongside cultural histories of District Six, memorial projects and social history research (Rassool and Prosalendis 2001: part 1). But all these accounts have reflected a commitment to bigger questions of social justice in the city of Cape Town, to addressing the history of forced removals in general, the need for urban regeneration and the desire to heal the city. This is a commitment to land restitution and the reconstruction of community. It is based on the recognition that the land restitution process represents perhaps the only means of restoring the poor to the centre of the city from which they had been removed. It is also a commitment to contributing to the building of civil society. Like other cities in South Africa, Cape Town saw the dramatic erosion of community and the structures of civil society, such as sports clubs, choirs, dance bands and cultural and debating societies. The District Six Museum has emerged as an attempt to address the need for such social regeneration.

What has also emerged in these accounts of the museum's history was a productive ambivalence about the categories of 'museum' and 'exhibition'. This ambivalence has expressed itself in two ways. When the District Six Museum Foundation was created and the museum itself established, the choice of the category 'museum' did not necessarily also express a specific commitment to the institution of the museum in the formal sense of the word. The foundation certainly wanted a project through which it would be able to contest the past and use history as a means of mobilisation around the traumatic landscape of District Six. Records of the early days of the museum's existence reveal a debate about what the priorities of the museum should be and where it should allocate its energies and capacities. While some were concerned about the links between the District Six Museum and other museums in South Africa and beyond, a strong position was articulated that the mission of the museum was *not* to network with museums, but to mobilise the masses of ex-residents and their descendants into a movement of land restitution, community development and political consciousness.

Nevertheless, it was indeed fortuitous that a District Six *Museum* was created as a cultural institution at the same time as the challenges of museum and heritage transformation in South Africa were being identified, and the frameworks for such processes of transformation created. As a museum, it was an independent, non-government organisation. It was not burdened by the baggage of old collections and outdated classificatory systems. And as a new community-based independent museum, it did not face any pressure to conform to the state authorities and emerging, centrally directed, national heritage policies or frameworks. These circumstances necessarily saw the District Six

Museum, explicitly and implicitly, engage with processes of museum and heritage transformation in South Africa. As a small, community-based initiative, the museum nevertheless saw itself as being of national significance, telling a national history of forced removals. The District Six Museum had appropriated and mobilised one of the premier institutions of 'Western civilisation' for its own cultural purposes. And as an independent space of knowledge-creation, which was confident about its achievements and ways of working, and was also attempting to address its shortcomings, the museum wanted to tell its story nationally, thereby intervening in the field of cultural representation.

The ambivalence about being a 'museum' also expressed itself in the approaches of trustees of the museum. Trustee Irwin Combrinck has said about the District Six Museum: 'It is not a place where you just come to view artefacts. It's something that you become involved in' (cited in Goodman 1997: 17). This view has been echoed by another trustee, Peggy Delport, who has been the central curator of the museum's key exhibitions, and who has regularly referred to the processes of inscription, performance, annunciation and theatre that are the lifeblood of the museum's work. To these can be added the argumentation and debate about the past of the district, of Cape Town, and of South Africa, that have filled the spaces of the museum. It is these, sometimes ephemeral, processes that have given the museum's distinctive curatorial features – the map (Figure 8.2), the cloth, the street signs, the hanging portraits (Figure 8.3) and the hand-coloured enlarged streetscapes – their meaning.

Whereas *Streets: Retracing District Six* was the core exhibition of the museum during its early history, a new exhibition, *Digging Deeper,* was created for the freshly restored and renovated Buitenkant Street church building in 2000. *Digging Deeper*, as a self-conscious and self-reflexive exhibition, sought to

Figure 8.2
Inscribing the floor map –
a distinctive curatorial
feature of the District Six
Museum.

Figure 8.3
Hanging portraits and
enlarged streetscapes:
the Digging Deeper
exhibition at the District
Six Museum in Cape
Town.

address a restlessness within the museum that wanted to tell the story of District Six with greater complexity. Whereas *Streets* had tended to focus on spaces and lives constructed in public, *Digging Deeper* sought to examine the private and interior spaces of people's lives. In making *Digging Deeper*, the museum chose to inquire into its collections and to ask deeper questions about the district, rather than merely to produce more facts.

The aim in *Digging Deeper* has been to avoid taking a single, safe narrative approach. Rather, the museum has set out consciously to disrupt and unsettle certain conventions about District Six's past: that the district was a 'coloured' place, that District Six was a 'slum', and even the idea that social life in District Six was without contradiction. In adopting such an approach, the District Six Museum has asserted that it is not a space of innocence. The memorial text at the entrance to the museum reflects the desire to ask difficult questions: 'we seek to work with our memories, our achievements *and our shames*, our moments of glory, courage and love for one another, *and also the hurts we inflicted upon each other*' (emphasis added). In the District Six Museum, exhibitions come to life through what is generated and provoked within its spaces: in the arguments and interjections, in the memorialising and working with memory, as former residents remember, tell and interpret. The aesthetic forms, textures and interrelationships are generated primarily by voices, while photographs, artefacts and documents help layer the framework and act as triggers (Delport 2001).

In the work of the District Six Museum, certain features have emerged as core values and approaches that underpin its memory work. Informed by the social character and political history of District Six that it has come to understand, the museum is convinced that one of the most important contributions it can make to the fields of culture and history in South Africa is to articulate a position which questions the validity of race and racial categories. One of the most important missions of the District Six Museum is to question race at every turn and to assert a politics of non-racialism and anti-racism in every facet of its work. The museum holds on to and propounds the possibility of a non-racial community, as it emerges out of and is reflected in the history of District Six. This commitment also necessitates identifying dominant modes of framing society, when claims are made to being new and transformatory, and when they are premised on similar, if not the same intellectual foundations of colonialism and apartheid. The dominant discourse of diversity, with apartheid categories left frozen and naturalised, suggests more a continuity with the past than a clear effort to break with the past.

The District Six Museum has shown an awareness that its capacity to continue to be effective depends on how it is nurtured as an independent space of representation and contestation about history and knowledge of society. The museum has sought to open up questions of relations of knowledge as contained within and generated by all facets of its work, and about the possibilities and limits of self-representation. In part, this has also been an attempt at a self-critical and reflexive pedagogy on the part of an institution which has brought together community-connected academics – some of whom see themselves as 'activist intellectuals', but who often bear the restrictive marks of the academy, and former residents, many of whom have been activist intellectuals for decades with their roots in District Six-based political and cultural organisations. The synergies and contests of such a membership mix have been at the heart of the curatorial methods of the District Six Museum (Figure 8.4).

Figure 8.4
District Six Museum educator and former resident Linda Fortune tells stories to young visitors in Nomvuyo's room

As a site of knowledge of society, the museum, by its very nature, has confronted the legacy of ethnographic representation in all of its work, and has resisted its construction as a convenient field site for the study of culture and the politics of transition by 'experts'. The increasing scale of visiting academics and graduate students, bent on finding spaces of engagement in South Africa, has established the country as a growing, highly specialised site of tourism. South African academics, students and public scholars have increasingly found themselves in the position of native informants, facilitating a double relationship of ethnography, as a research encounter, as well as a cultural encounter in a post-colony in transition (McEachern 1998: 48–72). The museum has also been mindful of the need to challenge meanings that are attributed to the museum within relations of tourism more generally, which might also derive from a quest for an encounter with 'the other'. Implicitly, the work of the museum has been concerned to develop a productive ambivalence about academic forms of knowledge appropriation as well as the power of tourist discourses of diversity (Delport *et al*. n.d.).

It is thus out of its 'core business' of memory work conducted in support of the struggle for the restitution of land rights in District Six that the District Six Museum has committed itself to reconstituting and recalling community in District Six in the heart of Cape Town (Figure 8.5). The notions of 'recall' and 'remember' have been used to refer to both the museum's memory work on District Six as well as its desire to see the community of District Six restored, and called back to resettle, redevelop and heal the scarred landscape at the foot of the mountain. From the perspective of the museum, the recovery and restoration of memory is just as important as, and needs to be a vital component of, the recovery and restoration of land. Apart from the mixed land use, which the history of District Six reflects, it also reveals core values of non-racialism,

Figure 8.5
District Six Museum as site of knowledge: engaging theatre and performance.

tolerance, heterogeneity, and a way of life that was 'also about the exploration of the self'. District Six 'provided a civic space in which people not only performed particular roles and functions, but were also able to account for their roles' (Soudien 2001). In claiming these values in the history of District Six, the museum has posited a concept of community that must inform District Six's reconstruction.

RE-MEMBERING DISTRICT SIX

In a 'landmark ceremony' in District Six on 26 November 2000, that was presided over by President Thabo Mbeki, the final stage of the District Six land restitution process was launched. Title to 40 hectares of District Six land was handed back to claimants who had been tenants in District Six at the time of removals. This brought the process of land restitution ever closer to ensuring that thousands of mainly working-class families, described under apartheid as African or coloured, would return to District Six after successful land claims. At the ceremony, ex-resident and District Six Museum trustee Anwah Nagia joined Mbeki and Land Affairs Minister Thoko Didiza on the podium to address the assembled land claimants and former residents of the district. In the build-up to the ceremony, Nagia had eloquently expressed the views of both claimants and the District Six Museum:

> History must begin to judge us as victorious over apartheid social engineering and separate development. We are celebrating the return of stolen land from the people who were defenceless, voiceless and disenfranchised in the land of their birth. Let this victory teach us to share and shape a common destiny for a united people.
>
> (Geldenhuys 2000b)

With estimates of between 8,000 and 10,000 people set to move back to the city, the process of land restitution had seemingly entered its final stages and was moving forward with greater pace (Geldenhuys 2000a, 2000b). It seemed clear that the 'recalling' of the community of District Six would not be held up for much longer. The memory work of the District Six Museum has hitherto taken place on the basis of the empty traumatic landscape of District Six and the desire for its healing. The redevelopment of the area, the building of houses and the reconstitution of a community of District Six have posed new challenges for the District Six Museum of inserting issues of memory into the redevelopment process.

By insisting that the reconstruction of District Six is not only a bricks-and-mortar issue, the museum has embarked on a new phase of its own development, which it has characterised as 'Hands On District Six'. Working with the District Six Beneficiary and Redevelopment Trust, the museum has proposed plans for the creation of a memorial park, and for the inscription of memory markers into the redeveloped landscape. On this basis, the redevelopment of District Six stands in contrast to other urban rejuvenation initiatives in central Cape

Town, such as Mandela-Rhodes Place, which have begun to inscribe the city with signs of corporate luxury and exclusivity.

The District Six Museum has emerged as one of a range of institutions and sites in the public domain in post-apartheid South Africa concerned with public memory as a basis for imagining and reconstructing a new society. From an independent location, it explicitly and implicitly contests the ethnic and racialised ways in which South African society continues to be depicted, in the tourist gaze and beyond, in spite of the demise of apartheid. In the cultural practice of its curatorial work, it also challenges the ways in which national heritage tends to be centrally constructed and handed down by the state in the form of institutions and sites which celebrate the lives of heroic leaders. Through its memory work, the District Six Museum holds on to and propounds the possibility of a non-racial community as it emerges out of and is reflected in the history of District Six. In arguing that the social reconstruction of District Six needs to be informed by its history, the District Six Museum has created a space of reflection, annunciation and memorial that insists on the possibility of self-representation in South African public culture. This will ensure that the process of reconstructing and re-membering District Six will not only occur through the work of experts.

REFERENCES

Bundy, C. (2000) 'The Beast of the Past: History and the TRC', in W. James and L. van der Vijver (eds) *After the TRC: Reflections on Truth and Reconciliation in South Africa*, Cape Town: David Philip.

Callinicos, L. (2000) *The World that Made Mandela: A Heritage Trail – 70 Sites of Significance*, Johannesburg: STE Publications.

Cape Argus (1995) 'Experience Tribal Life in Xhosaville', 18 December.

Delport, P. (2001) 'Digging Deeper in District Six: Features and Interfaces in a Curatorial Landscape', in C. Rassool and S. Prosalendis (eds) *Recalling Community in Cape Town: Creating and Curating the District Six Museum*, Cape Town: District Six Museum.

Delport, P., Rassool, C. and Soudien C. (n.d.) 'District Six and Its Pasts: Identity, Memory and Transgression in Public Culture', unpublished discussion memo.

Friedman, H. (1996) 'Land of Milk and Honey', *Mail & Guardian*, 'Open Africa': 19.

Geldenhuys, Henriette (2000a) 'Thousands to Move Back to District Six', *Cape Times* 22 November.

—— (2000b) 'Putting the Heartbeat Back into the City', *Cape Times* 24 November.

Goodman, David (1997) 'Cape Town's District Six Rises Again', *Ford Foundation Report*, vol. 28, no. 2.

Koch, E. (1996) 'Spitting a Cud to the Winds in QwaQwa', *Mail & Guardian*, 'Open Africa': 20.

Land Claim Committee (1995) 'Land Claim and Submission to the Minister of Land Affairs by the Land Claim Committee and the Southern Kalahari Bushmen', 7 August.

Legacy Project Committee (1998) 'The Portfolio of Legacy Projects: A Portfolio of

Commemorations Acknowledging Neglected or Marginalised Heritage', (discussion document, January).

McEachern, C. (1998) 'Working with Memory: The District Six Museum in the New South Africa', *Social Analysis* 42 (2).

Mayibuye Centre (1997) 'Draft Discussion/Working Document Only: Proposal for the Smithsonian South African Culture Programme at the 1997 Festival of American Folklife'.

Mimeo (1999) 'Nelson Mandela Museum: Exhibition Brief and Proposal'.

Morphet, T. (1995) 'An Archaeology of Memory', *Mail & Guardian* 30 February.

Mtshali, L. (1998) 'Statement by Minister Mtshali on Legacy Projects: issued by the Minister of Arts, Culture, Science and Technology', www.polity.org.za/govdocs/pr/1998/pr0615a.html.

National Monuments Council (1998) 'Claim Your Heritage', poster.

Nelson Mandela Museum Exhibition Committee (n.d.) 'Nelson Mandela Museum: Exhibition Brief and Proposal' (Exhibition Committee discussion document).

Ngubane, Dr B. S. (2000) Speech by the Minister of Arts, Culture Science and Technology, Visit to Flagship Institutions, 27 January, www.dacst.gov.za/speeches/minister/jan2000/flagship.htm.

Rassool, C. (1997) 'The Individual, Biography and Resistance in South African Public History', *South African and Contemporary History Seminar*, University of the Western Cape, 7 October.

—— (1998) 'Cultural Performance and Fictions of Identity: The Case of the Khoisan of the Southern Kalahari, 1936–1937', *Conference on Voices, Values and Identities: The Social Ecology of Heritage Interpretation*, Berg-en-Dal, Kruger National Park.

Rassool, C. and Prosalendis, S. (eds) (2001) *Recalling Community in Cape Town: Creating and Curating the District Six Museum*, Cape Town: District Six Museum.

Rassool, C. and Witz, L. (1996) '"South Africa: A World in One Country": Moments in International Tourist Encounters with Wildlife, the Primitive and the Modern', *Cahiers d'Etudes africaines*, 143, XXXVI-3.

SATOUR (1996) 'Explore South Africa: A Promotion by the South African Tourism Board', *Culture*, 1st edn, April.

Saturday Business (1996) 'The White Face of SA Tourism' (supplement to *Saturday Weekend Argus*) 22/23 June.

Soudien, C. (2001) 'Holding on to the Past: Working with the "Myths" of District Six', in C. Rassool and S. Prosalendis (eds) *Recalling Community in Cape Town: Creating and Curating the District Six Museum*, Cape Town: District Six Museum.

Truth and Reconcilation Commission (1998) *Truth and Reconciliation Commission of South Africa Final Report* (5 vols), Cape Town: Juta & Co.

Chapter 9: A Second Life

Museums, Mimesis, and the Narratives of the Tour Guides of Robben Island

Harry Garuba

While it looks old, heritage is actually something new. Heritage is a mode of cultural production in the present that has recourse to the past. Heritage thus defined depends on display to give dying economies and dead sites a second life as exhibitions of themselves.

(Kirshenblatt-Gimblett 1998)

On the front page of the *Cape Times* of Thursday 11 July 2002, is the picture of a former inmate of Robben Island locked in a prison cell.[1] Standing inside the cell in a pensive mood, with his hands behind his back, the man is engaged in a protest performance that he knows carries a dense historical significance and symbolic meaning in the social imaginary of contemporary South Africa (Figure 9.1). Its symbolic import is such that it conditions much of the discourse of the new post-apartheid nation and, knowing this, he deploys all the signs that enhance the efficacy of this performance. Though the hands are simply held behind his back, we can imagine them being in handcuffs; behind the bars, he exudes the quiet determination that narratives of Robben Island have circulated with such consistency about the courage of the political prisoners of the apartheid years. Outside – in front of the bars of the cell – is an aluminium plate and an aluminium cup representing, presumably, the kind that the prisoners' food and water used to be served in. Only his clothes and his shoes tell us that this performance is being enacted in another 'time' and 'place', a time that is both the now and not-now, and a place that is both here and not-here. In this coeval time and place, the plate and cup are both empty, speaking of deprivation and – if we may extend the analogy – signifying also the 'empty artefacts' that every museum displays, awaiting the fullness of narrative. For it is narrative that gives 'voice' to the artifacts that museums display.

Under this highly suggestive picture is the caption: '**PROTEST:** Former political prisoners (*sic*) Afrika Hlapo of Gugulethu, who was jailed for 11 years on Robben Island, was one of 17 former prisoners who locked themselves in the

Figure 9.1
Robben Island prison
tour guide and former
prisoner Afrika Hlapo
protests by locking
himself in a cell.

cells yesterday in protest at alleged mismanagement in the island administration.'
In the report that follows, the journalist, Melanie Gosling, writes:

> Former Robben Island political prisoners locked themselves into 17 maximum security cells
> yesterday morning and began a 24-hour hunger strike in protest at what they described as
> corruption and mismanagement in the running of the Robben Island Museum.
>
> (Gosling 2002: 1)

The hunger strike of the here and now echoes and evokes the hunger
strikes of a different time and place. The report continues:

> Tours of the prison museum were cancelled in the afternoon, but earlier tour groups
> looked surprised to find people locked in what they thought was an empty museum,
> and the corridor was filled with the sound of clicking cameras as tourists snapped the
> former prisoners standing behind bars or lying on their blankets on the cell floors.
>
> (Gosling 2002: 1)

The clicking cameras recording what was once hidden from public view
and banned from public scrutiny bear witness to that time, to the uncovering of
that truth that was suppressed. In a strangely unintended way, they were fulfilling the didactic purpose of the museum to bring that past into public knowledge; they were also confirming the linear progression from concealment to
revelation which is the narrative of apartheid and the struggle for liberation. It is
noteworthy that the writer here says that the tourists 'looked surprised' to see
real people actually locked up in what 'they thought was an empty museum'.
Perhaps some may have known that the people 'locked up' in the cells in the
here and now were some of the same people who had been locked up in the
there-then, several years ago. If they knew, maybe their perplexity would have

deepened on realising that these same people also work, here and now, as tour guides on the island.

There is a sense in which what the unsuspecting tourists saw that morning before tours were cancelled is an ironic fulfilment of the 'realism' and 'authenticity' that administrators had desired when the decision was first taken to employ former prison inmates as tour guides for the prison now turned museum. But this reading will rest on the assumption that the use of ex-prisoners as tour guides was motivated by the need to create the 'authenticity effect' for tourists by intimating a direct relationship of identity between the representations of the past of Robben Island that these ex-prisoner tour guides provide, and that past itself. Being participants in that past, their narratives, it is assumed, will transparently reflect that past, which is itself seen as a closed, stable and knowable, objective fact that simply needs to be revealed. The 'realism' of their narratives and their authenticity therefore would be a selling point here, so to speak.

This presupposition may or may not be strictly true; it may or may not be the primary reason why the prisoners were employed as tour guides in the first instance. But what is undoubtedly true is that the Robben Island tourists, the audience to which the narratives of the tour guides is directed, often experience the urge, indeed, are urged to, and usually do ask questions relating to the guide's personal experience, once they realise that their tour guide was a former inmate. This audience expectation of the personal experience is built into the tour and permeates and structures the entire narrative. In this regard, what the tourists saw that morning was a re-enactment, a direct imitation of the past – rather than a simple narrative of it – by the *subjects* of that past now turning themselves into *objects*. At this point, the audience expectation built into the tour is fulfilled by the protest performance. As stated earlier, it is clear that the former prisoners-now-turned-performers are aware of the symbolic significance of Robben Island, its evocative power as a primary site in the making of a public history and discourse that has become central to the new South Africa. In fact, in their 'muted' re-enactment, they also unwittingly fulfil the museum 'requirement' of putting objects on display. By 'displaying' themselves in this manner, they paradoxically perform an agency that strips them of *human* agency by reinforcing their presence as objects. In this paper, I intend to argue that this double manoeuvre of simultaneously inscribing agency and objecthood in the bodies of the former inmate is at the very heart of the narratives of the tour guides of Robben Island.

To begin, I find it necessary to recount the circumstances in which this essay was conceived. The idea for this chapter developed in 2001 when I first visited Robben Island and found former inmates being used as tour guides. The sense of unease I felt about this was confirmed over the 12-month period when I had occasion to repeat the tour several times with visiting friends and family who could never resist the urge to see the prison in which Nelson Mandela had spent so many years. My unease arose from my inability to understand the logic behind the use of former prisoners as tour guides in the place of their incarceration, a place that, I assumed, could only be associated with traumatic memories for them. To make the sufferers tell the story of their deprivation and personal pain all over, again and again, several times a day, to an audience of tourists did not seem to me a particularly good way of memorialising the event and the island, no matter what the intended lessons for the audience were. On the contrary, I felt that it was more likely to trivialise it and/or aggravate the pain.[2] My search for understanding has taken many twists and turns since then. In the process, I have visited the island over a dozen times, spoken to the tour guides in informal conversation, asked questions, and so on. In this essay, I present only one account of the many directions this search has taken. The essay thus combines the subjectivity of a personal journey of understanding with the 'objectivity' of a research inquiry.

The major question I ask here can be phrased as follows: Between the hegemony of the narrative of the anti-apartheid struggle and the role of Robben Island in it, on the one hand, and the discursive economy of the heritage industry and global tourism on the other, is there a space for the truly personal lives and subjectivities of the ex-prisoner tour guides to emerge in their narratives and memories of their time on the island? In short, can personal, private memories be produced and narrated against the grain of the public, collective memory in this instance? One other way of posing this question is to ask if the tour guides do have personal memories and narratives that are capable of resisting discursive appropriation or capture by the dominant narratives? If they do have such memories, can these be narrated and under what conditions? And, if they don't have such personal memories that can be articulated in narrative, why don't they?

This account focuses specifically on exploring these questions. In examining these issues, the account suggests that there are ways in which real human subjects with their own personal experiences and memories, their own unique individuality, often become subjected to the power of a discourse. It also looks into some of the ways in which individual, 'subaltern' memories and selves are articulated into a dominant narrative that appropriates and recreates them in its own image. The narratives of the ex-prisoner tour guides thus function here as an opening into larger questions of memory, subjectivity and agency which I can only broach here rather than examine fully.

MIMESIS AND THE SPACE OF NARRATIVE

The 'mythology' of Robben Island is so large that it is perhaps idealistic to expect that any individual will be able to live outside of its power. The island is one of those overtextualised places and sites which become impossible to 'see' or narrate without the conditioning of prior texts and discourses. But since the expectation of the unique individual perspective of an ex-prisoner is one of the advertised items of the tour, it is therefore not really off the mark to begin with this expectation.

This account thus rests on the presupposition that by using ex-political prisoners as guides, the audience expects or is led to expect that the narratives will bear traces of the personal experience of the ex-prisoners in all its authenticity and truth. Taking this premise for granted, the line of inquiry I will be pursuing here draws upon ideas from two disciplinary domains: the idea of mimesis taken from literary theory and the idea of museums as places of mimetic display. If it is true, as Barbara Kirshenblatt-Gimblett (1998) asserts in the quote that I use as epigraph, that heritage 'depends on display to give dying economies and dead sites a second life as exhibitions of themselves', it follows that a certain kind of mimesis is fundamental to the production of heritage and the museum as one of its 'store houses'. A site museum is particularly important in this regard because both the objects on display and the site itself acquire a second life, functioning as representations of themselves and their previous lives. In literary theory the classical Greek concept of *mimesis*, usually translated as imitation or representation, is seen as the foundation of literature and art. In literature, mimesis is conceived as a relationship of imitation between an object (real or imagined) and its representation, implying something (not the real thing) standing in for something else (the real thing). Mimesis, thus conceived, involves a separation between object and representation creating a relationship of disjuncture or, if you like, one of non-identity between them. This space of disjuncture is the space occupied by the social codes, conventions, interpretive devices, and so on, that work to create the imaginative correspondence between them. This is the space of narrative, the space where a discourse is constructed to provide the ground of intelligibility.

With regard to the museum, however, the use of the concept needs to be complicated to take in the case of an object standing in for itself. I use the term mimetic display in this sense to take in the case of the museum where instead of representing something else the object 'represents' itself.[3] Here the 'real' object is recreated as a representation of itself or its previous self and thus becomes an object of discourse. In the present, the object may be the 'same' but the discourse that frames it reproduces it in this scene as a representation of itself in the past. As object and representation at one and the same time, it possesses both a self-identity as a real object, so to speak, and a representational identity as an object of discourse constructed as part of a signifying process.

The distinction that I have been trying to draw between conventional conceptions of mimesis as different from the case of museum displays and the extension I have tried to make to the concept to hint at their underlying similarity are important when the objects on display are truly non-speaking objects. Non-speaking objects, being voiceless, may be described as 'empty' in the sense that they cannot represent themselves in narrative. Displayed as artefacts from a significant past, their presence in the present is given meaning by a narrative construction of that past. Instead of the conventional 'gap' between object and representation in conventional mimetic theory, here time separates them: same object, different temporalities. This, in essence, is the second life that

Kirshenbatt-Gimblett speaks of. For 'mute' artefacts, this temporal disjuncture creates the occasion for narrative; a narrative constructed in the present by someone else. But what happens when real people are displayed? Speaking subjects by the very fact of their possession of speech belong to a different order, at least because they can be assumed to have the power of self-representation. Being capable of speech and self-representation in a shared language, we assume that they can in fact become subjects constructing their own personal narratives, be to some degree individualised and independent of the constructions of others. In advertising '[i]nteraction with an ex-political prisoner' as one of the features of the tour, the Robben Island Museum encourages this assumption by seeking to portray these ex-prisoners as subjects, constructing their own narratives in an unconstrained dialogic interaction with an audience – a tourist or group of tourists.

Setting out with this assumption, would we find an instance where the power of the personal narrative, or the prodding or questioning from a tourist, disturbs the stability of the dominant narrative of Robben Island? Would an errant text emerge from the margins represented by the speaking subject to undo this hegemonic master text?

THE TOUR

These days the Robben Island tour begins at the Nelson Mandela Gateway, at the Victoria and Alfred Waterfront, Cape Town. From the ticketing office on the ground floor, you go down a stairway to a modest hall through to the boats. The boats are named after a seventeenth-century Khoi interpreter who was to become a prisoner on the island, Autshumato, and a nineteenth-century prisoner, the Xhosa chief, Makana, who drowned while trying to escape from the island. These figures represent the era of the first encounters of the indigenous Khoi communities of the Western Cape with the Dutch, and the later period of the resistance to colonial expansion by the amaXhosa in the Eastern Cape.

As the boat sets out, a video starts to play. The video recording tells the story of the island from its beginnings to the present. It starts off in geological time, the prehistoric separation of the island from the continental land mass and details its uninhabited natural beauty, creating the picture of a pristine pearl in the ocean. Images of stunning natural beauty fill the screen as the story unfolds. The narrative then moves on to the period of human history; the coming of the ships and the beginning of human habitation on the island. The sullied time of human history is presented as two serial episodes, one representing the Fall, followed by a second, the subsequent struggle for the return to grace and redemption. It is a neat teleological narrative that compresses natural and historical time in one linear sweep: it has all the makings of a modernist narrative. Interestingly, the narrator of this story is the island itself personified, speaking with the authority of a presence that begins in the unfathomable past, in a natural time outside of history, treads through historical time and human activity, and hints at a future secure in the knowledge of a manifest destiny.[4]

Thirty minutes later, the boat arrives on the island where buses and the guides are on hand to welcome the tourists. Depending on the numbers, the tourists may be divided into two or three groups. In the buses, one group may begin with a tour of the island taking a clockwise direction while the other takes an anti-clockwise direction. If there is a third group, this group walks right on into the prison and begins with the prison tour. A tour guide will be at hand to conduct each of the groups. If a group is particularly 'lucky', it will have an ex-prisoner as tour guide for the island tour and another for the prison tour. Whatever the case may be, the tour is sold – as I have said – with the promise of 'interaction with an ex-political prisoner' and, in my experience, there is usually one available at the very least, either to conduct the island bus tour or the walk-through prison tour.

Though each tour follows the same generic template of sites and speeches, the measure of its success lies in the ability of the guide to provide information in a clear and concise manner, interspersing this with stories and anecdotes that keep the interest of the audience. Sometimes there are guides able to balance good rhetorical skills with a sense of time that allows them to cover and comment as much as possible on the chosen sites while regaling the tourists with interesting anecdotes; and at other times there are garrulous guides who have to rush the group through because they have spent too much time at one site or on irrelevances. Then, there are the tight-lipped who simply provide the relevant information without flourish or embroidery. Whatever the type of guide, on the island tour you often get to see/be shown the following with their accompanying narratives: the kramat (and tales of a Muslim holy man and other holy men of religious zeal and political resistance from the East), the Anglican church (built and owned by the church to serve the lepers quarantined on the island), the lepers' graveyard (segregated in life, integrated in death), the Robert Sobukwe House (and information about the infamous Sobukwe Clause, and a story or two about Sobukwe's days on the island), the Stone Quarry and the Lime Quarry (and stories about prisoner self-education projects with a name or two of present political figures thrown in for effect), and information on the flora and fauna (water-guzzling imported trees). You are also likely to hear about the visit of the Clintons (and the mishap with the car being transported by helicopter to the island), Mandela's return visit (and the traditional symbolism of the 'memorial' piles of stones by the Lime Quarry placed there by Mandela and his entourage during this return visit), and possibly a word about winds and winter on the island; the present residences and residents of the island, and so on.

The bus comes to a stop at the prison gates and the tourists alight to meet a waiting guide who will take them through the prison. Greetings are exchanged, introductions made, the tourists are asked which countries they come from and then the prison section of the tour begins. Again this is a combination of short talks, providing sketches of history, giving information on the objects and places shown to the tourists, and the anecdotes and narratives that spice them all. You may hear a short history of the building of the Maximum Security Prison in the early 1960s before you begin. Within the prison itself, you are shown the general or communal section and the isolation cells section where the famous Rivonia Trialists were housed in the infamous section B; the visitor centre, the administrative offices, the infirmary, the courtyard in the B-section with a photograph of Mandela talking to Walter Sisulu, the games yard and more. You are told about prison conditions and the regime of rules and regulations, about discrimination in food rations between black and coloured prisoners, about the number and frequency of letters and visits allowed, the censorship of letters and the strict regulation and surveillance of visits, the question of illness and the infrequency of doctors' visits, the changing prison conditions from the harsh brutality of the 1960s to a general improvement of conditions over the decades as a result of the struggles of the prisoners and the protests outside. The emphasis all the time is on the resilience, creativity and ingenuity of the prisoners and their willingness to share and to help one another. On one occasion, a guide tells me that he was sick during his incarceration and 'Mr Nelson Mandela came and took [his] bucket and his in both his hands and emptied it for [him]'. For a moment, very briefly, my eyes lit up at this instance of personal recollection. But later, I wondered if I hadn't heard or read this somewhere else – one variant of a tale type, so to speak – among the many tales of Mandela's generosity of spirit and his readiness to help at moments such as this.

As would be expected, one of the highlights of the tour is the Mandela cell, where tourists click away with cameras, many posing beside the cell and having their photos taken, and asking questions about the authenticity of the items in the cell. Is that the blanket that Mandela really used? Is that his plate? And that cup, is it the one he drank from as a prisoner? No, they are not the real items; they have been placed there to show what those times were like. Those are the regulation issue blankets provided to the prisoners, and the same type of plates and cups that they used were also placed in the cell. During the tour, the image of Mandela looms large and, if the tourists are mostly Americans, every question seems to be about Mandela and no one else. Locals often ask about other public figures besides Mandela, largely other struggle leaders or political leaders who have recently been in the news. The guides often seem to be galvanised by these local questions into narratives that are outside the strictly political. You could catch the animated tones with which one spoke about Defence Minister Mosiuoa Lekota's soccer skills, interspersing his narrative in the games yard with gestures and demonstrations of various moves. He is careful to add at the end of this story that the games were also an excuse for conducting planning and strategy sessions. They also furnished an occasion for people to reach out to members of organisations other than their own.

The tour comes to an end with a short lecture on the new South Africa, the necessity for forgiveness and reconciliation as a condition for moving forward. Depending on how good the guide's memory is and how wide his knowledge of the international anti-apartheid movement is, he will thank the tourists and try to ensure that he mentions each of their countries individually as having contributed to the struggle against apartheid and the creation of a better South Africa. There can be no better tribute to their contribution than to build a non-racial, democratic South Africa. The Robben Island Museum, we are finally reminded, stands as a testament to their struggle and the triumph of the human spirit over adversity and oppression. Ahmed Kathrada's statement on this is boldly printed on a giant billboard just outside the prison.

MEMORY, NARRATIVE AND SUBJECTIVITY

On returning from one of my many visits to the island, I had an overwhelming feeling that perhaps I was looking in the wrong place, that I had the wrong expectations, that the tour was simply too programmed, too packaged, too short and too oriented to the public for any glimpse of an individual subjectivity to emerge. At this point, it had become clear to me that the promise of personal interaction with the ex-prisoner tour guide was an invitation that could not be taken up or met in full. Like a rhetorical question, it contains the promise of an answer that is forever deferred. What if I had the opportunity to speak with the guides outside the confines of the tour? Would this yield better results? Even though my project was initially limited to the narratives of the ex-prisoners, a probe into the rationale for using them as guides at the site of their incarceration, and seeking answers from the stories they told in this role, what if I went beyond these tour narratives to explore the stories they told when they were not functioning in this role? I decided to do just that, to test if the constraints of the role were solely responsible to this elision of the uniquely personal from their narratives.

From the conversations and interviews I conducted, did I obtain any new knowledge of them as individuals with their own personal fears and aspirations? Yes, I did: about their economic circumstances, their families, the kinds of lives they now lived in the township, and so on. But did I get anything significantly new about their memories of their time on the island that was not already part of the stories in public circulation? No, I didn't: and this became the occasion for asking how a generic template of memory is imposed upon individual subjects who, having lived through an experience, should have their own personal memories of it. Wasn't this the goal of prison? To create homogenised, generic subjects, stripped of all individuality? Why would a post-apartheid discourse partake of this homogenisation? But then again, I felt that it may be too soon to assume that a generic template of memory that erased any truly personal recollections had been discursively imposed. What if I had all the while been asking the wrong questions, questions that did not allow the personal to emerge even though I believed that this was what the questions were supposed to bring out? I decided to shift the focus of inquiry from the tour guides themselves and my own questions to the questions that the tourists asked.

Shifting focus in this manner led to some interesting discoveries. It was interesting to find that, even though – unlike the guides – the tourists do not have to follow a template of sites and objects to be shown and a 'script' of their stories and narratives, they all almost invariably asked similar questions. Indeed so similar were the questions asked on my several visits that it became possible for me to anticipate the questions. They were within a very limited spectrum that ranged from questions about the guide himself, the years of his imprisonment, his offence, and so on, to those questions aimed at obtaining further information on a specific object or site that had been pointed out by the guide, or for some narrative about a period, a person or conditions in the prison at a particular time. Then, of course, there were the usual Mandela questions. Even more interesting was the realisation that I could murmur the answers along as the guides spoke. Though not exactly in the same words, my answers corresponded to a large degree with the answers that the guides provided to the questions asked. This should not have been as surprising as it was to me because I had visited the island so often that I may also have learnt and internalised some of these narratives and performances. But my surprise was not occasioned by the answers to questions about objects, cells and histories. Rather it was from the fact that I could answer questions about individual experience and memory. I could tell which cell the prisoner was held in, the highlights of his period of incarceration, his activities – in short, his memories. I could narrate his memories in a fairly similar manner to his telling of them. On realising this, I began to wonder if this 'free' interaction had not been 'pre-scripted' all along in a kind of scenario planning that pre-plots the expectations that prospective visitors who come to the island will bring with them, and narratives and performances are rehearsed along these lines to meet these expectations.

The notion of anticipated questions to which performers formulate responses in advance is fairly common and is often highly successful when the nature and composition of the expected audience is easy to establish. When audiences vary widely, the possibility of error and the unforeseen increases. This is where a clearly focused narrative with a guiding principle becomes essential because it imposes its own (often unspoken) rules about what can be said within the context. From the minutiae of everyday life and experience, it selects the usable from the unusable and from the flux of memory, it draws a line between authorised speech and the unspeakable. I therefore decided to explore the possibility of 'pre-scripts' and the notion of discursive rules that set the limits of the sayable or, for that matter, the askable.

'PRE-SCRIPTS,' NATIONALIST NARRATIVES AND USABLE PASTS

When the last prisoners walked out of Robben Island in 1991, and its use as a prison facility was discontinued, public debates about the future of the island that had begun earlier in the 1970s and 1980s took on a new urgency as the struggle over the structures, symbols and meanings of post-apartheid South

Africa were taking shape. Tracing the history of these debates and mapping the various positions adopted by the partisans, Harriet Deacon says:

> During the 1970s, as political tension rose surrounding the use of the island as a prison for anti-apartheid activists, a public debate about an alternative role for it was generated. There was a political contest between broadly right-wing proposals to make Robben Island into a leisure resort or nature reserve and broadly anti-apartheid suggestions to build an educative museum or a peace centre there within an ecologically and historically sensitive development. This debate was part of a contest over the public memory of the island which because of its symbolic importance had important consequences for national identity.
>
> (Deacon 1998: 165)

When this debate was finally resolved in favour of the museum option, an evaluation process was conducted before the museum tours were open to the public. The Robben Island Museum (RIM) Exhibition Unit developed a set of criteria to drive these evaluations. Framed as a questionnaire given to all participants in the process, the aim was to evaluate the exhibitions against these criteria and make recommendations for improvements before the exhibitions opened to the public. The questionnaires covered such areas as the exhibition concept, what it aimed to communicate, the role of guides, whose 'voices' would be speaking or heard, and so on. There were also questions aimed at determining if the prison experience had been adequately conveyed and if it was engaging enough to elicit empathy, the role of ex-prisoners, questions of audience and access, text, images, design and curating, and those focused on issues of ecology and conservation.

The first phase of the evaluation was conducted on Tuesday 23 July 1999. In a memo from the RIM Exhibition Unit addressed to all evaluation participants concerning the second phase which was to take place on Monday 16 August, Gaby Cherminais of the RIM Exhibition Unit summarised the observations, suggestions and points raised from the first phase of the evaluation process. Among the many issues raised in connection with the tours were that the voices of ex-political prisoners needed to be incorporated into the narratives and that there should be a clear sense of periodisation, i.e. differentiating between the experiences of the prisoners in the 1960s and the 1980s. There was also concern that specific aspects of the histories of the prison experience – hard labour in the Stone Quarry, and the use of criminal prisoners by the authorities, for instance – were not mentioned. One suggestion was that the B-Section prison tour be used as an occasion for visitors to engage with the 'intimate personal experiences of the political prisoners' in an 'emotive/reflective manner' (Cherminais 1999). Other questions related to the clarity of purpose in the tours, that there was no core concept and coherence to the narrative; the experience of the evaluators being that it was, at that stage, more chaotic than moving towards a climax as it should. Suggestions and recommendations were then made with regard to these and other aspects.

From these evaluations it is clear that issues having to do with what were labelled the personal experiences of ex-prisoners and the integration of their voices into the narrative were taken into consideration in the planning process and not simply added on to the later brochures produced for visitors to the museum. It is also important to note that there were concerns about narrative coherence and the need for what was described as a 'core' to the narrative, and that the telling/showing should be sequenced in such a way as to create a sense of narrative progression to a climax. This concern with narrative structure and coherence had to be aligned with another equally serious concern that the personal voices and experiences of ex-prisoners somehow be heard. However, the personal voice and experience could not be randomly and incoherently attached to the main narrative thrust: it had to be integrated into it. These two ideas – of coherence and closure to the narrative on the one hand and of free interaction with the ex-prisoners and open-endedness on the other – would, on the surface, appear to pull in different directions. How to solve this question of a closed narrative that is still somewhat open?

This is where the idea of a guiding principle or concept comes into play; it becomes the enabling ground around which the various signs, images and their clusters of meaning cohere. Even though the stories may be different and dispersed – even individualised – they achieve a unity in discourse. In fulfilling this function, the discourse also exercises control over the various, dispersed narratives by semiotically and symbolically reining them in and thus preventing a descent into incoherence. Michel Foucault (1991) perhaps provides the best example of what I am struggling to state here. In his description of the way in which a discursive formation is individualised, Foucault says:

> What individualizes a discourse such as political economy or general grammar is not the unity of its objects, nor its formal infrastructure; nor the coherence of its conceptual architecture, nor its fundamental philosophical choices; it is rather the existence of a set of rules of formation for *all* its objects (however scattered they may be), *all* its operations (which can often neither be superposed nor serially connected), *all* its concepts (which may very well be incompatible), *all* its theoretical options (which are often mutually exclusive). There is an individualized discursive formation whenever it is possible to define such a set of rules.
>
> (Foucault 1991: 54)

Though Foucault is here speaking of the process through which larger discursive formations are individualised, I wish to suggest that the poetics of nationalism plays a similar role in these narratives because it provides a specific grammar with such 'a set of rules of formation' for speaking – and, indeed, asking questions – about Robben Island. These rules may be explicitly articulated as may have happened in the evaluation sessions or they may be implicitly disseminated through the assumptions and practices that predominate in the contexts in which the institutions function. If we think of the tour guides as implicated in these rules by the more direct, explicit route, we can see the museum visitors and tourists as being more indirectly interpolated. These therefore exert a form of control over the narratives and the 'free interaction', a control that may vary in degree from the hegemonic to the merely dominant.

From the section subtitled 'Summary of issues raised around the B-Section guided tour' of the memo sent out to the participants before the second phase of the evaluation process, it is obvious that this grounding discourse had not yet been fully constructed or articulated at the first phase. Here are some of the issues raised and suggestions made.

Concept

1 There was no clarity on the purpose of the guided tour. It does not work as a coherent experience, there is no sense of journey and insufficient contextual information about why people were imprisoned.
2 It is not an emotive experience because there are too many things (moments/issues) to apprehend. The way in which information (oral/visual/textual) is layered and sequenced creates a chaotic experience.
3 It was noted that many of the problems are due to inadequate periodisation.
4 It does not communicate the adversity and suffering, or the experience of imprisonment effectively.

Suggestions

1 RIM as a site of pilgrimage/journey:
2 That the journey into the prison must start in Cape Town and historical/factual information should be provided prior to arrival on island. The prison then becomes a space in which to engage with the intimate personal experiences of the political prisoners – emotive/reflective.
3 That visitors are welcomed at the entrance and then move to B-Section courtyard and engage with prison guides in courtyard and in B-Section.

The narrative

1 Is there a main narrative/core narrative and what is it?
2 What makes up a core narrative?
3 Do we need a core narrative?

Selected comments

1 The narrative has no climax/crescendo.
2 The triumph over oppression/adversities in prison is not communicated clearly.
3 The language is too formal, needs simplification.
4 Is the key story about prison life? Or the reason people were incarcerated?
5 The core/main narrative needs to be strong.
6 The concept of one main narrative is a conservative idea.

(Cherminais 1999)

Finding that grounding principle of coherence was therefore of major importance to the planners. They had realised from their first evaluation that because there were so many events, incidents, issues and memories spanning so many years and so many different personae, the story of Robben Island told to the tourists could easily degenerate into chaos and incoherence if an active principle of order was not found. That they were worried about this is evident in these observations, comments and suggestions. Perhaps they needn't have been so overly concerned because at that point in time the process of inventing a new South Africa was being actively pursued and the establishment of the Robben Island Museum was part of this negotiation of a new national identity. What was required was a reinvention of Robben Island in the image of this new national identity. The grounding principle for ordering such a diverse mass of material was thus to be found in nationalism. Nationalist discourse is not only capable of drawing upon and drawing together apparently contradictory sources of evidence and material, it also identifies usable pasts, draws subtle or not too subtle lines of inclusion and exclusion between authorised speech and the unspeakable.

Robben Island, of course, provided a perfect staging ground for the nationalist tropes of exile and homecoming and its history could easily be made to exemplify the movement from oppression and alienation to freedom and wholeness. Constructing a 'pre-scripted' narrative along these lines is not altogether a difficult affair. But as we have seen, a 'closed' narrative was only one part of the equation because there was an equal concern with open-endedness and dialogue, with the ex-prisoners and tourists cast in interactive, performatory roles. Giving them an agential role meant that the closed narrative could be opened up and irruptions could arise to unravel this closure. The idea of pre-scripts, of nationalist narratives and usable pasts, may account for the narratives of the tour guides but it cannot explain why their memories all seem so similar, nor why the questions from such diverse audiences are all posed within a limited ambit of possibilities. How could the possibility of irruptions be so contained? I suggest that the answer, once again, can be found in nationalism and the normalising processes of post-apartheid governmentality.

To understand the 'harmony' between the private memories of the ex-political-prisoner tour-guides of Robben Island, their personal experiences of incarceration, their public narratives to tourists, and the questions that these tourists ask, we need to understand the complex articulation between the power of discourses and technologies of power on the one hand, and the political technology of individuals and technologies of the self in general on the other. This kind of complex articulation across various fields and directed at various targets, Foucault claims, is characteristic of the political rationality of the modern. Foucault (1988) describes the modern regime of power as one that is simultaneously totalising and individualising.

> The main characteristic of our modern political rationality in this perspective is neither the constitution of the state, the coldest of all cold monsters, nor the rise of bourgeois individualism. I won't even say that it is a constant effort to integrate individuals into the political totality. I think that the main characteristic of our political rationality is the fact that this integration of the individual in a community or in a totality results from *a constant correlation between an increasing individualization and the reinforcement of totality.*
>
> (Foucault 1988: 161–2; emphasis added)

In short, the illusion of freedom created by the individualising process which inscribes the availability of choice only serves as a reinforcement of the tyranny of the totality, since choice is limited to an already constituted terrain which produces its own set of possibilities. Foucault's insight, I believe, may well explain why I did not find what I had been searching for – that is, evidence of an individual subjectivity formed outside of the metanarrative of Robben Island.

CONCLUSION

To briefly recall, the line of inquiry that I have been pursuing by focusing on the tour guides is one that seeks to determine if there is a space for the truly personal experience to emerge in the narratives of the tour guides of Robben Island who had been inmates in the prison. For these tour guides, can there be an individual memory uncontaminated by the dominant narrative of the anti-apartheid struggle and of Robben Island as a primary symbolic site of that struggle? Can they for a few moments be subjects of their own narratives? This is what the promise of 'free' interaction with these ex-prisoners would lead one to expect. But can this 'freedom' of interaction, of self-representation, exist outside of the discourse and the narrative structure that authorises it? Can one find instances of the private and personal outside of the recognisable pattern of collective memory? Or discern a subjectivity that is individualised and specific to the particular guide? Does their paradoxical positioning as 'objects on display' and as subjects with a speaking voice in their own histories mean that they will be able to enact an agency different from the voiceless passivity of the regular museum artefact?

The provisional answer that emerges from these explorations is: not likely. A second life, it appears, is only available to artefacts, sites and human subjects so long as they 'live' within the discourse that produces that life.

BIBLIOGRAPHY

Buntman, F. (2003) *Robben Island and Prisoner Resistance to Apartheid*, Cambridge: Cambridge University Press.

Cherminais, G. (1999) 'Memo – Re: Phase 2 in the Exhibition Evaluation Process', mimeograph, RIM Exhibition Unit.

Davison, P. (1993) 'Human Subjects as Museum Objects: A Project to Make Life-Casts of "Bushmen" and "Hotentots", 1907–1924', *Annals of the South African Museum* 102 (5).

Deacon, H. (1998) 'Remembering Tragedy, Constructing Modernity: Robben Island as a National Monument', in S. Nuttall and C. Coetzee (eds) *Negotiating the Past: The Making of Memory in South Africa*, Cape Town: Oxford University Press: 161–79.

Deacon, H., Penn, N., Odendaal, A. and Davison, P. (1996) 'Robben Island Timeline', in *EsiQithini: The Robben Island Exhibition*, Cape Town: South African Museum, Mayibuye Books: 12–39.

Foucault, M. (1988) 'The Political Technology of Individuals', in L.H. Martin, H. Gutman and P.H. Hutton (eds) *Technologies of the Self: A Seminar with Michel Foucault*, London: Tavistock Publications: 145–62.

—— (1991) 'Politics and the Study of Discourse', in G. Burchell, C. Gordon and P. Miller (eds) *The Foucault Effect: Studies in Governmentality*, Chicago, IL: University of Chicago Press: 53–72.

Gosling, M. (2002) 'Protest', *Cape Times* 11 July: 1.

Jacobs, J. (1992) 'Narrating the Island: Robben Island in South African Literature', *Current Writing* 4: 73–84.

Kathrada, A.M. (1996) 'Opening Address' in *EsiQithini: The Robben Island Exhibition*, Cape Town: South African Museum, Mayibuye Books: 5–11.

Kathrada, A.M., Deacon, H.J. *et al.* (1996) *EsiQithini: The Robben Island Exhibition*, Cape Town: South African Museum, Mayibuye Books.

Kirshenblatt-Gimblett, B. (1998) *Destination Culture: Tourism, Museums, Heritage*, Berkeley, CA: UCLA Press.

Lindfors, B. (1999) *Africans on Stage: Studies in Ethnological Show Business*, Bloomington: Indiana University Press.

Mandela, N. (1994) *Long Walk to Freedom*, Randburg, South Africa: Macdonald Purnell.

Pickering, J. (1997) 'Agents and Artefacts', *Social Analysis* 41: 46–63.

Chapter 10: Social Institutions as 'Places of Memory' and 'Places to Remember'

The Case of the Ottery School of Industries

Azeem Badroodien

> Memories are true memories, that is, they are memories and not inventions or fantasies. Whether the memories accurately represent past events or not, however, is irrelevant; the process of construction of the meanings of those events is the focus of memory work.
>
> (Crawford *et al.* 1992: 51)

Social institutions are important repositories (subjects) of memories and also valuable 'albums' of broken instances, promising possibilities, and lived moments in the lives of those associated with them. As 'memory sites', social institutions have important stories to tell about the people linked to the facilities, their geographical and social location, and the ways in which institutions in the modernising city informed different aspects of their lives. Such images of institutional and city life offer helpful insights into how sets of social practices are constructed and deconstructed to regulate objects and people, about the ways in which time is defined and rewritten into space at particular moments in the modernising city, and how this informs and informed the emergence of various social formations in South Africa. Indeed, I suggest in this chapter that a social institution like the Ottery School of Industries (located in Cape Town), and an understanding of its evolution, provides communities, the researcher and the historian with a unique site of memory to unravel vital aspects of identity-making and social landscaping in the formative years before apartheid.

Treating physical locations (such as social institutions) as sites of memory, however, could easily become a collage of 'happy or sad moments' in the lives of those who inhabited such facilities; markers with which to capture nostalgic but disparate stories about largely unrecorded pasts (Figures 10.1 and 10.2). It is suggested that social institutions (as places to remember) should instead be employed as signposts by which to understand social context and historical period, and as a conduit to collect and contextualise memory and meaning in geographical space. When used alongside the available and recorded histories of social institutions and the different forms of documented information (located at various facilities) about their associated development and operational processes, memories about social institutions offer key insights into how unity and diversity operate in a constant and dynamic confrontation, and the different forms of discursive spillage between social institutions and the envisioning of space in the metropolis.

In this chapter, I focus specifically on the thinking around the establishment of the Ottery School of Industries in the period before June 1948. In so doing, I

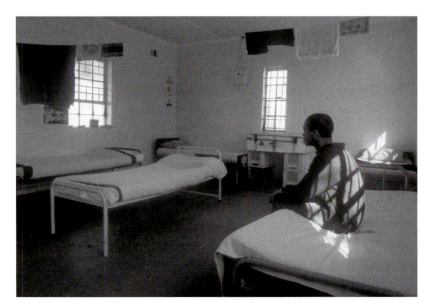

Figure 10.1
Spartan living conditions of boys in hostels at the Ottery School of Industries.

Figure 10.2
The sparsely furnished dining hall at the Ottery School of Industries served between 120 and 150 boys in 2000. In the 1960s the same hall would have been filled with benches and tables for 800–900 boys and 200 staff members in different sittings.

address how discourses of 'colouredness', the segregated space of the Cape Flats, poverty and criminality, operated in confrontational tandem on the outskirts of Cape Town to inform the establishment of the facility.[1]

THE ROLE OF SOCIAL INSTITUTIONS

In contemporary South Africa political and social mobilisation in and around urban spaces invariably points to the 'poor' social conditions of the indigent to indicate the material and metaphorical existence of 'disorder', 'danger' and 'disease'. Presented in this way, poverty, social need, anti-social norms, risk behaviour and criminality in the city are presumed to be inextricably linked. That is because, while the city in the contemporary era is the place where 'new lifestyles are to be played out, workplace and home-place reunited and where the symbolically enriched cultural capital of the urban world is held to epitomise a new *dolce vita*' (Keith 1993: 10), it is also home to a populace that Charles Murray (1990: 68) disparagingly referred to as 'a depraved, unconforming, illegal, and unemployable underclass' that invariably represents decay, insecurity and squalor.

Yet fundamental issues of inequality, racism and injustice in the contemporary city are rarely addressed. Neither are the ways in which inequality, racism and injustice have been inscribed over time into the logic of metropolitan life. Rather, it is deemed reasonable within the logic of a 'new urbanism' that the indigent in the city represent significant danger to the livelihood of the 'more decent' and those who make 'more substantial economic contributions' to the growth of the city (Smith 1989; Wilson 1987; Gilroy 1987; Cooke 1988; Keith 1988). In that regard, the impoverished in the city are cast quite simply as unscrupulous hangers-on, unemployable dirt-trackers and harbingers of criminal intent:

> They are not the moral incorrigibles of the past and they are known to be disadvantaged. They are not to be morally condemned but they are to be contained. They are not to be patronisingly 'treated', but they are to be avoided. They are not detestable but they are disposable. They are quite simply 'dangerous', 'suspicious', 'aggressive', threatening' and 'dodgy' yet they do not need to break the rules to be so defined.
>
> (Lianos and Douglas 2000: 104)

I have argued elsewhere (Badroodien 2001: 5–6) that the root of this conceptualisation in South Africa can be traced back to the emergence of a modernising metropolis in the colonial period, to the moment when the modernising state had to first directly confront the problem of the racially marginalised in the city, and had to work through how to reproduce racial marginalisation in more shared and confined spaces. In that respect, Goldberg (1993: 46) notes that a core element of the colonial era was that 'racial others' were primarily defined in terms of biology and their different histories (where acknowledged), and were regulated in a space apart from their European masters. From the 1920s in South

Africa however, with the migration of people of colour and rural origin to urban areas, exclusion and exclusivity became internalised within the very structures of metropolitan planning (Western 1981: 42).

More specifically, I assert that the criminalisation and racialisation of poverty in cities like Cape Town is most clearly visible in the different kinds of state social institutions in the city and in the ways in which state care is and was provided for the poor, disadvantaged and marginalised.[2] In that respect, criminalisation and racialisation are processes that are clearly tied to (and perpetuated through) the ways in which elements of social ordering under the modern state were historically inscribed into models for urban planning, health care, housing, education and social welfare projects in the city (Badroodien 2001: 11).

It is noteworthy in that regard that a sophisticated network of institutions has been in existence in South Africa since the early 1920s to address the social needs of populations drawn to the city and urban life, and to regulate and control them so that they do not pose a threat to 'normal' city life. These networks of social institutions were the first key 'melting pots' for social reconstruction work in urban areas; places where identity and social formations were tested, reformulated and reconfigured. Factors such as the diverse groups of people that populated the institutions both inside and outside their material boundaries, the geographical spaces in which institutions were located, and the differing levels of social contestation and interaction, impacted significantly on the ways in which such institutions were constituted.

Knowledge about the role and impact of social institutions on the lives of the communities they came to serve would make a significant contribution to understanding the contemporary city. The historical relevance of such institutions lies in knowing how diverse and contesting communities made sense of and confronted the adverse realities of the metropolis and subsequently fashioned different but quite tangible forms of self. It also reveals how racial hierarchies in different social spaces were reproduced, challenged or subverted under apartheid and before. The complex processes by which race is constructed as a social and political relation in the city is of particular relevance. Importantly, social institutions, and the processes that informed their provision and establishment, are inextricably linked to the ways in which modernist thought evolved and took hold in South Africa. The following section provides a context and broad framework in which to understand the emergence and role of social institutions in a modernising South Africa.

MODERNITY, SOCIAL INSTITUTIONS AND THE CITY

Modernisation is a process invariably associated with 'becoming better', or more enlightened, or achieving the 'good society' in comparison with earlier less developed stages in social evolution (Rodger 2000: 14). Featherstone (1988: 197) defines modernity 'as the progressive economic and administrative rationalisation and differentiation of the social world', where the 'collection of empirically grounded knowledge and the systematic application of rational scientific principles leads to the improvement of the human condition'.

The concept of modernity is most often linked to the notion of a modern welfare state. That is because the architects of the original welfare state were part of a wider intellectual movement that had its origins in the eighteenth-century Enlightenment, a period in which 'the application of reason, scientific enquiry and humanistic understanding had as its objective the improvement of the human condition and the eradication of what Beveridge later called the five great giants of idleness, want, disease, ignorance, and squalor' (Rodger 2000: 18).

While the growth of modern society is more commonly associated with developments in science and medicine and their role in 'perfecting mankind' (Dubow 1995: 14), it is the emergence of state apparatuses to monitor and regulate society that probably best embodies modern accomplishment. Rodger (2000: 19) notes that over time modernist thought came to realise that the state apparatus was the most important and direct instrument in giving social welfare interventions political direction from the centre, and thereby improve the human condition of state citizens:

> Modernism is perhaps the highest expression of the Enlightenment's rationalist and utilitarian ambitions, and is best exemplified by the confidence in the capacities of the state (through the intervention of government agencies) and the possibilities of science to resolve key social and societal conditions.
>
> (Garland 2001: 40)

In South Africa after 1910 it was the above kind of modernist vision that informed the redefinition of the role and nature of the South African state (Chisholm 1989: 98). From 1910 the modernising state was expected to play an important part in 'observing', 'controlling' and 'transforming' the actions and movements of its citizens, by increasingly using the range of new techniques and modern forms of knowledge available to regulate and socially structure the emerging South African society. This focus was not only about increasing state intervention and participation in the everyday lives of citizens, but also about getting the emerging society to acknowledge altruism, solidarity and collectivism as the key founding principles of its embraced modernity.

For example, when the state sought to establish a network of social institutions for 'poor whites' on the Rand from the 1920s to deal with what it perceived was moral degradation through association and 'mixing with other races' in urban areas, it was equally concerned about the high levels of poverty and impoverishment in all working-class areas of Johannesburg. While the solution tried at the time was to establish institutions and programmes for 'poor whites' to remove them from 'contexts of risk' in which they associated with 'the degenerate races' (Bundy 1986; Chisholm 1989; Malherbe 1977; Davies 1979), while also developing state interventions in the workplace and the economy that dealt more directly with their impoverished conditions, municipalities were equally keen to impact upon the quality of the lives of all other residents in urban areas at that time. The main point here is that calls to deal with poverty in urban environments, and some of the imagined consequences thereof, have been a persistent feature in the history of the modern city in South Africa. Importantly, such calls for social intervention have invariably been couched in a modernist vernacular of the need for social order and social salvation, or the need for community participation, altruism, social solidarity, and accessible and quality state provision for citizens.

This kind of vocabulary made it possible for the modernising state to be equally alarmed by the number of white, coloured and African urban dwellers living in poverty from the 1920s. It also marked the beginnings of a state imagination that conceived of quite different interventions for the various population groups based on racial and social hierarchy and a very particular set of ideological assumptions about modernity, economic growth, capitalism, industrialisation and urbanisation in South Africa. The relevance of the above to contemporary discussions of the poor in urban areas is in understanding how racial and social hierarchies became embedded in a very particular form of state social provision under colonialism and apartheid:

> Race making and racism has never been about race alone. Rather, they have always been part of the consolidation of bourgeois projects, the forming of nation states, and the uncertain cultivation of identities forged around what Stuart Hall has called the 'structures of dominance'.
>
> (Stoler 1995: 204)

Indeed, I argue that the overarching concern with 'poor whites' and their supposed 'progressive submersion in the colour of their urban surroundings' in the early part of the twentieth century (Chisholm 1989: 118) served to link in determinate ways the issues of race, poverty and 'unruly' urban environments in South Africa. This linking of race, poverty and disorder from the 1920s became a vital ingredient of the 'metropolitan vocabulary' thereafter (Badroodien 2001: 11–12), and is still evident in contemporary discussions about the city in South Africa. It is notable in the latter regard that the link between race and social distress has remained part of the language of modern social welfare provision and social upliftment simply because it is firmly embedded within the knowledge bases and techniques of state social provision (Badroodien 2001: 416). The aim of the rest of the chapter is simply to show how the understandings of race, poverty and urbanity that informed the establishment of the Ottery School of Industries in Cape Town in 1948 were manifested in the language of (modern) state provision at the time.

A LANGUAGE OF RACE AND SOCIAL PROVISION

The above description of the 'modernist' meshing of racial, social and economic impoverishment in urban space was pervasive by the 1940s, when the modernising state began providing social institutions for the coloured population as a way of addressing the high levels of poverty in the greater Cape Town region and 'the coterminous influences of urban spaces' that apparently brought to the fore 'inherent coloured criminal and unsociable behaviour' (Union of South Africa 1938: 10).

It was a delineation that differing constituencies and communities in Cape Town had become particularly adept at hearing and using by that time. One reason was that the percentage of the total coloured population in urban areas in South Africa in the period 1921 to 1936 had increased from 45 per cent to 54 per cent (of which 89 per cent resided in the greater Cape Town metropolitan area), and members of municipalities in the various urban spaces of Cape Town were anxious about the impact of this increased migration on social order.[3] Newspapers regularly pointed to the substantial increase in serious crime for the period 1939 to 1942 (by 63.9 per cent) and asserted that this was partly due to the influx into the Cape Peninsula of 'native' and coloured rural youth as a result of the Second World War (Cape Archive 1944).[4]

One finding of the Wilcocks Commission Report of 1937, that a considerable section of this urban population was 'submerged' in poverty, also generated deep concern among both the white and affluent coloured urban populations of Cape Town. At the time unemployment and impoverishment among the coloured population at the Cape was steadily increasing (which was accentuated by the worldwide economic Depression of the early 1930s), and members of the coloured middle class in particular were worried that this increase in poverty and 'social disharmony' would spiral out of control (Lewis 1987: 150). Subsequently, when suggesting ways of responding to the dangers posed by this 'submerged' population (see Stedman Jones 1971: 285–6), both the white and affluent coloured populations (see Adhikari 1993: 179) pointed to similar images of urban degradation, disease, mayhem and the need for 'salvation'.[5] A Teachers' League of South Africa (TLSA) pamphlet observed in 1946 that the 'progressive development of any nation or people is retarded significantly, and its energy sapped, by the kinds of dire attacks of immorality, drunkenness, hooliganism, gambling and extravagance as is prevalent among the coloured underclass' (Adhikari 1993: 154).

Likewise, a conference organised by the National Liberation League (NLL) in Cape Town in 1942 to discuss what it called 'coloured intemperance' asserted that the effects of rapid urbanisation, poverty and the lack of adequate social welfare and education facilities, had to be urgently addressed if its deleterious impact on the impoverished of Cape Town was to be countered (Lewis 1987: 205). The main source of this intemperance was felt to lie in the disorganised family and social environment. An undated memo pencilled by the Coloured Advisory Council (CAC)[6] in the 1940s noted:

> In responding to the hanging of a coloured fisherman for the rape of a white girl in Hout
> Bay in 1944, the Coloured Advisory Council wishes to note that the environment, home

life, and individual personality of the accused must be taken into account in explaining his deed. It must also be noted that family disintegration, marital separation, promiscuity, lack of education, pure ignorance, sexual neuroses, lack of outlets for manly energies, and lack of access to civilized past-times, often play a significant role in members of the coloured population indulging in such baser vices of life. Such developments need to be urgently addressed.

(Cape Archives: undated CAC memo ref. 11/8)

In 1937 the Wilcocks Commission had asserted that urgent remedial intervention was required in Cape Town if the delinquency rate among the coloured population, which was estimated to be more than 19 times that of the white population, was to be addressed. The commission pointed to the sophisticated forms of institutional provision made available to the white population in South Africa by that time and suggested that similar facilities be provided for the coloured population (Union of South Africa 1938: 20). More specifically, the commission observed in 1937 that the Department of Railways and Harbours had developed a system of 'coloured training camps' that provided valuable and practical ways for counteracting the influences of street gambling, intemperance, dagga smoking, vice and delinquency among the coloured population.[7] The commission asserted that similar facilities for coloured youth would inculcate them with 'much needed discipline and self-control' (Union of South Africa 1938: 24, 196; Pretoria Archive 1945). In this regard, the chairperson of the CAC, G. Golding, noted in 1947 that:

> Youths of every race have an urge for adventure. It was for the European however to decide whether the coloured youth should satisfy their urges in dissolute gangs with the police as their common enemy, as at present, or in disciplined government-controlled environments, ready and eager for 'respectable' social service, and able to go back into their families, lead ordered lives and bring up their own respectable children.
>
> (Cape Archive: undated CAC memo)

The key difference from the earlier discourse on 'poor whites', social institutions and the city (in the 1920s) was that the 'origin' of the 'coloured slide into degradation' was said to lie not as much in 'racial mixing' as in the nature of 'this mixed race', in 'their many inherent frailties' and in the inadequacies in their home lives, immediate social environments and individual personalities (Union of South Africa 1938: 38).[8]

Social institutions for the coloured population were thus expected to not just 'save' individual welfare recipients from 'illicit urban environments' or from their individual 'degenerate ways', but also 'heal' the entire urban community from whence they came (Union of South Africa 1938: 21–2). The principal of Porter Reformatory in Tokai, W. D. Marais (1942: 59), noted that:

> The coloured community is presently experiencing a cultural conflict where uncertainty about their culture has led to significant disharmony. Intra-community conflict over issues like good morals, social ideals, and approaches to things like honesty, honour, law

and order and good strong families has resulted in a large proportion of the submerged coloureds living at odds with the established order. As long as drunkenness, stabbing, immorality, dagga selling and purse robbing are regarded as normal life practice to a large proportion of the coloured population and most of them turn a blind eye to such things, so long will filth and degradation be a daily part of the lives of the present community.

(Marais 1942: 59)

Indeed, the appeal of institutionalisation that provided for the 'moral training', 'character building' and 'work resocialisation' of members of the 'submerged coloured' population was particularly strong in the 1940s.

MAKING RACE THROUGH WELFARE AND SOCIAL PROVISION

Two observations can be made with regard to the provision of institutional care for the coloured population from the 1940s. First, in being earmarked specifically for the coloured population, social institutions and welfare provision from the 1940s subsequently came to reify the notion that the coloured population was a separate and distinct 'ethnic' group with unique problems of its own. Second, and coupled to this notion of 'distinctiveness', social institutions helped define the 'key character traits' associated with the 'coloured submerged' class that needed 'fixing' before such subjects could return to 'normal' life in the metropolis. The latter function served to not only develop a hierarchy by which to locate this distinctive population (by distinguishing the 'deserving, law-abiding and respectable' from the 'undeserving, unruly and unkempt'), but also inserted some very particular and compelling 'images of colouredness' into the language of state and metropolitan institutional planning (Jensen 2001: 54). Moreover, in noting that the 'submerged coloured population' invariably came from unfavourable home environments where street gambling, intemperance, dagga-smoking, vice and delinquency were rife, the Wilcocks Commission of 1937 fortified perhaps one of the most enduring images of the coloured working class in South Africa, namely that of 'irresponsible, irrational, unstable, lazy, happy-go-lucky, jovial, unemployed, and easy to tempt urban dwellers' (Union of South Africa 1938: 82–5). This image has for decades framed the ways in which the city has understood and dealt with the needs of the 'coloured underclass'.

By calling for state intervention to 'retard' and 'remedy' the unruliness and lack of discipline embedded in the homes of the 'typical coloured' working-class family, the Wilcocks Commission of 1937, and subsequent official and unofficial discussions around the supposed needs of the coloured population, set into motion the establishment of a wide array of state social institutions and interventions have come to play a key role in reinforcing, defining and reshaping what it supposedly means to be a 'kleurling' (coloured) in Cape Town (Union of South Africa 1938: 24). Jensen powerfully and convincingly argues that:

The knowledge produced by commissions of inquiry on the state of the coloured population in the city (and affirmed through welfare and educational practices) has helped to
confirm the inherent racial, gendered and social objectification of coloured men as
always already potential gangsters. With the dispersal of this logic into everyday
coloured life through government agencies, this institutionalized knowledge has been
reproduced through welfare and educational operations and through the everyday
working of institutions like the police and justice system.

(Jensen 2001: 78)

It is important to note in the above regard that modalities of what was deemed 'to
be coloured' were shaped not only by the ways in which subjects were defined, and
identities reinforced or challenged, but were always also 'shaped in relation to the
actions and discourse within the diverse coloured population and the social contexts
and social positions that they inhabited' (Salo 2004: 56; Adhikari 1993: 111).

It is this description of the ways in which notions of race, urban environment and social disorder meshed in the 1940s with issues of poverty, 'individual
personality', family disintegration, and the different modalities of identity
making, to 'naturalise' racial and social hierarchies, that serves to contextualise
the discussion of the establishment of the Ottery School of Industries in June
1948 and the kinds of contextual debates that informed its inception.[9] It is to this
that the chapter now turns.

A THEATRE AND GEOGRAPHY OF RACE

The Ottery School of Industries was formally established in June 1948 at the Ack-
Ack military camp in Plantation Road, Ottery, Cape Town. In the period 1946 to
October 1948 the camp had been used by the Central Organisation of Technical
Training (COTT) to provide trade training to ex-volunteer coloured soldiers upon
their return to Cape Town after the Second World War. At the time, the Union
Education Department (UED) was responsible for the administration of the COTT
programme, though the camp remained part of the Wynberg Military Base and
fell under the Department of Defence (Badroodien 2001: 66).

When the UED first began scouting the Western Cape for a potential site
for the state institution in early 1946, the principal of the Porter Reformatory
observed that the need for the facility was so urgent at the time that 'every
attempt had to be made to find a site that had established infrastructures' (Cape
Archive 1947). With regard to the Ottery site though, Van Antwerp (Pretoria
Archive 1946a) warned that:

The camp is completely surrounded by shebeens, and day and night robberies in that
area are frequent occurrences. If the camp is to be converted into an institution for
coloured boys, the surrounding fence would need to be reinforced so that pupils can
come into contact as little as possible with the people of that vicinity. The police can be
asked to clear the area of shebeens as much as possible.

(Pretoria Archive 1946a; see also Pretoria Archive 1946c)

In 1946 the two-hectare Ottery plantation lay on the outskirts of the city lodged between the vast lands of an important military base that housed a predominantly white population and the beginnings of coloured residential areas in Cook se Bos, Grassy Park and Parkwood Estate. The site was in a secluded area, so much so that to gain access to the Ack-Ack facility, one had to either travel along a dark, gravel road from the Cook se Bos side of the plantation (an area not well populated at that time and perceived as 'dangerous'), or via the road that ran through the Wynberg Military Base. The former option was especially difficult in the rainy winter months, while the latter option required the correct documentation to gain access to the military base.

Members of the Coloured Advisory Council regularly visited the site as it was used as a training centre for coloured tradesmen and ex-soldiers in the period directly after the Second World War.[10] Thus, when the CAC came to hear about the intention to use the camp as an institution for young, impoverished and neglected coloured boys, it highlighted the 'unsuitable' surroundings of the site and the difficulties in accessing it. In a letter from the Secretary of Education to the Secretary for Public Works dated 30 December 1946, the Union Education Department noted that:

> As a result of pressure exercised by the Coloured Advisory Council on this department during the last few years, various camps in the Cape Peninsula and farther afield have been visited by inspectors to determine whether the camps would answer our purposes. The camps at Ottery and Saldanha have been found to be highly and completely unsuitable, while those at George and Westlake conditions were found to be much more favourable.

> (Pretoria Archive 1946c)

The CAC asserted that, because the Ottery camp was covered in water during the winter months it was both 'unhealthy' and 'unhygienic' to expect state citizens and subjects (and children especially) to live there. Coupled with the proximity of 'unfavourable' 'shebeen-infested' surroundings, the CAC noted that the whole point of providing residential care for boys from the 'submerged coloured' population was to 'treat' them in environments that were isolated from their home situations.

The CAC suggested that the state investigate the possibility of using the grounds of the George Flying School (*Lugskoolkamp*) in the southern Cape, or the Westlake military camp in Tokai near Cape Town, for the establishment of the institution. Upon investigation it was found however that the George site had already been earmarked for a white housing scheme, and that the grounds of the Westlake military camp were being utilised to service the needs of white soldiers returning from the Second World War (Pretoria Archive 1946c). Residents were deeply opposed to a coloured facility being built in George and having 'lower-class members of the coloured population in their close proximity' (Pretoria Archive 1947a). They expressed these concerns in language that asserted that 'the values of their properties would decline substantially if the institution was established there'. Likewise, in the mid-1940s, efforts were being made to convert the Westlake military camp into a home for white war orphans, or white immigrants, or as a housing scheme for white ex-soldiers looking to start anew after their 'patriotic' exertions abroad. Notably, residents of the Tokai area were also keen to prevent another institution for 'lower-class' coloured boys being established in their immediate vicinity (the other being Porter Reformatory in Constantia).[11]

Attempts to secure either of the two camps for a social institution for coloured boys were thus abandoned (Pretoria Archive 1947b) and renewed approaches were made to secure the Ottery site. However, given the earlier resistance from the CAC, state officials were keen to emphasise a more 'modernist' logic for establishing the institution at the Ottery site. It was noted for instance, that in order for coloured boys to be re-integrated into their communities after institutionalisation, boys needed to live in close proximity to the kinds of environments in which they would eventually live and work, and also have an experience of 'living in the city' (Pretoria Archive 1947b). More pointedly, they needed to be able to work on weekends in the kinds of jobs that they would eventually fill as adults. It was asserted that boys needed to live close to their families and their communities if these groups were also to be reconstituted and 'monitored'. Given that the majority of 'lower-class' coloured families lived in dire poverty at that time, state officials further felt that 'the re-socialisation of coloured boys and their families would be compromised' if parents could not (financially) afford to visit their sons regularly (Pretoria Archive 1947b). Institutions had to be close to the residential areas of the 'lower-class' coloured population if interaction between the institutionalised and their families was to be encouraged.

In the above regard, a Union Education Department official, paraphrasing a letter dated 30 November 1945 from Gordon Taylor, chief liaison officer for the Office of the Director-General of Demobilisation (Pretoria Archive 1945), noted in 1948 that:

> If the coloured people are to become good citizens, and the criminal class among them in Cape Town is to be whittled down, they must be given the hope of a better future and something approaching equality of opportunity and respect. We introduced the coloured population in Cape Town to hopes of a higher standard of living and it would be cruel and unwise not to pursue every possibility of ensuring that they lead better and more ordered lives.
>
> (Pretoria Archive 1948)

Notably, the Union Education Department observed that establishing the facility in Ottery would engage with 'the great interest that is being shown by both the coloured middle-class and sections of the working class in the activities provided at the Ottery camp and their willingness to get involved in resolving some of their own social problems' (Pretoria Archive 1948).

Once this logic of establishing the Ottery School of Industries at the Ottery site became amenable to all relevant parties, the challenge was then to ensure that the boys institutionalised at the facility received state care that had 'the required impact' on their lives. How the Union Government 'imagined' this process is addressed below.

THE IMPERIOUS GAZE: CREATING MODEL COMMUNITIES

I have argued elsewhere that the Ottery School of Industries was a key testing site in the history of Cape Town where an envisaged 'image of the coloured family' was constructed for the coloured underclass (Badroodien 2001). Below I present two examples of how the language of race, class and poverty was written into the discursive space of the Ottery facility.

External model communities

In 1958, the Principal of the Ottery School of Industries, F.A. Bester, noted that:

> The whole point of establishing the institution next to Ottery (a white area) in the first place was because street fighting, lazing around, gambling, drunkenness and other such social evils, which are a part of the daily life of a coloured area, is not prevalent here. Employees of the social institution can therefore point to the surroundings (use the surrounding area as a reference point) to present criteria/good examples for coloured children by which they should live [sic].
>
> (Cape Archive 1958a)

Bester noted that a key reason for locating the institution on the boundary of a white residential area was also to enable coloured boys to work over weekends in the gardens and houses of white residents 'where they could learn how to work and earn well-deserved money' and 'be inducted into the work environment that they will fulfil once "released" from the facility'. Furthermore, the Ottery institution 'needed a stable and orderly white neighborhood on its border to demonstrate (and serve as a real life example) to the boys ... [of] what they should aspire to achieve in their own community' (Cape Archive 1958b).

On the more practical level, the location of the institution was also linked to the Ottery School of Industries being the first social institution in South Africa with a mix of white and coloured staff residing at the institution. White staff members simply could not (and would not) reside on the institution's premises if it were not bordered by a white residential area like Ottery. It was further felt that the institution needed to be in an area where both the white staff and the mostly middle-class, coloured, teaching staff would be comfortable if the two groups were to agree to live on the site (Cape Archive 1948).

From early 1949, the Ottery camp was divided into two parts, one for the coloured and the other for the white staff members and their families. The coloured staff members initially used an access road from the Cook Se Bos side of the institution, while the white staff lived at the end closest to the military base, and used the base as an exit point.

Internal model communities

The make-up of the institutional staff at the Ottery School of Industries resembled the racial and social hierarchies embedded in the physical structure of the site. First, there was the management team that consisted of a contingent of well-qualified white Afrikaners. This team consisted of the principal, four deputy principals each responsible for the academic, psychology, hostels and technical trade units, and the administration staff.

Second, there was the professional team of white psychologists trained at Afrikaans-speaking universities like Stellenbosch and Potchefstroom who administered IQ tests, developed 'scientific' admission policies, provided psychological counselling, and managed the release and placement of children. This professional team used their institutionalised charges at Ottery as 'scientific guinea pigs' to develop further research on coloured children in state care, which later served to inform the establishment of state facilities for coloured children elsewhere. Third, there were the white trade instructors who were mostly English-speaking, although there were also a few Afrikaner tradesmen in middle-skill trades like upholstery and carpentry. This group was followed in rank by white hostel wardens and kitchen and laundry heads.

Hostel wardens and kitchen heads supervised a large coloured staff who served mainly as caregivers, cooks, matrons and laundry workers. They were largely unskilled and were mostly women working in traditionally female and domesticated occupations in the laundry, kitchen and hospital. Coloured men served as the chief caregivers and disciplinarians in the boys' hostels. These men were all unqualified and were responsible for the coloured boys' daily living needs.

Lastly, and above this unskilled coloured component, there existed a core staff of qualified coloured male teachers and assistant trade instructors. This group was expected not only to educate the boys under their care but also to serve as their main role and class models. They were meant to provide coloured boys with the main re-socialisation mechanism (education), while also serving as the key portrayers of coloured 'civilised living' (Cape Archive 1948).

The race, gender and institutional imperatives of the institution thus ensured that, while coloured staff members were the primary caregivers and educators, the white staff living and working in the institution served as 'living examples' for coloured staff on how to best fulfil their parental responsibilities.[12] In this way, institutionalised boys were constantly reminded about the race and class status of the coloured population within society.

SOCIAL INSTITUTIONS AND MEMORY

It will not have escaped the reader of this chapter that they have read nothing about the workings of the Ottery School of Industries, about what it was meant to do, whom it was supposed to serve and how it impacted on the lives of its subjects. It will also not have gone unnoticed that the memories of those that inhabited the institution from June 1948 have not been presented here, nor has a case been made for what these memories tell us about the city in the 1940s.

Readers will certainly not know any more about the close links between the Ottery facility and Porter Reformatory, Bonnytoun Place of Safety, the Coloured Cape Corps Cadet camp, the Coloured Work Colony at Westlake, the De Nova Rehabilitation Clinic for Coloured Alcoholics, the Athlone (Guidance) Clinic, Pollsmoor Prison, various children's homes, school clinics, social welfare centres, the grant and foster care system, and the myriad of other social interactions that inform the complex web of social institutions spread across the Cape Flats. They won't have read about the ways in which staff and institutionalised boys moved between and across these social institutions in Cape Town, about the knowledge they shared with such facilities, and the various resources they collectively fought for.

They will not know that coloured boys institutionalised at the Ottery facility regularly played soccer at the nearby William Herbert Sportsground, a field where Bafana Bafana players like Mark Williams, Benni McCarthy and Shaun Bartlett learnt their trade. They will not know about the many talks that William Herbert gave at the Ottery site, urging the boys to stick to 'civilised' norms if they hoped to continue getting access to the nearby sportsfield. They will also not know about David van der Ross and the Sonn brothers (and so many other middle-class coloured icons) serving on the Ottery Board, a body that determined which boys were institutionalised at the facility, when they could be released and under which conditions.

Readers have also not been informed about how students from nearby middle-class coloured schools like Livingstone High regularly accessed the facilities (Olympic-sized pool, numerous grassed fields and technical education workshops) of the Ottery School of Industries in the 1960s because their schools had none of these facilities, nor about the complex ways in which students from these schools interacted with institutionalised boys.[13]

When it is argued that the Ottery School of Industries in Cape Town was an important institutional 'test site' where uncomfortable fits between class, race, gender and notions of respectability were confronted, where particular notions of 'race-making' were tried and tested, and where attempts to 'rebuild' the coloured family were initiated in Cape Town, it is certainly not a frivolous or academic suggestion.

Rather, the point being made is that as communities, historians, policy-makers, we simply do not know enough about these processes. Social institutions can provide important clues by which to draw together some understanding of the Cape Flats and Cape Town from the 1940s. They provide these possibilities because they were formative in the lives of so many of those institutionalised in the web of social institutions spread across the city, both in shaping how they understood and engaged with their subsequent lives, and in moulding the pasts, foibles and needs of individuals in ways that were supposed to make them 'more decent' and 'respectable' future citizens and 'urban dwellers'.

Social institutions in Cape Town are important sites of memory: now there's a novel idea!

BIBLIOGRAPHY

Adhikari, M. (1993) *'Let Us Live for Our Children': The Teacher's League of South Africa, 1913–1940*, Cape Town: UCT Press/Buchu Books.

Badroodien, A. (2001) *A History of the Ottery School of Industries in Cape Town: Issues of Race, Welfare and Social Order in the period 1937 to 1968*, unpublished PhD dissertation, University of the Western Cape.

Bester, F.A. (1961) *Die etiologiese agtergrond van die gedragafwykende Kleurlingkind en die implikasies daarvan vir sy heropvoeding*, unpublished PhD thesis, Potchefstroomse Universiteit vir Christelike Hoer Onderwys.

Bundy, C. (1986) 'Vagabond Hollanders and Runaway Englishmen: White Poverty in the Cape before Poor Whiteism', in W. Beinart, P. Delius and S. Trapido (eds) *Putting a Plough to the Ground: Accumulation and Dispossession in Rural South Africa, 1850–1930*, Johannesburg: Ravan Press.

Chisholm, L. (1989) *Reformatories and Industrial Schools in South Africa: A Study in Class, Colour and Gender in the period 1882 to 1939*, unpublished PhD thesis, University of the Witwatersrand.

Cooke, P. (1988) 'Modernity, postmodernity and the City', *Theory, Culture and Society* 5: 475–92.

Crawford, J., Kippax, S., Onyx, J., Gault, U. and Benton, P. (1992) *Emotion and Gender: Constructing Meaning from Memory*, Newbury Park, CA: Sage.

Cross, M. and Keith, M. (eds) (1995) *Racism, the City and the State*, London: Routledge.

Davies, R. (1979) *Capital, State and White Labour in South Africa, 1900–1960: An Historical Materialist Analysis of Class Formation and Class Relations*, Brighton: Harvester Press.

Du Plessis, W.K.H. (1958) *Die Nywerheidskool as Onderwys- en Opvoedingsinrigting in Suid-Afrika* (Schools of Industries as Educational and Welfare Institutions in SA), unpublished PhD thesis, University of Potchefstroom.

Dubow, S. (1995) *Illicit Union: Scientific Racism in Modern South Africa*, Johannesburg: Wits University Press.

Featherstone, M. (1988) 'In Pursuit of the Postmodern: An Introduction', *Theory, Culture and Society* 5 (2–3): 195–215.

Garland, D. (2001) *The Culture of Control: Crime and Social Order in Contemporary Society*, Chicago, IL: University of Chicago Press.

Gilroy, P. (1987) *There Ain't No Black in the Union Jack*, London: Hutchinson.

Goldberg, D.T. (1993) 'Polluting the Body Politic: Racist Discourse and Urban Location', in M. Cross and M. Keith (eds) *Racism, the City and the State*, London: Routledge.

Gross, F.A. (1944) *Society and the Criminal*, Cape Town: Stewart Printing.

Jensen, S. (2001) *Claiming Community – Negotiating Crime: State Formation, Neighborhood and Gangs in a Capetonian Township*, unpublished PhD dissertation, Roskilde University, Copenhagen.

Keith, M. (1988) 'Civil Disorder as a Social Problem in British Cities', in D.T. Herbert and D.M. Smith (eds) *Social Problems and British Cities*, Oxford: Blackwell.

—— (1993) 'From Punishment to Discipline', in M. Cross and M. Keith (eds) *Racism, the City and the State*, London: Routledge.

Kotze, F.G. (1995) *Social Welfare Policy for a Post-apartheid South Africa: A Developmental Perspective*, unpublished PhD mini-thesis, University of the Western Cape.

Lewis, G. (1987) *Between the Wire and the Wall: A History of South African 'Coloured' Politics*, Cape Town: David Philip.

Lianos, M. and Douglas, M. (2000) 'Dangerisation and the End of Deviance: The Institutional Environment', in D. Garland and R. Sparks (eds) *Criminology and Social Theory*, New York: Oxford University Press.

Macarov, C. (1995) *Social Welfare: Structure and Practice*, Thousand Oaks, CA: Sage Publications.

Malherbe, E.G. (1977*) Education in South Africa, Volume II: 1923–1975*, Cape Town: Juta.

Marais, W.A. (1942) 'Juvenile Delinquency', in *Medico-Legal Monographs Number 2*, Cape Town: University of Cape Town.

Murray, C. (1990) 'Underclass', in C. Murray (ed.) *The Emerging British Underclass*, London: IEA Health and Welfare Unit.

Patan, A. (1964) *Hofmeyr*, Cape Town: Oxford University Press.

Platt, A. (1969) *The Child Savers*, 2nd edn, Chicago, IL: University of Chicago Press.

Rodger, J.J. (2000) *From a Welfare State to a Welfare Society: The Changing Context of Social Policy in a Postmodern Era*, Basingstoke: Macmillan Books.

Salo, E.R. (2004) *Respectable Mothers, Tough Men and Good Daughters: Producing Persons in Manenberg Township*, unpublished PhD dissertation, Emory University.

Smith, S.J. (1989) 'The Politics of Race and a New Segregationism', in J. Mohan (ed.) *The Political Geography of Contemporary Britain*, Basingstoke: Macmillan.

South African Institute of Race Relations (1938) *Minutes of a Conference on Urban Juvenile Native Delinquency Held by the City of Johannesburg in 1938*, Johannesburg: SAIRR.

Stedman Jones, G. (1971) *Outcast London: A Study in the Relationship between Classes in Victorian Society*, Oxford: Oxford University Press.

Steinberg, J. (2004) *The Number: One Man's Search for Identity in the Cape Underworld and Prison Gangs*, Johannesburg: Jonathan Ball Publishers.

Stoler, A.L. (1995) *Race and the Education of Desire: Foucault's History of Sexuality and the Colonial Order of Things*, Durham, NC: Duke University Press.

Union of South Africa (1938) *Report of the Commission of Inquiry Regarding the Cape Coloured Population of the Union, 1937 – G 68EUG 54/37* (the Wilcocks Commission), Pretoria: Government Printer.

Van Krieken, R. (1986) 'Social Theory and Child Welfare: Beyond Social Control' *Theory and Society* 15 (3): 401–29.

Western, J. (1981) *Outcast Cape Town*, Pretoria: Human & Rousseau Publishing.

Willemse, W.A. (1932) *Constitutional Types in Delinquency: Practical Applications and Bio-Physical Foundations of Kretschmer's Types*, London: Kegan Paul, Trench, Trubner and Co.

—— (1938) *The Road to the Reformatory*, Pretoria: Van Schaik Ltd.

—— (1940) *Die Sorg van ons Kinders en Jeugdiges* Tweede Trek- reeks no. IV, Bloemfontein: Nasionale Pers.

Wilson, W.J. (1987) *The Truly Disadvantaged*, Chicago, IL: University of Chicago Press.

Primary sources
Cape Archive

Cape Archive (1944) TBK KUS, Ref: SWL2/9, Part 1, Vol. 312, 'Major Dolby on the Skolly Menace', memo dated 25 January 1944.

—— (1945) TBK KUS, Ref: SWL2/9, Vol. 1, 'Coloured Advisory Council: Liaison Section: Special Problems Associated with Crime, Juvenile Delinquency and Penal Treatment in Relation to Coloureds', memo dated May 1945.

—— (undated) TBK KUS, Ref: SWL2/9 Part 1, Vol. 312, undated memo from CAC (11/8).

—— (1947a) TBK KUS, Ref: 79/2/11, Part 1, Vol. 125, letter dated 8 February 1947 from Secretary of Education to Secretary of Public Works.

—— (1947b) TBK KUS, Ref: SWL2/9, Part 3, Vol. 314, memo dated 18 September 1947 and *Cape Times* article dated 17/9/1947.

—— (1948) TBK KUS, Vol. 125, Ref: 79/2/11, Part 1, 'Inspeksieverslae, 1947–1961', letter dated 4 February 1948.

—— (1958a) TBK KUS, Ref: 79/2/1, Vol. 123, letter titled 'Ottery as a Potential Coloured Area and the Impact of This on the School of Industries (sic)', May 1958 from F.A. Bester to the Union Education Department.

—— (1958b) TBK KUS, Ref: 79/2/1, Vol. 123, memo dated 9 May 1958 recapping the establishment and development of the facility, titled 'Stigting en Algemeen A30 Part 2, 1953–1960'.

Pretoria Archive

Pretoria Archive (1945) SAB UOD, Ref: E283/8/4/1/1, Vol. 1, letter dated 30 November 1945 from Gordon Taylor, liaison officer for the Office of the Director-General of Demobilisation to the Union Education Department.

—— (1946a) SAB UOD, Ref: E283/8/4/1/1, Vol. 1, letter dated 4 March 1946 from principal of Porter Reformatory, Van Antwerp, to the Secretary of Education (ref. A17).

—— (1946b) SAB UOD, Ref: E283/8/4/1/1, Vol. 1, letter dated 4 March 1946 from principal Van Antwerp to the Secretary of Education titled 'Vocational Training for Ex-volunteers, Cape Technical College and Ottery for Coloured Ex-volunteers'.

—— (1946c) SAB UOD, Ref: E14/19C/1, Vol. 218, letters dated 20 November 1946, 23 December 1946, 30 December 1946.

—— (1947a) SAB UOD, Ref: E14/19C/1, Vol. 218, letter dated 23 January 1947 from the Secretary of Defence to the Secretary of Education.

—— (1947b) SAB UOD, Ref: E14/19C/1, Vol. 218, letter dated 20 February 1947 from the Secretary of Education to the Secretary of Defence.

—— (1948) SAB UOD, Ref: E14/19C/1, letter dated 3 August 1948.

—— SAB UOD E283/8/4/1/1, Vol. 1.

Interviews

Interview with Dr F.A. Bester, principal of the Ottery School of Industries between 1948 and 1968, on 9 May1996 at his home in Pinelands.

Interview with R.O. Dudley, deputy principal of Livingstone High School, Claremont, on 5 September 1998.

Chapter 11: Living in the Past

Historic Futures in Double Time

Lynn Meskell

> Forget the past. Don't only forgive it. Forget it as well. The past did not happen. You only dreamt it. It is a figment of your rich collective imagination. It did not happen. Banish your memory. It is a sin to have a memory. There is virtue in amnesia. The past. It did not happen.
>
> (Mda 2000)

The status and success of socio-political transition in South Africa has been interrogated by Grant Farred (2004: 592) who, following Carl Schmidt's influential work *The Nomos of the Earth* (2003), examines how the narrative of 'progress' from a racist past to a nonracial present and future has become the critical modality in the post-apartheid era.[1] The 1994 elections signalled to the nation and to the world at large that one regime was ending while another was set in motion, with the *caveat* that economic, cultural and racial differences were to have lasting impacts and uncertain resolutions. Many have pointed out too, that the old fault lines of inequality and discrimination have been papered over with other forms of social injustice and hierarchy, namely those of rich and poor (Daniel *et al.* 2005). Farred argues that South Africans are living in a 'double temporality', an evocative notion for archaeologists and ethnographers alike. This positioning is key for those of us investigating post-apartheid shifts in the cultural productions of history and heritage, museums and tourist locales, constructions of nation and indigeneity, and identity and politics. 'Post-apartheid South Africa has produced a consciousness of the history that preceded and informs the current conjuncture, an awareness of living with the past in the post-apartheid present – and into the foreseeable future, for that matter' (Farred 2004: 593).

My own broader project is poised at this very conjuncture (Meskell 2005, forthcoming), the moment in which South Africans find themselves acknowledging, reconciling and even re-crafting specific histories and pasts. The project works between the disciplines of archaeology and ethnography to examine the ways in which the past becomes present and how the past is crucial in forging a viable future, possibly even a profitable and healing one. It also recognises a certain duplicity, where certain pasts are rehabilitated, despite the inflection of negative heritage (Meskell 2002b) in some cases, for the sake of nation-building and popular embrace. Conflictual sites that become a repository of negative memory in the collective imaginary constitute negative heritage. As site of memory, negative heritage occupies a dual role. It can be mobilised for positive didactic purposes (for example, Auschwitz, Hiroshima, District Six, Constitution Hill (Figure 11.1)), or erased if such places cannot be culturally rehabilitated and thus resist incorporation into the national imaginary (for example, Nazi and

Figure 11.1
Constitution Hill.

Soviet statues and architecture). Farred's notion of a double temporality is particularly useful here. It lays bare the impossibility of remaking the nation without recourse to its multiple pasts, not simply the apartheid years but the long *durée* of colonialism and its negative impact on indigenous people across southern Africa. For an archaeologist and ethnographer, this is a particularly salient time to track this interplay of times – past time and future time – as they coalesce for socio-political purpose.

The present has become highly politicised as the moment that is not the past, but is constantly situating itself in relation to history. South Africans are making and living history in the now, reflexively understood in opposition to the past – but always in some form of dialogue with it. Moreover, there is a great desire and longing that the future might become the present, right here, right now. This movement back and forth in time is palpable within the discourses of archaeology, heritage studies and museology as disciplinary wholes. It represents a sense of historicity that is ever present. At every turn, South Africans are painfully aware of creating historic futures and the concomitant responsibilities and repercussions that accompany that fabrication. For Mbembe (2004: 374), it is particularly salient in urban contexts where fragments of the city are being reworked as spaces for the experience of displacement, substitution and compression (none of which are easy repetitions of a repressed past), yet reflect a traumatic amnesia, nostalgia or even mourning in relation to the past. In this chapter I examine these processes in relation to one particular monumental site dedicated to the Great Trek in Pretoria, but also more generally in relation to urban museums such as the Hector Pieterson and Apartheid Museums.

Using an archaeological metaphor, I would like to consider the materiality of these sites, but also their histories redolent of past conflicts and repressions, as discrete strata that are repeatedly exposed, especially through the endeavors of contemporary cultural producers. Throughout the democratic period, the South African government and its cultural formations (for example, the South African Heritage Resources Agency SAHRA), have sought to preserve the past, tangibly and intangibly, rather than choosing the more radical option of cultural erasure. In many contexts, from post-Second World War Germany and Italy, to post-Soviet Russia and, more recently, Taliban-controlled Afghanistan (Meskell 2002b), as well as in the early 'liberation/invasion' of Iraq, statues and monuments associated with oppressive regimes were systematically dismantled or destroyed. Relatively few erasures of this kind have been enacted in South Africa, save the toppling of the Verwoerd statue in Bloemfontein in September 1994. At the time, threats from the Conservative Party made the notion of material retribution clear. As Conservative Party spokesman, Brig Cyprus, warned then: 'It is obvious that the insults now being meted out to the Afrikaner ... could lead to counteractions that could destroy any possible future reconciliation in the country' (ANC Press Briefing 1994). The materiality of national symbols and their perceived power to unite, and possibly even heal, has not been lost on the ANC government since coming to power.

Since 1994, concrete efforts have been made to incorporate divergent and often hurtful histories rather than privilege or re-balance the scales in terms of specifically African histories. This assimilative strategy often appears under the rubric of the 'rainbow nation', and sees full expression in the African Renaissance speeches of President Thabo Mbeki. It should be remembered that South Africa was the last nation to experience democracy on the continent, while being one of the wealthiest with its mix of First World and Third World. There are other rhetorics of exceptionalism: South Africa is a country in Africa yet different from other African situations. These myths of exceptionalism also find resonance in cultural rhetorics (Lazaus 2004: 617). The African Renaissance narrative is of particular interest to archaeologists as it calls for a cultural re-engagement with the rest of the continent, alongside enhanced economic and political connections. At its heart is a reliance on a suite of cultural (read archaeological) achievements from southern Africa and beyond: San art, Great Zimbabwe and so on link to the monumental efforts of ancient Egypt, Carthage and Axum (see Mbeki 1996, 1998). Stemming from Mbeki, but originally spearheaded by Mandela decades before, the theme of an African Renaissance is one that is regularly pronounced upon by South African leaders as another beacon of light in the dark continent. With full rhetorical flair Mbeki famously addressed the Constitutional Assembly in 1996:

> I am an African … I owe my being to the Khoi and the San whose desolate souls haunt the great expanses of the beautiful Cape … I am formed of the migrants who left Europe to find a new home on our native land …. I am the grandchild of the warrior men and women that Hintsa and Skehukhune led…. My mind and my knowledge of myself is formed by the victories that are the jewels in our African crown, the victories we earned from Isandhlwana to Khartoum, as Ethiopians and as the Ashanti of Ghana, as the Berbers of the desert …. I am the grandchild who lays fresh flowers on the Boer graves at St. Helena.
>
> (Mbeki 1996)

This speech connects to the other potent cultural myths of rainbow identity, a rainbow nation where black can expropriate and endorse Khoi, San and white histories and presumably vice versa, with the ultimate aim of cultural therapy, healing historic wounds and promoting interracial understanding. Such easy isomorphism may have rousing appeal, yet fails to take seriously histories of cultural difference, not to mention colonial genocide and apartheid repression, for the sake of a willing amnesia. 'Rainbow nation-ness' is the epitome of an imagined community à la Benedict Anderson, as Lazaus eloquently lays bare (2004: 620). Once again, the duality of history is underscored here, revelling in the glories and malleability of the past on one hand, and projecting them forward as exemplary models for progress on the other. An obvious discomfort stems from living in the space of two histories, of inescapable pasts on the one hand, and erased, unknowable ones on the other: concurrent excess and lack. Farred (2004) refers to this situation of living simultaneously with history and not-yet-history (post-apartheid) as a dual orientation, flipping between backward-looking and forward-looking practices, bifurcated code switching. Returning to Schmidt, he argues that South Africa represents a failed decolonisation project that is inevitably conceived as a lack, albeit produced by an excess: an excess of history, an overburden of pastness, and inscription of history always onto the present. 'The past is too constitutive of the present' (Farred 2004: 594).

This notion of the past as present, even perhaps past as future, is particularly redolent in the urban spaces of contemporary South Africa. For materialisation of this yearning one might look to the current proliferation of museums and sites of commemoration and the complex symbolic repertoire of practices at play.

MUSEUMS, MEMORY AND ANOMIE

Monumentality is intimately tied to memory, but also with forgetting and moving forward, which has come to epitomise post-apartheid South African society. Yet some have argued, in the context of Europe (Huyssen 1995: 258), that in preserving the monument the social obligation to engage in more active remembrance is partially removed. The monument's inherent exteriority affects the internal experience of individuals. Recently, Holocaust monuments have been accused of topolatry, especially at the sites of extermination, and this has ramifications for museums and memorials in South Africa. This view holds that monuments betray the memory, since memory is internal and subjective and thus incompatible with public display and musealisation. Memory, it has been said, is a type of anti-museum (De Certeau 1984: 108).

The current obsession with musealisation is in part a response to the burgeoning production of historical accounts and the uneven contribution of competing groups and individuals who have unequal access to the means of historical production. For Trouillot (1995), writing on the violence and oppression of colonialism in the Americas, such forces may be less visible than gunfire, class or political crusades, but they are no less powerful. He articulates the reasons why heritage is so forcefully implicated in these struggles and the material residues and physical reminders of more encompassing historical junctures:

> The bigger the material mass, the more easily it entraps us: mass graves and pyramids bring history closer while they make us feel small. A castle, a fort, a battlefield, a church, all these things bigger than we that we infuse with the reality of past lives, seem to speak of an immensity of which we know little except that we are part of it.
>
> (Trouillot 1995: 29)

Sites such as these are congealed memory. What sets archaeology apart from other disciplines seeking to represent the nation or culture, such as history or anthropology, is its materiality (Meskell 2002a). The residues of the past are often monumentalised and inescapable in daily life. Individually, the past is memory – collectively, it is history. Both are constructs entangled with identity issues in contemporary society.

Reflecting divergent positions on institutions such as South Africa's Truth and Reconciliation Commission (TRC), scholars have generally been fractured in their responses to the role of memory in post-apartheid society. Mamdani (1996), Ndebele (1998) and De Kok (1998) recognise the dilemma contained by the public desire for confession, forgiveness and forgetting, whereas Brink (1998) argues for healing and social transformation through narrative and a requisite forgetting. All are subsumed within psychological or psychoanalytic tropes and the connected phenomenon of amnesia. Returning to the past, De Kok (1998: 71) warns that the

> edifices of apartheid are being dismantled, papers are shredded, signs painted over, departments renamed. American collectors are buying the old 'whites only' sign that South Africans now repudiate. Those intent on promoting reconciliation at all costs see those who wish to preserve the history of the past as spoilers at best, revenge merchants at worst. But for the project of reconciliation to succeed, individuals and the nation require the physical evidence of our suffering and complicity to be displayed as part of a new pattern.

If we take two examples of memory-making – the Hector Pieterson and Apartheid Museums – both potent examples of the double temporality of urban spaces, we can see how architectural and spatial practices combine to produce embodied and visceral effects. Both inhabit the spatial economies of trauma. Described as a squat, bunker-like structure, the Apartheid Museum is a mix of harsh concrete, red brick and galvanised steel. Sandblasted and intentionally rusting, it is ultimately reminiscent of a Holocaust memorial, inflected with a per-vasive visual sense of discomfort and unease. The stark exterior of the museum immediately brings to mind images of detention, oppression and division. As you enter the building, you are immediately subjected to the most basic principle of apartheid – segregation. Your entrance card labels you either 'white' or 'non-white' and you must enter through the relevant gate. In this spatial manipula-tion, the individual momentarily experiences the embodied regimes of apartheid, the intimate disciplinary regulation of bodies inhabiting place. It is a dramatic evocation of the re-living of past events, of persons re-living past time and present time simultaneously, and being compelled to reflect on possible futures in the midst of that spatio-temporal matrix.

Gruesome in its accuracy and detail (film footage and photographs), trau-matic in its architecture of segregation, and ultimately hopeful in its desire for a new political and social configuration, this is a museum that affects in visceral and performative ways. Toward the end of the exhibit, a series of newspaper art-icles, replaced daily, underscores the ongoing nature of the post-apartheid project, that its goals are not fully realised and that all citizens must be vigilant. It is another instance of the relentless temporal duality within which many South African citizens find themselves.

A similar experience awaits visitors to the Hector Pieterson Museum. Spa-tialising trauma seems to be the objective here. The notion of containment has been effectively jettisoned so that one is constantly forced to look out from one constructed cultural space to the other, socio-economically deprived and politically charged terrain of Soweto, location of the unprecedented violence and social trauma of the student uprisings of 1976. Opened 26 years later in commemoration of the schoolchildren who were killed during peaceful protests against poor education and compulsory teaching in Afrikaans, the museum is named after the first child killed, Hector Pieterson.

Trapped in past and present time simultaneously, one might think both had collapsed: the township is still impoverished and the physical fabric of segregation remains. Looking out from one window, we witness where the student protesters marched, another is directed at the police station from which the armed assault was mobilised to attack and disperse the protestors. It is thought that some 500 to 600 young protestors were killed in Soweto alone during the uprising. The most haunting reminder, however, is a scarring line, gouged into the cement outside, visible in situ and from a museum window, that marks the line of the bullet that killed the young Hector Pieterson. The linkage is clear between historical events, the living community of Soweto and the situatedness of the museum itself. One is made uncomfortable at all opportunities within the museum and its environs: rusting iron, dripping water, confined spaces, uncomfortable seating, all are designed to inflect visceral horror through phenomenological and embodied means.

Spatio-temporal convergence is powerfully enacted here since visitors traverse the same ground, look out upon the same vistas and often feel threatened by being so obviously out of place. These are not events or places that will be easily forgotten, the struggle for recognition and yearning for change endure. Yet some have criticised the imposition of emotion here, rather than the evocation. The images are undeniable, but, perhaps because little interpretation is necessary, cultural critics such as historian Elsabe Brink feel bullied into their emotive responses. Evocation is a mark of the museum's success and of the power materiality wields in the world of intangibles and past time. But these are new, highly reflexive and experiential somatic domains.

THE VOORTREKKER MONUMENT: EDIFICE PATHOLOGIES

I now turn to an historic monument with nationalist and apartheid associations that has been subject to numerous afterlives. Contemporary attempts at re-signification, one could argue, have been less than successful.

Built in the late 1930s, the imposing fortress-like stone structure that makes up the Voortrekker Monument sits atop Pretoria's highest hill. It was designed to commemorate the Great Trek, which took place in the late 1830s, an event that was re-staged again for its centenary with racial and political overtones. As such it has strong resonance with the Van Riebeeck Festival (Witz 2003).

In the 1940s the monument became an oppressive icon of one culture's domination over another's, when the Afrikaans-dominated National Party gained control of the South African government and instituted its policy of racial segregation. Many of these prominent individuals had links with the Nazis and other fascist groups, a fact which is betrayed in this edifice where the eternal flame of white progress still burns. David Bunn suggests (1998: C4) that early twentieth-century Afrikaner memorial traditions effectively set themselves against rival African kingdoms and against the forces of British imperialism. He reminds us that the monument and the large amphitheatre nearby constitute a site of extreme contestation. Both provided the

> staging ground for rallies of Afrikaner extremists opposed to extending equal citizenship rights to blacks on the eve of South Africa's first multiracial election. Many now assert that the sites should be erased because they symbolise the roots of racial oppression and the ideologies of apartheid.
>
> (Bunn 1998: C4)

The Voortrekker Monument exemplifies the fraught histories of colonial monuments and that their celebratory architecture bears the burden of several racially specific contradictions. Its structure was originally likened to the Pyramids, Great Zimbabwe, the Mausoleum of Halicarnassus, Les Invalides, the Taj Mahal and the Great Wall of China (Delmont 1993: 86). By invoking these buildings and their concomitant cultures of greatness, Afrikaner culture sought to take its place alongside. And like those celebrated cultural survivals, the creators of the monument hoped that the values embodied in it would also be memorialised.

> Imagined as a white tradition, it is thought to surpass the ethical understanding of native communities, for which it is an obscure promise of future independence; at the same time, white monuments run the risk of becoming invisible or being neglected, because they rely on the memorial practices of an embattled minority group of settlers and their children.
>
> (Bunn 1998)

This paradox has general implications for the symbolic functioning of all monuments in the contemporary setting, particularly because monuments such as the Voortrekker can never be receptacles of collective meaning, or even mourning. They are inflected with contradiction, as Bunn exhorts, because of their reluctance to imagine the idea of citizenship outside the boundaries of race.

At this juncture, I want to offer a potent example of the willing suspension of disbelief, or the desire to forget or rework negative heritage in the present. The Voortrekker Monument has been vigorously deconstructed elsewhere (Van der Watt 1997), but here I want to focus on one very recent display in its museum, a set of illustrated panels that rationalises the colonisation of South Africa (Figures 11.2 and 11.3). Intended as an explanatory framework for global 'migration', the display reiterates the narrative that European settlers arrived at the Cape at much the same time as other African groups were entering South Africa from the north. In fact, there were so many ethnic migrations that the

Figure 11.2
Voortrekker Monument:
African migrations
display.

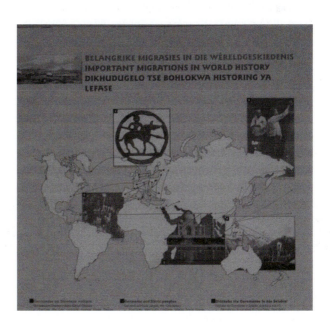

Figure 11.3
Voortrekker Monument:
World migrations display.

European entry was simply one of many. These texts couch the invasion of the country in the language of migration – a harmless movement of people from one place to another. Ten years after the overthrow of apartheid, myths perpetuated through Bantu education remain intact (see Dubow 1995; Hall 1984, 1993). Archaeologically, we know that Bantu-speakers were in South Africa well before the arrival of colonists, some 2,000 years ago, and this information is now well circulated. One has to question why that set of correctives has not been implemented? As Dubow (1995), Hall (1988, 2001) and Shepherd (2002a, 2002b, 2003) have respectively shown, archaeology and anthropology as related disciplines were deeply imbricated with the National Party strategy of institution-alised racism in South Africa. These deeply flawed constructions of history and culture have had a lasting legacy, felt to this day, but most palpably felt during the apartheid years since they were used to create racial hierarchies and structure living experiences for both black and white South Africans.

First, the museum actively presents a picture of 'tribal interaction' (so popular under apartheid) as a set of historical fractures and faultlines that cannot resist the interventions of external colonial forces (Mamdani 1996). Second, the devastating impacts of contact were absent: regimes of brutality, disease and decimation of indigenous population, exploitation of resources and so on. As an Australian, educated in the language of invasion rather than colonisation and certainly not migration (Smith 2004: 22), this struck me as the perpetuation of an appalling lie, largely in the service of a 'rainbow nation' narrative. It is indeed a dangerous fabrication, presumably embedded within a new political sensitivity towards an integrationist and healing policy. And third, we are all implicated in the narrative through the citation of other areas across the globe where 'migra-tion' took place throughout history. For example, the movement of Austrone-sian-speaking people across the uninhabited islands of the Pacific was considered a migration, and so it was. But directly underneath the Austronesian example is a similar claim of 'migration' by Europeans to Australian shores, which were defi-nitely not *terra nullius* and thus not a simple migration. Within this neat, palat-able scenario, South Africa conveniently implicates the rest of the world, and its history, in its national shame. It conflates history, erases specificity, and abne-gates responsibility for the ensuing policies of apartheid and so on. One has to ask how much has really changed? Consider an earlier text which argues that the 'Great Trek was not an armed invasion into the vast open areas of South Africa, but a trek in search of a new home, a homeland of promise … it was a climax of a gradual development towards national independence' (Smail 1968). As Smail concludes, 'they helped in the opening up of southern Africa to habitation by civilised peoples and by their combined efforts they opened up new areas of set-tlement, paving the way for the development of the land and the proper cultiva-tion of the soil'.

These migration displays make direct claims to the world as a single global entity. They seek to place South Africa among many countries that have been similarly forged, yet they also make claims that suggest the country was a tribal free-for-all and that such groups were pitched against each other, therefore trivi-alising the role of a new competing (European) party. Against the backdrop of global movements past and present, is the not-so-subdued rhetoric of cultural diversity and the various threads that have been woven together in the 'rainbow nation' fabric. Of course, we all know that when you spin a rainbow, the colour produced is white and the image of the rainbow itself is an illusion. The spin on history here is very clear. What is disturbing is that it is possible to craft and present such narratives of the past, suggesting that no one is thinking about the repercussions at the local level, inflected with the malaise that a memorial as provincial as the Voortrekker Monument is of little consequence. It is an issue of silencing, a particularly effective strategy in the crafting and selecting of appropriate histories. Indeed, every step of the historical process involves a level of silencing or editing of material considered extraneous, from the identification of a topic, to the sources selected, the examination of the archive and the writing and presentation stages: 'Silences are inherent in the creation of sources, the first moment of historical production' (Trouillot 1995: 51).

In a very broad sense, the Voortekker Monument is a marker of systemic violence and a material signifier of events that sedimented the policies of institutionalised racism. As Bunn (1998) states, the political significance of the 1938 trek was its invention and affirmation of white nationalist traditions. It celebrated a newfound unity and created the illusion of a collective identity through the political staging of vicarious spectacle – some might suggest it has continued to fulfil its task (see also McClintock 1995). The monument's immense materiality still exerts social and political energy, ostensibly doing the work of perpetuating the colonial fantasy of superiority and suppression.

This is further borne out in various forms of sexualisation of the monument that refract the specifically masculine aggression and sexual violence that has come to inhere in Afrikaner male identity more generally. Directed at the towering edifice and all that it comes to stand for, *Bittercomix* creators Anton Kannemeyer and Conrad Botes have been accused of doing nothing more than 'flashing rude signs at the Voortrekker Monument' (Barnard 2004: 721), instead of standing together with the wider populace in their fight for an inclusive democracy. The 'rude signs' in question refer to a drawing of a giant lizard of the Godzilla variety, 'tumescent and prodigiously endowed … threatening the young with his cry of *"Fokkof laities"* ("Fuck-off lightweights!")' (Barnard 2004: 725). The 'king lizard' holds his inordinately proportioned penis while standing on the monument, dwarfing it and causes electrical sparks to fly from its stolid architecture. Serving as a pedestal, one can see this cultural icon as a metaphorical base for patriarchal intimidation.

Previously, Annie Coombes has shown how mainstream Afrikaans pornography has seized upon the site and used it for its own purposes of ethnic absolutism. In 1995 the *Hustler* stable magazine *Loslyf* (translated as 'loose body'), featured 'Dina at the Monument' – a woman with breasts exposed who is the great-great-grand-daughter of Hendrik Potgieter (Coombes 2003: 40). Dina is portrayed as a child of the wilderness set amidst the tall grass, replete with leopardskin shorts, khaki vest and wild hair. She speaks out on the subject of monumental heritage: 'All the people who are so eager to punish the Afrikaner *volk* by demolishing and desecrating our monuments are playing with fire. They should know: if you interfere with my symbols, you interfere with me' (cited in Coombes 2003: 43). As a site of intensely negative memory in the new South Africa, the threat of violence (here gendered and sexualised) and potential for retaliation around the material past and its monuments has been ever-present since the first democratic elections (Matshikiza 2002; see also Brig Cyprus above).

Despite its enshrining of racist propaganda, the Voortrekker Monument has not been erased. Instead, a new space called Freedom Park is being built on a large hill directly opposite. The concept is a 'one-stop heritage precinct' where 'Freedom Park shall strive to accommodate and chronicle all of humanity's experiences'. 'It serves as an international icon for humanity and freedom and to inspire people all over the world to rediscover their humanity (www.freedom-park.org.za).' Designed to provide a therapeutic context for healing and reflection, the rationale of Freedom Park sets out explicitly to 'address the gaps, distortions and biases and provide new perspectives of South Africa's heritage' (see www.freedompark.org.za). The Garden of Remembrance has already been used for the commemoration of fallen heroes of the struggle. Its underpinning concepts are symbolic reparations coupled with cleansing and healing. 'Symbolic reparations' were conceived to assist people in dealing with their pain and trauma by reflecting on their past memories and experiences, and to heal by creating a common patriotism and participation in rebuilding the nation. Reinforcing this healing vision of the past for the future, the hope is that 'Freedom Park should be a spiritually uplifting and inspirational experience for its visitors' (www.freedompark.org.za). In retaining the Voortrekker Monument (still visited by busloads of tourists and students) and mirroring it with Freedom Park, we have another example of the willingness to incorporate rather than erase negative heritage within the 'rainbow' narrative. As Mandela himself has noted, there has to be white in the rainbow nation (see Witz 2003).

Throughout the official website there are swerving movements between a painful confrontation of past brutality and a desire to move forward in a remedial and positive manner. For example, the site will provide

> a national memorial seeking to facilitate a communal process of commemorating the pain and celebrating the victories of the past by preserving the memory of victims of conflicts and human rights abuse caused by slavery, colonialism and racism and honouring the victims, heroes and heroines of the struggle against apartheid.

There are obvious tensions here between a full and accurate remembering of the past, a necessary degree of therapeutic amnesia and an altogether new forging of a united nation. Here is a threefold mandate, to 'provide a pioneering and empowering heritage destination that challenges visitors to reflect upon their past, improve their present, and build on their future as a united nation' (www.freedompark.org.za). Encapsulating the dilemma of a new South Africa, the juxtaposed sites of the Voortekker Monument and Freedom Park represent the past and the future, a dual temporality: living within old and new regimes, and the struggle between memory and forgetting.

ARCHAEOLOGY AND FUTURE TIME

Many commentators see a danger in this conflation and blending, that the historicity of the past will be elided and that with forgetting comes the potential for future fallbacks. Archaeologists as public intellectuals must involve themselves in these dialogues and determinations and, while that seems an obvious and well-worn position to most in academia, many in South Africa and elsewhere would like to imagine their work existing outside socio-political frameworks (see Huffman 2004). The revolutions of history, as De Certeau states (1984: 201), its economic and demographic mixtures, lie in layers within and remain there congealed in customs, rites and spatial practices. Beyond the salient metaphor, this is very much the domain of archaeological praxis. As Shepherd documents, in the late 1960s and early 1970s archaeology re-established itself in

> South African affairs, this time in a very different context, as part of the general cultural apparatus of a modernising apartheid state with money to spend on museums and universities. This would involve archaeology in a new and different set of compromises and accommodations, which would in turn shape the nature of the discipline.
>
> (Hall 2000, 2001; Shepherd 2002b)

Although some academics were outspoken in their protests (Hall 1984, 1988), archaeology has suffered as a result of its apolitical stance during that era and now must reconfigure itself to meet the demands of a burgeoning tourist industry, new and complex constituencies, the recognition of multiple pasts and the ever-present spectre of a heritage that hurts. It remains an ever-present challenge to South Africans who are in the business of memorialising the past, to keep multiple versions of the past alive rather than to privilege a select set of master narratives that offer a sense of unity at the cost of eliding the fracture and dissonance (Nuttall and Coetzee 1998: 14).

We have to ask what constitutes significant history? What counts as heritage, or history with a purpose – a particularly apt concept in the South African context? Is its facticity important or are the emancipatory rhetorics of 'rainbow nation-ness' and African Renaissance all that matter in this ultra-democratic, postcolonial state? Are people prepared to experience, perhaps even be positively healed by, a fundamentally rewritten past in which they are immersed on a daily and present basis? Perhaps the ruptures that inhere in drastically rewritten pasts are considered too destabilising or, in the case of the Voortrekker displays, apathy and lack of attention to deconstructing apartheid's master narratives represent the major impediment? It remains unclear whether South Africans are reflexively choosing to live with the past in the post-apartheid present, or whether such double temporalities are inescapable. A more positive example is the new Constitution Hill project strategically built on the site of the Old Fort, Johannesburg's infamous prison complex, bearing the new mantle of human rights and protection of the constitution (see Figure 11.1). Presented as a heritage precinct and, as such, always understood within the context of the past

(Gevisser 2004: 507), its mandate is fixed intently on safeguarding future demo-cracies. One wonders when the past can safely inhabit the realm of history or whether futures are always shot through with past times. It reminds one of the classic *rites de passage* structure where physical death and decay is followed by separation and then incorporation back into society, thus making citizens, past and present, whole again. The process is enacted perhaps more for those surviv-ing, as a therapeutic stratagem, than for those who have passed into future time.

Today we are faced with a powerful and evocative repertoire of sites that challenge any seemingly straightforward or quotidian notions of the material past. Subsequently, their interlocutors need to reconfigure the notion of the museum or the monument in light of new political, social and economic configu-rations. South Africa provides perhaps the most complicated postcolonial context one might envisage, more so than Australia or the United States, and is particu-larly deserving of global attention. None of the sites described in the text would inhabit the traditional taxonomy of archaeology, although they are very much sites of cultural production. Each exudes its own form of negative heritage. One is a monument which is often associated negatively with the historic roots of apartheid ideology, and its concomitant exhibits that attempt to ameliorate recent destructive histories of oppression. The other two are intended as curative curations, museums with a clear historical and didactic purpose in the recogni-tion of and recovery from the atrocities of the apartheid regime. Through this analytic lens, I join with the other members of this volume in a close reading of new urban spaces and memory practices at an important juncture, in a new political climate and when newly commissioned monuments and museums are proliferating at an ever-increasing rate.

REFERENCES

ANC Press Briefing (1994) ANC Press Briefing Monday 12 September 1994. www.anc.org.za/anc/newsbrief/1994/news0912. Pretoria.

Barnard, R. (2004) '*Bitterkomix*: Notes from the Post-apartheid Underground', *South Atlantic Quarterly Special Issue. After the Thrill Is Gone: A Decade of Post-apartheid South Africa* 103: 719–54.

Brink, A. (1998) 'Stories of History: Reimagining the Past in Post-apartheid Narrative', in S. Nuttall and C. Coetzee (eds) *Negotiating the Past: The Making of Memory in South Africa*, Cape Town: Oxford University Press: 29–42.

Bunn, D. (1998) 'Whited Sepulchres: On the Reluctance of Monuments', in H. Judin and I. Vladislavic (eds) *blank_Architecture, Apartheid and After*, Rotterdam: NAi Publishers.

Coombes, A.E. (2003) *History after Apartheid: Visual Culture and Public Memory in a Democratic South Africa*, Durham, NC and London: Duke University Press.

Daniel, J., Southall, R. and Lutchman, J. (eds) (2005) *State of the Nation: South Africa 2004–2005*, Cape Town: HSRC Press.

De Certeau, M. (1984) *The Practice of Everyday Life*, Berkeley: University of California Press.

De Kok, A. (1998) 'Cracked Heirlooms: Memory on Exhibition,' in S. Nuttall and C. Coetzee (eds) *Negotiating the Past: The Making of Memory in South Africa*, Cape Town: Oxford University Press: 57–71.

Delmont, E. (1993) 'The Voortrekker Monument: Monolith to Myth', *South African Historical Journal* 29: 76–101.

Dubow, S. (1995) *Scientific Racism in Modern South Africa*, Cambridge: Cambridge University Press.

Farred, G. (2004) 'The Not-Yet Counterpartisan: A New Politics of Oppositionality', *South Atlantic Quarterly Special Issue. After the Thrill Is Gone: A Decade of Post-apartheid South Africa* 103: 589–605.

Gevisser, M. (2004) 'From the Ruins: The Constitution Hill Project', *Public Culture, Special Issue. Johannesburg: The Elusive Metropolis* 16: 507–19.

Hall, M. (1984) 'The Burden of Tribalism: The Social Context of Southern African Iron Age Studies', *American Antiquity* 49: 455–67.

—— (1988) 'Archaeology under Apartheid', *Archaeology* 41: 62–4.

—— (1993) 'The Archaeology of Colonial Settlement in Southern Africa', *Annual Review of Anthropology* 22: 177–200.

—— (2000) *Archaeology and the Modern World: Colonial Transcripts in South Africa and the Chesapeake*, London: Routledge.

—— (2001) 'Social Archaeology and the Theaters of Memory', *Journal of Social Archaeology* 1: 50–61.

Huffman, T.N. (2004) 'Beyond Data: The Aim and Practice of Archaeology', *South African Archaeological Bulletin* 59: 66–9.

Huyssen, A. (1995) *Twilight Memories: Marking Time in a Culture*, New York: Routledge.

Lazaus, N. (2004) 'The South African Ideology: The Myth of Exceptionalism, the Idea of Renaissance', *South Atlantic Quarterly Special Issue. After the Thrill Is Gone: A Decade of Post-apartheid South Africa* 103: 606–28.

Mamdani, M. (1996) *Citizen and Subject: Contemporary Africa and the Legacy of Late Colonialism*, Princeton, NJ: Princeton University Press.

Matshikiza, J. (2002) 'An Epitaph of Smoke and Mirrors', *Mail & Guardian*, Johannesburg, 21 June.

Mbeki, T. (1996) 'Statement of Deputy-President Tabo Mbeki, on Behalf of the African National Congress, on the Occasion of the Adoption by the constitutional Assembly of "The Republic of South Africa Constitution Bill 1996"', Cape Town, 8 May.

—— (1998) 'The African Renaissance Statement of Deputy-President, Thabo Mbeki', SABC, Gallagher Estate, 13 August.

Mbembe, A. (2004) 'Aesthetics of Superfluity', *Public Culture, Special Issue. Johannesburg: The Elusive Metropolis* 16: 373–405.

McClintock, A. (1995) *Imperial Leather: Race, Gender, and Sexuality in the Colonial Contest*, New York: Routledge.

Mda, Zakes (2000) *The Heart of Redness*, Oxford: Oxford University Press.

Meskell, L.M. (2002a) 'The Intersection of Identity and Politics in Archaeology', *Annual Review of Anthropology* 31: 279–301.

—— (2002b) 'Negative Heritage and Past Mastering in Archaeology', *Anthropological Quarterly* 75: 557–74.

—— (2005) 'Archaeological Ethnography: Conversations around Kruger National Park', *Archaeologies* 1.

—— (forthcoming) 'Trauma Culture: Remembering and Forgetting in the New South Africa', in D. Bell (ed.) *Memory, Trauma, and World Politics*, Cambridge: Cambridge University Press.

Ndebele, N. (1998) 'Memory, Metaphor, and the Triumph of Narrative', in S. Nuttall and C. Coetzee (eds) *Negotiating the Past: The Making of Memory in South Africa*, Cape Town: Oxford University Press: 19–28.

Nuttall, S. and Coetzee, C. (1998) 'Introduction', in S. Nuttall and C. Coetzee (eds), *Negotiating the Past: The Making of Memory in South Africa*, Cape Town: Oxford University Press: 1–15.

Schmidt, C. (2003) *The Nomos of the Earth*, trans. Ulmen, G.L., New York: Telos Press.

Shepherd, N. (2002a) 'Disciplining Archaeology; the Invention of South African Prehistory, 1923–1953', *Kronos* 28: 127–45.

—— (2002b) 'The Politics of Archaeology in Africa', *Annual Review of Anthropology* 31: 189–209.

—— (2003) 'State of the Discipline: Science, Culture and Identity in South African Archaeology, 1870–2003', *Journal of Southern African Studies* 29: 823–44.

Smail, J.L. (1968) *Monuments and Trails of the Voortrekkers*, Cape Town: Howard Timmins.

Smith, L.J. (2004) *Archaeological Theory and the Politics of Cultural Heritage*, Routledge: London.

Trouillot, M.R. (1995) *Silencing the Past: Power and the Production of History*, Boston, MA: Beacon Press.

Van der Watt, L. (1997) 'Savagery and Civilisation: Race as a Signifier of Difference in Afrikaner Nationalist Art', *de arte: Journal of the Department of Art History and Fine Arts UNISA* 55: www.unisa.ac.za/default.asp?Cmd=ViewContent&ContentID=7253.

Witz, L. (2003) *Apartheid's Festival: Contesting South Africa's National Pasts*, Bloomington: Indiana University Press.

Part III

Burial Sites

Chapter 12: On a Knife-edge or in the Fray

Managing Heritage Sites in a Vibrant Democracy

Abdulkader I. Tayob

This chapter is a reflection on the dispute between the Muslim Judicial Council (MJC) and the St Cyprian's School (SCS) development project on the evidence of Muslim graves on a disputed piece of school property. Part of the title, 'On a Knife-Edge', may give the impression that we were dealing with a dangerous issue: heritage sites poised between life and death. I do not want to leave that impression even though some would have thought so in August 2000, when a public demonstration was organised at the gates of the SCS. The vociferous protest provided fertile images and copy for newspaper editors and the public at large. When the dispute was amicably resolved at the end of 2000, a small report to that effect was buried deeply in the newspapers. Muslim radio stations, which had previously aired discussion with great interest and enthusiasm, also ignored the value of an agreement between Muslims and Christians. The process and resolution are worth recalling and evaluating.

I would like to invoke an alternative image for this dispute, away from the rollercoaster of media representation. My experience in this project has left me with the impression of a robust and open debate in the public sphere about a disputed site. All the niceties of democratic tolerance were dropped as the parties expressed their deepest fears and anxieties over a process that angered and frustrated them. Here democracy was expressed in the willingness to speak out openly and clearly on an issue. The debate ignored the divisions of class, power and sophistication. It was an honour for me to be part of the process, and now to reflect on it with the privilege of hindsight.

The St Cyprian's dispute was a relatively minor issue as far as the commemoration of heritage sites in the city of Cape Town and South Africa are concerned. It dwarfs in comparison with the symbolic importance of Robben Island, rock art and land restitution programmes in many parts of the country. And yet, its lessons yielded valuable insights into some of the fundamental questions that affect heritage management and identification. Perhaps because of its relatively minor importance in the conceptual map of the country, the St Cyprian's case allowed us to reflect on the meaning of historical significance, modes of evidence, and the ramifications of spatial occupation. It provides an opportunity to focus on how an open public discussion can take forward heritage identification and management.

St Cyprian's School in Cape Town wanted to extend its facilities towards Table Mountain. As is required by law, it requested permission from neighbours to proceed with the development, and to include a small portion of city land by way of prescriptive rights. Neighbours raised some objections, but the relevant government bodies dismissed them. One particular neighbour, Colleen Stolzman, was upset by the manner in which her objections were overturned. She suspected that the school enjoyed undue leverage and influence in the bodies in various government sectors that were entrusted to make decisions. In 1998, the school sent its plans to the Muslim Judicial Council to discuss future developments and how these might impact on interests in the Muslim community. The MJC did not immediately respond. As a leading body representing the Muslims of the Western Cape, it was dragged into the affair without any deep knowledge of any graves or the conflict. The school had initial contact with the Cape Mazaar Society, which was responsible for the upkeep of the existing shrine of Sayyid Abdul Malik on the edge of the school grounds. It organised annual meetings at the shrine, for which it used school grounds, and maintained the physical condition of the shrine. The Cape Mazaar Society was not aware of the existence of the grave site until the dispute erupted (Limbada 2000). The meetings, however, were held between the MJC and the SCS with the Cape Mazaar Society present as an interested party.

The MJC became more directly concerned when it heard from Colleen Stolzman and Dawud Zwaval that the proposed site was an old burial ground. After that, it tried to persuade the school to alter or terminate its plans. Colleen Stolzman seems to have played a significant role in the dispute. The MJC was persuaded by her enthusiasm and her commitment to try to halt the development. Colleen Stolzman appeared to have made a considerable impression on the members of the MJC, and she ensured that the issue was not shelved. From Dawud Zwaval, the MJC heard that the graves on the proposed site of the development were closely related to the shrine of Sayyid Abdul Malik. Perhaps it was the burial ground of his family, or his disciples. It was common knowledge within Cape Muslim society that saints were not buried alone. Their disciples preferred to be buried nearby. Soon, a strong perception was created of graves on the disputed territory. On its part, the school appointed an archaeologist, Mary Patrick, who meticulously worked with the parties to uncover the possible heritage significance of the area. This particular condition was required in terms of a new Act concerning graves and heritage sites (National Heritage Act no. 29, 1999). The dispute may in fact be the first test case for the application of the new Act. Some of the problems were a direct outcome of insufficient structures and mechanisms to apply the Act.

Several meetings were held from the end of 1998 until 2000. During this time, the MJC was requested to produce evidence in support of the claims on the site. When the claims about the existence of graves were made, it specifically involved the South African Heritage Resources Agency (SAHRA), requesting that it also present such evidence (SAHRA 2000). In the absence of any direct evidence of such graves, the school began clearing the ground under the supervision of Mary Patrick. The MJC and the general Muslim community in the city interpreted this as a resolve to go ahead with the project. A demonstration was called at the school on 7 August, and the dispute threatened to erupt into religious conflict. Saleem Mowzer, an elected member of the Cape Town City Council, and the Anglican Archbishop of Cape Town, Njongonkulu Ndungane, intervened. A process was begun that eventually led to an agreement, signed at the end of 2000.

Around April 2000, the school invited me to present my view on the graves, and asked if I would be prepared to attend a meeting with the MJC. I reviewed the matter with colleagues from archaeology and architecture, and decided to find out how the MJC was presenting its claim. After some careful reflection, I joined a research group set up by the MJC to collect data and evidence for the claim. Over a period of time, Noëleen Murray and I impressed upon the team the importance of carefully doing and documenting archival and oral research. This included examining the nature of the sources, the kinds of conclusions that could be reached, and their importance in arriving at a decision about the alleged graves. It took us about five months to collect data, which consisted of archival material, secondary sources on the area in question, as well as a few oral reports.

During this time, the pressure from the SCS and the MJC to produce evidence was mounting. After the demonstration on 7 August, a final period of 30 days was set aside for the MJC to produce evidence of graves. Thirty days later, such evidence was still not ready. The public conflict prevented any balanced consideration of the evidence. Then, a technical committee consisting of archaeologist Mary Patrick and representatives from the MJC was set up to look into the research conducted thus far. Based on these materials, an agreement was finally reached. In the absence of any evidence from both archival and oral testimony that linked the *particular* site to ritual activity, or to any provable claim about graves, the MJC and the school agreed that the development would go ahead. At the same time, however, the parties agreed that the dispute had placed a spotlight on an important spatial occupation of the general area by slaves. The agreement was brokered through the mediation of Archbishop Ndungane and Saleem Mowzer. A combination of research, goodwill and conflict-resolution strategies produced a final agreement in December 2000.

HISTORICAL SIGNIFICANCE

Heritage sites, by their very nature, carry historical significance and present exciting opportunities to understand how people perceive the past. There has been a major revision of South Africa's past, mostly conducted by excellent historians and other social scientists working with those previously excluded from official versions of history. Contestations around heritage sites, however, offer a chance to bring such revisionism into public space. In all their opaqueness and tangibility, disputed heritage sites bring historical perceptions and competing construction of meanings to the general public. They provide an ideal opportunity to test and evaluate the revisions generally confined to academic discourse. The identification of a heritage site as a contested space affords the opportunity to test the possibilities and limits of such revisions or reformulations.

The St Cyprian's case was one opportunity for re-thinking the meaning of Cape Town as a unified city. The school was thinking of its particular space, and insisted that legal processes had been meticulously followed. It called upon the Department of Environmental and Cultural Affairs and its successor, SAHRA, to check on its compliance. It tried to arrange a number of meetings to discuss the matter with the MJC, and asked for concrete evidence of graves on the disputed site. In turn, SAHRA appealed to the MJC for information to be submitted by 30 November 1999, a deadline extended to 10 December 1999 (Kane-Berman 1999).[1] During the first half of 2000, correspondence between the MJC and SAHRA indicates that evidence was still being pursued (SAHRA 2000). However, the two parties were talking past each other. The MJC was not focused on the particular space in question. In addition to the legal issue, it wrestled with popular perceptions and regular ritual visitation of the graves dotting the mountain landscapes around Cape Town. These perceptions suggested that the presence of graves on the undeveloped school property was not a far-fetched notion. Prejudice in favour of Christianity and its privileged role during apartheid was also brought to bear on the debate. Most importantly, however, the area in dispute was part of a previously designated white area in apartheid South Africa.

The claim to the graves was seen as a rightful claim to land lost by black people in general during apartheid. The legal position of the school was pitted against a post-apartheid sense of entitlement, land restitution and past privilege. To its credit, St Cyprian's was sensitive to such claims. However, its financial and planning commitments and the lack of any substantial evidence from the MJC for the particular site, allowed little room for manoeuvre. Clearly, though, there were two competing claims to the significance of the site, one determined by a general vague perception of the other party as a privileged land-occupier, and the other by a legal claim to occupation and freedom of use.

MODES OF EVIDENCE

The school and the MJC approached the dispute from different perspectives. The school was operating in a familiar context of law, government agencies and independent research specialists. There seemed a neat and clinical approach to development plans, government permission and research. The school related to research in the way described by Anthony Giddens (1990). For Giddens, modern society is characterised by a reciprocal relationship between sociological abstraction and society: 'Sociological knowledge spirals in and out of the universe of social life, reconstructing both itself and that universe as an integral part of the process' (Giddens 1990: 15–16). The school hired a professional archaeologist to ascertain the presence of graves, and presented these findings at regular meetings. They were presumably prepared to change their plans in the face of strong evidence. Armed with this powerful process, the school's claim was easily understood in the new constitutional democracy. The law reigned supreme in post-apartheid South Africa. And the record of how the school played its role from a legal perspective was clear: any evidence of graves would have presumably led to a change of plans.

The school was not to be faulted with respect to compliance of legal requirements. But there was another, less clearly articulated dimension of the school's power operating in the dispute as well. Firstly, a certain level of frustration and irritation developed within the school with respect to its compliance. In an interview with a member of the school council and executive committee, such feelings were voiced:

> I think there was enormous frustration that things were just not happening at all, and of course it was very difficult operating for – and representing – a parent body that was enormously diverse. Some parents are a lot more sympathetic than others and inevitably quite an element within the school body said 'For heaven's sake, we've got our rights, so just get on with it'.
>
> (Baumann 2000)

In principle, such frustrations and irritations with the legal process within the school were hidden from public debate. Their absence from public debate was in striking contrast with the sentiments and suspicions of the MJC and its supporters. In order to assess the conflict in full, we need a better sense and clarity about such 'uncivil' sentiments both within the school and within the MJC. Both are important for contrasting and explaining the dispute over heritage sites in the public arena. As it stands, the frustrations and irritations within the school were downplayed within a post-apartheid context coming to terms with competing claims. The school was sensitive and aware of such contexts, and felt no need to express such misgivings. But the opposing party, which regarded the school as a bastion of wealth and privilege, was aware of such misgivings and suspicions from the school. Yagya Adams, the chief negotiator for the MJC for the greater part of 2000, worked with these suspicions:

> And they were not really prepared to budge on much. What they were basically claiming, in a very arrogant way, was that 'look – if that is what you (the MJC) are assuming then come up with your facts'. And this was part of the investigation of the position of the land and the disappearance of court legal papers that led to a great deal of suspicion. ... There was very little relationship-building from the school's side.
>
> (Adams 2000)

The MJC felt the power and arrogance of the other party. Working within a previously advantaged white area, the imbalance was particularly pronounced for the MJC. The MJC claim must be situated within the widespread and well-accepted fact that property ownership in the city of Cape Town was skewed in favour of white interests. The school became a symbol of such interests, and the evidence, or lack thereof, was immaterial in the face of such a fact.

The SCS was less aware of its power bearing upon the opposing party. It was less aware of its powerful position in relation to the law and due process, in comparison with the MJC. Nicolas Baumann (2000) shared his general vision of the development of the school since 1976. Such a long vision lent it a certain degree of authority and power over the course of developments within the city. In an interview with Melanie Atwell and Clive Jones of the Cape Town City Council's heritage conservation structures, we had a clearer indication of such power as felt within the City Council:

> looking back at it, I can see that St Cyprian's, with Nicolas [Baumann] being connected to the school as the architect, he is entirely familiar with what the process is and where you are in the process at the time that the problem is. The MJC would not necessarily have had knowledge of those administrative processes involved in getting development approval. And I think that they were at a disadvantage in the point of view of ... in demanding the development to stop, not having information that in fact the rights had been transferred and that the city can't intervene in the kind of way that they'd [have] liked the city to intervene. It's just from a position of no information about where it is in the process and who does have the power to stop it. If it were the other way around I think that St Cyprian's would have certainly had people like Nicolas who would have known exactly where to be able to intervene and to put a stop (to the process). The MJC were doing it by putting pressure through the media, through the protest at the gate, using vocal popular mechanisms rather than administrative and legal mechanisms. So I think they were at the disadvantage in going in at the beginning ....
>
> (Atwell and Jones 2001)

Even the goodwill of the SCS towards the MJC was an expression of its power. Before the promulgation of the new act in 1999, the SCS approached the MJC to discuss the impact of its development. At the time, the MJC was not aware of graves, or of the significance of the area for an historic Muslim claim. In contrast with the power of the school and the legal tradition in which it stood, the MJC represented a different kind of public player. Powerful within the confines of Muslim community structures, the MJC had moved into unfamiliar territory. It held on to the notion of lost records, graves that were perhaps stealthily removed, and title deeds that were not acknowledged. And it responded to hard facts by raising awareness in the public arena. Since the advent of democracy, Muslim leadership has created a greater public image through its own radio stations, and through the media of the city. It appealed to the Muslim sense of historic denial to rally around a site. Radio programmes and Friday sermons were marshalled for its responses. While it was unable to effectively challenge the school at meetings where the rule of law prevailed, it had no shortage of public attention through its traditional channels to create a perception of its embattlement.

The dispute posed a challenge for researchers as to how and where the divergent powers, debates and discussions could be brought together. The story of dispossession could not be restricted to that which could only be expressed in legal terms. The research team, and then the technical team in the dispute, had the opportunity and responsibility to give expression to these hidden subtexts of public memory. One ironically concrete way of accessing the subtexts was by looking at oral testimonies. Oral records are a powerful means of invoking alternative narratives. And the oral record had been institutionalised in the new act that the MJC and the SCS were trying to uphold. While the SCS was demanding concrete evidence, and the MJC was agonising about its absence, the new act had enshrined oral testimony in law: 'to protect, preserve and promote the content and heritage which reside in orature in order to make it accessible and dynamic' (National Heritage Council Act, no. 11, 1999, 4 (c)). Neither of the parties, until late in the dispute, realised that the implementation of the act also implied a thorough appraisal of the oral evidence at hand. Even the post-apartheid agencies that were entrusted to take oral traditions seriously continued to insist on concrete evidence. Neither the City Council nor SAHRA went far enough in understanding the point of view of the MJC. In spite of the reference to oral evidence in the act, the lack of concrete evidence was a weapon wielded against the MJC.

In the absence of concrete evidence, oral traditions can become a powerful tool to unearth hidden perceptions of the past. The view of the past captured in written historical records is simply not enough. But oral testimony should not be expected to yield magical results. Rather, the collection of these stories can help to construct alternative perceptions of the past. Holstein and Gubrium's recommendations for an active interpreter seem to consitute an ideal tool to assist in the construction of such alternative perceptions:

> Challenged by the interviewer, pointed in promising directions, and at least partially aware of the interpretive terrain at hand, the respondent becomes a kind of researcher in his or her own right, consulting repertoires of experience and orientations, linking fragments into patterns, and offering 'theoretically' coherent descriptions, accounts, and explanations. Far from merely reporting a chronicle of what is already present (hidden or obscured as it might be), the respondent actively composes meaning by way of situated, assisted inquiry.
>
> (Holstein and Gubrium 1995: 29)

The identification of heritage sites, then, furnished the occasion to evoke powerful narratives waiting to be told. Principally, heritage sites determined by archival records risk telling only one kind of story: the story of the victors. Even though the oral respondents in this case did not locate their narratives at the site in question, they were instrumental in giving concrete life to new perceptions of the mountain previously ignored on the margins of Cape society.

We realised that our success in resolving this issue would come from an understanding both of the structural imbalance between the parties, and of the meaning of the process for the school and the MJC. For the MJC, oral evidence and defective evidence were proving useful tools in staking a claim against the school. The idea of 'oral history' and one's own 'indigenous oral historian' in the person of Dawud Zwaval, were marshalled in the place of evidence. Meanwhile, suspicions about re-zoning and prescription rights fanned the flames of continuing privilege. In general, oral history suspicions towards the City Council, and allegations of tampering with evidence, were used to shore up the Muslim claim.

MJC members believed that their research team would supply the evidence demanded of them in the meetings with the school. Our participation soon convinced us that we had the opportunity to do something much more fundamental. Instead of supporting one view or another, we worked with the organisation to come to terms with and participate in the process. This meant appreciating both the possibilities and limitations of research, and the responsibility of taking control of the process.

The MJC had neither the organisational framework nor the capacity with which to review and judge the process and the research reports. We decided to assist it in assessing the research at its disposal. It would constitute a modest attempt to understand the material at hand. Auwais Rafudeen went through the secondary literature on the property, while I took on the oral sources. Another group focused on the history of land ownership of the property, while a fourth group tried to work closely with the City Council and SAHRA to look into the legal opportunities for the MJC. This systematic approach to the existence of graves, under the leadership of a sub-committee of the MJC, afforded the focus lacking in the organisation. Not all of these groups were entirely successful in completing their tasks. The critical demands of the dispute, and its public nature, led to frequent changes in the group working with and for the MJC. For example, the issue of property ownership, and the acquisition by prescription, was imagined to be larger than it really was. At the end, there was sufficient material with which to test the key claims about graves even though some doubts, particularly pertaining to ownership of land, remained.

Reviewing the secondary literature, Rafudeen concluded:

> My own perusal of documented sources compels a similar assertion: we do not have any *documented* evidence for the existence of such graves. These conclusions corroborate archaeological research, which confirms that the existence of any graves on the designated location is geo-scientifically unlikely.

Rafudeen's conclusion could create the impression that oral traditions could support claims to occupation of the site. However, my own work on the different ritual and oral traditions in the area led to a similar conclusion. I found that the oral traditions pointed to a sustained relationship between this previously designated white area and the Muslim community. The claim against the school could not be understood as a manipulation of individuals trying to exploit a situation. Rather, oral and ritual traditions reversed the view of a racially divided city. Throughout apartheid, certain individuals staked a claim to the mountain through ritual, walks and herb collections. There was much in popular perception that amplified the importance of the area as a significant site for Muslim religious and oral tradition.

However, nothing pointed to the SCS site. There was no narrative recollection or ritual occupation of the particular site under dispute. The oral tradition that I was able to access was not specific enough about the place. The Cape Mazaar Society, guardians of the Sayyid Abdul Malik shrine, had no recollection of the significance of the site before the dispute. And Achmat David's notice of Abdul Malik of Batavia in the nineteenth century seemed more accurate than that given by Zwaval that he predated the arrival of Jan van Riebeeck in the middle of the seventeenth century.

We took this information and these considerations to the leadership of the MJC for their evaluation and decision. Such evidence and materials were still considered in the light of the public debates and suspicions. Gaps in the research, as in almost all kinds of research, were debated and considered. But eventually, the MJC had to make a decision about the site in question. And at that moment, the decision could only be made from the documents. Although some MJC members continued to conflate citywide historical disputes with the SCS site, the leadership eventually felt empowered to take a decision. The significance of the SCS dispute for the role of the MJC in the city may have to be considered at a later stage. I am convinced that it represented a major turning point for some members at least.

A careful evaluation of the material by the MJC allowed the assessment of a communal perception. A summary dismissal of the lack of evidence could not bring about a resolution. A careful consideration of the oral reports and other materials shared by a community produced a middle ground. It created a space for bridging the gap between community representatives and a school that were talking past each other. More than just supplying information, heritage researchers and management should play an important role in identifying imbalances, miscommunications and lack of organisational capacity within the parties in a dispute. Heritage management should at least be aware of different approaches to city landscapes, even if it cannot solve all the problems.

MEANING OF SPATIAL OCCUPATION

I come now to my third and final point about heritage sites. Taking heritage sites as spaces that possess meaning for the protagonists, I had the privilege of listening to alternative perceptions of place. The school's legal argument defined space as a fixed geological area registered in archives and deeds offices. The MJC accepted these conditions, and asked its researchers to produce a counter-narrative. The people who used the site, however, inscribed a different sense of location that merits consideration. I want to draw on my understanding of sacred space to suggest how heritage space may be extended beyond legal considerations.

The significance of space, in particular religious space, has received the attention of a number of scholars. Eliade (1959) has identified the classical notion of sacred space in the study of religion as the locus of experiencing ultimate reality. According to Eliade, absolute chaos and relativity threatened the modern world of homogeneity. In contrast, sacred space, best exemplified in religion, provided a sense of absolute value. This was achieved by setting aside a space distinct from everyday usage: the key difference between sacred and profane. Secondly, sacred space was intrinsically better than profane space. In addition to these qualities of demarcation and hierarchy, sacred space signified a hierophany where contact between the horizontal and vertical dimensions of reality could be recalled and realised (Eliade 1959). Jonathan Z. Smith (1987) accepted the category of sacred space but argued that it was not a primordial, timeless entity that reminded one of a divine encounter. This timeless quality of sacred space was an illusory experience of the nature of 'place' as a fixed and changeless entity. When returning to a place where something significant had taken place, one often recreated another experience thereof. It would be a mistake to assume that returning to the same place duplicated the experience. Such a return or recollection produced a new encounter within the same geographical location. The total encounter was an experience of a new place. Similarly, sacred places in religious experiences, according to Smith, were continually founded and produced in collective ritual activity and the human acts of remembrance and recollection. 'Place' was never given, it was valued and produced in social contexts: 'place is not best conceived as a particular location with an idiosyncratic physiognomy or as a uniquely individualistic node of sentiment, but rather as a social position within a hierarchical system' (Smith 1987: 45). Taking this notion of a socially delineated and hierarchically organised place one step further, Chidester (1994) insisted that sacred places were located and articulated in culturally contested contexts. Accordingly, the primary means of remembering the 'Holy', or the 'Real' or the 'Divine' at a place was as much open to inversion and hybridisation as it was to recollection and definition (Chidester 1994). Symbols, including sacred spaces, were open to competition and contestation; two processes which defined sacred spaces as much as the hope or memory of the supreme, ultimate encounter.

The study of sacred spaces has much to offer to an understanding of heritage sites such as the one being debated in this chapter. A review of the dispute from this perspective allows some reflection of how the dispute was contesting and creating a new space over the old. Colleen Stolzmann was an unlikely source for the first ritual occupation. After an unsuccessful attempt to stop the development blocking her view or her privacy, she discovered a presence, an occupation of sorts, in the empty woods through a drumming ceremony. Powerful feelings and sentient beings were reported to her that injected a new life and new direction to her private, middle-class privilege. Her sightings or hearings were confirmed by a group of Muslim spiritualists who encouraged her to seek further, but they themselves remained in the background throughout the dispute. Stolzmann, however, kept the memories of these presences alive among members of the MJC, and the wider Muslim community through the radio. She was supported by Dawud Zwaval who recreated the site with a medley of recollections that touched on the sensitive memory shared by Muslims in the city. He had accompanied his grandmother on walks on the mountain nearby. She had introduced him to the power of herbal remedies that could fight life-threatening disease. Rarely did he seem to visit the mountain for purely religious reasons. But he also created, through bits of archival snippets and religious lore, an alternative memory of a pious mountain (*jabal salih*) that sheltered early Muslim political exiles and the Khoi in a romantic Garden of Eden. Table Mountain, the geographical landmark of a new booming city, was transformed into a religious space. *Jabal salih*, a sound Arabic construction, and the product itself of a new wave of Arabisation among Muslims, evoked an exotic and powerful memory of people who were embattled. Such embattlement found fertile ground in contemporary political and social circles. The MJC reluctantly took over leadership in this dispute from the Cape Mazaar Society, which did not want to upset its good relations with the SCS.

After the dust had settled, the society needed to return to the school to continue to honour the memory of Sayyid Abdul Malik and any others possibly still resting there. Furthermore, the leading members of the negotiating team had just joined the Democratic Alliance (the party opposing the ANC in local politics), which drew considerable criticism from the anti-apartheid activists within the MJC. Investing the public space with a new religious mantle was inviting in the new political landscape, but was fraught with problems. The first problem was the lack of evidence, countered by the real sense of marginalisation felt. Particular members of the MJC were also sometimes troubled by the fact that they were championing the cause of grave reverence. Within theological circles in the Muslim community in general, and in the MJC in particular, this was by no means an issue that had been resolved despite a long tradition of shrine visits stretching back to at least the nineteenth century.

The creative reading of the new space was constructed through a number of strands and sources, and merits greater scrutiny. In previous paragraphs, I have pieced together a number of leads that I have picked up from the narrative and ritual construction of this contested space. With the emphasis in this chapter on the process, there is no opportunity to explore these dimensions. But I hope to have given sufficient indication of the richness of the oral lore that developed around the site and around the legal process. These leads do indicate, moreover, that, after the dust over the site dispute had settled, some issues would remain unresolved.

CONCLUSION

This revisiting of the dispute over graves on the grounds of the SCS has raised some fundamental issues about heritage identification and management. In the first instance, it forced us to remember that heritage sites are historical sites that afford an ideal opportunity to develop alternative approaches to South African history in the public sphere. Even though the risks might be high, such revision should not be relegated to academic discourse. Taking heritage sites as contested spaces meant that all perceptions needed to be viewed as constructed perceptions privileged by the dominant ethos. In the case of the SCS dispute, the legal rights of the school had to be contrasted with the loosely constituted oral perception of a previously disenfranchised part of society. As required by the new act, heritage identification thus had the duty to develop alternative perceptions from oral traditions. The project had to follow the ramification of the hegemonic discourse in the kind of evidence presented. Written sources had to be matched and challenged by a careful and meticulous appreciation of the oral witness. Most importantly, organisational capacity had to be created and nurtured in order to transform communities' relationships with the law, government and research traditions. And finally, I suggested how the study of religious space was helpful in understanding the definition of space through narrative construction and ritual occupation. As I have shown, the SCS case shows that the results will not always be what those previously disadvantaged in the South African past might have desired. However, taking such traditions seriously could ensure that we all win.

REFERENCES

Chidester, D. (1994) 'The Poetics and Politics of Sacred Space: Towards a Critical Phenomenology of Religion', in A.T. Tymieniecka (ed.) *Analecta Husserliana*, Netherlands: Kluwer Academic Publishers.

Eliade, M. (1959) *The Sacred and the Profane: The Nature of Religion*, trans. W.R. Trask, New York: Harcourt Brace & World Inc.

Giddens, A. (1990) *The Consequences of Modernity*, Stanford, CA: Stanford University Press.

Holstein, J.A. and Gubrium, J.F. (1995) 'The active interview', vol. 37, *Qualititative Research Methods*, Thousand Oaks, CA: London and New Delhi: Sage Publications.

Kane-Berman, J. (1999) Cape Town: Letter dated 7 December.

Limbada, M. (2000) Interview with chair of the Cape Mazaar Society, Cape Town: 16 June.

Smith, Jonathan Z. (1987) *To Take Place: Toward Theory in Ritual*, Chicago, IL: University of Chicago Press.

South African Heritage Resources Agency (SAHRA) (2000) Cape Town: Letter dated 15.

Interviews

Adams, Yagya (2000) Interview with Antonia Malan and Abdulkader Tayob, Cape Town.

Atwell, M. and Jones, C. (2001) Interview with Antonia Malan and Noëleen Murray.

Baumann, Nicolas (2000) Interview with school council and executive committee member, Cape Town.

Chapter 13: Leaving the City

Gender, Pastoral Power and the Discourse of Development in the Eastern Cape

Premesh Lalu

> Knowledge is not meant for comprehension, it is made for cutting.
>
> (Foucault 1972: 216)

Far from being self-evident, Mahmood Mamdani's phrase 'the rural in the urban' may be construed as a figure of speech that delineates the ways in which the rural functions as a silent referent in the discourse of the urban.[1] Post-apartheid city planners might heed the caution entailed in Mamdani's critique of South African exceptionalism, especially his thesis that apartheid was a variation on the theme of indirect rule that similarly defined systems of colonial governmentality in tropical Africa and apartheid South Africa (1996: 27). In the genealogy of these apparent connections, Mamdani traces the dynamics associated with the exercise of power of the homeland system as it overflowed into the streets of the

Figure 13.1
Men and women of Qora in the Eastern Cape march to Idutywa demanding an end to the abuse of women.

apartheid city, with, as we know, dire consequences for many. I wish to argue that the phrase 'the rural in the urban' does not merely call attention to the co-incidence of two otherwise discrete entities but to specific relations of power and subjection.

At the level of discourse (as opposed to say, sociology), the phrase 'the rural in the urban' recalls the concept of *heterotopias*, which 'links abstract spaces to concrete places in politically productive ways' (Deshpande 2000: 170). Measured against this formulation, constructions of the urban as operating exclusively in the empty homogenous time of capital are, in my view, hopelessly inadequate. The utopias forged in empty and homogenous time depend on tonalities of pastoralism, in which promises of salvation are exchanged for sub-jection.[2] In this chapter, I argue that such relations of exchange between salva-tion and subjection are products of deeper histories of colonialism, apartheid and (under-) development. If 'the rural in the urban' functions as a specific exemplar of *heterotopias*, it is because the phrase cuts through the empty homogenous time of capital to recall the relational sites within which specific forms of power are articulated.

I propose that we leave the city, if only temporarily, to explore the forms of pastoral power that are indexed by the topography of graves and memories of chiefs and kings in the rural Eastern Cape.[3] I turn to the discourses surrounding these graves to track the relation between the emergence of the tonalities of pastoral power and the rationalisation that attends to the rural. If pastoral power refers to the modes of subjection that rely on the promise of salvation (Foucault 1997: 67), the rationalisation of the rural implies an apparatus by which that subjection is achieved. As forms of rural governmentality, the coupling of pas-toral power and rationalisation find expression in the following bifurcations: mis-sionary discourses and native administration, segregationism and nationalist memory, apartheid and chieftaincy, tourist development and gender relations. These combinations have produced modes of subjection that arguably supple-ment urban governmentality by cutting through its presumed operation in empty homogenous time.

The problematic that organises this chapter arises from a visit to the graves of Hintsa and Sarhili, two nineteenth-century Xhosa kings in the former bantus-tan of the Transkei, in 2004. On 2 July, we encountered about 100 men and women of Qora marching to Idutywa bearing banners, inscribed on old ANC election posters, demanding an end to the abuse of women (Figure 13.1). First, the marchers wished the magistrate to return the body of a young woman who had allegedly been strangled to death by her partner in what was commonly seen as a case of femicide. Second, they demanded that her alleged tormentor be arrested. What interested us, as we expressed solidarity with the demands of the marchers from Qora, were the targets of this protest, singled out as the magistrate and the tormentor.

The encounter on the N2 national road that snakes through the Eastern Cape was given new meaning a few days later at Sarhili Primary School in

Figure 13.2
Nomathotho Njuqwana
stands alongside the
recently erected
memorial to Sarhilli.

Tsholora on the banks of the Mbhashe River. This was the site of the grave of
the nineteenth-century Xhosa king, Sarhili, whose reign spanned a considerable part of the 100 years of war that engulfed the Eastern Cape from the late
eighteenth to nineteenth centuries. Joe Savu, a councillor for the Mbhashe
municipality, and the local 'chief' and caretaker of the grave, Nomathotho
Njuqwana, guided us to the graves (Figure 13.2). In expressing our interest in
Sarhili's grave, we made it a point to distinguish ourselves from the development workers, ethnographers or representatives of NGOs who have become
increasingly familiar in these parts of South Africa and whose presence locals
negotiate with ease. Our purpose was to set to work on Mamdani's phrase
'the rural in the urban' by relating it to a strategy coined by Gayatri Spivak
which calls for 'learning to learn' from the subaltern (Mamdani 1996: 218;
Spivak 2000: 34). We understood at the outset that both Mamdani and Spivak
might be asking for a work of criticism that relinquished reliance on the
subjective presuppositions of ethnography and social history while seeking out
strategies to resist elite discourses.

Following the visit to the graves, the residents of Tsholora, many of whom
were women, took advantage of the presence of the local councillor to inquire
about the future development of the area. With the image of the Qora marchers
etched in our memory, we managed a question about the impossibility of thinking of development without a history of colonial and apartheid violence that
haunts the region. The response to the suggestion seemed to distinguish
between different historical sensibilities: '*our* sense of history', we were told, 'is
tied to culture and land'. This was qualified by a gendered statement about
history which served to elaborate upon a presumed difference between an urban
and rural historical sensibility.

> When men left to work on the mines and when children went to school we women
> took responsibility for the livestock and tilling the land. We became farmers, taking care
> of all the aspects of agriculture.
>
> (Tsholora interview 2004: the respondent asked that her name be withheld)

A concept of history founded on notions of culture and land, it seemed at the time, glossed over the rationalisation that attends to images of the rural. The difference between the rural and the urban implicit in this statement obscured the way the rural functions as a specific exercise of power. Thought of as an articulation of power, the rural may serve as a 'problematic fiction' that reveals the fragile character of the urban on the one hand, and allows us on the other to trace the forces that enable its emergence (Brown 2001: 100).

TOPOGRAPHIES OF A RURAL LANDSCAPE

David Bunn (2002: 57) has emphasised the centrality of graves in the history of the Eastern Cape by calling attention to their indexicality in realising the topography of the region. Graves, Bunn tells us, in respect of the nineteenth-century Eastern Cape frontier landscape, were indexical and therefore critical to the formation of a settler public sphere and the subjection of local Xhosa idioms of life and death to missionary and administrative ritual universes. In Bunn's essay, graves are indexical in that they enable readings of landscapes. He traverses the landscape of the nineteenth-century Eastern Cape, west of the Kei River, connecting graves to a colonial topography on the one hand and, on the other, relating these markers to the unfolding narrative of mortuary rituals of Xhosa and settlers respectively. Critical to the elaboration of this network of meaning, he narrates the stories of three graves of Xhosa chiefs roughly spanning the second half of the nineteenth century: Tyhali's, Namba's and Sandile's – three chiefs of the Rharhabe branch of the house of Phalo. I find Bunn's notion of indexicality productive and particularly useful for thinking about graves in relation to topography and landscape. His reappraisal of the importance of graves as markers also enables us to think of their function enabling the convergence of forms of rationalisation and the pastoral tonalities of power.

It is true that colonial topographies were products of rather violent affairs. The cartographic representations of the Eastern Cape, for example, were deeply implicated in the project of colonial expansion, especially after 1835 when the Xhosa paramountcy of Hintsa east of the Kei River was increasingly drawn into the tensions along the frontier. It is not surprising that the first sketch of the king, and also the topographical map of the scene of his killing in 1835, were produced by the surveyor general C.C. Michell. The surveying of the Eastern Cape was embroiled in other acts of violence. Two days after the killing of Hintsa, a member of the British entourage that had accompanied the king in a bid to retrieve cattle allegedly stolen from settlers and hidden near the Mbhashe River, was killed 'trying to add to his carefully constructed map of the country through which the troops had passed since the commencement of the war of 1834–35'. Major T.C. White, we are told by James Alexander of the Royal Geographic Society, was killed while conducting a survey, and in the process, his maps, equipment and intricate sketches also disappeared. As Alexander was to write, quoting the three troopers who had survived the attack:

> The major had placed [them] at different points of observation; and with the corporal beside him, and his surveying table before him, he was looking down a krantz, or precipice; when a dozen Kaffirs crept on him from the bush and long grass, threw an assegai from behind through his back, and ran up and finished their work. They also stabbed the corporal through the heart.
>
> (Alexander 1838: 172)

The bodies were discovered, we are told, stripped and bloody, and the double-barrelled guns, the major's gold chronometer, surveying instruments and map carried off. By 1848, the first comprehensive map of the 'Eastern Frontier of the Colony of the Cape of Good Hope (and part of Kafirland) from Algoa Bay to the Great Kei River' was issued by J. Arrowsmith (Schrire 1965: 7). Arrowsmith's map was compiled from manuscript surveys and sketches supplied by Michel before him. The spectre of violence was never far from his efforts to map the Eastern Cape. Michel's complicity in the advances made by colonial forces in the war of 1834–5 east of the Kei River, meant that these scenes of colonial violence would indelibly mark the cartography of those landscapes that extended beyond the purview of colonial officialdom. In the Eastern Cape, ideas of the rural emerge not only, I would argue, out of a specifically romantic or nostalgic imaginary, but also out of a sense of insecurity and violence.

That such cartographic undertakings were served by acts of violence perhaps explains why graves of Xhosa chiefs who had fallen in battle became devices for accessing the topography of the Eastern Cape. But what strikes me as critical in Bunn's reading of the interplay of graves and topographies is the way in which graves serve as sites from which to extract the pastoral tonalities of power and the ways in which they function as a source of subjection specific to what we have come to call 'the rural'. We might say that the rationalisation of the rural was not merely a product of instrumental reason but also the development of pastoral power.

In February 1864, for example, the Reverend Tiyo Soga called attention to the proximity of two graves which, he pointed out, were of great significance. 'Tyhali and Chalmers', he claimed, 'were buried together', that is in close proximity to each other (Williams 1983: 101).[4] But the circumstances of the utterance of these words were not entirely congenial. Soga tells us that when the missionaries arrived at the upper Thomas River (sic), Oba, the son of Tyhali, made his imposing and dignified appearance, accompanied by a considerable entourage on horseback. Oba looked at the visitors intently as if, according to Soga, 'seeking admiration'. But soon lightness descended on the meeting and there was an exchange of greetings and salutations. Then Mr Brownlee, the recently appointed commissioner to the Ngqika, rose before about 116 men, paused and spoke in Xhosa: 'What I have come to do, son of Tyhali, does not require many words, and yet it is a great thing' (Williams 1983: 100). The deed that did not require 'many words' was the introduction of the Rev. John Chalmers as the new missionary to the land where his father, William Chalmers, had been buried. Rev. John Chalmers, upon being introduced to those gathered and rising to speak, recalled days gone by, emphasising that he was joining the sons of Tyhali in mourning the death of a father 'both of whose dust was lying at the Tyhume they had now left'.

Soga made much of this 'concrete detail', perhaps recognising that 14 years earlier, the scene of Tyhali's grave had been the source of a violent confrontation between settlers and the chief's subjects. In 1850, soldiers residing at Woburn had plundered Tyhali's grave. The incident resulted in a response from those living on the banks of the Tyhume River and ended in a bitterly violent confrontation (Mostert 1992: 1028–30). The missionary J.F. Cumming recalled some of the reasons for the violence that broke out on Christmas morning 1850 in the following manner:

> Before concluding these notes, I may mention that the indiscretion of some of the Woburn settlers tended greatly to foment the vengeance of the Xhosa around them. When Tyhali, one of the most intelligent and most esteemed of the sons of Gaika (Ngqika) died, he was buried on the other side of the Chumie opposite Woburn. His grave was preserved by his people in their manner. They placed his assegai, his saddle and bridle, and whatever other furniture belonging to him which he greatly prized, along with his body. If there is one degree of dishonour in the estimate of the people more than another, it is that of desecrating the grave of their Chief. Some of the Woburn settlers, either not knowing or not caring what they did, went and dug up Tyhali's grave, and either looted these articles or scattered them about. It is said that when Tyhali's people heard of this, they muttered their threatenings deep and strong, and only waited for an opportunity to wreak their vengeance against all these military villages.
>
> (MSB 139, 6(430) 6(16), J.F. Cumming Papers, NLSA, Cape Town)

The visit by Soga and John Chalmers in 1864 aimed to make amends for the offence and conflict of 1850. The deaths of Tyhali and Rev. Chalmers, and no less their graves, once the scene of bitter struggle, now augmented the missionary ideals of conversion and civilisation. The graves were made to serve as points in the application of a missionary discourse and its attendant transformation of the rural into a recognisable Christian spirit. Soga was of course critical to elaborating and initiating this pastoral pact.

Brought into the fold of Christianity by the Rev. William Chalmers of the Glasgow Missionary Society and later educated at Lovedale Missionary Institution and the Glasgow Free Church Seminary, Soga was the consummate representative of a pastoral ethos. His ability to persuade Tyhali's subjects to accept the presence of the missionary was related to the complex way in which colonial administration and Christian beliefs overlapped in the administration of the frontier. Charles Brownlee, the Ngqika commissioner, not only authorised missionary activity in the lands of the Rharhabe chieftains but actively sought their conversion. It is not surprising that Brownlee was present at the opening of several mission stations west of the Kei River. The presence of Brownlee at the laying of the foundation-stone of the mission station at Emgwali some years earlier in 1861, enables us to gauge the effects of the convergence of missionary discourses and native administration. Brownlee may have been comforted to hear Soga say:

> I have a growing conviction in my mind – strengthened every day by observation – that we should introduce amongst our people whatever in any degree tends to give them new notions of civilization, and whatever tends to enlarge and enlighten their minds, provided it be done with simplicity, order and propriety.

> (Williams 1983: 87)

To treat missionary discourses as located in the tensions of empire, between liberal humanitarianism and conservatism, between metropole and colony, has become a widely acceptable proposition in contemporary African history. The resultant pluralisations of missionary histories that followed the work of Jean and John Comaroff (1991) have provided indispensable considerations of the implications of the way missionary discourses produced a normalisation of power. More recently, Derek Peterson has argued that missionary discourses provided texts for processes of translation as a popular activity that was 'a continual, and continuing strategy of political argumentation' (Peterson 2004: 9). Both attest to the complex and often provisional forms of subjection that flowed from missionary discourses. While we may have to attend to similar investigations in relation to missionary histories in the Eastern Cape, we might say that the convergence

Figure 13.3
View of the Mbhashe
River and site of Sarhili's
last Great Place.

between missionary discourses and native administration rested on the manner in which both produce the object of which they speak. That of which they both speak in the case of the Eastern Cape was the *native as a specifically rural subject*.

If this construction proved more successful west of the Kei River where the missionary presence was more pronounced, efforts to extend the logic of pastoral power to the region east of the Kei would have to confront the figure of the sovereign king. In 1865, after a three-day journey, Tiyo Soga and John Chalmers crossed the Kei River, to meet the son of Hintsa, King Sarhili, for discussions about the possibility of establishing a mission station among the Gcaleka at the king's request. After the devastating consequences of the 1856 prophecy of Nongqawuse, Sarhili, originally driven beyond the Mbhashe River, was given a tract of coastal land where he could settle with what Soga believed to be between 10,000 and 15,000 supporters (Figure 13.3). Comparing the successes, or indeed failures, of their evangelical quest, Soga noted that 'whilst darkness resting on the Gaika's is indeed deep, that brooding on the Gcaleka's is unrelieved by scarce ray of light' (Williams 1983: 110).

Sarhili, gathering from Soga's assessment, remained suspicious of the pastoral pact and at a meeting in October 1867 he inquired into the relations that those who converted to Christianity would have towards the chief and to the missionaries (Williams 1983: 128). Soga claimed that the response given to this question was purposefully framed to take account of Sarhili's concern about the loss of control over his subjects and land. Although Sarhili agreed to the terms for the establishment of a missionary station in his territories, he apparently used the occasion to express his concern:

> All missionaries who had come into his country introduced themselves in the same way; that what [Soga] had said had been said by others before, but that, as time went on, a break took place as regards the people and the land; that he gradually lost his influence over his people and his right over the land he had given them to settle on; that the people preferred another authority to that of the chief, and also took the land away with them.
>
> (Williams 1983: 128–9)

By specifically recording this concern in his correspondence, Soga may have been projecting his own fears about his posting to Sarhili's lands. Sarhili's recourse to the tropes of pastoral power was incongruent to its expression in the combination of missionary discourse and native administration. Perhaps, such judgement rested with the complicity of the Wesleyan missionaries in the killing of Sarhili's father, Hintsa, in 1835, leaving him understandably suspicious of the pastoral pact. The 'darkness' ascribed to the Gcaleka was a sign that the pastoral pact would have to await a moment of nationalist memory. Nationalism secured a renewed sense of pastoral power by constructing an image of a benevolent sovereign capable of reclaiming the pastoralism that had since been usurped by the combined efforts of missionaries and native administrators.

NATIONALIST RESPONSES AND THE EMERGENCE OF PASTORAL POWER

If the pastoral pact encountered an impasse in the figure of Sarhili, who eventually was overthrown through an act of war in 1877–8, then I would argue that the resurrection of the memory of Hintsa and Sarhili in the aftermath of the creation and consolidation of native reserves in 1913 and 1936, also extended the nationalist theme of pastoralism. The creation of native reserves and the intensification of land deprivation through the 1936 Native Land Amendment Act activated a return to the memory of the precolonial sovereign endowed with the spirit of resistance, world history and difference to colonial articulations of power.

The year 1936 was of course appropriate for another reason. It marked the 100th anniversary of the killing of Hintsa and the official commission of inquiry into his killing. The reincarnation of the precolonial past in nationalist narration coincided with emerging state discourses of segregation and the rise of a nascent mission-trained nationalist intelligentsia whose class mobility was being seriously thwarted.

S.E.K. Mqhayi, a foremost contributor to what Jeff Peires (1979) calls *Xhosa historiography*, opted for forms of representation that set out to revise colonial narrations of precolonial histories. Historical narration was itself an act of resistance especially in as far as it denied the forensic procedure by which the colonial archive organised such stories as the killing of Hintsa (see Lalu 2003). The killing of Hintsa, in the sixth colonial war of 1834–5, is shrouded in controversy. Gunned down in the dense thicket of the Nqabara River, it is unclear whether the British forces responsible for the shooting also mutilated and beheaded the dead king. In nationalist narration of the killing of Hintsa, however, the story has pivoted on the history of precolonial Xhosa chieftaincy, especially the Gcaleka branch of the house of Phalo.

On the occasion of the 100th anniversary of the killing of Hintsa, Mqhayi dedicated a lengthy poem titled *U-Mhlekazi uHintsa* in which the demand for a memorial is addressed:

> The days of The Grumbling of Nobutho have come;
> The Treader of the land till it becomes a floor.
> The Welcomer of different nations,
> The Home of different races,
>
> The Father of different homeless wanderers.
> Praise Hintsa, nations of the world!
> You British, why are you so silent?
> What is it, you Mfengu?
> Bomvana, I hope you are not forgetting,
> Even you Sotho of Qhudeni,
> Can you be so silent on Hintsa's day?
> When we are talking about his prime?
>
> ....
> [An address to the Ngwane]

Ross's son says you should build a Memorial.

I say Ross's son Bringer of Reform!

Leopard's Face was saying it himself, –

The white chief of Gcalekaland.

They said Mfengu and Xhosa unite!

And organise Hintsa's Memorial Service.

And organise a great ceremonial feast,

So that he should never be forgotten in Xhosaland,

So that his good name should remain forever,

Which is also inscribed in European books.

Peace, European gentlemen!

You are trying to incite us though we are old men,

Old Xhosa men who need to be cooled down.

Peace, nations, for mentioning you!

It's not spite but glorification.

Khawuta's son should have his own day, –

He should be acknowledged by the whole of Africa,

Because they have learned about the white man from him, –

The nations benefitted, he was blunted.

(Mqhayi 1937,[5] translated by Jeff Opland)

The chiding tone surely alludes to the exercise of control in the recording and writing of history. Thus, while Hintsa is featured in European books as a villain, we must assume Mqhayi calls for a remembrance based on the primacy of resistance and his judicial qualities as king. Hintsa's killing revealed the face of colonial domination and its civilising mission. Referring to Brownlee, the white chief of Gcalekaland, and his desire to ensnare the memory of Hintsa in an orchestrated unity between 'Xhosa and Mfengu' that secured colonial interests, Mqhayi deliberately makes the memory of Hintsa a site of reinventing the figure of Hintsa. A memorial cannot, it seems, contain the memory of Hintsa, especially the memory of his killing at the hands of British forces. In this way, Mqhayi makes Hintsa available for an anticolonial narrative that, I have argued elsewhere (Lalu 2003), seeks to take on colonialism on the stage of world history – that is on the very ground that colonialism had staked out for itself. Hintsa became the very incarnation of the struggle against colonial domination and its legacies.

There is more to Mqhayi's narrative. In his commemorative poem, the universality of the question of sovereignty enables a convergence of two discrepant discourses of power – one anticolonial and the other judicial. The effects of casting Hintsa in the role of sovereign echoes Mqhayi's earlier text, *Ityala Lamawele,* which cast the king in a juridical role in the trial of the twins (1931) over birthrights. In the preface to that text, Mqhayi explains his attempt to prove that Xhosa society was founded on judicial concepts not too dissimilar to that which British settlers proclaimed as the sign of their difference.

Mqhayi was clearly responding to the colonial caricature of the Xhosa king as a despot.

In many ways, the nationalist reinscription of Hintsa that flowed from the texts of Mqhayi, and later John Henderson Soga (1931) and the artist George Pemba, provided a foundational fiction for subsequent elaborations of the position of the king in nationalist narration, especially his characterisation as a diplomat and as a just and 'democratic' king. In Partha Chatterjee's (1993) formulation, which we would do well to bear in mind, nationalist discourse operates at both the level of the problematic and the thematic.

It is possible to discern the consequences of this reinscription in what became of Sarhili, Hintsa's son, in which the sovereign is both the sign of a problematic and conjoins the thematic in nationalist narration. Like the circumstances surrounding the killing of Hintsa in 1835, the memory of Sarhili is equally caught up in the intricacies of colonial history. One such instance relates to Sarhili's response to the prophecies of Nongqawuse, a young *intombi yabafana* (young woman of marriageable age), in the so-called cattle-killing episode of 1856 (Bradford 1996: 361). Nongqawuse, it is claimed, received an instruction to kill all cattle and burn all grain while residing at the Gxarha River with her uncle Mhlakaza. The prophecy carried hope that the dead would arise, a promise that encouraged Sarhili to see apparitions of his father as he stood on the banks of the Gxarha River, looking out over the ocean (Peires 1989: 87).

While historians like Peires have called attention to Sarhili's critical part in winning support for the prophecies, writers like S.E.K. Mqhayi held Nongqawuse and British colonial officials almost entirely responsible for destruction wrought by the cattle-killing prophecies. Mqhayi represented Nongqawuse as a dupe of British missionaries and colonial officials who, in conjunction with her uncle Mhlakaza, brought the Xhosa nation to its knees by requiring the killing of cattle stocks and the destruction of crops in Xhosaland.

If such statements sought to share some of the blame for the catastrophic events of 1856, H.I.E. Dhlomo, who wrote a play called *The Girl Who Killed to Save* in 1935, reinstated Nongqawuse as critical agent in the destiny of the Xhosa polity. Again the segregationist environment of 1935 was not inconsequential when Dhlomo wrote:

> Nongqawuse may reduce at a sweep what legislation and missionary endeavour have so far failed to fight against – the power and influence of the witchdoctor, the tyranny of custom and tradition, the authority of the chief, the isolation of the Xhosa nation … Nongqawuse will give the AmaXhosa that dependence which spells progress.
>
> (Dhlomo cited in Feinberg 1996: 60)

While Dhlomo positions Sarhili as secondary to the power wielded by Nongqawuse in the days of the prophecy, other representations of the king and prophetess emphasised equality. A painting by George Pemba completed in 1989, drawn from an earlier work based on Dhlomo's play, presents her not as a 'dupe but as an earnest and dignified young woman who allows her prophecy to be presented to the chief (Sarhili), unaware of the dire consequences which will follow' (Dhlomo cited in Feinberg 1996: 60). Important for our purposes is the way a gendered subaltern subject complicates the representation of the king. Sarhili's museumised entry, however, and his ambiguous memory in nationalist history, contrasts strongly to the gendered readings that are enabled by his grave. I will return to this point later.

At the Castle of Good Hope in Cape Town, the portrait of Sarhili by Frederick I'Ons, showing a dejected and defeated king, is accompanied by a text, drawn from nationalist narration, that recalls the redeeming and benevolent qualities of a king who was capable of surrendering to the will of his people:

> Chief Sarhili's entire life was affected by the inhumane death of his father, yet he protected and treated with consideration any European in need of his help at the mercy of his people. C.H. Malan, a British Officer (*sic*), later wrote: 'Sarhili did not attack or threaten the British government, he did not injure a white man. In personal character he is in every sense a noble man and it has been his most earnest endeavour for the last twenty years to keep on good terms with the English nation.'
>
> (Castle of Good Hope, Text Panel 41, October 2002)

In that very same exhibit, however, the memory of Sarhili shifts to the devastating outcomes of his rule:

> The 1857 Eastern Cape disaster [referring to the cattle-killing episode] should be told for its tragedy and its meaning. Therefore, the chief's support for the Nongqawuse cattle killing episode led him to admit responsibility for the suffering of his people. Thus he said: 'I was a great chief, being as I am the son of Chief Hintsa who left me rich in cattle and ordering my people to do the same, and I shall be left alone as my people must scatter in search of food; thus I am no longer a chief. It is all my fault; I have no one to blame but myself.' Such words reveal the obligation of trust chiefs had towards their people.
>
> (Castle of Good Hope, Text Panel 41, October 2002)

We might say that the memory of kings is furtively deposited in the designs of the segregationist state. Recalling the precolonial kings as juridical, equivalent to modes of colonial governmentality, I wish to argue, produced little difference in the story of colonisation and its aftermath except to reaffirm the convergence of subjection and the rationalisation of the rural. In the writings of S.E.K. Mqhayi or the museumised representations of colonial violence, the aim was to portray the sovereign in a manner that would ensure that he is counted on the stage of world history. With this recasting of the sovereign, nationalism extends the pastoral pact that began with missionary discourse and native administration.

GRAVE MARKERS: FROM APARTHEID TO DEVELOPMENT

Roger Southall and Zosa De Sas (2003) conclude that the erosion of chiefly authority has continued in post-apartheid South Africa as the chiefs are contained and fail to establish legitimacy from below. The victory, it seems, is premature. The memories of kings and chiefs that punctuate new development discourses have seen the absorption of the very pastoral power that once produced the subaltern subject through discourses of culture and land. The historical premise of development discourse, I suspect, cannot but replicate the predicament in which the subaltern will be returned again and again to the exercise of pastoral power.

Pastoral power, with its notions of salvation, perhaps proves effective only when it enters a specifically biopolitical paradigm, where life and its mechanisms are brought within the reach of a calculus of the exercise of power. Southall and De Sas (2003) argue that the ninth frontier war – which incidentally was the final onslaught against Sarhili's power – 'saw the determination of the British to break the power of the chiefs by establishing a system of direct, magisterial rule, thereby securing peace and "civilization"'. The Transkei, they argue, was divided into 27 districts, each headed by a white magistrate who served as both judicial and administrative officer responsible for collecting taxes and reporting to the chief magistrate in Umtata. Increasingly the headmen became functionaries of the Native Affairs Department and later, under apartheid's homeland system, the chiefs became wedged to bureaucratic machinery and with time, a repressive state apparatus for their sustenance. The sense of containment led Ezekiel Mphahlele to similarly bemoan the 'pressurised talk about Bantustans (homelands)' which established 'fences of barbed wire across the country, across allegiances, across the landscape of African nationalism' (1974: 52). Apartheid represented the most intense discourse in the rationalisation of the rural.

In the interstitial space between a statist programme of containment and the emergence of chieftaincy as a bureaucratic caste, the markers of the effects of colonial violence assume a particular significance. While the apartheid state sought to acknowledge and therefore contain the institution of chieftaincy as a

Figure 13.4
Tsholora – site of the
Xhosa Great Place on the
Mbhashe River.

source of customary law, chiefs found a source of legitimacy in the outlines of cultural history. In 1985, the head of the Xhosa royal house, Xoliliswe Sigcawu, unveiled tombstones at the graves of the fallen Xhosa kings, Hintsa, his son and grandson, Sarhili and Sigcawu. The tribute in the form of a headstone at Hintsa's grave at the site where he was shot by British forces in May 1835, was similarly replicated for Sarhili's and Sigcawu's graves in an area called Tsholora on the Wild Coast (Figure 13.4). The unveiling of the tombstones to the Gcaleka fallen, east of the Kei, coincided with the troubles that beset the Transkei independent state around 1985. West of the Kei, the inauguration of the Ciskei homeland under the leadership of Lennox Sebe was marked by the unveiling of a monument, Thaba kaNdoda, after the alleged retrieval and relocation of the remains of the Ngqika chief, Maqoma, from Robben Island. Under apartheid, we might say that the rural was rationalised through the figure of the sovereign that was once revised to contest the segregationist measures of the land acts in 1913 and 1936.

Journeying to the graves of Hintsa and Sarhili in July 2004, we were to learn of the extent to which the graves of chiefs and kings are critical to current local development initiatives. Their importance can be gleaned from a report of the Amathole District Municipality's announcement of its budget for 2004. The Local Economic Development and Environmental Cluster Plans to diversify the district's tourism initiatives by developing, among others, the Maqoma Loop in Tyhume and the Kat River Valley, the Phalo Route in the Mnquma and Mbhashe areas, and the Sandile Route, which covers areas in Nkonkobe, Amahlathi and Buffalo City (Amathole District Municipality insert, *Daily Dispatch* 2004: 7). The sites and the plans for their development were featured in a television documentary prepared by the local state in the Eastern Cape. The overall plan highlights the further allocation of funds to upgrade the graves of Phalo, Hintsa and Ngqika (Amathole District Municipality insert, *Daily Dispatch* 2004: 7). As in 1985, many of the graves that have been earmarked for upgrading and incorporation in tourism development are associated with a patrilineal genealogy on the one hand, and on the other, with the violent history of nineteenth-century colonialism. Inserted into a roadmap of the Eastern Cape, the proposals of the Amathole District Municipality highlight the troubling question of the specific histories to which they give rise. Most of the graves are markers of very specific instances in the 100 years of war in the nineteenth century, largely provoked by British colonists in what the tourist signposts around Grahamstown unashamedly announce as 'Frontier Country'.

While Phalo's grave marks the foundations of the Rharhabe and Gcaleka houses, roughly along the contours that later came to define the homelands of the Ciskei and Transkei under apartheid, the graves of Ngqika and Hintsa recall the heady days of colonial conquest. So too do the graves of Ndlambe, Sandile, Sarhili and Sigcawu. As their respective graves are incorporated into a tourist roadmap, the promise, as it were, holds forth an unproblematised paternity as a dominant construction and understanding of history. At the same time, the graves are significant markers of the history of colonialism and critical catalysts in recalling the hardships that were, and continue to be, endured in a region which is often glibly passed over by development experts as one of the poorest provinces in the country. As if to seal that fate, the British government offered an apology for 'colonial injustices committed against the Xhosas', but while it would not give reparations for past injustices, it would offer developmental assistance to the Eastern Cape as a whole (*Cape Argus* 2001).

The discussion at Sarhili Primary School that followed our visit to the grave of Sarhili would throw the genealogy of the pastoral pact and its relation to development discourses into sharp relief. As the meeting at the school unfolded, and as increasing numbers of women joined in the discussion, it soon became clear that subaltern sentiment was carved in the interstices of development discourses and histories of colonialism and apartheid – unsettling each, we might add. The chief produced a history of male descendants to designate its significance, almost expecting his visitors to be interested in the patrimony that defines the area.

Sarhili was buried at the gate of his kraal, we were told. He was buried at the place where he had his homestead. Before his death, the land was defined by the homestead and two dams for cattle and cows. But it was also marked by the homestead of Dalasile who is buried in the area. Descendants of Dalasile, Gudlulwandle, Ndabangaye, Sibethe and several other notables were also buried in the vicinity. While Sarhili's sons, Gwebinkumbi and Zwelidumile, were born and initiated in Tsholora, they nevertheless moved to Nqadu, the current great place near Willowvale. It was Dalasile's descendants who were left to look after the site, tending to the graves of the late king, who had died in 1893, and ensuring that the royal possession was regarded as such (Njuqwana interview 2004).

The graves opened up the space of reclaiming a wounded and fractured paternity, only to falter on account of the history of the effects of colonial violence on women. Sarhili's grave is integrally tied, as stated already, to the narrative of the destruction of an independent Xhosa kingdom and to that fateful event called the cattle-killing of 1856, in which the king ordered the wholesale destruction of cattle and grain following the prophecies of the young Nongqawuse. Whether thought of in terms of a colonial genocide or as a national suicide, Sarhili's role alongside others as a catalyst in the unfolding events is hard to deny. The current overseer of the grave described the memory of the deceased king in a sympathetic light. 'Sarhili was not a bad man ... there is no blame towards him' (Njuqwana interview 2004). Any reference to Nongqawuse was dismissed as myth or as 'stories' that could not be verified. Perhaps this was the silent expression of the war between the believers and unbelievers that Zakes Mda (2000) recalls in his fictional account of contemporary Qolorha, a place not too far south from Tsholora.

The refusals to speak about the cattle-killing and destruction of crops in 1856 are perhaps symptomatic of the way the graves of ancestors, the markers of history, have been aligned with the demands of tourism development. During the meeting, every suggestion to work at the point at which the two epistemes – history and development – did not lend themselves to each other, seemed futile. It seemed that the history of development had recast the history of colonialism and apartheid as banal and inconsequential. In a tactical shift that had been decided by our earlier encounter with the marchers to Idutywa, I asked about the graves of women. Where was the grave of Nomkhafulo, Sarhili's daughter, who had been crippled by her abusive husband Ngangelizwe, the Thembu king? By inviting her back to his homestead, Jeff Peires (2003: 352) tells us that the ageing Sarhili, in launching an attack on the Thembu Great Place, invited the intervention of the Cape Colony and the compensation of 40 head of cattle for the abuse. Did the graves of women have any bearing on the history of colonialism, on the understanding of history, or development, among those who today live on the fringes of Dwesa-Cwebe, setting of the graves of Hintsa and Sarhili?

It was at this point that the comment about 'our concept of history [as] tied to culture and land' surfaced. Initially, I read this comment about women becoming farmers as a tacit acceptance of the conflation of history and development. The women of Tsholora who attended the meeting at the school seemed to have been persuaded that development would be the source of their salvation and that the history surrounding the graves of chiefs and kings was a means to this end. Perhaps, with this apparent surrender to an elite discourse, they seemed to have accepted the pastoral pact that was bolstered by the demand for tourist development.

A notion of history bound to land and culture recalled the convergence of the pastoral tonalities of power and the processes by which the rural is rationalised. Yet, the marchers of Qora placed this pastoral pact in jeopardy, unsettling its cohesion and also the production of subjectivity authorised by its power. This was not merely a protest restricted to the demand to end the abuse of women but also one that targeted the modes of power that produced this violence in the first place.

RETURNING TO THE CITY

In this chapter I have argued that the rural is a silent referent in the discourse of the urban. What the discourse of the urban represses is the history of the modes of power that have come to define the rural as such. The process of discernment of gendered subjectivity that accompanies this convergence may help us to explain the overwhelming marginality of women in discourses of the city. The notion of the rural in the urban leads us to question the modalities of power by which the post-apartheid city is being reimagined.

We may do well to consider the phrase 'rural in the urban' in terms of an analogous, but critical, formulation emanating from Giorgio Agamben's resolutely critical insight that 'today it is not the city but rather the camp that is the fundamental biopolitical paradigm' (2000: 181). This, he argues, throws a sinister light on the models by which social sciences, sociology, urban studies and architecture today are trying to conceive and organise the public spaces of the world's cities without any clear awareness that at their very centre lies the same bare life (even if it has been transformed and rendered more human) that defined the biopolitics of the great totalitarian states of the twentieth century.

If, as Mahmood Mamdani (1996) has argued, the homeland system of indirect rule produced a bifurcation between citizen and subject, we might say that a naturalised division of labour between chiefs and commoners in recollections of the precolonial past helped to engender that distinction. In other words, as the graves of Hintsa and Sarhili recall the violence of colonial domination they also inadvertently register the experience of subalternity as subjects of pastoral power, no less of the gendered experience of colonial and apartheid subjection. It is here, in the confluence of the history of colonial violence and the emergent pressures of development discourse, that the graves of kings lend themselves to a process of learning to learn from subalternity. I believe that such a task entails learning to anticipate the demise of developmental discourses and to institute subaltern gesture in history as constitutive of a new geography that displaces the sacred spatial strategies and techniques of urban governmentality that have thus far defined the modern nation.[6]

POSTSCRIPT: THE RURAL IN THE URBAN OR THE RETURN OF THE REPRESSED

On 30 March 2000 the *Cape Times*, Cape Town's morning newspaper, carried an image of a mock Xhosa village on the slopes of Table Mountain under the heading, 'The Village People'. Its caption read:

> **XHOSA WAY OF LIFE:** 'An African village sprung up on the mountain slopes of Table Mountain yesterday bringing traffic on the M3 to a virtual standstill. Groote Schuur Estate was the scene of an Italian commercial shoot for an Italian Internet company, Kataweb. The company engaged about 60 Khayelitsha artists to display the Xhosa way of life in a traditional village. Wide-eyed motorists were amused, and perhaps relieved, to hear that the invasion was only temporary.'

The photograph is blatantly stereotypical in its characterisation of the modernity of what it calls 'an African village'. But more importantly, between the internet and the wide-eyed motorists, the traffic in notions of culture and land reveals another level of complicity by which the rural is being rationalised.

REFERENCES

Agamben, G. (2000) *Means without End: Notes on Politics*, trans. V. Binetti and C. Cesarino, Minneapolis: University of Minnesota Press.

Alexander, J.E. (1838) *A Narrative of a Voyage of Observation Among the Colonies of Western Africa ... and a Campaign in Kafirland*, London: Henry Colburn Publishers.

Bradford, H. (1996) 'Women, Gender and Colonialism: Rethinking the History of the British

Cape Colony and Its Frontier Zone, *c.*1860–1870', *Journal of African History* 37 (3): 351–70.

Brown, W. (2001) *Politics out of History*, Princeton, NJ: Princeton University Press.

Bunn, D. (2002) 'The Sleep of the Brave', in P. Landau and D. Kaspin (eds) *Images of Empire: Visuality in Colonial and Postcolonial Africa*, Berkeley: University of California Press.

Comaroff, J. and Comaroff, J. (1991) *Of Revelation and Revolution: Christianity, Colonialism and Consciousness in South Africa*, Chicago, IL: Chicago University Press.

Deshpande, S. (2000) 'Hegemonic Spatial Strategies: The Nation-space and Hindu Communalism in Twentieth-century India', in P. Chatterjee and P. Jeganathan (eds) *Subaltern Studies XI: Community, Gender and Violence*, New York: Columbia University Press.

Feinberg, B. (1996) *George Mnyaluza Pemba Retrospective Exhibition Catalogue*, Cape Town: South African National Gallery and Mayibuye Centre, University of the Western Cape.

Ferguson, J. (1999) *Expectations of Modernity*, Berkeley: University of California Press.

Foucault, M. (1972) *The Archeology of Knowledge*, trans. A.M. Sheridan Smith, New York: Pantheon Books.

—— (1997) 'Security, Territory, and Population' in P. Rabinow (ed.) *Ethics: Subjectivity and Truth: The Essential Works of Michel Foucault, 1954–1984*, New York: New Press.

Lalu, P. (2000) 'The Grammar of Domination and the Subjection of Agency: Colonial Texts and Modes of Evidence', *History and Theory* 39: 45–68.

—— (2003) 'In the Event of History', unpublished PhD thesis, University of Minnesota.

Mamdani, M. (1996) *Citizen and Subject*, Princeton, NJ: Princeton University Press.

Mda, Z. (2000) *The Heart of Redness*, Oxford: Oxford University Press.

Molema, S.M. (1963) *The Bantu: Past and Present*, Johannesburg: Struik Publishers.

Mostert, N. (1992) *Frontiers: The Epic of South Africa's Creation and the Tragedy of the Xhosa People*, New York: Alfred Knopf.

Mphahlele, E. (1974) *The African Image*, London: Faber and Faber.

Mqhayi, S.E.K. (1937) *U-mhlekazi u-Hintsa*, Alice: Lovedale Press.

Peires, J (1979) 'The Lovedale Press: Literature for the Bantu Revisited', in *History in Africa*, vol. 6.

—— (1989) *The Dead Will Arise*, Johannesburg: Ravan Press.

Peterson, D. (2004) *Creative Writing*, Portsmouth: Heinemann.

SAPA. (2001) 'We're Sorry, Brits Tell Xhosas, but That's All', *Cape Argus*, 19 September.

Schrire, D. (1965) *The Cape of Good Hope: 1782–1842, From De la Rochette to Arrowsmith*, London: Map Collectors Circle.

Southall, R. and De Sas, Z. (2003) 'Containing the Chiefs: The ANC and Traditional Leaders in the Eastern Cape', *The Eastern Cape Historical Legacies and New Challenges Conference*, 27–30 August.

Spivak, G.C. (2000) 'From Haverstock Hill Flat to U.S. Classroom, What's Left of Theory?' in J. Butler, J. Guillory and K. Thomas (eds) *What's Left of Theory: New Work on the Politics of Literary Theory*, New York and London: Routledge.

Williams, D. (ed.) (1983) *The Journal and Selected Writings of the Reverend Tiyo Soga*, Grahamstown: A.A. Balkema.

ADDITIONAL SOURCES

Amathole District Municipality insert, *Daily Dispatch*, Monday 5 July, 2004: 7.

Castle of Good Hope, Text Panel 41, October 2002.

Interview with Nomathotho Njuqwana, Sarhili Primary School, Tsholora, 3 July 2004.

Interview with members of Tsholora community, Sarhili Primary School, Tsholora, 3 July 2004. (The respondent asked that her name be withheld.)

MSB 139, 6(430) 6(16), J.F. Cumming Papers, National Library of South Africa, Cape Town.

Chapter 14: The World Below

Post-apartheid Urban Imaginaries and the Bones of the Prestwich Street Dead

Nick Shepherd and Christian Ernsten

one of the characteristic features of a metropolis is an *underneath* … beneath the visible landscape and the surface metropolis, its objects and its social relations, are concealed or embedded other orders of visibility, other scripts that are not reducible to the built form, the house façade, or simply the street experience of the metaphorical figure of the *flaneur*.

(Mbembe and Nuttall 2004: 363–4)

When Achille Mbembe and Sarah Nuttall call on scholars working in the tradition of urban studies in South Africa to consider the 'underneath world' of the city as a route to fresh insights and a means of evading the limited purview of the tradition, they have in mind the city of Johannesburg and the underneath world of the mines. The shafts and tunnels, the army of labour that disappears into the earth and is disgorged at shift's end, constitute a world within a world, a world beneath, but also a foundational world, a reminder of the reality of sweat and toil. If capital achieves its surface apotheosis in the airy fantasy of skyscrapers and shopping malls, then its grounding reality (its deeper reality) remains the sweated labour of the workers on the darkened stopes. It is in this context that they propose the migrant worker as the exemplary figure of African urbanism and modernity. The vortex of the mines draws in workers from across the subcontinent, and returns them – if it returns them – broken in body and spirit or newly powerful, freighted with new goods and ideas; at any rate transformed, and in turn transforming. The pulse of the mines becomes the pulse of history itself. Colonialism, apartheid, the wars of dispossession and the wars of capital and labour: all responding to the imperatives and opportunities of the world below.

In this chapter we respond to the notion of the world below, as a heuristic device and as an opportunity to think through the city in new ways, but in a different context. We look at a series of events in Cape Town concerned with the contested exhumation of an early colonial burial site. Like all cities of any time depth, Cape Town exists as a palimpsest, a layering of successive horizons and events. To dig down from the surface is to encounter wall footings, occupation floors, the debris of past societies, the remains of the dead themselves. This is the world underneath, not as the working world of the mine, but as the stratified world of the archaeologist. And it is a conception of the city not as the single (visible) horizon of the strolling *flaneur*, but rather in terms of notions of depth, dimensionality, succession. It remains only to add that the temporal relation between these different layers is unstable, is capable of shock and surprise. Sudden eruptions, surfacings, unexpected returns: these are among the processes that characterise life in post-apartheid society, whether through the institutionalised resurfacings of the Truth and Reconciliation Commission, or through more impromptu resurfacings like the Prestwich Street exhumations. In all cases they are accompanied by the release of energies, by reminders of unfinished business and unrequited yearnings. In a recent work, Svetlana Boym (2001: 77) writes: 'In cities in transition the porosity is particularly visible; it turns the whole city into an experimental art exhibit, a place of continuous improvisations.' Porosity and improvisation, 'other scripts' and 'other orders of visibility': it is with these notions in mind that we turn to the case of the Prestwich Street dead.

TIME-LINE PRESTWICH STREET

Green Point is a part of Cape Town strategically located between the central business district and the new Victoria and Alfred Waterfront development at Cape Town's harbour. For much of the seventeenth and eighteenth centuries it lay outside the formal boundaries of the settlement, a marginal zone which was the site of the gallows and place of torture, situated on a prominent sand dune. It was also the site of a number of graveyards, including the graveyards of the Dutch Reformed Church and the military, and of numerous undocumented, informal burials. Those buried outside the official burial grounds would have made up a cross-section of the underclasses of colonial Cape Town: slaves, freeblacks, artisans, fishermen, sailors, maids, washerwomen and their children, as well as executed criminals, suicides, paupers and unidentified victims of shipwrecks (Hart 2003). In the 1820s, Green Point was subdivided and sold as real estate, in time becoming part of the densely built urban core. In the late 1960s and early 1970s black and coloured residents of Green Point were forcibly removed, and relocated to the bleak townships of the Cape Flats, a series of events which has entered popular imagination via the fate of the residents of District Six, on the other side of the city. Green Point is currently undergoing a process of rapid gentrification, driven by escalating property prices. For many former residents, this means that, even as the political space has opened up in which they might reacquire property in the city centre, so they face new forms of economic exclusion.

In mid-May 2003, in the course of construction activities at a city block in Green Point bordered by Prestwich Street, human bones were discovered. The developer, Ari Estathiou of Styleprops Ltd, notified the South African Heritage

Resources Agency in accordance with the newly passed National Heritage Resources Act (Act No. 25 of 1999), and construction was halted. Also in terms of the Act, the developer appointed the Archaeology Contracts Office (ACO), a University of Cape Town-affiliated contract archaeology unit, to perform the archaeological investigation. The ACO applied for and was issued a permit by SAHRA for a 'rescue exhumation of human remains' (SAHRA 2003e). The Act provides for a 60-day notification period, and for a public consultation process. Antonia Malan, a UCT-based historical archaeologist, was contracted by the ACO to run the public consultation process, which she did in the name of the Cultural Sites and Resources Forum (CSRF), an advocacy organisation with a track record of involvement in heritage issues. The South African Heritage Resources Agency is the national statutory body in charge of the protection and management of heritage resources in South Africa, and replaces the apartheid-era National Monuments Council.

On 11 June, exhumation of the bodies began. Seven weeks later, on 29 July, a public meeting was held at St Stephen's Church in central Cape Town. At this point the remains of approximately 500 individuals had been exhumed. Most bodies were shallowly buried without grave markers or coffins. Earlier burials were intercut by later ones. The site was fenced with wire-link fencing and was open to public view. Estimates of the total number of bodies stood at 1,000 (up from an initial estimate of 200) on the 1,200-square-metre site. In the meantime, a Special Focus Reference Group (SFRG) had been set up, consisting mainly of UCT-based archaeologists and human biologists. Malan and the SFRG framed the agenda for the public meeting in terms of consultations regarding the relocation of the bodies and the memorialisation of the site.

The public response was angry. The minutes of the first public meeting record '[a] general feeling of dissatisfaction, disquiet and disrespect' (Malan 2003). Questions were asked as to why the demolition permit had been approved without the requirement of an archaeological survey, why the exhumations had continued through the 60-day notification period, and why the first public meeting had come so late in the process. Opposition to the exhumations came from several quarters: community leaders, many of whom had been active in the struggle against apartheid; Christian and Muslim spiritual leaders; academics from the historically black University of the Western Cape; heritage-sector NGOs; and Khoisan representatives.

The minutes also record comments by a number of unnamed individuals:

Woman at back: On what basis does SAHRA decide on exhumation? Issues of African morality and African rights ....

Man in green shirt: Developer contacted SAHRA and did marketing strategy for this evening. I don't buy these ideas .... Archaeologists can go elsewhere to dig ....

Rob of the Haven Shelter (a night shelter for homeless people): Many questions come from black people who hang around the site. Why are white people, and white women, scratching in our bones? This is sacrilege ....

> *Zenzile Khoisan:* These archaeologists, all they want to do is to dust off the bones and check them out with their scientific tests and to put them in the cupboard! (*Storming out of the hall, he shouted*): Stop robbing graves! Stop robbing graves!
>
> (Malan 2003: 4, 5, 6)

On 1 August 2003, SAHRA announced an 'interim cessation' of archaeological activity on the site until 18 August, to allow for a wider process of public consultation. This was later extended to 31 August. On 16 August, the CSRF convened a second public meeting. It also collected submissions by telephone, email and fax as part of its mandate of public consultation. Just over 100 submissions were collected. Mavis Smallberg from Robben Island Museum said

> my strong suggestion is to cover up the graves .... Apart [from] the recently renamed Slave Lodge, there is no other public space that respectfully marks or memorialises the presence of slaves and the poor in Cape Town society .... Only scientists are going to benefit from picking over these bones – of what purpose and use is it to the various communities to which the dead belong to know what they ate 150 years ago or where they came from?'
>
> (Smallberg 2003)

Imam Davids wrote on behalf of the Retreat Muslim Forum to say '[we] view the work and approach of the CSRF, based at UCT, with dismay ....' (Davids 2003).

On the other side, there was a sharp reaction against those who had been critical of the process, and against the growing anti-exhumation lobby. A comment by the UCT-based human biologist Alan Morris, is logged as follows:

> Members of public/prominent academics (especially UWC) suggested development stop and site is made into memorial. They have totally misjudged the reason for having a public process. NOT opportunity to control development of the city, but IS opportunity to join process of memorialisation ... don't let pseudo-politicians benefit at [our expense].
>
> (Malan 2003: 4)

The developer submitted a report to the CSRF, via Project Facilitator André van der Merwe, 'to provide the developmental perspective'. Many of the luxury apartments that comprised the residential development had been presold. At the time construction began, R21-million worth of sales contracts had been concluded, and were at risk due to the delay. As well as carrying the costs of the delay, the developer was also paying for the archaeological work and the public consultation process. The report expressed the hope for 'a sensible solution' (Van der Merwe 2003: 1).

On 9 August, the synod of the Cape Town diocese of the Anglican church, under the leadership of Archbishop Njongonkulu Ndungane, the successor to Desmond Tutu, unanimously passed a resolution condemning the exhumations and calling for '[the] appropriate institutions and organisations to be guided by African values and customs with regard to exhumations, burials and cemeteries', and for '[our] government, through its heritage agency ... to maintain the integrity of the site as that of a cemetery' (Wheeder 2003).

On 29 August, SAHRA convened a third public meeting at St Andrew's Church in Green Point 'to wind up the public participation process' (SAHRA 2003b). The verbatim transcript of the meeting records a number of comments from the floor. An unnamed respondent said:

> There is this kind of sense that it is a *fait accompli*. There were 60 days. The 60 days are over, now it's will the developer be kind enough to us. Now to me this is not about the developer. This is about those people lying there and the people that were part, historically, of that community ... [the interests of the developer] must be of secondary importance. The same with the archaeologists as well ... they have a social responsibility first before they have a responsibility towards the developer.
>
> (SAHRA 2003b: 15–16)

Another respondent said:

> there are multiple implications for this burial ground and its naked openness in the centre of the city ... in this city there's never been a willingness to take up [the issue of genocide and the] destruction of human communities that were brought from across the globe .... This is an opportunity to get to the bottom of that and time means different things to different people, institutions, stakeholders. Time for the dead – we need to consider what that means.
>
> (SAHRA 2003b: 17–18)

Michael Wheeder, who was later to play a central role in the Hands Off Prestwich Street Ad Hoc Committee, said:

> Many of us of slave descent cannot say 'here's my birth certificate'. We are part of the great unwashed of Cape Town .... The black people, we rush into town on the taxis and we need to rush out of town. At a time many decades ago we lived and loved and laboured here. Nothing [reminds us of that history] ... and so leave [the site] as a memorial to Mr. Gonzalez that lived there, Mrs. de Smidt that lived there. The poor of the area – the fishermen, the domestic workers, the people that swept the streets here. Memorialise that. Leave the bones there .... That is a site they have owned for the first time in their lives *het hulle stukkie grond* (they have a little piece of ground). Leave them in that ground. Why find now in the gentility of this new dispensation a place which they have no connection with?
>
> (SAHRA 2003b: 18–19)

Mongezi Guma, one of the facilitators of the meeting, said in his closing remarks: 'How do we deal with the intangibles of people's lives that were wasted? ... [This is not just about] an individual or family. It is not just about that. It is about people who got thrown away literally .... I'm trying to move SAHRA away from simply a legalistic decision' (SAHRA 2003b: 20–1).

On 1 September, despite a clear weight of opinion at the third public meeting opposed to the exhumations, Pumla Madiba, the CEO of SAHRA, announced a resumption of archaeological work at the site. In a statement to the press, she said that '[out] of respect the skeletons will be moved .... Many of the people who objected were highly emotional and did not give real reasons why the skeletons should not be relocated (*sic*)' (Kassiem 2003: 1). The period leading up to the announcement saw a growing anxiety on the part of SAHRA over the cost of expropriation, and the possibility of legal action on the part of the developer. A leaked internal memo to SAHRA's Archaeology, Palaeontology, Meteorite and Heritage Object Committee (the permit-issuing committee in this case) expresses the concern that, should the site be conserved as a heritage site, it would have 'disastrous consequences for the developer who will presumably appeal against the decision and may instigate litigation against SAHRA and the city'. The committee is informed that it is 'imperative that a responsible decision be made by SAHRA and the city … The matter is urgent, as the apartments in the development have been pre-sold and every delay means that the expenses are increasing' (PPPC 2003).

On 4 September, the Hands Off Prestwich Street Ad Hoc Committee (HOC) was launched. At this point opposition to the exhumations shifted outside the officially mandated process of public consultation, to civil society and the politics of mass action. On 12 September, the Hands Off Committee lodged an appeal with SAHRA calling for a halt to the exhumations and 'a full and extended process of community consultation' (HOC 2003). The appeal document notes that '[for] a large section of Cape Town's community, whose existence and dignity has for so long been denied, the discovery and continued preservation of the Prestwich Street burial ground can symbolically restore their memory and identity'. It continues: '[the] needs of archaeology as a science seem to have been given precedence over other needs: the needs of community socio-cultural history, of collective remembering and of acknowledging the pain and trauma related to the site and this history that gave rise to its existence'. In opposing the exhumations, it argues that '[exhumation] makes impossible a whole range of people's identifications with that specific physical space in the city. Such a removal echoes, albeit unintentionally, the apartheid regime's forced removals from the same area' (HOC 2003: 8).

The 23 October was set as the date for a tribunal hearing to consider the appeal. In the run-up to the hearing, the Hands Off Committee organised regular candlelit vigils at the Prestwich Street site on Sunday evenings. A billboard was erected outside St George's Cathedral, a symbolic site of anti-apartheid protest, with the slogan: 'Stop the exhumations! Stop the desecration!' Lunchtime pickets were held in the city centre. On 19 November, the SAHRA-convened Appeals Committee handed down a written ruling. The excavation permit awarded to the ACO was revalidated and the rights of the developer upheld. The Hands Off Committee reconvened as the Prestwich Place Project Committee (PPPC) to launch an appeal directly to the Minister of Arts and Culture. A letter of appeal was lodged with the Ministry on 12 January 2004. Supporting documents call upon the Minister to expropriate the site and 'to conserve Prestwich Place as a National Heritage Site' and a site of conscience (PPPC 2003).

By this stage all of the human remains on the original site had been exhumed and were in temporary storage in Napier House, a building on the adjacent block, itself to be demolished as part of the Prestwich Place development. During the SAHRA appeal process, the ACO had applied for permits to disinter human remains believed to exist under West Street, and the adjacent block containing Napier House. This was expected to result in the exposure of a further 800 to 1,000 bodies. On 21 April 2004 – Freedom Day in South Africa – the remains were ceremonially transferred from Napier House to the mortuary of Woodstock Day Hospital, on the other side of the city. Some of the remains were carried in procession through the city centre in 11 flag-draped boxes, one for each of the official language groups in the country. Muslim, Christian and Jewish religious leaders blessed the remains in a ceremony at the site prior to the procession. On 22 July, the developer was informed that the appeal to the Minister had been dismissed and that construction activities on the site could continue. Terry Lester of the PPPC was reported to be 'deeply saddened'. He said: 'We're acting the whore in this instance, bowing down to the god of development and selling a segment of our history' (Gosling 2004: 1).

Subsequently, the focus of attention has shifted to issues of memorialisation and access. On 6 April 2005, two of Morris's graduate students, Jacqui Friedling and Thabang Manyaapelo, made a presentation to a combined meeting of SAHRA and the PPPC as part of an application to conduct basic anatomical research on the Prestwich Street remains. Their application was turned down, mainly on the basis of a negative response from the PPPC. An activist in the PPPC described this to me as a 'rearguard action': having failed in their initial objective of halting the exhumations and preserving the integrity of the site with its remains, their concern was to protect the remains against further invasive procedures. At a meeting on 17 September, SAHRA's Executive Committee resolved 'not [to] approve basic anatomical research on the human remains exhumed from the Prestwich Place site', effectively extending this decision into a moratorium on future research (SAHRA 2005). In response, Friedling said: 'SAHRA has denied all South Africans the right to know about their heritage .... The information we can get from these bones will make these people come alive again' (Gosling 2005).

POINTS OF FRACTURE

Clearly, the events around the Prestwich Street exhumations constitute a complex playing out of social and political interests, forces, values and ideas. Coming ten years after the democratic transition of 1994, they serve to capture many of the conflicts and debates in post-apartheid society, to explore its faultlines, to point up its unresolved tensions and antagonisms. There are a number of ways of framing these events although, in keeping with the complexity of post-apartheid contexts, each needs to be qualified and explained. At one level, they appear as a conflict between the forces of memory and the forces of modernisation, development and urban renewal. At another level, they appear as a conflict between the forces of civil society, expressed through People's Power and the politics of mass action, and various state agencies and institutions of governance (SAHRA, Heritage Western Cape, the Office of the Minister).

A third way of characterising the conflict would be in terms of a dispute over the role of the sciences in post-apartheid society. In fact, it was not so much pro- or anti-science (as some of the protagonists suggested), as a dispute over notions of social accountability in the sciences, and the different interests for whom knowledge is produced. A feature of the Prestwich Street dispute was the manner in which this was expressed as conflict between universities (the histori-cally white University of Cape Town versus the historically black University of the Western Cape), and between disciplines (archaeology versus history). A full account of these oppositions would need to take on board the different institu-tional histories of the two universities, and the different historical trajectories of the disciplines of archaeology and history in South Africa. A key difference between these disciplinary histories has been the relative openness on the part of the discipline of history to engage with prevailing social and political contexts, whether through the Marxist and revisionist histories of the 1970s, the People's History movement of the 1980s, or the strong public history school which emerged in the 1990s.

A notable feature of the research process around Prestwich Street is what we might call the 'archaeologising' of the remains. Particularly notable was the absence of social historians on the SFRG, and the lack of systematic oral historical research despite the obvious leads given by many who spoke in the public meet-ings of their memories of growing up in the area. More generally, discussions of the scholarly and scientific value of the burial site were consistently framed in terms of the archaeological and physical anatomical value of the human remains, just as it was archaeologists who were invited to give expert opinion, write pro-posals and sit on panels and platforms.

A fourth way of framing the events is in terms of issues of race and iden-tity, and of local, regional and national concerns and interests. It is relevant, for example, that nearly all of the archaeologists working on the site and involved in the public consultation process, as well as nearly all of the members of the SFRG and key facilitators from the CSRF, are white. It is also relevant that the majority of the members of the Hands Off Committee and the Prestwich Place Projects Committee are coloured (to use an apartheid racial designation denoting a complex amalgamation of *mestizo* identities with the descendants of Khoisan groups, people imported as slaves from the Dutch possessions at Batavia, and others), and that the CEO of SAHRA and the Minister of Arts and Culture are black (or African, to use a current designation).[1] However, rather than finding in these events a simple fable of racial antagonism, we would argue that they rep-resent a complex convergence between slave histories, coloured identities and regional 'Cape' politics on the one hand, in tension with national heritage prior-ities articulated in terms of 'Africanisation' and accounts of essentialised black African cultural histories, on the other. It is the kind of complexity in which the

New South Africa abounds, and which has seen the convergence between new (black) and historical (white) elites, and the continuing marginalisation of black and coloured working classes, as was arguably the case at Prestwich Street.

RIVAL LANGUAGES OF CONCERN

We encounter Prestwich Street through a substantial, and growing, archive, which takes the form of records, minutes, reports, transcripts, submissions, film recordings, photographs, reminiscences, email exchanges and so on.[2] One thinks of the different theatres or spheres of performance through which events were played out: the theatre of excavation, framed by the wire-link fence, with its crowd of curious onlookers; the theatre of public consultation, with its more-or-less conscious echoes of the TRC process; the theatre of street protest, with its more-or-less conscious echoes of the anti-apartheid movement. At an early stage two distinct and opposed discourses emerged: on the one hand, the institution-ally situated heritage management discourse of the pro-exhumation lobby; on the other hand, a nascent or emergent public heritage discourse based on an empathetic identification with the dead, and the needs of social restitution and reconciliation. Each, in turn, gave rise to what has been termed rival 'languages of concern' (Shepherd forthcoming a). Those arguing for exhumation did so on the basis of the scientific value of the remains as a source to access 'hidden histories'. The proposal circulated by the SFRG at the first public meeting states:

> These skeletons are also – literally – our history, the ordinary people of Cape Town, whose lives are not written in the official documents of the time. They did not leave possessions or archives. If we want to recover their history, then one of the most powerful ways to do so is through the study of their skeletons.
>
> (Sealy 2003: 1)

In this case, the semantic slide from 'our history' to 'their history' is instructive. A number of tropes emerged and were recycled by archaeologists throughout the process. At the second public meeting, Belinda Mutti, an archaeologist, argued in favour of exhumation 'to give history back to the people' (Malan 2003: 12). Liesbet Schiettecatte argued that '[leaving] bones leaves information unknown. Studying them brings them back to life …' (13). Mary Patrick argued to '[continue the] exhumation – otherwise half a story is being told' (13). At a public level, this desire to 'give history back to the people' and 'bring the bones to life' was mediated by the technical discourse of cultural resource management, with its rituals of 'public consultation', and its circumscribed notions of value, need and interest. The double valency given to notions of 'respect' and 'dignity' by SAHRA and others had its counterpart in a pragmatic language focused on 'real reasons', 'sensible decisions' and the fact that 'life must go on'.

In opposition to this discourse, the Hands Off Committee emphasised the language of memory and personal reminiscence. They sought to articulate an alternative set of values (African values, spiritual values), and alternative notions of space/time (the notion of the site as a heritage site or a site of conscience; and in one memorable intervention, the notion of 'time for the dead'). They insisted on recalling a more recent past of apartheid and forced removals, as well as a deep past of slavery and colonialism. More generally, they sought to insert the events at Prestwich Street into a prevailing debate in post-apartheid society around notions of truth, reconciliation and restitution. Building on this, it is possible to observe a number of instructive convergences in the events around Prestwich Street. The first is a convergence between the practices of troping that we have described, and a positivist conception of archaeology as science, resulting in the production of observable data and 'information'. The notion of history that emerges – the history that is to be 'given back to the people' – becomes severely curtailed, as essentially archaeological data relating to the provenance of the burials and physical, chemical and anthropometric measurements of the bones themselves.

A second convergence is between the discourse of cultural resource management and a political strategy of containment. Particularly instructive in this case, we would argue, was the manner in which the language and practices of cultural resource management actively discouraged the emergence of radically new identities and refigurings of the public sphere, through a narrowed conception of need, interest, value and the mechanics of public participation. The notion of 'heritage' that emerges is itself narrowed and ambivalent, internally divided between the promise of individual restitution and reconciliation and the practice of restricted access and bureaucratised control.

For ourselves, writing as archaeologists and heritage practitioners in South Africa with a position on Prestwich Street that is different from the majority of our colleagues, in that we have been opposed to the exhumations, and supportive of the arguments of the HOC, what has interested us most in the events around Prestwich Street has been the glimmer of an alternative set of possibilities – of 'newness' – present in the discourse of the HOC. Prestwich Street encourages us to revisit and re-examine core disciplinary practices and ideas, and to consider alternative ways of knowing the archaeological past, and approaching the problematics of heritage and memory in post-apartheid society. It raises the possibility of alternative archaeologies, even of alternative epistemologies. We associate archaeology with a radical – a prying – 'will to knowledge', every excavation a mini-enactment of the Enlightenment injunction to know, to uncover. Prestwich Street makes the argument for an alternative kind of archaeology: an archaeology of silence, of secrecy, of closure (rather than disclosure). Adapting a term from Derrida, the archaeologist Keisuke Sato has written of 'archi-violence' as the violence done against sites and remains in the process of archaeological investigation (Sato 2006). This violence is physical and material, but it is also disciplinary and epistemological, the violence of certain methodologies and of certain ways of knowing.

How has the archi-violence of Prestwich Street differentially affected the communities of the living and the dead? In what sense do physical and chemical measurements of human remains and notes on their provenance constitute history, and more specifically a history which is 'given back to the people' as 'their history'?

Are there cases in which the current of sympathy between the living and the imagined community of the dead might be more profound in the absence of such information? How do we mediate between the multiple possible ways of 'knowing the past' in the case of a site like Prestwich Street, beyond simply asserting the priority of archaeology as science? As archaeologists in the postcolony, how do we take account of the discipline's own history – its gaps and silences, its unexamined practices – in formulating our approach? Do we enter the debate from the perspective of the priority of positivist science, flourished like a banner before us, or more modestly, as belated arrivals at a society-wide discussion on science, citizenship and accountability? The events around Prestwich Street raise a tangle of epistemological and ontological issues, but these resolve themselves around a simple set of questions: Are the bones of the Prestwich Street dead artefacts? Or are they ancestors? And under what conditions might they be both?

POST-APARTHEID URBAN IMAGINARIES

And so, what of post-apartheid urban imaginaries? On the desk in front of us lies a large-format, glossy brochure for *The Rockwell: Luxury De Waterkant Living*, produced by Dogon Gavrill Properties, the estate agents responsible for selling the development (Dogon and Gavrill 2005). The Rockwell, which is currently under construction on the Prestwich Street site, will consist of 103 'New York-style' apartments, plus parking bays, a private gym, a restaurant, a deli and a swimming pool (Figure 14.1). The historical point of reference for the development is the Jazz Age of early twentieth-century New York. According to the brochure:

Figure 14.1
The Rockwell: Luxury De
Waterkant Living.

Inspired by the early 1900 buildings of downtown Manhattan, The Rockwell displays an inherent richness and warmth. It has been designed to have an upmarket industrial New York feel (sic). Textured raw rock, brick and plaster are set against smooth glass and tempered steel.

This is because:

At the turn of the previous century, they did design right. Not only because it was classical in form and function. Not only because it was the birth of a new age and an explosion of fresh ideas. But because they did it with soul.

Figure 14.2
Clean, depopulated interiors brushed free of history.

Doing it 'with soul' becomes a refrain, and the rest of the brochure makes reference to 'Rock & Soul', 'Pure Soul', 'Rich Soul', 'Style & Soul', 'Rhythm & Soul' and (obscurely) 'Deli & Soul'.

The brochure continues:

> It was the beginning of a new era. A time of industry. It was the industrial revolution (*sic*). And with this era came the music, the freedom of spirit and the romanticism. It is in this spirit that The Rockwell was conceived.

By way of summary, it declares in bold type: The craftsmanship must have character. The design must have heart. The Rockwell has it all (Dogon and Gavrill 2005: 2).

The brochure is richly illustrated with photographs, which fall into two types. The first are pictures of clean, depopulated interiors (Figure 14.2). Linen and pale wood, dusted free (as it were) of history, of unwelcome associations and the stain of the earth below. The other category of pictures illustrates the notion of 'luxury De Waterkant living': caviar perched on a wedge of toast, a bowl of ripe figs, rounds of sushi on a plate, coffee emerging from a spigot, a reclining woman looking out from a hot-pink boudoir (Figure 14.3).

This sort of thing is familiar from promotional campaigns – the overblown language, the hype and the jive – at the same time it is profoundly jarring, not so much postmodern pastiche as a cynical annihilation of history. The full force of the notion of 'forced removals' – a phrase used by the HOC to describe the exhumation and relocation of the Prestwich Street dead – strikes home. It is as though history, memory, every rooted association between a group of people and a site on the landscape is evacuated, pulled up at the roots, to be replaced by a copywriter's whimsy. Prestwich Street becomes a site of instantiation of a new kind of post-apartheid urban imaginary, one in which history is imagined by the victors and beneficiaries, and in which victims have no place outside of the borders of memorial parks and heritage precincts. It is also, profoundly, a site of globalisation. It has become a commonplace that the period of political transition in South Africa coincided with the concerted effects of globalisation. Part social experiment, part vale of tears, Prestwich Street, like the adjacent Victoria and Alfred Waterfront development, becomes a site of instantiation of a new kind of global urban imaginary, in which places are stripped of specific histories and local identifications, and repackaged and rebranded to meet the tastes of a generalised elite, imagined in terms of the markers of 'cosmopolitanism': sushi, espresso and 'New York-style' living (Figure 14.4).

This is not a new or even an unusual phenomenon in post-apartheid society. Martin Hall and Pia Bombardella have written about the effects of the 'experiential economy' at sites like GrandWest Casino, Gold Reef City, and 'Montecasino' (a Tuscan-themed casino and entertainment complex near Johannesburg) (Hall and Bombardella 2005, and this volume). Leslie Witz has tracked the origins and development of Cape Town's 'township tour' circuit (Witz, this volume). Nigel Worden's pioneering studies of Cape Town's Victoria and Alfred

Figure 14.3
'Deli & Soul' at The
Rockwell.

Waterfront examined the ways in which heritage was constructed and contested at a prime tourist destination (Worden 1996, 1997). What makes Prestwich Street different is the imminence of the materiality of the past, and the tragic/ironic distance between the charnel house in the ground and The Rockwell's 'Deli & Soul'. What makes it different, too, is the passionate identification of the living descendants and inheritors of the HOC and the felt presence of the Prestwich Street dead, scary and implacable as the dead always seem, especially in their resurfacing, but also curiously vulnerable in their cardboard boxes in the Woodstock Day Hospital.

Figure 14.4
The Jazz Age refigured
as a signifier of
cosmopolitan style.

IN THE POSTCOLONY

Elsewhere, Shepherd has argued that Prestwich Street and the actions of the Hands Off Committee need to be understood as one of a number of popular or 'grassroots' social movements in post-apartheid society (Shepherd forthcoming b). The District Six Foundation, the parent body of a community social history museum that works with 'the experiences of forced removal and with memory and cultural expression as resources for solidarity and restitution' (Rassool 2006: 1), is one significant example that comes to mind. Another is the Treatment Action Campaign, a public information and advocacy organisation that has challenged the denialism of the government around HIV/AIDS and campaigns for affordable anti-retroviral treatment (TAC 2006). These various organisations have in common a concern with contesting the nature and extent of citizenship in the post-apartheid state, exploring the possibilities of participatory politics, and testing rights and entitlements under the new constitution – in the broadest sense, giving shape and substance to a post-apartheid public sphere.

In an immediate sense, there were a number of things at stake at Prestwich Street, and not the least of these is the shape and nature of post-apartheid urban imaginaries and the public sphere. The surfacing of the buried dead is always experienced as a traumatic moment, as an eruption into the fabric of the present of the past in its most literal and inescapable aspect. But it is also a moment that takes us to our deepest selves and, socially speaking, confronts us with profound energies. In a transitional social context (and what society is not in transition?) these are among the energies that transform us and the society of which we are a part, that aid us in our task of 'becoming'. Swirling, heterodox, contested: the energies of the Prestwich Street dead are still among us. For the living, the task becomes how to interpret these energies as a force for the good rather than as a threat, how they might be harnessed to generate not only heat but light, and a greater understanding of the place in which we find ourselves as fellow citizens who stand on opposite sides of a divided history.

In a specific sense, the failure of Prestwich Street is a failure for heritage managers in Cape Town. In a more general sense, it is a failure to roll back, in however provisional a way, a discourse of globalisation and development which sees local histories and bodies of lived experience as little more than resources to be mined of their picturesque or marketable aspects and otherwise ignored or replaced, and for which cities exist as clusters of shopping and leisure precincts increasingly dissociated from prevailing social contexts. If the exemplary figure of urban modernity in southern Africa is the figure of the migrant worker, as Nuttall and Mbembe suggest, then the exemplary figure of this latter set of processes is the victim of forced removals. In this, Prestwich Street stands as an iconic instance, in part because of the multiple removals and displacements which have characterised the site and its histories. These include the removal of the colonial poor to the outskirts of the city, the forced removal of black and coloured residents of Green Point from the apartheid city, the removal of the Prestwich Street dead from their site of interment and the replacement of local histories and identifications by the simulacrum of The Rockwell – a chain of displacements taking place in the margins of the city, at the edges of Empire, in the global periphery.

For the post-apartheid city, Prestwich Street is a cutting edge, always an uncomfortable place to be. It plays itself out in terms of notions of imagined community, the unrequited legacies of slavery but also of forced removals, complex negotiations between local urgencies and global dynamics, the relation between rooted histories and simulacra like The Rockwell, a politics which is profound and troubling but also strategic and opportunistic, and in terms of rival ideas of science and a contested set of disciplinary and institutional histories. But it is also – and pre-eminently – a story of state control, exercised through the capture and institutionalisation of the dead and their possessions, the bureau-cratisation of private yearnings, and the instantiation of particular regimes of care and languages of concern. One form of convergence between the discipli-nary interests of archaeology and the workings of the state may be seen in those primary means of control: the map, the plan, the grid-line. It is the lines of the plan or grid, finally, that determine the differential fate of objects and consign them to particular regimes of care. A closing image, then, as a way of taking leave of Prestwich Street: the dead of Green Point extend far beyond the city block constituted by the Prestwich Street site, a fact which is currently causing anxiety and controversy on the part of city managers and developers. Neither does the interment of the dead respectfully follow the lines of a map, so that bodies fall either side of the notional boundaries that constitute city blocks, plots of private land, edges of streets. Such, indeed, is the fate of a handful of the Prestwich Street dead. One looks closely at the sides of the excavation to see the signs of truncation: a torso which extends under the roadway, legs which have been exhumed and form part of the collection in the Woodstock Day Hospital. We are reminded of a line: 'To remember is to dismember'.

REFERENCES

Boym, S. (2001) *The Future of Nostalgia*, New York: Basic Books.

Davids, M.N. (2003) Fax from Imam Davids to Antonia Malan, Cape Town.

Dogon, D. and Gavrill, G. (2005) *The Rockwell: Luxury de Waterkant Living*, Cape Town: Dogon Gavrill Properties.

Gosling, M. (2004) 'Exhumation of Prestwich Street Skeletons Has Been Given Go-ahead, Says Developer', *Cape Times*: 1.

—— (2005) 'UCT Students Exasperated as Sahra Blocks Bones Study', *Cape Times*.

Hall, M. and Bombardella, P. (2005) 'Las Vegas in Africa', *Journal of Social Archaeology* 5: 5–25.

Hart, T. (2003) *Heritage Impact Assessment of West Street and Erf 4721 Green Point, Cape Town, prepared for Styleprops 120 (Pty) Ltd, December 2003*, Cape Town: University of Cape Town.

HOC (2003) *Substantiation of Appeal Submitted by the Hands Off Prestwich Street Ad Hoc Committee*, Hands Off Prestwich Street Ad Hoc Committee, Cape Town.

Kassiem, A. (2003) 'Public Given Time to Appeal against Moving Graves', *Cape Times*: 6.

Malan, A. (2003) *Prestwich Place. Exhumation of Accidentally Discovered Burial Ground in Green Point, Cape Town [Permit no. 80/03/06/001/51]. Public Consultation Process 9 June to 18 August 2003. Prepared by Dr Antonia Malan Cultural Sites & Resources Forum for the South African Heritage Resources Agency and the Developer*, Cape Town: Cultural Sites and Resources Forum.

Mbembe, A. and Nuttall, S. (2004) 'Writing the World from an African Metropolis', *Public Culture* 16: 363–4.

PPPC (2003) *Submission to DAC Tribunal*, Cape Town: Prestwich Place Project Committee.

Rassool, C. (2006) 'Community Museums, Memory Politics and Social Transformation: Histories, Possibilities and Limits', in I. Karp, C. Kratz, L. Szwaja and T. Ybarra-Frautso (eds) *Museum Frictions: Public Cultures/Global Transformations*, Durham, NC: Duke University Press.

SAHRA (2003a) *Minutes of Meeting of the Prestwich Place Exhumation Project, 8 August 2003*, Cape Town: South African Heritage Resources Agency.

—— (2003b) *Minutes of South African Heritage Resources Agency Public Consultation Meeting Held on 29th August 2003 at St Andrew's Presbyterian Church, Somerset Rd, Green Point*, Cape Town: South African Heritage Resources Agency.

—— (2003c) *Minutes. Prestwich Place Burial Ground: Meeting between SAHRA, HWC, City Council and Department of Public Works*, Cape Town: South African Heritage Resources Agency.

—— (2003d) *Minutes. Prestwich Place Burial Site: Meeting with Archaeologists and Academics*, Cape Town: South African Heritage Resources Agency.

—— (2003e) Permit No. 80/03/06/001/51 issued by the South African Heritage Resources Agency (SAHRA) Archaeology, Palaeontology, Meteorites and Heritage Objects Permit Committee to T.J.G. Hart of the Archaeology Contracts Office, Cape Town: University of Cape Town: 1–4.

—— (2005) *Minutes of Presentations and Discussions for Proposed Research Pproposals on the Prestwich Place Human Remains*, Cape Town: South African Heritage Resources Agency.

Sato, K. (2006) 'The Site of Memory, the Site of Things: Against Identity Politics', *World Archaeological Congress Intercongress on Cultural Heritage*, Osaka: 1–4.

Sealy J. (2003) *A Proposal for the Future of the Prestwich Street Remains*, Cape Town: University of Cape Town.

Shepherd, N. (forthcoming a) 'What Does It Mean to Give the Past Back to the People? Archaeology and ethics in the Post-colony', in Y. Hamilakis and P. Duke (eds) *Archaeology and Capitalism: From Ethics to Politics*, London: UCL Press.

—— (forthcoming b) 'Archaeology Dreaming: Post-apartheid Urban Imaginaries and the Bones of the Prestwich Street Dead', *Journal of Social Archaeology*.

Smallberg, M. (2003) Email from Mavis Smallberg to Antonia Malan, Cape Town.

TAC (2006) Home page of the Treatment Action Campaign, www.tac.org.za.

Wheeder, M. (2003) Email from Michael Wheeder to Mogamat Kamedien, Cape Town.

Worden, N. (1996) 'Contested Heritage at the Cape Town Waterfront', *International Journal of Heritage Studies* 2: 59–75.

—— (1997) 'Contesting Heritage in a South African City: Cape Town', in B. Shaw and R. Jones (eds) *Contesting Urban Heritage*, Ashgate: Aldershot: 31–61.

Part IV

Transit Spaces

Chapter 15: Transit Spaces

Picturing Urban Change

Matthew Barac

Images by David Southwood

Climbing overhead, the aircraft banks left towards Johannesburg, and levels off as it outruns the roar of its takeoff. Tracking across the sky, it is now nothing more than a droning whistle. Other sounds drift over rooftops and up through the cats' cradle of power lines, carrying a more human tempo. Music and radio talkshows are intermittently drowned out by the gusting south-easter; down at street level singsong conversations, schoolkids on mid-morning break and the rush of water filling bucket after bucket at the public standpipe tell the ordinary story of another day in Khayelitsha.

Figure 15.1
Victoria Mxenge
Settlement, Khayelitsha,
2002.

A small boy in a blue hood shoots out of an alley, drunk with giggling laughter. He is pursued by three others and a split-second later they all disappear between two shacks on the other side of the dusty clearing. Women leaning against a recycled timber wall as they wait to draw water take turns finishing one another's sentences in Xhosa, with the occasional English word thrown in: words like – 'nerves', 'transport', 'airtime' (Figure 15.1). Church vestments dance on a washing line, cellphones ring and bleep, dogs bark.

In the darkroom later and then afterwards peering through an eyeglass at a contact sheet, this daytime scene is reconstructed. Quotidian township episodes downloaded from a digicam play back on a laptop. Editing software allows us to freeze frames and zoom in, to split the screen with a vertical horizon so that sky and street appear side by side, moving at different speeds. Looking down into this world – this public place – from the cherry-picker hoist hired for a day's shooting, the cinematic sense of space and time is no less pronounced (Figure 15.2). A camera in the hand seems to suggest that any given moment can be stopped, or even run backwards so that people stiffly retrace their steps, cars back up and water is sucked out of the plastic bucket and up into the mouth of the standpipe.

This kind of image, in the cinematic genre of the establishing shot, encourages a way of regarding the scene as an assemblage of conditions: conditions that, captured in the form of a moment, point to their possibilities. The photograph offers a surface against which reality's circumstances stake a claim (Figure 15.3). The situation, a continuum linked extensively to the corners of its world

Figure 15.2
From New Way Road,
New Way, 2002.

Figure 15.3
Corner of NY1 and NY3A,
Gugulethu, 2005.

and intensively to the depth of its meanings, gathers the conditions into a unity that is expressed as a place. Place thus frames mediation between the situation's conditions and possibilities. To be situated is to know where you are and where you have been; place is thus a venue for history-making (Katz and Smith 1993: 77). These images toy with place's promise, looking for the tension between the particulars of a setting and its universal dimension: the horizons of the city that are common to all.

Hence these spaces exude anticipation. They shimmer as though the humdrum reality depicted conceals something more alive, something that answers to a deeper call in relation to the situation. In Pieter Bruegel's painting *The Fight between Carnival and Lent* (1559) figures crowd and structure the scene. The tableau portrays Shrove Tuesday's climax of carnival celebrations as a specific moment, yet one that sums up a world made of differences and negotiations. The common ground of Bruegel's canvas accommodates myriad episodes that fill out the narrative of Lent's annual victory over Carnival. Modern cities are haunted by the loss of Breugel's convivial spectacle and often appear abandoned, as in Giorgio de Chirico's cityscapes – places to get lost in.[1] Yet in this emptiness, and in the silence of photography's frozen moment, the clamour of what might be rings out. These images seem to say: something is going to happen.

In today's South Africa, change is on the agenda: transformation presents itself as a discourse of wholesale renewal at every level, from the personal to the political, from how you know your neighbour to the continental rhetoric of the

Figure 15.4
Corner of New Way and
Lansdowne Road, New
Way, 2005.

African Renaissance. Cities provide a platform for change's enactment. It is in public places that the transition to a new order is played out. These sites of adjustment track the everyday traffic of people and things, of gossip, cash and ideas about what works. Movements resonate with the reciprocity between a traumatic past and a promised future. Planning policies follow, picturing the emerging city's intersections and termini as economic thresholds. The idea of spatialising transport and commerce becomes the vehicle for movement of a different kind – a movement from township to town (Figure 15.4).

Building or writing or thinking the city's transformation, we trace pathways that are often conventionally directed, as 'progress' would have it, and equally often nomadic, responding to other modalities of search. Achille Mbembe and Sarah Nuttall promote an individuated writing of the city that they call 'voice-lines', a strategy that draws out 'the extent to which cities must be negotiated but also how citiness … has to do with motion – not the simple traversal of space, the act of going from here to there, but the negotiation of disparate sites and zones, in which (one) behaves in different ways' (Mbembe and Nuttall 2004: 370). Such 'citiness' is always a movement, one that, in James Joyce's written Dublin, recapitulates the city's foundation and unity not as an image but as a 'cityful passing away, another cityful coming ….' (Joyce c.1922: 156). Today's mobility defeats apartheid's territorial straitjacket, which sought to locate and trap black people. It drives an exchange between self and city, navigating between urban conditions and urban possibilities. Many discourses convene this relationship as a spatial proposition: a space of 'becoming' (Gotz and Simone

2001) or of 'change' that the city must pass through in a phenomenal and historical movement – a 'transit space'.

Such movement stokes the increasingly frenetic and, for commentators such as AbdouMaliq Simone, definitively African urban metabolism of the moment. (Simone 1998).[2] Ostensibly built on resistance to colonial power's gravity field, this dynamism paradoxically emerges from and reproduces tradition. It depends on the associations and institutions, from family to nation, that affiliate individuals to one another and in history. Accounts of the struggle against apartheid's efforts to control physical and social mobility testify to involuntary journeys and containments: to exile, forced removal, the 'transit camps' at which squatters were deposited, and the cycles of migration on which so many local tragedies and distant fortunes were founded.

Apartheid's demise and Nelson Mandela's election anticipated a new era of freedom. This transformation is a process that the country has addressed at every level, but in many ways such change is beyond the control of the state. Nevertheless, institutional efforts to intervene and guide the consciousness of the citizenry are high on the agenda, bringing the past into consequential debate with the future.[3] The question as to what this freedom is and how it should be put to use continues to emerge as a core national speculation. For the township-dweller the new conditions emerge in a range of imaginings, on occasion according to the motif of an ideal city or a new monument, or as an encounter with urban policy, with a plan.

Planning's theoretical power is predicated on its potential for synthesis, the notion that it draws together the social and the scientific, and at a scale not only of the collective but in relation to the past. Conceptualising this task as 'design', in which a plan is generated as the future's blueprint, casts the planner as almost demiurgic. Weighed down by such responsibility, the discipline has for some time been engaged in attempts to adjust its theoretical models, to ponder how citizens might have a hand in shaping what may come to pass. Urban design today is mindful of this agenda. Analysing agency-led projects in Johannesburg, Gotz and Simone (2001) developed the notion of 'spaces of becoming' as a plan-category particular to the agenda of national transformation. Similarly, Cape Town's policy suite of 'spatial development frameworks' calls for the interpretation of public space as a generator of 'town'. Transport interchanges and community hall forecourts are designated 'places of informal theatre' in which behaviours that catalyse or rehearse citizenship can be performed (Southworth 2002; City of Cape Town 1999: 51). Such efforts go further than simply providing for perceived needs. Planning is also engaged in the representation of national unity – an irony when in the past it worked so hard to erase common ground.[4]

As plans orchestrate the city's rescue, movements from township to town, under the rubric of progress, assume a contest between tradition and the new – one in which modernity always wins. Accounts of the aspirations, anxieties and avarices that pervade transformational township culture emerge in many quarters. Anthropologist Fiona Ross (2002) shadows squatters' efforts to build connections between themselves and with the changing world according to the discourse of *ordentlikheid* (respectability); novelist Zakes Mda (2000) laments not only the loss of innocence but also the ironic sacrifice of heritage to tourism in *The Heart of Redness*.[5] Such conflicted accounts of transformation press the case for a reappraisal of emancipation, one that emphasises freedom's ethical obligations rather than its economic opportunities.

For outsiders and insiders alike, South Africa since 1994 has been a laboratory experiment, testing democracy, building culture, rethinking politics, delivering a miracle: all thematised according to freedom. Mandela's quasi-mythic heroism in the nation's narrative of redemption has supplied riveting copy for pundits worldwide. In 2004, a spate of events and publications marking 'ten years of democracy' provided a reflective pause against which the status of transformation's probation could be assessed (Pieterse and Meintjies 2004; Bremner 2004; Morris 2004). Economists, politicians, artists, freedom-fighters, urbanists, drug-dealers and others have engaged in speculations as to how to achieve the right conditions for freedom to flourish. Popular belief in the notion of a formula by means of which the South African experiment would be assured success is linked to the perception of governance. The public mandate tasks the leadership with putting transformational mechanisms in place, with pulling the levers designed to deliver a fully functioning democracy. This is where planning comes into its own: it is exactly about getting the urban machine to work as an engine of prosperity. Spatial planning assumes a key role in picturing the nation's possibilities, figuring the city's public spaces as the backdrop to South Africa's emergence. In this line of thinking, space is called upon to both situate and foster citizenship. Didactic buildings, streets and parks teach people a new way of life. This ever-present drama unfolds in a public realm critiqued by Vanessa Watson (2002: 149) as comprising 'space-time containers bounding the activities which go on within (them)'. Watson, just as she writes up her own account of the South African experiment, is pointing to the epistemological problem of our way of putting our world – our city – before us, as an object of study.

Printed and hung on a wall, the large-format photographs shown here are big enough to approach as if travelling around the place portrayed, finding subplots played out in its corners, imagining oneself involved in activities outside of the centre. A view down into public space configures it as a little world or a simulation, as if the place is a receptacle for collectivity. People move about and make their lives, but in a manner that suggests habituation to the camera which observes a respectful distance from the home's privacy. This distance affords all concerned – photographer and writer, the lived space, and its inhabitants – room to move (Figures 15.5 and 15.6). Yet the pictures highlight a problem. Positioned far away enough for images to read as fields of colour-abstract, but close enough to implicate the viewer in a slightly arguable situation, the lens feigns impersonal detachment as it spies on reality's circumstances. This proximate distance, a tension that echoes with the paradox of hope and loss present in the conditions of transformation, discloses something of the melancholy of urban

Figure 15.5
Corner of Site C and
Lansdowne Road, Site C,
2005.

Figure 15.6
Corner Terminus and
Emms Drive, Nyanga,
2005.

change. The certainty of former expectations has begun to yield to an ambivalent liaison with the future, and hope is dogged by disappointment.[6] Tomorrow's promise ebbs away as these 'transit spaces' become inscribed in a discourse of deferral.

Establishing a critical distance and at the same time moving in for a closer look, we find that the township reveals not much more than ambivalence as to what its economy, its public life and its topography have to offer. A prevailing sentiment is that of rejection: those who can, leave the township for the town, those who dream of a better life dream of living it elsewhere. Yet many belong here, whether they like it or not.[7] Their existential foothold in what they know as their 'world' is in the township's communities, in its institutions, its history and its geography. It is within a reciprocal exchange between the township's improvised places and the imaginary metropolitan spaces promised by freedom that the key to a meaningful urban future is to be found.

Our thinking about cities must account for a more elaborate topography of institutions and urban phenomena if it is to accommodate the conflicts of every-day life. Imagined and made 'transit spaces' include the space of change that civil society seeks out as its own image. Such a bold ambition must negotiate the risk of masking its situational integrity with a picture of reality as it could be, a picture made into an urban scenography that claims to hold the clues to deliver-ing freedom's promise.

REFERENCES

Bremner, L. (2004) *Johannesburg: One City, Colliding Worlds*, Johannesburg: STE Publishers.

City of Cape Town (1999) 'Municipal Spatial Development Framework' (Muni-SDF), Cape Town.

Gotz, G. and Simone, A. (2001) 'The Implications of Informality on Governmentality: The Case of Johannesburg in the Context of Sub-Saharan Urbanisation', paper presented at the *ESF/N-AERUS International Workshop*, Leuven and Brussels, 23–26 May.

Joyce, J. (c.1922) (1988) *Ulysses*, J. Johnson (ed.), Oxford: Oxford University Press.

Katz, C. and Smith, N. (1993) 'Grounding Metaphor: Towards a Spatialized Politics', in M. Keith and S. Pile (eds) *Place and the Politics of Identity*, London and New York: Rout-ledge: 67–83.

Mbembe, A. and Nuttall, S. (2004) 'Writing the World from an African Metropolis', in *Public Culture* 16 (3): 347–72.

Mda, Z. (2000) *The Heart of Redness*, Oxford: Oxford University Press.

Morris, M. (2004) *Every Step of the Way: The Journey to Freedom in South Africa*, Ministry of Education, Cape Town: HSRC Press.

Pieterse, E. and Meintjies, F. (eds) (2004) *Voices of the Transition: The Politics, Poetics and Practices of Social Change in South Africa*, Johannesburg: Heinemann.

Ross, F. (2002) 'Making Home in the New South Africa', Africa Seminar paper, Center for African Studies, University of Cape Town, May.

Simone, A.M. (1998) 'Urban Processes and Change in Africa', *CODESRIA Working Paper Series*, Dakar: Council for the Development of Social Science.

Southworth, B. (2002) 'Urban Design in Action: The City of Cape Town's Dignified Places Programme – Implementation of New Public Spaces towards Integration and Urban Regeneration in South Africa', *Urban Design International* (8): 119–33.

Watson, V. (2002) *Change and Continuity in Spatial Planning*, London and New York: Routledge.

Chapter 16: Paths of Nostalgia and Desire through Heritage Destinations at the Cape of Good Hope

Martin Hall and Pia Bombardella

'Desire lines' – the theme of this volume – traverse the spaces between that which is projected and planned, and that which is circumstantial and accidental. This space, heterotopia in Foucault's concept of the instable zone of creativity (Foucault 1986), both builds on the organised project of modernity, and subverts it. Desire and nostalgia are interleaved, resulting in contradictions and uncertainties. In this chapter, we explore the nature of some of these spaces through contemporary entertainment complexes – shopping malls and casinos – the architectural children of a new democracy re-inserted in the global consumer economy. Entertainment complexes embody the contrasts between wealth and poverty and frequently evoke heritage in their pitch for the attention of the consumer. Our argument is that these spectacular inventions are both manifestations of the global entertainment industry – interpreted with a local patina – and also opportunities for new, popular, public spaces. They are amalgams of nostalgia and desire – shaped, and shaping, aspects of city living. As physical spaces, they are true 'desire lines' (Hall and Bombardella 2005).

Svetlana Boym has defined nostalgia as 'a longing for a home that no longer exists or has never existed':

> modern nostalgia is a mourning for the impossibility of mythical return, for the loss of an enchanted world with clear borders and values; it could be a secular expression of a spiritual longing, a nostalgia for an absolute, a home that is both physical and spiritual, the edenic unity of time and space before entry into history.
>
> (Boym 2001: xiii and 8)

The projection of a lost, mythical world will inevitably be drawn to heritage – material remnants of the past that can be re-imbued and saturated with associations and interpretations. Such longing blends into desire, and desire into the wish to possess and consume (Stewart 1993). And – inevitably – contemporary advertising plays on this relationship, persuading consumers to miss that which they have never owned, and never lost:

in thus creating experiences of losses that never took place, these advertisements create what might be called 'imagined nostalgia', nostalgia for things that never were. This imagined nostalgia thus inverts the temporal logic of fantasy (which tutors the subject to imagine what could or might happen) and creates much deeper wants than simple envy, imitation, or greed could by themselves invite.

(Appadurai 1996: 77)

It is hardly surprising that contemporary South Africa should be particularly susceptible to this heady combination of nostalgia, desire and consumerism. Emerging as a new nation in 1994, with the impossible formal public histories of white domination and colonial celebration, new senses of home were urgently required. Reintegration into the world economy at a time when the new experiential economy was driving the renaissance of Las Vegas as a family destination, heritage theme parks from Europe to Japan, new technologies of entertainment offered entertainment, enthralment and consumption. With high crime rates and sharp contrasts between wealth and poverty, gated and protected entertainment and shopping destinations offered refuge and possibility to both the established and the new consumer classes. Specifically, the National Gambling Act of 1996 re-regulated the casino industry, offering 40 licences and requiring a contribution to community development that was, in many cases, met through heritage themes, museums and other resources that could be deemed educational. Massive investments of local capital, usually in partnership with international entertainment interests based either in London or Las Vegas, resulted in the construction of extensive complexes outside major cities, characteristically combining high-end shopping, a wide range of food options, cinema complexes and a casino (Hall and Bombardella 2005; see also Hannigan 1998, Ritzer and Stillman 2001, Sagalyn 2001). In Venturi *et al.*'s felicitous phrase, these complexes are 'decorated sheds' – large, steel-framed hangars in which are assembled the technologies of theatre and illusion (Venturi *et al.*1977).

Here, we track this 'mourning for the impossibility of mythical return' through a cluster of heritage associations. Our argument is that, despite first appearances, these nostalgic evocations are more complex than they seem, forming a heterotopia characterised by the contradictions of new identities in the process of formation – desire lines that link the past with the future.

GrandWest Casino and Entertainment World is one of South Africa's new entertainment complexes, developed within the framework for gambling that was established in the 1996 Act. GrandWest is in Cape Town's northern suburbs, midway between the old wealth on the slopes of Table Mountain and the massive informal settlements of in-migrants seeking employment and opportunity. The complex has the characteristic design features of such entertainment destinations – a central casino and gaming area surrounded by a range of entertainment options that include cinemas, restaurants and shops selling designer goods. Because the redevelopment of the site incorporated earlier facilities, there is also a large ice-skating rink, a draw card for children, families and team events that is augmented by fast-food outlets. GrandWest is enclosed within a high-security perimeter and has a high degree of surveillance with CCTV and a large and visible security staff – considered important attributes by many, given South Africa's high rates of crime. Visiting GrandWest – in common with similar destinations the world over – is essentially a theme-park experience with an edge, a day out for the family with the dangerous edge of gaming, or a night out in a simulated town.

GrandWest's pitch is heritage:

> This superior family entertainment complex has, as its main theme the rich architectural heritage of the Western Cape .... With all this beauty and style that surround this larger than life gaming and entertainment complex, no wonder, the rest of the destinations in South Africa's fairest Cape seem just a little smaller once you've been to GrandWest .... GrandWest Casino and Entertainment World is a recreation of historic Cape Town .... From the impressive old Post Office building and the Grand Hotel to the streets of District Six, GrandWest Casino and Entertainment World is both a step back in time, and a leap into the future with smart-card gaming ....
>
> (www.suninternational.co.za)

Thus – and with startling self-awareness – GrandWest situates itself precisely in the nexus of nostalgia and desire; an enchanted world, larger than life itself, that recalls the magic of the past and projects it into the future, and the possibility of fabulous riches to be attained through gambling.

This evocation of heritage rests on four themes. Firstly, a reconstruction of the Fort of Good Hope refers to the initial settlement of the Cape by the Dutch East India Company in 1652. Simulated stonework refers to the standing Castle of Good Hope (for which construction began in 1666), while the shell of a caravel alongside the stretch of walling (Figure 16.1) refers to the Dutch East

Figure 16.1
GrandWest – evoking
1652.

India Company fleets that put into Table Bay on the long sea route from the Netherlands to Batavia, and for which the Cape settlement was established as a victualling station.

There is little attempt at realism here. The architectural details are incorrect – the first fort at the Cape had earthen walls and the ramparts of the 1666 Castle were not detailed in this way. Further, the Castle moat was not connected to Table Bay and could not have been used as a mooring (see Hall *et al.* 1990). It is tempting to interpret this aspect of GrandWest's architecture as an allusion to the architectural reconstruction of the Castle – an exercise of dubious historical accuracy completed in the 1980s, that attempted to reconstruct an idealised Dutch East India Company architecture floating somewhere in the eighteenth century, stripped of the Victorian accretions that came with the British colonial occupation of the Cape in the nineteenth century. However, this would probably be an over-interpretation. It seems more probable that GrandWest's theme designers wanted an arresting, large-scale set of symbols that would catch visitors' attention in an unambiguous reference to the earliest colonial settlement at the Cape of Good Hope.

The second design theme takes the visitor from the mid-seventeenth century to the mid-eighteenth century through frequent references to the baroque style of architecture known as 'Cape Dutch'. This style of colonial architecture developed in the earlier eighteenth century as an elaboration of a utilitarian, peasant vernacular. Despite similarities to the high baroque architecture fashionable in the Netherlands a century earlier, it is more probable that the Cape's eighteenth-century colonial architecture was a Creole style, combining a range of northern European influences and memories with interpretations by slave artisans from the Dutch East Indies. Reaching its most elaborate form in the country manor houses of the late eighteenth century, 'Cape Dutch' was abruptly superceded by the Georgian façades introduced with the British occupation in 1795 – the British regarded the Cape's baroque as laughably outmoded (Hall 2000). 'Cape Dutch' was discovered again in the early to mid-twentieth century as the iconographic architecture of Afrikaner nationalism, and is now celebrated as the genteel style of the Cape winelands.

As with the seventeenth-century military theme, there is no attempt to achieve historical accuracy in GrandWest's Cape Dutch theme. This is a 'vulgar historicism' in the tradition of holiday homes, shopfronts and service facilities that were common embellishments in the Cape region – and elsewhere in South Africa – until the late 1980s. The advantage of adopting a 'low' form of Cape Dutch is that it is versatile, and able to incorporate retail outlets and fast-food opportunities without the hindrance of attempting accuracy. As a result – and counter to GrandWest's self-promoting claim that these are larger-than-life versions of the 'real' architecture of the Cape region – the design reference is to the bourgeois architecture of the Cape's white suburbs and small, segregated towns of Afrikaner nationalist revival and formal racial segregation.

GrandWest's third design theme again takes the visitor forward, this time

Figure 16.2
Reconstructions of
nineteenth-century
urban façades.

to the mid to late years of the nineteenth century. But here, in contrast with the seventeenth-century militarism of eighteenth-century Cape Dutch, there is a considered and quite striking principle of accuracy in reconstruction (Figure 16.2).

Cape Town in the later nineteenth century was an established British colonial settlement with aspirations to greater prosperity that were manifested in high colonial Victorian architecture. A substantial merchant class – buoyed by the discovery of gold and diamonds in the interior – serviced the port as well as the requirements of trade, building stores, warehouses, banks and municipal buildings which portrayed a suitable impression of respectability and prosperity (Bickford-Smith 1995). This architecture was recorded by early photographers, and is reflected in the extensive collections preserved in the Cape Archives. In developing this nineteenth-century theme for the outward-facing perimeter of their entertainment complex, GrandWest's designers used photographs from the archive collections to create streetscapes in which close attention has been given to the accuracy of the façades – full-scale constructions of 'perfect forms' of nineteenth-century buildings devoid of the patina of time. This is both Ventura and Scott-Brown's 'decorated shed' at its best, and Walter Benjamin's fear of an age when the replica supercedes the original (Benjamin 1999).

In their fourth heritage theme, GrandWest's designers have reverted to the adaptable eclecticism that is more characteristic of this entertainment destination. 'The District' – a precinct close to the casino and comprising restaurants and specialist retail outlets – seeks to evoke Cape Town's District Six with narrow streets, washing lines and vernacular façades (Figure 16.3). This part of the city grew up in the second half of the nineteenth century and was known for the

Figure 16.3
The District, GrandWest.

diversity of its immigrant communities – a typical harbourside area of low-income tenancies, small industries and services (Bickford-Smith 1995). District Six's particular note, however, came with its destruction by the apartheid government from 1966 onwards in terms of the Group Areas Act. In picking up this theme at GrandWest, the entertainment complex seeks to draw on the success of the District Six Museum, which has become the model for successful community museums in South Africa, contributing to the continuity of memory and identity of a displaced community, and closely associated with the complex process of land claims and restitution following the democratic transition in South Africa after 1994 (Rasool and Prosalendis 2001).

Taking these four themes together – and seeing them as a combined presentation, as any visitor to the entertainment complex does – there is little justification for GrandWest's claim that this is a 'recreation of historic Cape Town' that is more impressive than its originals. With the exception of the full-scale reproduction of the nineteenth-century façades on the casino's outer face, GrandWest's design rather refers to the 'vulgar', secondary interpretations of Cape heritage – the nationalistic reconstruction of the Castle, for example, collapsed and collated as quick visual impressions, and to the mid-twentieth-century suburban interpretations of seventeenth-century colonial architecture.

This becomes even more apparent when the representational lineage of the casino's 'District' is taken into account. As Nasson has shown, District Six has long stood for the stereotype of the 'Cape Malay':

> exclusively a merry community, with a rich, vigorous and rowdy popular life; a higgledy-
> piggledy riot of buildings and architectural styles, thronged with characters with an

insatiable appetite for conviviality and an insatiable thirst for alcohol; a District Six of January Coon Carnivals, of cackling flower sellers like the durable and celebrated Maria Maggies, of blaring horns from hawkers' carts during the snoek season ... a colourful, legendary place, characterised by the perpetually open front door and cuddly youth from the Globe Gang, helping frail old women across Hanover Street with their weekend shopping from Spracklens or the Parade.

(Nasson 1990: 48)

This was picked up again in the 1980s in the widely popular *District Six – The Musical*, and the lyrics of one of its most popular songs, 'The Heart of District Six':

From Hanover Street/ Comes a lovely sound/ Can you hear the music that I hear/ A rhythm and a beat/ Of the people all around/ Melodies are ringing in my ears/ And it goes klop klop/ Beating out a rhythm/ Klop klop a rhythm that is living/ It's the heart that beats in District Six.

(see Hall 2001)

GrandWest's 'District', then, draws on the romantic and racialised tradition of representing 'Cape Malays' as cheerful, care-for-nothing drunkards, out of politics and out of time.

Nostalgia's timelessness, coupled with a consumer-oriented desire, allows the paradox of a yearning for a 'future home' that is envisaged through references to the past. This can be illustrated through a second entertainment destination, Century City. This gated complex of offices, shops, cinemas and accommodation is some ten kilometres north of Cape Town. Again one of the new, large-scale corporate projects planned after South Africa's isolation from the world ended in 1990, Century City has a chequered history, intertwined with the complex and sometimes dubious land deals of the 1990s (Marks and Bezzoli 2000; Witz *et al.* 2000). Its first phase was Ratanga Junction, a theme park inspired by Busch Gardens in Tampa, Florida (formerly known as 'Africa: the Dark Continent'), and based on a colonial Congo theme in which Africa is entered via the 'Orient' (the 'Marrakesh-style bustling market' of Salim Pashai's Souk), leading on to Ratanga River Congo Services, and the Ratanga Officers' Club, and finally, to the rides which offer the thrill of fear ('valley of fear', 'absolute terror never felt so good') (Witz *et al.* 2000). By the time Century City itself opened in October 2000, it had been reinvented as Africa's first 'intelligent city'. The basis for this claim was the complex's high-speed, high-capacity connection with the Internet, comprising a gigabit Ethernet network (revolutionary at the time) and office towers designed as an 'intelligent precinct' wired with high resolution ISDN lines (www.canalwalk.co.za).

Century City is a utopian concept. Thus the first issue of the *Canal Times* (April 2001): Century City was carefully planned

for more than 30,000 people who will live and work there. The City is planned to be ecologically sensitive, with 90 per cent of waste recycled and a system of navigable canals using recycled effluent that is further purified through a wetland refuge that features pans, birdlife and indigenous flora. There is a strong emphasis on security, with a 'zero tolerance' policy to crime, extensive CCTV coverage, foot, horseback, motorcycle and car patrols and a central control centre.

In one of many favourable reviews,

> Century City in Cape Town is one example of the new city concept. Once development is complete, a Century City resident need never leave the safe, cosy complex. Retail in the form of Canal Walk abounds, while Ratanga Junction and the bird sanctuary offers all the fun a Cape Townian [sic] can take. The new business parks that are being built in the enclosure will ensure that there is no possible reason to risk the great wide world. And it makes the perfect place for a working, city-wide, high-bandwidth network.
>
> (Young 2001)

Canal Walk shopping centre is at the heart of the Century City complex. Not surprisingly, given the expressed intention to develop an entertainment destination, close attention has been paid to detail. Exterior façades draw fully on the eclecticism allowed by postmodern architecture (Figure 16.4). In their essay on Century City's design, Marks and Bezzoli (2000) describe it as 'a carefully constructed fiction of pre-modern European urbanity, evoking a city of bygone days … pseudo-Tuscan flavour'. They identify a number of themes in Century City's general development plan: 'a sort of Edwardian London meets the canals of Amsterdam … an aesthetic soaked in nostalgia'; 'Venice meets Disneyland'; 'medieval Italy meets nineteenth-century European neo-classicism'. Marks and Bezzoli observe that

> images such as these are intended to conjure up emotionally satisfying visions of bygone times, a nostalgia for the traditional city … they are designed for inattentive viewers, tourists or city travellers who browse these real-life stage sets, scarcely aware of how the relics of the past have been indexed, framed and scaled.
>
> (Marks and Bezzoli 2000)

Century City's external architecture is, in essence, a massive three-dimensional billboard, again in the tradition of Venturi, Scott Brown and

Figure 16.4
Canal Walk, Century City.

Izenour's decorated shed. But Canal Walk is also inward-looking. Once the visitor has passed through one of the 15 entrance points with its security checks, there is no vista to the outside world – a striking feature of the design, given the way in which Century City as a whole capitalises on its vista of Table Mountain. Inside, Canal Walk is a double-storey arcade in a figure-of-eight design. This results in a continuous, double-level loop promenade of about two kilometres which, in the present context, can fairly be described as a 'desire line'. This promenade, bounded on either side by restaurants and retail outlets, has several integrated design themes, each unified by elaborately decorated ceilings. These include 'Art of the World':

> here the works of great European artists from the exquisite works of the Renaissance Masters to the dreamlike works of the Pre-Raphaelites gaze down on shoppers … So out of the ordinary is Canal Walk that it is not uncommon to see visitors whipping out cameras or just standing for long periods admiring the beauty of some or other design detail. More often than not it is the magnificent artworks which cover the upper reaches of the malls that have caught their attention.
>
> (*Canal Times* #1, 2001)

A second theme – of particular interest here – is Egypt. But rather than direct references to Egypt, which would perhaps have been expected in a development that ostensibly celebrates Africa, Canal Walk's ceilings celebrate Victorian-era representations of colonial Egypt. As with GrandWest's allusions to representations of eighteenth-century architecture, there is a double-remove here – a celebration of Europe's view of Africa, itself seen as Art.

This serpentine desire line of Victorian nostalgia loops through the heart of Century City – the food court and cinema complex. And here the 'longing for home' is projected into the future, with a theme of exposed ducts, space travel

Figure 16.5
Food Court, Century City.

and giant video screens, recalling *Blade Runner's* metropolis (Figure 16.5). This is Appadurai's 'imagined nostalgia' in action. The effect of walking the desire lines of Century City is to pass through misty images of nineteenth-century colonial Egypt – a luxurious, exotic world that can never be regained – and into a future place that is not yet attained. Adjacent retail outlets offer the gratification of possession by means of shopping.

It may seem easy to assign the heritage themes of GrandWest, Century City and similar entertainment destinations to simple commercialism – inappropriate appropriations of the work of museums, monuments and 'respectable' celebrations of cultural precedence. However, the interplays of memory, identity and desire are more complex than this. This is well demonstrated by looking again at one of GrandWest's heritage themes – the references to District Six and its multiple associations.

Archetypical romanticisations of District Six certainly play to racialised stereotypes. But at the same time, former residents of the area also present images of past lives – authenticated by personal experience and memory – which have the rough edges sanded away (Hall 2001). When *District Six – The Musical* opened in the segregated 1980s, it was as popular in 'coloured' theatres as it was in 'white' venues. Idealised recollections of 'the District' are apparent in the oral traditions of one-time residents. For example, Linda Fortune (1996: 58) writes in her published memoir:

> people who grew up and lived in District Six knew everyone who belonged in the area. So did the gangsters, who grew up there and lived there. They recognised strangers immediately, and some of them would linger about, waiting to rob an unsuspecting victim. They never bothered any of us living in District Six.

Indeed, gangsters are cast as agents of redistribution, robbing Jewish-owned shops in what was termed 'free entertainment' by residents. For example, Shrand's shoe shop on the corner of Tyne and Hanover streets was frequently burgled, often in broad daylight:

> no bystander ever told the truth and no one ever saw or knew anything when questioned by policemen. If the Law asked which direction the thieves had gone, someone would always point the opposite way. Later in the week you would see children and grown-ups wearing brand new shoes that were obviously stolen. They would even dare to walk right past Shrand's shoe shop and stop to do window shopping!
>
> (Fortune 1996: 62)

As Raphael Samuel (1994: 17) has warned, there is a danger in assuming that commemoration is 'a cheat, something which ruling classes impose on the subaltern classes'. Rather, he suggests, 'heritage might be seen as a vehicle for the pursuit of the visionary, an idiom for the expression of otherwise forbidden, or forgotten, desire. It allows utopia to occupy the enchanted space which memory gives to childhood, promising a new age which will be simpler and purer than the present. It joins the practical and the visionary, the future and the past' (Samuel 1994: 294). In the present context, we need to differentiate between different sorts of 'desire lines' – different ways in which nostalgia and desire become intertwined.

Here – again – Svetlana Boym's work on nostalgia is helpful. Boym (2001) distinguishes between two types of nostalgia. 'Restorative nostalgia' attempts a reconstruction of the lost home, while 'reflective nostalgia' thrives on the longing itself: 'restorative nostalgia puts emphasis on *nostos* and proposes to rebuild the lost home and patch up the memory gaps. Reflective nostalgia dwells in *algia*, in longing and loss, the imperfect process of remembrance' (Boym 2001: 41).

Drawing on nationalistic revivals, and particularly from Eastern Europe, Boym shows how 'restorative nostalgia' is invariably cast as a quest for truth and the restoration of monuments to the lost home, often as part of claims for present rights. It is clear that the recollections of past residents of District Six belong to this category of restorative nostalgia. Linda Fortune's published memoir is part of the wider purpose of the District Six Museum, arguably the most successful of South Africa's contemporary community commemoration projects (Rasool and Prosal-endis 2001). The District Six Museum originated in sustained opposition to apartheid-era forced removals, and to proposals for redevelopment without community participation, opposition that crystallised in the Hands Off District Six movement of the late 1980s. Opened at the end of 1994, the museum became widely popular with people who had been dispossessed by apartheid removals, providing a combination of 'memory work' and political engagement (Figure 16.6). One example is the museum's 'seniors project':

> in stitching together the torn fabric of the District Six community, the museum has had to reach across time and space. Our efforts at building a museum would be in vain if people who were relocated to the flats could not seek assistance in visiting this exhibit, particularly those who have difficulty with transportation because of age or infirmity. Through the use of a bus made available by the [South African] National Gallery, hundreds of senior citizens have visited the exhibition. These moving visits begin to rebuild the sense of community that was lost when the neighbourhoods were destroyed.
>
> (newsletter, District Six Museum Foundation, January 1996)

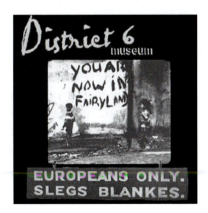

Figure 16.6
District Six Museum.

This cursory visit to the District Six Museum's decade of community development work and political engagement well demonstrates the chasm between
this form of recollection of the past and desire for social justice, and the objectives of those invested in GrandWest's 'District', despite GrandWest's claim to be
contributing to heritage in the spirit of the 1996 National Gambling Act. This difference can usefully be theorised by seeing GrandWest's heritage project as a
form of 'reflective nostalgia'. Boym shows how reflective nostalgia is more concerned with the individual – and individual time – than with the past condition of
the community: 'reflection suggests new flexibility, not the re-establishment of
stasis. The focus here is not on recovery of what is perceived to be an absolute
truth but on the mediation of history and passage of time' (Boym 2001: 49).
While Boym may not have intended the connection, this is consistent with the
precepts of the 'experiential economy' – the appeal to individual experience, and
the sale of individualised entertainment (Pine and Gilmore 1999). Reflective nostalgia is not bound by the constraints of 'truth' and 'evidence', but rather seeks
to evoke the spirit of the past in the interests of the individual. Boym, writing
from the perspective of Eastern Europe, prefers such reflection to nationalistic
obsessions with 'original stasis' and 'prelapsarian moment'. Interestingly, in the
political economy of heritage in South Africa, this preference is reversed. Restorative projects, such as those of the District Six Museum, contribute to social justice
by mobilising memory and memorabilia in the interests of contemporary
communities. 'Reflective nostalgia', in contrast, has been appropriated by investment interests as part of a global trend in individualised entertainment that pro-
motes consumption through desire for a state of life seen as better than the
present, but ever just out of reach. The two forms of nostalgia may use the same
symbolic sets – photographs, street signs, recollections, household treasures –
but the implications will be very different.

> Restorative nostalgia evokes national past and future; reflective nostalgia is more about
> individual and cultural memory. The two might overlap in their frames of reference, but
> they do not coincide in their narratives and plots of identity. In other words, they can use
> the same triggers of memory and symbols, the same Proustian madeleine pastry, but tell
> different stories about it.
>
> (Boym 2001: 49)

If, though, we need to dissect the concepts of nostalgia and desire to
identify distinctions in the ways in which heritage can be deployed, we also have
to be wary of a form of determinism, of an assumption of 'false consciousness'
on the part of those who visit GrandWest and Century City, and have done in
substantial numbers since these new entertainment destinations first opened. For
the desire lines that snake through the baroque arcades and laundry-strewn
lanes around GrandWest's casino and beneath the Egyptian ceilings of Canal
Walk are open to circumstantial and accidental uses not necessarily intended by
the planners of the experiential economy.

As is now well established, entertainment destinations are significant spaces in the contemporary economy (Hannigan 1998). Retail outlets, food and drink, movies and, in some cases, gambling, combined with secure parking, perimeter controls and internal surveillance and security, are forms of 'public places', albeit with a 'public' that is defined in practice by those who are excluded. The significance of such 'public places' in South Africa is accentuated by an urban environment inherited from the apartheid years: cities and suburbs designed for racial segregation, high levels of crime and continuing challenges in reclaiming inner-city neighbourhoods. In these circumstances, places such as GrandWest and Century City are attractive destinations for family outings, shopping or a night out.

The unintended consequence, then, of such 'desire lines' may be their contribution to the formation of identity in South Africa. As the old racialised divisions of apartheid are reassembled as socio-economic classes, those who have the resources to participate as consumers will become the familiars of these retail environments – of what George Ritzer (1999) has called 'cathedrals of consumption'. This point can be amplified by looking again at GrandWest. It is easy to dismiss the designers' hubris that theirs is a 'recreation of historic Cape Town'. Less obvious, perhaps, is their unintended construction of a new set of referents for an imagined past, a bizarre, concentrated mélange of romanticised Cape Malay and white suburban villa baroque, with a bit of colonial militarism thrown in. In its design, GrandWest is classic kitsch: 'a saturation of materiality, a saturation which takes place to such a degree that materiality is ironic, split into contrasting voices: past and present, mass production and individual subject, oblivion and reification' (Stewart 1993: 167).

This points to a new agenda for heritage studies in South Africa. Rather than limiting work to the past, with the risk of becoming locked in an academic form of 'restorative nostalgia', or remaining with critiques of the appropriation of heritage in the service of consumerism, heritage practitioners perhaps need to engage with urban designers, with planners and with the architects of the new 'cathedrals of consumption' which will – inevitably – be destination magnets in the cities of the future.

REFERENCES

Appadurai, A. (1996) *Modernity at Large: Cultural Dimensions of Globalization,* Minneapolis: University of Minnesota Press.

Benjamin, W. (1999 (1958)) *Illuminations*, London: Pimlico.

Bickford-Smith, V. (1995) *Ethnic Pride and Racial Prejudice in Victorian Cape Town*, Cambridge: Cambridge University Press.

Boym, S. (2001) *The Future of Nostalgia*, New York: Basic Books.

Fortune, L. (1996) *The House in Tyne Street: Childhood Memories of District Six*, Cape Town: Kwela.

Foucault, M. (1986) 'Of Other Spaces', *Diacritics* 16 (1): 22–7.

Hall, M. (2000) *An Archaeology of the Modern World*, London: Routledge.

—— (2001) 'Cape Town's District Six and the Archaeology of Memory' in R. Layton, P. Stone and J. Thomas (eds) *The Destruction and Conservation of Cultural Property*, London: Routledge: 298–311.

Hall, M. and Bombardella, P. (2005) 'Las Vegas in Africa', *Journal of Social Archaeology* 5 (1): 5–24.

Hall, M., Halkett, D., Huigen van Beek, P. and Klose, J. (1990) '"A Stone Wall out of the Earth that Thundering Cannon Cannot Destroy"? Bastion and Moat at the Castle, Cape Town', *Social Dynamics* 16 (1): 22–37.

Hannigan, J. (1998) *Fantasy City: Pleasure and Profit in the Postmodern Metropolis*, London: Routledge.

Marks, R. and Bezzoli, M. (2000) *Palaces of Desire: Century City and the Ambiguities of Development*, Johannesburg: Urban Futures.

Nasson, B. (1990) 'Oral History and the Reconstruction of District Six', in S. Jeppie and C. Soudien (eds) *The Struggle for District Six: Past and Present*, Cape Town: Buchu Books: 44–66.

Pine, J.B. and Gilmore, J.H. (1999) *The Experience Economy: Work Is Theatre and Every Business Is a Stage*, Boston, MA: Harvard Business School Press.

Rassool, C. and Prosalendis, S. (eds) (2001) *Recalling Community in Cape Town: Creating and Curating the District Six Museum*, Cape Town: District Six Museum Foundation.

Ritzer, G. (1999) *Enchanting a Disenchanted World: Revolutionizing the Means of Consumption*, Thousand Oaks, CA: Pine Forge Press.

Ritzer, G. and Stillman, T. (2001) 'The Modern Las Vegas Casino-Hotel: the Paradigmatic New Means of Consumption', *M@n@gement* 4 (3): 83–9.

Sagalyn, L. (2001) *Times Square Roulette: Remaking the City Icon*, Cambridge, MA: MIT Press.

Samuel, R. (1994) *Theatres of Memory*, London: Verso.

Stewart, S. (1993) *On Longing: Narratives of the Miniature, the Gigantic, the Souvenir, the Collection*, Durham, NC: Duke University Press.

Venturi, R., Scott Brown, D. and Izenour, S. (1977) *Learning from Las Vegas: The Forgotten Symbolism of Architectural Form*, Cambridge, MA: MIT Press.

Witz, L., Rassool, C. and Minkley, G. (2000) 'Tourist Memories of Africa', paper presented to the *Memory and History: Remembering, Forgetting and Forgiving in the Life of the Nation and the Community* conference, University of Cape Town, 9–11 August 2000.

Young, J.N. (2001) 'Building a City for the New Century', *ITWeb* January.

Chapter 17: Museums on Cape Town's Township Tours

Leslie Witz

In November 2000 a publication entitled *Travel Africa*, which claims to be 'The UK's Only Travel Magazine on Africa', ran a special feature on Cape Town.[1] The editor, Craig Rix (2000/1: 3), attempting to lure visitors to Cape Town, asserted that this 'is one of the most beautiful cities in the world. It has a real sense of history, a dramatic backdrop, extraordinary indigenous flora, magnificent beaches, outstanding vineyards and all things that make visiting a city so worthwhile.' Traversing a series of self-guided routes offered by the Cape metropolitan area's tourism authority, the feature-writer elucidated on these aspects, focusing on the 'heritage triumphs'. The vicarious traveller/reader was taken from the Victoria and Alfred Waterfront, the Castle of Good Hope, the 'colonial elegance' of Parliament, the 'antique *broekie lace*' verandahs of Long Street, the 'Victorian seaside' of Simon's Town, St James and Muizenberg, to the 'hidden gem' of Rhodes' Memorial and the 'fairytale white Dutch buildings and oak-lined streets' of Stellenbosch. These 'heritage triumphs' were clearly those that followed the paths of early European travellers, explorers, settlers and administrators (Debere 2000/1: 55–8).

But this was not all that the writer had to offer the traveller/reader. Since the early 1990s, with the unbanning of political organisations and the advent of democracy in South Africa, these European-based heritage trails have been incorporated into a repackaged and re-coded tourist image of Cape Town as 'The Mother City of Africa'. This finds expression, first, in a discourse of ethnic diversity and multiculturalism, where Cape Town becomes 'a complete prism containing life in every hue' (Debere 2000/1: 58; Gordon *et al.* 1996: 257–69). Second, a trip to Cape Town now involves an excursion into images of apartheid's past, such as Robben Island, where large numbers of political prisoners were incarcerated, and District Six, 'a once-vibrant area razed under apartheid's Group Areas Act' (Debere 2000/1: 58).[2] These two features of Cape Town's re-coded tourist image come together in the city's racially defined African and coloured townships. In the South African context, townships refer to dormitory locations on the margins of cities. They were initially established at the beginning of the twentieth century to accommodate and control African labourers from rural areas and were separated by roadways and belts of parkland from the suburban and industrial parts of the cities. At the beginning of the twenty-first century, these townships are being depicted for tourists as places of 'living culture … political resistance [and] modern life' (Kurin 1997: 273). Here is the opportunity for tourists both to 'wallow in an enthusiastic welcome over lunch at a Xhosa restaurant' and encounter the places where 'a major role in the struggle against apartheid was played out' (Debere 2000/1: 58, 66).

If the heritage triumphs are presented as places where one can traverse self-guided routes with a map and guidebook, the townships are introduced to tourists as potential sites of danger and disorder. They are described as 'maze-like' and places of inherent crime, 'although you won't get pounced on the minute you enter' (Debere 2000/1: 58). Thus, in order to 'experience another facet of Cape Town' and interact 'with cultures, communities and individuals living on the other side of the rainbow curtain', tourists are strongly encouraged to employ a 'trustworthy local escort' or to go on 'an organised tour' (Cape Rainbow Tours 2000; Grassroute Tours 2000; Debere 2000/1: 66). These sightseeing jaunts open up the frontier, marking 'the other side of the colour line', enabling the post-apartheid adventurer to enter areas 'previously inaccessible to whites' (Chapman 1999).

Although such tours are not among the main attractions in Cape Town – these remain the Victoria and Alfred Waterfront, Table Mountain and Cape Point – they have become increasingly popular among international tourists, especially those with an optional 'free day' in the city. Many tour operators, some large and well established and others smaller and newer, are jostling for routes, sites and destinations in the townships. In this battle to establish tourist zones on the township routes it would be expected that museums would play a crucial role. Not only are museums, in general, potential cultural destinations on itineraries (Kirshenblatt-Gimblett 1998), they also denote the temporal and spatial markings of an excursion and provide key elements of plots around which tour narratives are often constructed. Yet, while there are museums on Cape Town's township routes, there are no museums in the townships that are visited by tourist buses. The only museum in a township is in Lwandle, some 40 kilometres from Cape Town, largely beyond the boundaries of mapped routes. Given that Cape Town is now presenting itself to tourists as a destination rich in 'colour and culture' (Cape Rainbow Tours 2000), how does one begin to explain what seems to be a huge omission on township tours? And what role do the museums that are on the township route (but not in the townships) play in the narratives that are presented? In bringing these two questions together, one can begin to see how townships are being configured as essentially 'African places' – perhaps even as 'living museums' – in a new tourist discourse that invites visitors to 'Explore South Africa: Culture'.

TOWNSHIP TOUR ROUTES[3]

Township tours primarily present themselves as offering 'insights into post-apartheid progress and development' (Springbok Atlas Safaris 2000). Yet through the very routes they traverse, the sites they point out, and the destinations they call upon, these tours, almost inadvertently, confirm the spatial arrangements of apartheid. Explicitly, they are not offered as tours of Cape Town, but rather as separate, distinct, township tours. It is almost as if the tourist is being offered a journey to an exotic destination outside the boundaries of the city, where the attractions are beer-makers, traditional healers, dancing, taverns and shanty towns (Dondolo 2000: 12; Southern Tip Tours 2000). Whereas in the city and its immediate surrounds the 'impression' created for tourists is that 'the true heritage is not African but European' (Holiday 1994), the townships take one 'into Africa'.

After picking up tourists from hotels and backpacker lodges, township tours begin in the central city area with a visit to the Bo-Kaap. Situated on the slopes of Signal Hill, on the western side of the city the Bo-Kaap is a residential area that was occupied by people who were racially designated as 'Malay' under apartheid. This was a racial identity that owed much to the Afrikaans poet and journalist, I.D. du Plessis, who spent much of his time in the 1930s and 1940s constructing a Malay history, culture and physical type. D.F. Malan, whose government formally introduced a policy of apartheid in 1948, admired Du Plessis's work so much that he labelled him the *'slamse koning'* [king of the 'Malays'] (Jeppie 1987: 9, 17–28). But this is not the narrative that tourists are presented with in the Bo-Kaap. The area is generally presented as a 'Malay area' or 'Malay Quarter' (Southern Tip Tours 2000; Day Trippers 2001). Either on a brief walking tour or a drive through, tourists are told a history of colonial occupation of the Cape, the introduction of slavery and the beginnings of Islam at the Cape. There is a museum in the area, which is part of the Iziko Museums of Cape Town complex, but it is not a favoured destination for township tours. Most guides merely point to the museum and recommend a visit during free time.

Moving to the eastern side of the city, narratives shift from the days of colonialism to apartheid. In District Six, experiences of the apartheid policy of removals to assigned areas designated by the racial ordering of society form the basis of the accounts presented. On a drive through what has become a desolate landscape, tourists are told about a harmonious, multicultural community that was destroyed by apartheid. A visit lasting about 30 minutes to the District Six Museum further enables guides to dramatise this narrative.

At this stage, about one hour of a four-hour morning tour has passed, and it is time to leave the central city and move into the townships. The minibus leaves the city and travels along the lower slopes of Table Mountain towards the N2 motorway – named Settlers Way – which leads both to the airport and the townships. At this stage there is very little talking, marking a moment of

Figure 17.1
A township-touring
minibus in the township
of Langa.

anticipation that will take tourists away from the metropole into a peripheral
world of possible dangers and labyrinths that the guide will steer them through.
Once past the Mowbray and Rondebosch golf courses, the cooling towers and
sewerage works signify the gateway to the Cape Flats, a designation which
draws upon comparisons with the suburbs on the mountainside, both in terms
of landscape and locations of economic and political power.

As the minibus enters the township of Langa (Figure 17.1), the narrative
resumes, but the history of apartheid, which had been so powerfully presented
in the city, has now disappeared. Now, two aspects come to the fore, the one
based in a timeless past of tradition, the other in a world of social and economic
development. In a dramatic enactment of modernisation theory, tourists are
pointed to spiritual healers, initiation schools and places where they can imbibe
umqomboti [traditional African beer], alongside housing projects, soup kitchens,
recycling depots, crèches, catering schools, arts and craft centres and bed and
breakfast establishments – the latter all bound up in a discourse of tourism as a
possible 'passport to development' (De Kadt 1979; Mathieson and Wall 1982:
186). It is tourism that turns the 'traditional' into the modern. Thus Eziko Restaurant is proclaimed to be

> Langa's greatest meeting place where the people of the world can now meet to share
> the Township and South African dishes. In the Xhosa culture the word "eziko" holds a
> significant place because it is not only the central space of the household but also signi-
> fies warmth literally and figuratively. Fire and Food are considered as source of warmth.
>
> (Eziko Training Centre 2000)

The major stops *en route* are people's homes, drinking places – shebeens,
arts and craft projects and a crèche. These destinations are spread through the

various townships, thus enabling a sense of journey to be built into the itinerary. Visits to people's homes and various housing projects usually take place in Langa. Tsogo Environmental Centre provides step-down guides which many tour companies use. On a specially designed walking route, tourists are taken to see different classes of houses, and some of their inhabitants – among them, original working-class housing, old hostels, upgraded hostels, upper-class housing – referred to by the guide as the Beverly Hills of Langa, and the Joe Slovo squatter camp. In order to quench one's thirst, the obligatory shebeen is invariably the next stop. Although homemade sorghum beer has largely been replaced in the townships by clear beer manufactured by South African Breweries, several operators have specifically located places where tourists can drink what is termed the 'traditional brew'.

Once tourists have had their 'sip of Africa', they are driven through the coloured township of Bontheuwel *en route* to Gugulethu. Here the District Six narrative is called upon as many residents of District Six were removed to Bontheuwel. As the journey proceeds further north into Gugulethu, and then Khayelitsha (Figure 17.2), tourists visit a day-crèche where children are asked to perform a series of songs. This is then reversed when the tourists are called upon by the guide to sing for the children. The tour usually ends at an arts and crafts centre, such as the Philani nutrition centres, where tourists can observe, admire and perhaps purchase some of the wares of a women's weaving project (Philani Nutrition Centres 2000). From Khayelitsha, it is back onto Settlers Way, past the airport, the sewerage works, the cooling towers and the golf courses, to the drop-off at the hotel or lodge. At the end of their 'crosscultural voyage of discovery', tourists are presented with the possibility of extending the morning trip into

Figure 17.2
Visiting Vicky's Bed and
Breakfast in Khayelitsha.

the 'black township[s]': with a visit to Robben Island Museum to view 'Nelson Mandela's "home" for many years as a political prisoner' (Grassroute Tours 2000). These tours to Robben Island are organised and run by the museum and its staff, but the tour companies assist in making the booking arrangements. It is not clear how many tourists actually take up this option, but they are marketed together as a one-day package. Those tourists who choose to return to their hotel rooms can be well satisfied. Through their 'encounters across the African frontier', they have been configured as not mere adventurers and explorers, but as community developers. They have been cast as 'contributing directly to the "reconstruction and development" of a society and to the fundamental replacement of apartheid with a "culture of tourism"' (Rassool and Witz 1996).[4]

MUSEUMS ON THE TOWNSHIP TOUR

On the township-tour package there are thus only three museums which may be called upon, and none of them are located in the townships: the District Six Museum, the Bo-Kaap Museum and the Robben Island Museum. The latter two are not central to these tours, but the District Six Museum is always visited and provides the core for the narratives presented.

There are different claims as to where the origins of the District Six Museum lie (Rassool and Prosalendis 2001), but one of the stories is that it grew out of a political campaign to keep the land unbuilt as 'a powerful memorial to apartheid suffering' (Worden *et al.* 1999: 183). The museum serves 'as a memorial to Cape Town's most infamous removal, and nostalgic celebration of place' (Worden *et al.* 1999: 229). Although much has changed in the museum, three images from its early days remain the key signifiers. Its central image is the map where ex-residents have inscribed their addresses and places they recall. A large cloth serves not only as a comment book but also invites recollections of place. Street signs, which were secretly stored away by a man involved in the destruction of the district, serve as a material reminder of what once was, and assert the preservation of memory amidst the destruction wreaked by apartheid. People might have been physically removed from their spatial community but the District Six Museum functions as a reinstatement of that community as bound together by different memories of place.

Much has been written about the District Six Museum and the memories it evokes. Initially, a great deal was written about how the museum was able to capture a sense of community and memory through its minimal displays. The acts of visiting, listening, recalling and recording were the modes of establishing the community of memories. The museum also fed into the land reclamation process as recollections and artefacts provided the basis on which previous residents reclaimed their property. Some critics pointed to the way the museum seemed to evoke a sense of nostalgia, and appeared to neglect the dangerous activities of gangs of criminals who operated in the district. In addition, although this was never explicit, some critics maintained that the exhibitions and photographs on show tended to reinforce the myth of the district as a 'coloured place'.

Digging Deeper, the museum's permanent installation which opened in 2000, seeks to challenge many of the myths about District Six, in particular the one which associated District Six with a group of people who were racially classified coloured under apartheid. It does this in three ways. First, information boards reproduce a series of identity documents which explain the arbitrary operation of the system of racial classification. They also provide visual images of what the district looked like before the removals and after. Second, one of the reconstructed rooms of an inhabitant of District Six is that of someone who was classified black under apartheid. A reconstruction of Nomvuyo Ngcelewane's home 'places on record that "African" people made homes and lives in District Six, and that these were disrupted by the first forced removal in 1901 and later in the 1960s' (District Six Museum 2001). Finally, there is an attempt to show that the experience of the people of District Six was not unique and that millions of people throughout South Africa were physically removed from their homes as part of apartheid's social engineering. Through such displays, the museum is not only able to insert itself into broader national historical narratives, but also challenges the racialised ways in which much South African history, both in the past and now, has been produced. Instead of taking racial and ethnic identities as given and settled very early on, almost before history begins, they are shown to be changing and mutable.

The map on the floor and the information boards are the main props that township tour guides utilise for their brief introductory remarks. The map serves to emphasise a sense of multiculturalism in the area which was anathema to the advocates of racial segregation and later apartheid. The guides relate how in the twentieth century, firstly under the banner of slum clearance and later more explicitly through the Group Areas Act, thousands of people, most of whom were racially designated as African or coloured, were forced to move from District Six to the Cape Flats. District Six was declared a white group area in the mid-1960s and most of the existing houses were destroyed to make way for anticipated residential development. Guides use the information boards extensively to show how the policies of racial separation were implemented. In both cases, with the map and the boards, the narratives the guides present conform to many of the museum's intentions with these displays. After this brief introduction, tourists have about 20 minutes to explore the museum for themselves.

The District Six Museum plays such a crucial role in the township tour that it becomes impossible to imagine a township tour in Cape Town without it (although township tours have been in existence since at least the mid-1980s, before the museum was established). Not only does the District Six Museum act as an early stop on the route to engage the tourists' interest, but it also introduces two key elements on which the township tours are based. The first centres around the discourse of multiculturalism, with District Six representing a pre-apartheid past and future. That past is one of supposed racial harmony, where everyone lived together, the so-called 'rainbow nation', believed always in existence, almost destroyed by apartheid, and now re-emerging in post-apartheid

South Africa. The second element presented by the museum is to illustrate that what happened to District Six actually represent's apartheid. The rest of the tour shows the results of apartheid (equated with the destruction of District Six) and the attempts to construct a post-apartheid society. In this way township pasts become effects-driven and seem to lack their own dynamics. Townships are either cast in a timeless past of tradition or in a post-apartheid future of imagined modernisation won through 'trickle-down' effects from the growth of tourism.

The only other museum visited on the township tour is the Bo-Kaap Museum. Here, a step-down guide takes charge and shows visitors the items on display. The emphasis is on the beginnings of Islam at the Cape and, although the museum reconstructs a mid- to late nineteenth-century home, the representations are in the ethnographic present. Visitors are told a great deal about Muslim weddings, dress and spiritual practices. In so doing, the museum presents itself as depicting a cultural group largely identifiable through their religion. This explicitly contradicts the notion of the area as a 'Malay quarter'. Yet, at the same time, many of the customs, skills and dress that are presented in the museum are precisely those that came to be associated with the stereotypes of 'Malay' culture as defined by I.D. du Plessis in the 1930s and 1940s. Visited at the very beginning of the township tour, the museum thus sets the scene for encounters with 'rich traditions' and anticipates the journey as a series of cultural encounters (African Mosaic Tours 2000), where one will gain 'insight into the ethnic character of the city' (Cape Team Tours 2001).

The visit to the Robben Island Museum is offered as an option at the end of the township tour. Research remains to be done on how the Robben Island Museum operates when it is combined with the township tour. One indication is that, in the world of cultural tourism, Robben Island might be imaged, along with the townships, as an essentially African place. On 3 March 2001 an article appeared in the weekend edition of Cape Town's evening newspaper, the *Cape Argus*, which reported on the visit of a group of 1,000 German travel agents and tour operators to Cape Town in December of the previous year. According to the report, what impressed these visitors most was not Table Mountain, the beaches nor the winelands, but 'the experience of visiting Robben Island and the Cape's sprawling townships'. The article claimed that these two encounters had enabled the German visitors to 'experience the heart of Africa' (Carew 2001).

But, in this instance, the packaging is not exclusively in the hands of the tour operators. The Robben Island Museum markets itself and presents its own image that may affirm or counter that of the prevailing township-tour packages. Although Robben Island may increasingly be located as an essentially African tourist destination, this is not the primary way that it presents itself. Since the transformation of the island from a prison into a museum in 1996, it is the experience of political prisoners from the 1960s that has been the major ingredient of its imaging. The intention is not only to show the many hardships that the prisoners went through, but, perhaps even more importantly, to show how they managed to survive, overcome these adversities and retain their sense of humanity. This enables Robben Island to locate itself primarily as a 'living museum' of the modern nation state, encapsulating what appear as global values. As Ciraj Rassool (1997: 23) has pointed out, Robben Island has been re-envisioned as the birthplace of the new nation and the quest for national reconciliation, with Nelson Mandela 'reinscribed as the father of the reconciled nation'. This discourse of reconciliation moves beyond the bounds of the national state in Robben Island's promotional slogan, 'Triumph of the Human Spirit', and its successful claim to being a world heritage site.

The representation of Robben Island as the birthplace of national and global modernity may not entirely discount the image of the island as an essentially African place. Somewhat ironically, the significance attributed to Nelson Mandela inadvertently locates the museum within the latter discourse. The emphasis at Robben Island on Nelson Mandela places the museum in a biographical geneaology, through which 'the discursive construction of Nelson Mandela has moved through different phases, from born leader to sacrificial hero to Messiah, culminating in symbolic father with paternal authority in the public sphere' (Rassool 1997: 36). In somewhat contradictory terms, international tourists, encountering this Mandela on Robben Island in the guise of paternal leader, are fulfilling their expectations 'to experience Africa at grassroots level' (Carew 2001).

TOWNSHIPS AS 'LIVING MUSEUMS'

While there may be some contention about how museums outside the townships are represented and represent themselves on township-tour packages, once tourists enter the townships of the Western Cape there are virtually no museums to be visited.[5] This apparent lacuna is usually explained by tour operators in two ways that link museums to history. First, some claim that tourists do not want to see and be told about history as 'history is boring'. Second, the tourists have had their fill of history and museums in the city and the suburbs, but now they want to venture into 'real Africa' and meet 'the people'. Claims such as these locate the spaces of history and modernity within the metropolitan centre, with the spaces of tradition and supposed authenticity placed on the periphery. In places where people have been constituted as subjects of the national state for decades, township tours cannot accommodate museums as spaces of modernity and national citizenship.

This perspective on township museums does not merely emanate from the structures of the tourism industry. It is mirrored in the difficulties within townships of establishing museum communities. Museums have come to represent a place in the metropole, to which one may be taken to for a brief school excursion. They are not regarded as places of one's own community, but as places associated with and belonging to another. When museums are, at times, considered as township places, they are primarily viewed in functional economic terms as tourist sites. They thus have to present themselves within a dominant tourist framework that is 'overtly driven by commerce and the state' and that does not correspond with how the museum may project itself to its local communities – what Lippard (1999: 77) calls its covertly ideological function.[6]

Instead of presenting museums to the touring public, the townships in the Western Cape have become living museums on a grand scale. The primary sites and destinations are not classified by scenic or historical interest but through their ability to provide an opportunity to identify and to see 'the people' in carefully curated settings: at home, at school, on the streets, at work (but not in an industrial context) and at leisure. There is the mandatory visit to a few carefully selected people in their homes, ranging from a small tin and wood house to a room in a hostel or a new Reconstruction and Development Programme home. A daycare centre is chosen to put on a daily performance for the tourists. The 'short walk' through a series of designated streets, under the watchful eye of the guide, is intended to impart a 'feel' of the townships. At a craft centre, tourists are able to satisfy their expectation of encountering work and development. Simultaneously they can also 'feel good' by purchasing what appears to be a handmade memory of Africa. Finally, there is the social experience, set up in a 'safe' shebeen, where the tourists will be able to partake of township life but where they won't be harassed by a drunken and disorderly clientele.[7]

In this ethnographic spectacle, history, particularly that which relates to struggles against apartheid, is sidelined. This is particularly illustrated in the drive along Langa's Washington Street, a route taken by many of the operators. On the wall of a community centre, there is a huge mural, made by Ricky Dyaloi, Duke Norman and Timothy Zantsi for the 'Returning the Gaze' project of the Cape Town One City Festival in September 2000 (Minty 2005: 16). It depicts the march led by Phillip Kgosana from Langa to Cape Town in 1960 to protest against pass laws. The minibus passes the mural but it is not mentioned. On the righthand side of the street are the dilapidated remains of an office once used to issue pass books for workers, while nearby is the building where government-appointed Bantustan leaders stayed in the townships. Again there is silence. The destination is the Tsogo Environmental Centre and the walking tour of the living conditions, and nothing distracts the guide from this objective. On one tour the minibus turned off Washington Avenue to show the remains of a beer hall that was burnt down by protesting youth. This was used to illustrate the ways that beer halls had come to be regarded as instruments of the apartheid state. But this is the exception, as the tour through Langa largely revolves around shebeens, 'traditional healers', restaurants and housing developments.

Similarly in Gugulethu, the minibus usually speeds past the memorial erected to the Gugulethu Seven (Figure 17.3). This is a memorial to a group of youths who were executed by the police, the latter then stage-managing the scene to create the impression that they were acting in self-defence. A few hundred metres further on, though, there is usually a brief stop at a memorial to Amy Biehl, the exchange student from the United States who was killed in Gugulethu at the time of intense political violence in the early 1990s (Figure 17.4). Her parents have subsequently

Figure 17.3
Memorial to the Gugulethu
Seven, in Gugulethu near Cape
Town.

Figure 17.4
Memorial to Amy Biehl, in
Gugulethu near Cape Town.

forgiven her killers and set up the Amy Biehl Foundation. Thus, the memorial is used to illustrate a narrative of reconciliation, a favourite theme of township tours. Moreover, it contributes to the notion of the tour and the tourists as bearers of community development, even though they might not have to make the same sacrifice as the Biehls.

The only place on a township tour which does attempt to depict a sense of political history is the Tourist Information Centre at Sivuyile College in Gugulethu. The information centre has three sections. At the front there is an arts and crafts shop. In the rear a group of artists and potters are at work, and adjacent to them is an exhibition about Cape Town's townships and their histories. It is in the latter exhibition that the stories of Philip Kgosana, the Gugulethu Seven and Amy Biehl are told. In the context of depictions in township tours, and the unrelenting drive to represent 'African tradition', this exhibition challenges the viewer to begin looking at some of the internal dynamics in the making of township histories. But even in this exhibition, there is the demarcation between 'history' and depictions of 'the people'. After the events are shown in the first part of the exhibition, the remainder of the panels display a series of photographs of 'township people' in a range of different activities. Most of the people in the photographs are nameless, the geographical settings they appear in are anonymous and the temporal scene timeless, thus confirming a sense of townships as places without history. Moreover, the information centre was only visited by two of the tour operators on the 11 township tours which myself, colleagues and graduate students took between August 2000 and July 2001. Visits to the centre tended to be short and were mainly concentrated in the front of the centre, where arts and crafts are available for purchase. Despite the major effort being made to create a sense of history at Sivuyile, it is still the ethnographic gaze that prevails at the Tourism Information Centre and on township tours in the Western Cape.[8]

A TOWNSHIP MUSEUM OFF THE BEATEN TRACK

Some 40 kilometres outside Cape Town, alongside the motorway which leads past Langa, the airport and the winelands, is the only museum in a Western Cape township. The Lwandle Migrant Labour Museum serves as a reminder of a system of migrant labour, single-sex hostels and the control of black workers through an identity document which regulated access to employment and residence in urban areas – the infamous pass book.

Given the origins of Lwandle, it is appropriate that such a museum be located in the township. Lwandle was established in 1958, with hostel-type accommodation for workers who mainly serviced the nearby fruit and canning industry. These hostels were only intended for single men, as, in terms of apartheid, the African family was to be bound to the rural environment and the labourer was merely seen as a temporary sojourner in the city. As many analysts have pointed out, this not only meant that wages were kept low on the basis that the worker in town was merely supplementing his family's income, but that a minimal amount of money was spent on supplying housing and services in urban areas. The hostels provided very basic accommodation, with four to six men occupying a small confined space, with an entire block sharing rudimentary ablution facilities. In the 1980s, as the control of the flow of people from rural areas was eased, these hostels became even more overcrowded and the facilities were not able to sustain the increased population.

In the 1990s, as part of the Reconstruction and Development Programme, the new ANC-led government decided to upgrade the hostels and turn them into family accommodation (Figure 17.5). It was the latter move which provided the catalyst for the development of the Lwandle Museum. Charmian Plummer, a resident from Somerset West who had done considerable voluntary work in Lwandle over the years, felt that at least one hostel should be preserved in order to sustain a memory of how the system of apartheid had operated. She, together with Bongani Mgijima, a young resident of Lwandle and graduate of the Post-graduate Diploma in Museum and Heritage Studies (which is jointly offered by UWC, UCT and the Robben Island Museum), worked to establish a museum on the basis of a preserved hostel. When the opportunity arose to take occupation of an old community hall, their plans expanded and on 1 May 2000 the Lwandle Migrant Labour Museum was officially opened.

Three types of display featured at the Lwandle Migrant Labour Museum in 2000/1. The most striking and overwhelming image was that of an enlarged version of the pass book, the identity document through which the lives of Africans in urban areas were controlled, with a sign above indicating segregated beach facilities for people racially designated white. (Lwandle is near the town of Strand, which translated from Afrikaans means 'the sea'. Lwandle is the Xhosa word for 'sea'.) This enlarged book gazed upon a set of wheelbarrows containing artefacts that were used by the residents of hostels. These barrows are an

Figure 17.5
Lwandle: from hostels to homes.

installation work by Cape Town artist Gavin Younge. Finally, on a set of panels surrounding the barrows are photographs from the UWC-Robben Island Museum Mayibuye Archive, showing images of migrant labour, from poverty in the rural areas to influx control and resistance. This exhibition was designed to draw in members of the community whose individual stories would contribute to developing displays and building collections.

The museum has endeavoured to become a destination on the township-tour route (Figure 17.6). For instance, it offers a 'safe guided walk' through the 'whole township' with an excursion through 'an original historic hostel'. This is presented as an opportunity to 'learn more about the migrant labour system (1958–94), (Lwandle Migrant Labour Museum 2000). But this legacy of repression and resistance to apartheid is placed within an internationalised tourist representation of traditional Africa as a place of essentialised ethnic rhythms, tastes and crafts. The result, as Bongani Mgijima and Vusi Buthelezi (2001: 8), curators of the Lwandle Museum put it, is that the intention to portray the political and economic history of migrancy often has to make way for a tourist expectation of 'authentic Africa', where migrant histories might be exoticised to fit in with tourist expectations long conditioned by histories of travel. Thus, the museum includes images of 'traditional dress' in its promotional material, claims that it is a site of 'cultural activities' and offers, among other items, 'beadwork and other locally produced souvenirs' (Lwandle Migrant Labour Museum 2000). Despite these marketing efforts, the museum has not been able to insert itself as

Figure 17.6
Visiting Hostel 33, Lwandle.

a destination for township tourism in the Western Cape. This may be a result of its distance from central Cape Town, but perhaps it is also because it does not conform to images of what constitutes an 'African place'.

For museums in the townships, like the Lwandle Museum, the question of how they locate themselves within the international tourist image economy is a difficult one. The museum has embarked upon projects that seek to develop new notions of a public citizenry through the construction of a new set of public pasts. At the same time, the museum must also engage with international tourists and aspire to locate itself as a unique destination on routes into the past. While the museum definitely does not want to locate itself as an exotic destination, the tourist industry demands places of difference. The museum is having to constantly mediate the pasts it collects, presents and represents in order to ensure that it becomes a 'Destination Culture' (Kirshenblatt-Gimblett 1998).

CONCLUSION

As I was finishing off this chapter, a feature article appeared in a South African weekly newspaper, the *Mail & Guardian*, claiming that Cape Town was promoting itself to international tourists as 'a European outpost'. In the world of 'glossy images', 'clichéd expectations' and 'vacation fantasy', the 'real city', where a 'glistening grey sea of shacks' stretch 'out over the sandy wastes of the Cape Flats', was being 'swept out of sight' (Rostron 2001). Township tours are based on the premise of making this 'real city' visible. 'Experience another facet of Cape Town, one revealed to very few tourists', claims one company (Cape Rainbow Tours 2000). Another '[I]nvites you to look beyond the Rainbow Curtain' (Grassroute Tours 2000). And yet another has produced an information booklet for tour guides about 'another side of Cape Town: a side that we prefer not to show the tourist' (Johannes 2000: i). Whereas tourism training has generally been limited to snippets of knowledge about the 'most beautiful city in the world', the information booklet provides guides with a foundation that will enable them to show tourists 'a reality we have to face'. Although the author asserts that 'squatter camps' are 'not a very good way of introducing Cape Town to tourists and visitors', the booklet aims to assist guides 'in answering questions from tourists ... about the black townships and squatter camps of our city' (Johannes 2000: i).

There is no doubt that these township-tour companies and their guides are presenting, through their routes and destinations, a part of the city that stretches beyond Cape Point, Table Mountain, the Castle of Good Hope, Rhodes Memorial and the Victoria and Alfred Waterfront. But, in the stories that are presented, the sites that are visited, and the people that are called upon, the townships retain an aura of being hidden places, where there is a 'maze of dwellings, customs and traditions' and 'it is peremptory to go with a guide'. And more than anything, the routes along which one is guided take one into an essentialised Africa, where key stops are the 'witch doctor's store' and a 'shack where a few elderly men sit on the floor … conversate and drink Mqombotie [*sic*]' (*Event Magazine* 1998: 7). While slices of political history have started to make their way onto these routes – and the information booklet referred to above provides guides with a handy reference, the tours remain encounters where 'the West meets Africa'. In this world of tradition, museums which attempt to present a history of political struggle find very little space. Instead, in the townships one encounters the 'music, dancing, mysticism, hospitality, joy, laughter, hope … beauty … and friendliness of the people' (*Event Magazine* 1998: 7). As the inhabitants of the township have been cast in their assigned (traditional?) roles, and their homes, schools and social places converted into tourist sites, so a series of dioramas have been constructed and the townships of the Western Cape have taken their place on the beaten track of international tourism as living museums to 'township life' (Grassroute Tours 2000).

REFERENCES

Carew, D. (2001) 'Visitors More Interested in Robben Island than Table Mountain, Says Tourism Boss', *Saturday Argus* 3/4 March.

Chapman, K. (1999) 'Township Tours – Exploitation or Opportunity', *Cape Times* 8 July.

De Kadt, E. (1979) *Tourism: Passport to Development?*, Oxford: UNESCO–World Bank.

Debere, S. (2000/1) 'The Life and Soul of Cape Town' *Travel Africa* 14.

Dondolo, L. (2000) 'The District Six Museum, Cape Town', paper presented to the *Public History, Forgotten History* Conference, University of Namibia, 22–25 August.

Event Magazine: The Exclusive Guide to the Cape (1988) Cape Town: GDCB Project Management, February.

Gordon, R., Rassool C. and Witz, L. (1996) 'Fashioning the Bushman in Van Riebeeck's Cape Town, 1952 and 1993' in P Skotnes (ed.) *Miscast: Negotiating the Presence of the Bushmen*, Cape Town: UCT Press: 257–69.

Holiday, A. (1994) 'Desire to Shake off Colonial Trappings', *Cape Times* 8 July.

Jeppie, M.S. (1987) 'Historical Processes and the Constitution of Subjects: I. D. du Plessis and the Reinvention of the "Malay" ', unpublished Honours paper, University of Cape Town.

Johannes, C. (2000) *The History of The Black Townships and Squatter Camps of Cape Town*, Cape Town: Southern Tip Tours.

Kirshenblatt-Gimblett, B. (1998) *Destination Culture*, Berkeley, CA: UCLA Press.

Kurin, R. (1997) *Reflections of a Cultural Broker: A View from the Smithsonian*, Washington: Smithsonian Institution Press.

Lippard, L. (1999) *On the Beaten Track*, New York: New Press.

Mathieson, A. and Wall, G. (1982) *Tourism: Economic, Physical and Social Impacts*, London: Longman.

Mgijima, B. and Buthelezi, V. (2001) 'Mapping Museum – Community Relations in Lwandle', unpublished paper presented to the *Mapping Alternatives: Debating New Heritage Practices in South Africa* conference, hosted by the Project on Public Pasts (UWC) and the Research Unit for the Archaeology of Cape Town (UCT), 22–23 September.

Minty, Z. (2005) 'Hola Cape Town: It's Time to Take Back the Streets – Critical Public Art Practice in Cape Town from 1999', unpublished paper presented to the Institutions of Public Culture workshop, University of Cape Town, 7–9 July.

Mokaba, P. (1994) 'Tourism: A Development and Reconstruction Perspective', Johannesburg: ANC.

Rassool, C. (1997) 'The Individual, Biography and Resistance in South African Public History', South African and Contemporary History Seminar, University of the Western Cape, 7 October.

Rassool, C. and Witz, L. (1996) '"South Africa: A World in One Country": Moments in International Tourist Encounters with Wildlife, the Primitive and the Modern' in Cahiers d'Etudes Africaines, 143, XXXVI-3.

Rassool, C. and Prosalendis, S. (2001) Recalling Community in Cape Town: Creating and Curating the District Six Museum, Cape Town: District Six Museum.

Rix, C. (2000/1) 'The Fairest Cape', Travel Africa, 14.

Rostron, B. (2001) 'The Last Outpost', Mail & Guardian 20–26 July.

Solani, N. (2000) 'Memory and Representation: Robben Island Museum 1977–1999', MA mini-thesis, University of the Western Cape.

Worden, N., Bickford-Smith, V. and Van Heyningen, E. (1999) Cape Town in the Twentieth Century, vol. 2, Cape Town: David Philip.

Pamphlets

African Mosaic Tours (2000) Cape Town: pamphlet.

Cape Rainbow Tours (2000) 'See the Cape in Colour', Cape Town: pamphlet.

Cape Team Tours (2001) 'Township Tours: Cultural Tour of Cape Town', Cape Town: pamphlet.

Day Trippers: Your Alternative Tour Co (2001) Cape Town: pamphlet.

District Six Museum (2001) 'A Guide to the District Six Museum and the Digging Deeper Exhibition', Cape Town, pamphlet.

Eziko Cooking and Catering Training Centre (2000) 'Eziko Cooking: Share the Taste', Langa, Cape Town: pamphlet.

Grassroute Tours (2000) 'Grassroute Tours Invites You to Have a Look beyond the Rainbow Curtain', Cape Town: pamphlet.

Lwandle Migrant Labour Museum (2000) 'Lwandle Migrant Labour Museum and Arts and Crafts Centre', Cape Town: pamphlet.

Philani Nutrition Centres (2000) Cape Town: pamphlet.

Southern Tip Tours (2000) 'To the End of Africa', Cape Town: pamphlet.

Springbok Atlas Safaris (2000) 'Day Tours pamphlet', Cape Town: pamphlet.

Chapter 18: Public Reflections

Njabulo S. Ndebele

Writer, academic and public figure, Njabulo Ndebele is often called upon to make public representations. His return to South Africa in the early 1990s after a 20-year absence saw Ndebele beginning a process of public reflection around issues of identity and exile, and the ways in which these are played out against the background of political landscapes. He wrote in the popular media at the time: 'Perhaps home for me can only be some concept of belonging to some historic process; some sense of historic justice assuming, on the day of liberation, the physical space of a country' (DeKler 1997: appendix). He was writing in very personal terms about his displacement and the journey he made taking his family to the place of his birth – the house at 925 John Mohohlo Street, Western Native Townships – which he could not find.

The texts contained in this chapter are edited versions of two instances of public address in which Ndebele reflects directly and metaphorically on the state of being in South Africa, and in which the personal and the public are interwoven. The first piece, from 1997, reflects his opening remarks made for the exhibition *blank_Architecture, apartheid and after*, entitled 'Breaking free of the present'. In this piece, delivered in Rotterdam to an audience of architects, planners and cultural practitioners across a wide range of disciplines, he further elaborates on questions of home and belonging in a country whose space is tainted by an 'inherited presence' where 'inherited inequities and divisions still abound'. For Ndebele, the space of creativity is the only space in which we can 'break free' and 'make a home'.

Ndebele's intellectual sense of the critical involvement of landscape in writing, and his awareness of the ability of landscape to reflect interrupted narratives and fragmented histories, is made all the keener by his personal experience of exile and dislocation. He speaks here, in his public capacity as intellectual, to his personal feelings of alienation born of exile from his home, of the need to make a home within the personal space of creativity, and of the implications this has for the meaningful rewriting of the South African landscape. For Ndebele, the framing of landscape as 'blank' is the first step in a process of a rewriting which acknowledges the burden of pain, violence and dispossession encoded within landscape, as well as embraces the possibility of the recreation of new post-apartheid identities and narratives.

The second address was made on Freedom Day 2004 – ten years after South Africans elected their country's first democratic government – where, as author and intellectual, Ndebele delivered the sermon in Cape Town's famous St George's Cathedral to an audience of congregants, dignitaries, intellectuals and members of the public. His theme – perspective – captures the intersecting fault-lines of the occasion: the journey of the church from bulwark of colonialism to advocate of liberation; Ndebele's own journey from radical student activist to university vice-chancellor; the site of the Cathedral, positioned at the intersection of the commercial heart of the city and the legislative precinct of parliament; and the architecture of the building itself – Victorian complacency supplanted by today's humility of ministry in the face of massive poverty and hardship.

Ndebele speaks of the limited perspective imposed in the past by apartheid now emerging as new creative spaces which are animated both by the ability to view others from multiple perspectives, as well as the willingness to encounter and embrace difference.

Along with his extensive writings, the moments referred to above show Ndebele stepping into the role of the public intellectual, an individual 'with a vocation for the art of representing, whether it is talking, writing, teaching, appearing on television' (Said 1994: 10).

Both occasions are moments in which Ndebele becomes the 'representative figure that matters – someone who visibly represents a standpoint of some kind, and someone who makes articulate representations to his or her public despite all sorts of barriers' (Said 1994: 10). As argued by Said in his now famous 1993 Reith Lectures entitled 'Representations of the Intellectual', both these occasions are, for Ndebele and his audience, moments where private and public spaces overlap and become enmeshed, where 'personal inflection' and 'private sensibility' 'give meaning to what is being said' (Said 1994: 9).

*

[T]he logic of mass removals and resettlements is the logic of conquest, still playing itself out inexorably in the 1960s and 1970s. This strongly suggests that we still have millions of South Africans today whose experience of the South African landscape is that of space invaded by them. Space possessed through determined dispossession. Once invaded, the space has to be fiercely defended and protected from the encroachments of the dispossessed. [...]

By the same token, there are many millions more South Africans whose experience of the South African landscape is that of lost space which, in some undetermined future, has to be reclaimed. The space they were permitted to occupy without the exercise of choice, was often the space of deprivation, and violence. It presented them with a future of uncertainty and impermanence, with limited possibilities for planning the future. [...]

Both experiences of South African space present themselves to us as dominant features of our post-apartheid reality. They are so formidable, they cannot be wished away. Yet, their forbidding presence makes us so conscious of the future. It makes us so aware of the link between human history and the transformation of the landscape, and how that link may fashion identity. It makes us ask what will be the nature of our contribution to transforming this inherited landscape, and what questions will we ask as we set about that task. [...]

[H]ow do we set about creating a home? Right now, we do not have a common home. We are faced with an inherited presence which sends us conflicting messages. [...]

This exhibition [*blank_Architecture, apartheid and after*] brings to the fore the complex of images of our landscape which have dominated South African history: South Africa as outpost (space to be fortified: the 'laager', the Battle of Blood River). South Africa as 'promised land' on which churches, promising different kinds of heaven, are ranged on opposing sides. South Africa as anthropological 'homeland', the imagined authenticities of 'Bantustans', and 'homesteads'. The South Africa of internal migrations: Group Areas, 'black spots', 'removal and resettlement schemes', all yielding their harvest of hostels, 'informal settlements', 'squatter camps' hovels of wood or corrugated iron, and dormitory townships, that monotony of similarity. South Africa of the mine dumps. Gold. Diamonds. Coal. Chrome. South Africa, the land of plenty: huge multi-storied mansions, swimming pools, double garages, bathrooms 'en suite', parks, high-rise glass buildings, highways and shopping malls. [...]

Through these conflicting images and messages, we are presented with a formidable reality of the present. Yet it is a reality which presents us with the one available space of creativity to make a home. The only space through which we can break free of the very present. We break free from a white space to create a human space heavily informed by the visions of interrupted histories.

With this exhibition should begin what is perhaps the most important South African dialogue since the national dialogue that led to the writing of the constitution. This is the dialogue about writing the land. It is a project which affects all of us intimately. [...]

This historic exhibition … is the first of its kind to enable us to read the great stories of human settlement that have been written on our land in South Africa. The writers of these stories have been many, although some writers became more dominant than others. Indeed, the dominant ones have been able to spread their texts all over the land, enabling us to see them and read them more than others. … Such stories were often written at the cost of great pain. [...]

We want to affirm what freedom recently brought to South Africa: that there are other stories on our land; that new stories will be written on our land. We want to say: other stories will have to be retold. Interrupted narratives completed. [...]

[T]here will be blank pages; there will be half-told stories; and there will be full texts. These full texts, however, and I'm talking about the inherited landscape of cities, townships and squatter camps, will continue to command our attention, requiring us to reinterpret them. Indeed, over the centuries, they have become a reality too formidable to erase. Nor will it necessarily be desirable to erase it. So intricately bound with the nature of our needs, they have become ours. Sometimes we will need to find spaces in between the lines, or on the sides of the page, at the bottom or at the top, to insert urgent messages. Altogether, both the insertions and the new texts, will be part of a new order. It will be an order structured by those who never had the opportunity to write their stories on the land. That is the meaning of this exhibition. The beginning of a dialogue to make possible the writing of new stories over the landscape of a new country. [...]

(Rotterdam, 1998)

*

I want to explore with you the theme of perspective. The word 'perspective' has several, but closely related, meanings .... But the one I want to hold on to defines 'perspective' as 'the appearance to the eye of objects in relation to their relative distance and positions'. [...]

If you want to experience the meaning of perspective beyond this kind of technical definition, try to walk regularly on many of Cape Town's lovely walking trails. The first time I entered a forest I had never been to, I recall being hesitant, wondering, being of the kind often subject to a fertile imagination, what unknown threats lay there ahead of me. But then, you realise after a while as you move on and nothing happens to you except the increasingly joyful experience of being in communion with nature, that if there were any threats, they existed only in your imagination. [...]

At this point, let's return to our definition of 'perspective' and recall the key expressions in it that we identified. The first one 'appearance to the eye' is expressed with scientific objectivity as something that happens to the eye. In fact, it is your eye. Through your eyes, things appear to you. But things appear to you in relation to other things. [...]

Experiencing the world from multiple perspectives presents the world to you as something constantly changing depending on where you are when you are looking at it. But the miracle that suddenly strikes you is that you become aware that there is one thing that remains constant through all the multiple perspectives that you experience: it is the experience of yourself as the one that experiences all the changes. You, the experiencing self, are the constant feature in the transformation around you. Even if an experience changes you, you are still aware of yourself as changing. [...]

You are the one who remains constant through changing perspectives of reality. You are the constant consciousness that experiences change. Your consciousness is the stable factor in the transformation around you. It is the treasure that enables you to navigate through change.

What has all this to do with celebrating ten years of democracy? It has become common to look at the past ten years and count off the number of things we have achieved. [...]

Yet, I believe that the revolution that really occurred is often not fully appreciated. It is the extent to which each and every one of us appreciates just how much depends on how we experience ourselves as the stable consciousness amidst change. [...]

The greatest damage of apartheid is how it conditioned all of us to experience the world from a single perspective. That is how it killed our capacity for self-reflection. [...]

[O]ur new country … is about embracing uncertainty with some confidence because the ability to do so is the new source of creativity. Our country is about embracing multiple perspectives. […]

[O]ur freedom is about increasing the opportunities for experiencing multiple perspectives and learning to draw meaning from their interactions. […]

There is nothing more unifying than the values of tolerance, compassion, humility, and open-mindedness. If we allow these to mediate between us, we draw the fullest meaning of ten years of our democracy. […]

(Cape Town, 2004)

REFERENCES

DeKler, A. (1997) *South African Seasons, March 1997–March 1998*, Rotterdam: Netherlands Architecture Institute.

Said, E. (1994) *Representations of the Intellectual*, London: Vintage.

Chapter 19: A Renaissance on Our Doorsteps

John Matshikiza

The city (Johannesburg, that is) is moving.[1] Perhaps that means the whole country is moving – ugly, functional, here-today-gone-tomorrow Johannesburg being South Africa's powerhouse, cultural and economic hub, magnet for Africa's rough and ready, and barometer of what's up and what's down.

In the northern suburbs money is being turned into concrete and steel and throwing up office blocks, multistorey parking lots, and a bizarre and ever-increasing array of luxury townhouse complexes built in the ersatz style of Tuscan villages. Rivonia and Fourways have never had it so good. The white and black empowerment muscle behind this seems to be living out a fantasy world of dreams of a distant, civilised past out there in the Europe that it left behind. The luxury 4×4s that purr between its offices and restaurants and casinos have no idea that they are in Africa, and no interest in being relieved of their delusions.

Meanwhile, down here on the ground, the inner city is changing too. Hillbrow and Berea, once home to white bohemian civilisation, artists, poets, closet revolutionaries and old Jewish ladies who still remembered when they were not so old and could go down for a decent cup of coffee after the hairdresser, have become a hectic, extended, offshore suburb of Lagos and Kinshasa, with South Africa's traditional mix of whores and *tsotsis* ducking and diving in between.

Then there's Yeoville, just a few steps down the road, within easy shooting distance of the Telkom Tower and Ponte City.

Yeoville has become Johannesburg's new Sophiatown. It used to be white. Now it is distinctly black. Just as Sophiatown transcended its original purpose and became the home of an earlier African renaissance, like Harlem, with all its inevitable highs and lows, Yeoville has moved from easygoing gentility to slum – but a slum with a vibe and a disorganised sense of purpose.

The slum that Yeoville has become is where the people make it happen. Because they can. Because finally, out of the desperation of poverty, alienation and disempowerment on the fringes, they can step out into the street on their own terms, dress up in boubous and furs, and talk loudly out of their own mouths.

Johannesburg has become a tale of two cities – or perhaps it always was that way. The difference is that the two cities are now crammed up against each other, and not bothering to try to make any sense of the arrangement.

The elite hang out at the Rhema Church and the synagogues up there in the north. The povos hang out here in Yeoville, and do the best they can under the circumstances.

After a drab and ugly period of uncertainty, Yeoville seems to have rediscovered an identity. The filth and denigration so eloquently described by Es'kia Mphahlele when referring to his native Marabastad and all the other townships that blacks were locked into is certainly a feature of the new Sophiatown that is Yeoville. But a walk through its streets on a Sunday morning also reminds you of the kind of energy that made Sophiatown buzz in spite of all its problems.

There are churches everywhere, with loud music soaring out of the doors in the midst of the cacophony of hungover reprobates trawling the streets through the litter of last night's shattered beer bottles, and wondering where the next liquid relief is coming from. Cameroonian women in all their finery drag their carefully groomed children on a shopping expedition towards the West African marketplace, picking out healthy tomatoes and aubergines and chunks of halaal lamb for Sunday lunch, in this buzzing place that sits cheek by jowl with the queues waiting to stock up on essentials in the impersonal corridors of overpriced merchandise at white-owned Shoprite.

White-robed devotees of the various amaZiona churches who send their voices to God on the rugged hills overlooking the city stride through this stew of Sodom and Gomorrah with their chins held high in superior disdain. And the Rastas crack open an early libation of Hansa on the roof of what used to be a trendy bar and restaurant called Tandoor.

From on high, and far away in Pretoria and Cape Town, the leaders of the new dispensation that once was the Republic of South Africa dispense wisdom to the world about the African renaissance. Meanwhile, Africa is getting on with a renaissance of its own: alive, vibrant, dangerous and relentlessly colourful. Just like Sophiatown.

But it seems like the leadership is, after all, taking an interest in all of this. Yeoville, Troyeville, Hillbrow, Bertrams and other marginalised suburbs, which have effectively become in-house townships, are receiving serious attention in the plans of the Johannesburg Development Agency and whatever it trails behind it. The year 2010 and the soccer World Cup have suddenly made them sit up and think about how to make Johannesburg look like Barcelona, Paris and London.

So they are moving forward with some speed to gentrify Yeoville and those other places, bulldoze the old in the traditional apartheid way, and make them look acceptable by the standards of the civilised world.

There is a huge contradiction here, which nobody seems to be dealing with. While we would all like to see Yeoville looking cleaner and smelling prettier, we certainly don't want to see it lose its new and exciting African character.

It would be a disaster for Yeoville to end up looking, sounding and feeling like those ridiculous neo-Tuscan villages in the north, which have no reference to the soil in which they are lodged.

Yeoville and Kliptown and the people who live there, are what the African renaissance really is. It would be interesting to see that translated into some political vision for the future – and allow these to remain places where the people count.

Afterword

Lines of Desire

Martin Hall

A 'desire line' is an informal path rather than an official route; an intersection that reveals notions of space, memory and identity in the post-apartheid city; contested spaces of power and privilege, identity and difference; palimpsests of historical experience; lived spaces in the everyday performance of urban life (Shepherd and Murray, this volume). Lines of desire cut across the formal grid, challenging the search for order, engaging in a tussle for recognition and difference, and risking disappointment and destruction as the stamp of authority is reasserted.

Cape Town began as a grid imposed on the troubling disorder of the colonised landscape. Its orthogonal grid grew to include houses and gardens, Castle, Church and Slave House, and a Garden of walkways and planted beds, 'rich in fruits and flowers', enclosed by 'a wall a rood high and a moat half a rood wide' and defined by rules for its use and maintenance (Hall 2000, 2006). Visitors drew a comparison between this geometric regularity and the wild and untamed nature of Devil's Peak behind, 'a land that seems the most sterile and horrible in the world' (Raven Hart 1971: 276–7).

These early texts of the city included a long memoir by François Valentyn, first published in 1726. Valentyn was particularly drawn to the Garden, following his own line of desire that was both threatening and alluring: Table Mountain, 'barren and rocky', 'everything that is horrid and frightening', opposed to the 'very fine and delightful arbours roofed with foliage, where one can long sit hidden from everyone' and where 'Nature and Art seem to have brought together in unity all that can give pleasure' (Valentyn 1971: 107). To hide away in the public space of the grid and to wander off the walkways in search of delightful arbours invited contradictions, and Valentyn's pleasure was infused with anxiety. The 'womb of this African Mother-Garden' offered 'astonishingly large nurseries of melons' that gave 'exceptional relief' to 'the worn-out and scurvy-smitten seaman'. But such a man can never be 'sated' by the Garden because he 'continually experiences a new desire to be in it again' (Valentyn 1971: 105, 107).

Three centuries later, the Voortrekker Monument celebrated the expansion of the formal grid from city to nation, a network of roads and municipalities, farm boundaries, magisterial districts, group areas and homelands, 'a marker of systemic violence and a material signifier of events that sedimented the policies of institutionalised racism', creating 'the illusion of a collective identity through the political staging of vicarious spectacle' (Meskell, this volume). And again the ambiguity of desire, the symbol of the nation that is also a magnet for mainstream Afrikaans pornography, 'Dina at the Monument', Voortrekker descendant, bare-breasted child of the wilderness in the tall grass, with leopardskin shorts, khaki vest and wild hair: 'if you interfere with my symbols, you interfere with me' (Coombes 2003; Meskell, this volume).

Despite the assertions of official historiography, the Cape of 1652 was no empty land. Africa was replete with legends of cannibals and one-footed creatures, collated in the bestselling 'Mandeville's Travels', or the stories of the fabulous wealth of Prester John, always over the next range of mountains (Hall 2000). Valentyn's anxieties extended beneath his feet, as he sought to 'dredge up from the ground the things which have occurred here' (Valentyn 1973: 127). These included accounts of Portuguese shipwrecks a century earlier, Dona Leonor, ravished, who buried herself up to her waist in the sand and covered her upper body as best she could with her long hair, and her husband who

> went back alone to the forest, refusing to take anyone with him, and since then no word nor sign of him was perceived, from which it was decided that he was eaten by some wild beast, unless from sorrow he helped himself to his end in some other manner.
>
> (Valentyn 1973: 145)

And always present was the colonists' image of the Khoikhoi:

> in the early records one finds a repertoire of remarkable facts about the Hottentots repeated again and again: their implosives ('turkey-gobbling'), their eating of unwashed intestines, their use of animal fat to smear their bodies, their habit of wrapping dried entrails around their necks, peculiarities of the pudenda of their women, their inability to conceive of God, their incorrigible indolence.
>
> (Coetzee 1988: 22)

Today, as 300 years ago, the ground beneath the city is subject to 'sudden eruptions, surfacings, unexpected returns', whether through the exhumation of contested burials, or the 'institutionalised resurfacings' of the Truth and Reconciliation Commission (Shepherd and Ernsten, this volume). Graves are unstable markers in the landscape, 'entangled in the traffic between citizens and subjects' (Lalu, this volume). Thus the politics of Hintsa's lost head, the claims on his grave in the Eastern Cape, the complex discourse of reparation, colonial violence, development and tourism, and unresolved tensions of gender; the 'patriarchal dividend' that continues to assert the dominance of men and subordination of women by insisting that stories from the past are not resolved (Lalu, this volume).

Garden and landscape, then, embody metaphors for the tensions between order and disorder, between the geometry of the grid and random pathways of curiosity, between memories of that which has been experienced and desire for that which has yet to be attained, between what is still concealed beneath the ground and the surface, and its possibilities. Space and time intersect as social constructions, 'the space between the planned and the providential, the engineered and the "lived", and between official projects of capture and containment and the popular energies which subvert, bypass, supersede and evade them' (Shepherd and Murray, this volume).

*

The social construction of 'official' space has invariably been a figuration of the grid, whether in the layout of the formal garden, the colonial city, modernist planning, cadastral systems of mapping or the very boundaries of the African nation state, with lines of demarcation cutting through mountain ranges, deserts and forests without regard to the nature of the land and the rights and histories of those who have lived there long before. Desire lines violate the order of the grid, and are invariably forms of resistance, whether the transcripts of everyday misbehaviour (Scott 1990), or milestones marked and monumentalised as history, such as the Soweto marches of 1976 (Meskell, this volume). Violation of the grid invariably evokes discipline and punishment – Foucault's key analysis of the tension between order and disorder (Foucault 1979). Violence is inherent in the social construction of space. Recall the fate of Estienne Barbier, who led a minor rebellion by a group of colonists who were discontented with the company's restrictions on their own violent exploitation of the Khoikhoi. After being pronounced guilty, Barbier was

> bound upon a double wooden cross that was used for those condemned to be broken on the wheel; first his right hand and then his head were struck off with a hatchet; he was then quartered and his entrails buried under the gallows, while the head and hand were nailed to a stake which was set up in Heer Straat, a road that leads from the Castle to the interior. The four quarters were sent into the interior and fastened to stakes which were set up in the districts.
>
> (Mentzel 1919: 117)

Social space is institutionalised at different scales. Azeem Badroodien shows how the Ottery School of Industries sought both to formalise and contain 'colouredness' within the racial typology of apartheid, creating a 'metropolitan vocabulary' that is still evident in contemporary discussions about the nature of the city in South Africa. Such institutions were

> formative in the lives of so many of those institutionalised in the web of social institutions spread across the city, both in shaping how they understood and engaged with their subsequent lives, and in moulding the pasts, foibles and needs of individuals in ways that was supposed to make them 'more decent' and 'respectable' future citizens and 'urban dwellers'.
>
> (Badroodien, this volume)

At the next scale up – the level of the suburb – Steven Robins tracks the agency and resistance of those who have been – and are – the subjects of state and municipal social engineering and town planning. Through looking in detail at Manenberg, created from the forced removals of the group areas legislation and taken as an exemplar of social dysfunctionality, Robins highlights the challenge to governmentality in the contemporary city. On one side, the gated communities, surveillance and 'Californianisation' of Cape Town. On the other side, the disorderly, criminalised world beyond the limits of control:

> Manenberg regularly features in the media as a space of 'social pathology' and dysfunctionality, a representation that is reproduced through almost daily violence and gang killings. It is also associated with the highly militaristic and hierarchical prison gangs such as the '28s' and '26s' that have in recent years transformed themselves into sophisticated corporate structures connected to multinational drug cartels and crime syndicates such as 'The Firm', the 'Hard Livings' and the 'Americans'. Drug trafficking, alcohol sales and distribution, gunrunning, taxis and sex work are the major sources of revenue of this multibillion-dollar industry. With its extremely high levels of unemployment and poverty, Manenberg has become a ripe recruiting ground for the foot soldiers of the drug kingpins, the merchants and hitmen.
>
> (Robins, this volume)

Ottery and Manenberg were shaped by the grid of apartheid modernism – the geography of locations and relocations, class, race, segregated services and Group Area boundaries that structured the apartheid city and which will continue to shape the future city. Within these boundaries are the pleasure gardens of the present and future, such as the gated utopia of Century City and the GrandWest entertainment destination. Such places are 'amalgams of nostalgia and desire – shaped, and shaping, aspects of city living'. As such, they invariably invoke memory in the form of heritage – material remnants of the past that can be re-imbued and saturated with associations and interpretations. Contemporary South Africa is particularly susceptible to this combination of nostalgia, desire and consumerism, which provides new senses of home in a burgeoning, but markedly unequal, economy. Retail outlets, food and drink, movies and, in some cases, gambling, combined with secure parking, perimeter controls and internal surveillance and security, are new forms of public places, albeit with a 'public' that is defined in practice by those who are excluded (Hall and Bombardella, this volume). By evoking desire, entertainment destinations seek to legitimate the new grids of control and authority, the linear successors of the Dutch East India Company's Garden and the 'very fine and delightful arbours' encased within the protective walls of the perimeter.

Heritage is as much an evocation of the past as a relationship with the present, requiring not only the recall and representation of previous lives and circumstances, but also the motivation of today's participants, with their own desires and purposes. Consequently, the heritage of Cape Town's most widely known site of racial cleansing – District Six, from which more than 60,000 people were forcibly removed in the 1960s, 1970s and 1980s – can either be recalled for the purposes of fleeting consumerism at GrandWest (where it provides the theme for a food court and shopping mall) or for the reconstruction of community through memory and reconciliation (Rassool, this volume).

The potential contradictions inherent in heritage come together in Leslie Witz's account of township tours, a particular characteristic of the post-apartheid city. The township tour reasserts the grid of order and control. 'Trustworthy escorts' are offered to places of crime and potential danger. The township is presented as outside the orderly world:

> through the very routes they traverse, the sites they point out, and the destinations they call upon, these tours, almost inadvertently, confirm the spatial arrangements of apartheid. Explicitly, they are not offered as tours of Cape Town, but rather as separate, distinct, township tours. It is almost as if the tourist is being offered a journey to an exotic destination outside the boundaries of the city, where the attractions are beer-makers, traditional healers, dancing, taverns and shanty towns.
>
> Instead of presenting museums to the touring public, the townships in the Western Cape have become living museums on a grand scale. The primary sites and destinations are not classified by scenic or historical interest but through their ability to provide an opportunity to identify and to see 'the people' in carefully curated settings: at home, at school, on the streets, at work (but not in an industrial context) and at leisure. There is the mandatory visit to a few carefully selected people in their homes, ranging from a small tin and wood house to a room in a hostel or a new Reconstruction and Development Programme home. A daycare centre is chosen to put on a daily performance for the tourists. The 'short walk' through a series of designated streets, under the watchful eye of the guide, is intended to impart a 'feel' of the townships. At a craft centre, tourists are able to satisfy their expectation of encountering work and development. Simultaneously they can also 'feel good' by purchasing what appears to be a handmade memory of Africa. Finally, there is the social experience, set up in a 'safe' shebeen, where the tourists will be able to partake of township life but where they won't be harassed by drunken and disorderly clientele.
>
> (Witz, this volume)

At the same time, though, the itinerary of the township tour intersects with museums built from within the community as sites of reconciliation and reconstruction, and particularly with the District Six Museum, which Witz notes is inevitably a part of every route. As Rassool has also shown in this volume, the District Six Museum is both a memory project of a specific community and a recollection and interrogation of forced removals in general – and therefore of the violence and dislocation that is the essence of the national history of apartheid. In this, the District Six Museum looks to the future:

> one of the most important missions of the District Six Museum is to question race at every turn and to assert a politics of non-racialism and anti-racism in every facet of its work. The museum holds on to and propounds the possibility of a non-racial community, as it emerges out of and is reflected in the history of District Six.
>
> (Rassool, this volume)

At this site, then, the 'tourist gaze' confronts the reconstruction of community through memory, an intersection of the 'projects of capture and containment', and 'the popular energies which subvert, bypass, supersede and evade them'.

Potent, unstable spaces such as the District Six Museum are the creative nodes where new configurations of social space may emerge. Abdulkader Tayob's case study of negotiated heritage is one such instance. Here, the modernist tradition of rational planning deadlocked with the assertion of post-apartheid identity in the contestation of Muslim burial sites on the margins of the grid of the city. The rules and procedures of law, regulation, government agency and research required argument and evidence. But from the perspective of the Muslim Judicial Council, the scales of governmentality were weighted against the community. The MJC's currency was rather community solidarity, public opinion and the long history of repression and the denial of heritage:

> the identification of heritage sites furnished the occasion to evoke powerful narratives waiting to be told. Principally, heritage sites determined by archival records risk telling only one kind of story: the story of the victors. Even though the oral respondents in this case did not locate their narratives at the site in question, they were instrumental in giving concrete life to new perceptions of the mountain previously ignored on the margins of Cape society.

The way forward lay in a different conceptualisation, one of 'sacred space', a 'new space over the old' (Tayob, this volume).

The social construction of such new senses of space is work in progress, a set of tentative explorations that may result in a different order, but which may also fall back into the old, contested, regime that has been a defining feature of the city from its earliest days through to post-apartheid planning and regulation. The conundrums of this exploration are captured by a contemporary garden of remembrance – the Apartheid Museum. As Lindsay Bremner shows, the Apartheid Museum is representative of a new genre, an 'evolving cartography of sites' dedicated to apartheid memory and narrative: the Robben Island and District Six Museums in Cape Town and the Hector Pieterson Museum in Soweto (studies in various chapters in this volume), the Museum of the Peoples' Struggle in Port Elizabeth, the Fort Museum in Johannesburg, the Cato Manor Museum in Durban. Such cultural institutions evoke new kinds of public consciousness and new kinds of public encounters, 'excavating the apartheid consciousness, and subjecting it to an exhibitionary gaze'. Archival displays are of texts, film footage and photographs:

> where people tell their stories, bear witness to their apartheids, they tend to be its icons – Hendrik Verwoerd, Winnie Mandela, Mangosuthu Buthelezi. Other more ordinary unknown people acquire iconic status, as their hyper-scaled presences tell their stories in the documentaries that are shown in the museum's viewing rooms. This effectively objectifies apartheid, thereby making it more easily consumable.
>
> (Bremner, this volume)

The experience of the museum is structured and enhanced by a visceral re-creation of the containment and oppression of the 'apartheid condition':

> Its enveloping windowless wall (stone packed in steel cages) and south west corner lift shaft resembling a prison watchtower, make obvious connections to incarceration.... On entry, one's ticket classifies one as black or white, re-enacting the discrimination practised in every social space and on entry into every public building under apartheid. ... After ascending the entrance ramp and descending into the museum again, one feels 'claustrophobic panic'. The gratuitous ascent and descent this involves invoke a sense of manipulation and control, of being distanced from the world around one and entering a secret, restricted realm where everything is unknown and unpredictable. The frosted glass and aluminium reception desk and electronic news flash that face one on entry add to this feeling of alienation. They do not welcome. They are harsh, cold, mechanical and impersonal. The building's interior utilises unrefined, hard, neutral materials – red brick, steel, raw concrete, and intentionally crude detailing. It is institutional, industrial, and un-domestic. Its spaces are dungeon-like – dull, gray, sombre, devoid of natural light. The only spaces that are painted are the recreated solitary confinement cells, themselves bleak and sanitised. Natural lighting is kept to a minimum, often through openings located in positions that make it impossible to see out. The passage of time is obscured. Its acoustics are similarly deadened. Audio material is transmitted through overhead speakers that one has to stand directly beneath to hear. Outside of this space, sound is muted and multivalent – a dull, disturbing buzzing and bleeping permeates everywhere. The museum's exhibits are, for the most part, fixed to walls on purposefully crude steel brackets or contained within steel cages. These cages construct a maze of exhibits one moves around and through, claustrophobically en-caged in the exhibition oneself. ... They make one feel that there are unknown, hidden, impending knowledges within them; one enters with anxiety. Senses of alienation, dehumanisation, restriction and control prevail.
>
> (Bremner, this volume)

But all of this – instances of what Noëleen Murray (this volume) terms a 'moment of architectural design' – is also part of an entertainment destination, the improbable creation of the Krok brothers, impresarios and owners of the adjacent Gold Reef City Casino. Here, just across the road, the theme is Johannesburg some 20 years after its founding – a time when the first substantial buildings had been constructed, but it was still enjoying the excitement and adventure of the gold rush. The entrance is through an ornate lobby based on the 1906 Carlton Hotel. Beyond is a large, circular area with the hub based on the Joubert Park kiosk, also dating to 1906. The surrounding space is given over to the gambling tables and slot machines which form a busy public space reminiscent of a market square. The main heritage focus is around the perimeter, where there are three-dimensional replicas of 11 major historic buildings, each marked with a bronze plaque (based on those used by the South African heritage authority), an archival photograph of the original building, and a brief historical summary. This is a sanitised past – a city without exploitation, racism or violence – Johannesburg as a Wild West-frontier illusion of fun, camaraderie and equal opportunity for the bold-hearted. And this, of course, is the message of the casino itself – whoever you are, be bold enough to risk everything for the chance of a fortune and all that will come with it (Hall and Bombardella 2005).

The juxtaposition of these two cities – the devastation of apartheid and the mirage of casino heritage – recall the contradictions inherent in the social construction of space from the city's earliest days: François Valentyn's sense of forbidden fruits in the order of the Garden's grid, the vast social engineering project of apartheid, the tensions in post-apartheid town planning, the paradox of the township tour. Such contradictions, perhaps, propel the utopian tendency to want to start again, to draw a line over past spatial forms. The 1998 book and exhibition, *blank_Architecture, apartheid and after* sought such a new beginning through a set of themes – 'Invasions', 'Violence', 'International Tendency', 'Fortification', 'Promised Land' – and the striking 'visual conceit' of over 1,000 fluorescent tubes suspended from the ceiling, which 'sought to invert the associations of light, from the colonial trope of light in a dark continent, to light which is cruel, implacable, unforgiving' (Shepherd and Murray, this volume). In Njabulo Ndebele's words, this was 'perhaps the most important South African dialogue since the national dialogue that led to the writing of the constitution. This is the dialogue about writing the land. It is a project which affects all of us intimately' (Ndebele, this volume).

And yet, as Nick Shepherd and Noëleen Murray note in their introduction to this volume, *blank_* has had a limited effect on architecture in South Africa since 1998. Perhaps, as they write, this is because the 'disciplinary narrative' of 'just doing good architecture' tends to override a sense of context and response. But perhaps this is also because utopian visions – space without time – are always doomed to be hypothetical rather than realised. Perhaps it is because time always intrudes on space, and because the past, however unpalatable, is always with us.

*

The Dutch East India Company garrison that arrived in Table Bay in 1652 had a definite idea of how a civilised settlement should be laid out. When the company's surveyor was instructed 'to be kept conscientiously at his work of making maps', his reference points were the cities of northern Europe and their heritage of streets and canals, orderly housefronts and social order. Streets at the dusty Cape were named for the new colony (Olifantstraat), but also for the high culture of Amsterdam and Den Hague: Heerenstraat and Heerengracht. When it came to laying out the foundations for a new, stone-built Castle in 1666, the plans recalled longstanding fortifications, emblematic of military power and prestige. This early example of heritage-on-demand was celebrated in the oration that marked the event: 'Augustus' dominion nor conquering Alexander/ Nor Caesar's mighty genius has ever had the glory/ To lay a cornerstone at earth's extremest end!' Thus was the history of the Roman Empire expropriated to give historic depth to this fragile toehold on the continent of Africa (Hall 2006).

Time has been socially constructed ever since. As Shepherd and Murray show, the historical representations of the city can be understood as a series of tropes: 'Cape Dutch' architecture, with its historical allusions to an earlier European baroque, neo-classicism and the architecture of Empire, the tropes of nationalism and apartheid, rediscovering signifiers of European cultural origins and superiority, and the allusions and pretensions of contemporary style, 'a bizarre and ever-increasing array of luxury townhouse complexes built in the ersatz style of Tuscan villages' (Matshikiza, this volume).

Not surprisingly, social constructions of time continue to be contested. Rassool (this volume) explores these cultural workings of heritage, public history and identity formation under conditions of political transition:

> packaged as the recovery of a multicultural South Africa, culture and history were brought together into a timeless zone, a kaleidoscope of frozen ethnic stereotypes. A past–present relationship was established through the gaze on human culture scripted as traditional. But visits to the primitive in the diversity of South Africa were no longer cast as isolated encounters with 'natives in tribal setting'. In the 1990s, they were being framed as encounters with living cultures arranged in ethnically based cultural villages, township tours and village craft projects, all jostling with each other to take their place as the authentic past of the nation's visual splendour. It was expected by emerging cultural and tourism policy frameworks that this living spectacle would take place on an extensive scale, and that each 'community' would participate in a grand national celebration by finding cultural expressions.

Shepherd and Ernsten (this volume) focus in on one contested area, an exhumed burial ground on what was once the shoreline of Table Bay, a liminal zone where slaves and the colony's underclass were buried away from the gridded enclosures of the formal cemeteries. As they show, the conflict around the burial ground – as has so often been the case in similar situations around the world – comprised a thick rope of intertwined discourses, a conflict between the forces of memory and the forces of modernisation, development and urban renewal; a conflict between the forces of civil society and various state agencies and institutions of governance; a dispute over the role of the sciences in post-apartheid society; issues of race and identity, and of local, regional and national concerns and interests. As Shepherd and Ernsten write:

> the surfacing of the buried dead is always experienced as a traumatic moment, as an eruption into the fabric of the present of the past in its most literal and inescapable aspect. But it is also a moment that takes us to our deepest selves and, socially speaking, confronts us with profound energies.

Understanding how time is implicated in space, and how the material world of things is given meaning in these discourses of heritage constitutes a rich field of enquiry, benefiting from different theoretical approaches. Thus Murray (this volume) approaches the city through the eyes of the architect, evoking architectural 'moments', buildings standing as monuments. Meskell, from the standpoint of anthropology, explores how such monumentality works, how the past becomes present and how the past is crucial in forging a viable, potentially healing, future. Meskell's interest is in 'negative heritage', conflictual sites that are mobilised for didactic purposes (District Six, the Apartheid Museum). Such negative heritage, though, may in itself deny the valency of the past, diluting 'the social obligation to engage in more active remembrance.... The monument's inherent exteriority affects the internal experience of individuals' (Meskell, this volume). And Garuba calls up the literary device of memesis in his close study of the Robben Island Museum, the separation between an object and its representation, creating a relationship of disjuncture. Garuba sees this space of disjuncture as the space occupied by the social codes, conventions and interpretive devices that work to create the imaginative correspondence between things. This is the key 'space of narrative, the space where a discourse is constructed to provide the ground of intelligibility' (Garuba, this volume).

*

These explorations of the social construction of space and time show that what might seem at first settled and stable is, on closer examination, unstable and contested. Memory and desire are intertwined in a complex vortex. Sometimes the past is claimed to be closed and desire is the pure yearning of consumerism – the alluring shopfronts in the heritage mall. Elsewhere, the construction of the past is open and challenged, and the yearning is for the recovery of memory. This instability goes to the heart of the concept of the city – an issue taken up by Vanessa Watson, who challenges the fundamentals of the orderly grid and the rules of planning:

> a vast gap exists between the notion of 'proper' communities held by most planners and administrators (grounded in the rationality of Western modernity and development), and the rationality which informs the strategies and tactics of those who are attempting to survive, materially and culturally, in the harsh environment of Africa's cities.
>
> (Watson, this volume)

This is reflected in Dutch architect Rem Koolhaas's quixotic expedition to Lagos, city of 'exuberant existence':

> our first engagement with the city was from a mobile position. Partly out of fear, we stayed in the car. This meant, in essence, that we were preoccupied with the foreground.... Lagos seemed to be a city of burning edges. Hills, entire roads, were paralleled with burning embankments. At first sight, the city had an aura of apocalyptic violence: entire sections of it seemed to be smouldering, as if it were one entire rubbish dump.

But on his third visit, Koolhaas was able to hire the President's helicopter:

> from the air, the apparently burning garbage heap turned out to be, in fact, a village, an urban phenomenon with a highly organised community living on its crust ... what

seemed, at ground level, an accumulation of dysfunctional movements, seemed from above an impressive performance, evidence of how well Lagos might perform if it were the third largest city in the world.

('Fragments of a lecture on Lagos' 2003; cited by Gandy 2005: 40)

Who, then, should be the emblematic pedestrian, walking the desire lines of the colony and postcolony? Here is one story, still to be inscribed in Cape Town's public spaces of names and monuments. One who watched as the Dutch dug out the ditches of their first fortification in 1652 was Krotoa, a Khoi woman of substance. As the garrison sought to trade with the Khoikhoi, Krotoa came to play a pivotal, and complex, role. Inside the garrison, she became 'Eva' – maid to the commander's wife and interpreter. Back on the other side of the frontier, Krotoa was the daughter of a chief. Later, Krotoa married a minor Dutch official, was widowed, and in 1674 died destitute, reviled as a drunkard and prostitute. Nevertheless, Krotoa was a Christian and so was the first to be buried in the new Castle. The company's journalist at the Cape used the opportunity of her death to offer a philosophy. Noting that she had been 'transformed from a female Hottentoo almost into a Netherland woman', the diarist observed that her subsequent debauchery proved that 'nature, however closely and firmly muzzled by imprinted principles, neverthe-less at its own time triumphing over all precepts, again rushes back to its inborn qualities' (quoted by Malherbe 1990: 51). A more fitting epitaph is an extract from Karen Press's evocative narrative poem:

no word came for me from Oedasoa, ever

and so I stayed among those people
became a dutch wife, learned
to speak in long dutch sentences,
became a widow, standing like a wild buck
in the yard of the foreigners

they would not take me in, hottentot woman
nor would they let me run away, they broke my legs

mine are the crippled footprints
worn into the rocks along the harbour wall

the beginning was an exploding sun
I ran dancing into the fire
the end unravelled like an old root,
dry with sorrow, lasting forever

(Press 1990: 66)

Krotoa – the 'woman between' – dared to challenge the authority of the grid. She paid for her audacity in derision and rejection, and her 'crippled footprints' trace a desire line in the landscape. But the promise remains in the fire, in the 'exploding sun', in reaching for something that, by its very nature, can never be grasped and possessed.

REFERENCES

Coetzee, J.M. (1988) *White Writing: On the Culture of Letters in South Africa*, New Haven, CT: Yale University Press.

Coombes, A.E. (2003) *History After Apartheid: Visual Culture and Public Memory in a Democratic South Africa*, London: Duke University Press.

Foucault, M. (1979) *Discipline and Punish: The Birth of the Prison*, New York: Vintage Books.

Gandy, M. (2005) 'Learning from Lagos', *New Left Review* (33): 37–52.

Hall, M. (2000) *An Archaeology of the Modern World*, London: Routledge.

—— (2006) 'Indentity, Memory and Countermemory: The Archaeology of an Urban Landscape', *Journal of Material Culture* 11 (1–2): 189–209.

Hall, M. and Bombardella, P. (2005) 'Las Vegas in Africa', *Journal of Social Archaeology* 5 (1): 5–24.

Malherbe, V.C. (1990) *Krotoa, Called 'Eva': A Woman Between*, Cape Town: Centre for African Studies, University of Cape Town.

Mentzel, O.F. (1919 (1784)) *Life at the Cape in Mid-Eighteenth Century, Being the Biography of Rudolf Siegfried Allemann, Captain of the Military Forces and Commander of the Castle in the Service of the Dutch East India Company at the Cape of Good Hope*, trans. M. Greenlees, Cape Town: Van Riebeeck Society.

Press, K. (1990) *Krotoa's Story*, Cape Town: Buchu Books.

Raven Hart, R. (1971) *Cape of Good Hope 1652–1702: The First Fifty Years of Dutch Colonization as Seen by Callers. 2 Volumes*, Cape Town: Balkema.

Scott, J.C. (1990) *Domination and the Arts of Resistance: Hidden Transcripts*, New Haven, CT: Yale University Press.

Valentyn, F. (1971 (1726)) *Description of the Cape of Good Hope with the Matters Concerning It. Part I*, edited by R. Serton, R. Raven Hart, W.J. de Kock and E.Raidt, Cape Town: Van Riebeeck Society.

—— (1973 (1726)) *Description of the Cape of Good Hope with the Matters Concerning It. Part II*, edited by E. Raidt, Cape Town: Van Riebeeck Society.

Notes

Introduction

1   Architects working in this way include Gwen and Gabriel Fagan, Dirk Visser and others funded by prominent Afrikaner businessmen such as Anton Rupert, who embarked on grand-scale projects such as the restoration of Tulbach, Graaff-Reinet, Stellenbosch and folk projects such as the Klein Plaasie (small farm) Museum and the almost 20-year-long work at the Castle of Good Hope in Cape Town.

2   The Historical Archaeology Research Group (HARG) is based at the University of Cape Town and includes work by Martin Hall, Antonia Malan, Yvonne Brink and others.

3   Papers on the Union Buildings project are in the architectural Baker Collection, at the Department of Manuscripts and Archives, University of Cape Town Libraries.

4   This argument (about the African metropolis) has been the subject of a heated debate in recent issues of *Public Culture* as geographer Michael Watts has taken up Mbembe and Nuttall's arguments of African modernity and accused them of dismissing the empirical work on cities and apartheid (Watts 2005: 182–3). Their response has been that the task at hand is to reposition notions of African modernity in a critique of this literature for 'mainly its lack of comparative depth, the paucity of its theoretical reach, and its overall dependence on political economy' (Mbembe and Nuttall 2005: 198).

Chapter 1: Planning Fictions

1   Mitchell analyses these innovations as the vehicles of a modernist metaphysics that generates the modern experience of meaning as a process of representation (1998: xiii). Mitchell's analysis of world exhibitions and urban planning in colonial Cairo focuses on the 'modernist experience of the real' produced by the generation of what seems an unproblematic distinction between reality and its representation.

2   A key feature of these interventions has been the social and spatial separation of the middle class from 'the poor', and the creation of the private space of the home within which the nuclear family could be nurtured and protected. According to Roger Silverstone (1997: 7; cf. Pile *et al*. 1999: 31), this Euro-American suburban culture was, and continues to be, highly gendered. It is built around an ideology and a reality of women's domestication and confinement to household work and the private domain. Throughout Europe and North America, this suburban culture was buttressed by public policies, state resources and media images that attempted 'to resocialize women into the home, and into the bosom of the nuclear bourgeois family' (Pile *et al*. 1999: 31).

3   See *Community Development Report: Urban Regeneration*, 24 October 2000. The Manenberg zone was identified as 'the worse [sic] off in terms of poverty and dysfunctionality'. The six zones of poverty included SLP (Philippi, Crossroads, Nyanga and Brown's Farm), Manenberg zone (Gugulethu, Hanover Park, Heideveld and Manenberg), Langa, Kewtown, Woodstock/Salt River and Mitchells Plain. The key social indicators for the Manenberg zone, Kewtown, Woodstock/Salt River and Mitchells Plain included 'poor, high crime and dysfunctional'.

4   Sometimes I will use 'CCT officials' to refer to both Devcom and CCT officials. I do this because the Devcom team worked as part of a larger team that included CCT planners and officials from other CCT departments.

5   The city's definition of 'dysfunctional' is based on indicators such as the extraordinarily high levels of criminal and gang violence, tuberculosis, substance abuse, the prevalence of teenage pregnancies and domestic violence.

6   The city's attempt to undermine these community-based gang cultures can be seen as part of a more general process whereby community consciousness is first made through residential differentiation (along class, ethnic and racial lines) and then destroyed in the name of the national interest and capital accumulation (Harvey 1985: 123). As David Harvey notes,

> Community consciousness with all of its parochialisms, once created becomes deeply embedded, and it becomes just as difficult to piece it together in a configuration appropriate to the national interest (as perceived from the standpoint of capital accumulation) as it is to transform it into a class-consciousness antagonistic to the perpetuation of the capitalist order. In order, therefore, to maintain its own dynamic, capitalism is forced to disrupt and destroy what it initially created as part of its own strategy for self-preservation. Communities have to be disrupted by speculative activity, growth must occur, and whole residential neighbourhoods must be transformed to meet the needs of capital accumulation. Herein lie both the contradictions and the potentials for social transformation in urbanization at this stage in our history.
>
> (Harvey 1985: 123)

7   Advocates of both the new public management and the community participation models claim to depart from the 'traditional' public sector model, which is seen to be rule-bound and hierarchical and built around centralised power and authority. During the 1990s, the traditional model of bureaucracy inherited from the apartheid era was vigorously attacked from both the Left and the Right for being wasteful, inefficient, hierarchical and outmoded. In addition, it was seen to be incapable of dealing with complexities, uncertainties and contingencies by virtue of being pre-programmed through inflexible, standardised procedures (Paine 1999). It was within this management policy scenario that the city embarked upon a public–private partnership low-income housing development scheme in Manenberg.

8   In France, during the French Revolution, it was possible to 'liberate individuals' and create a 'new universal citizen' by eliminating all existing identities. According to Manuel Castells, France is probably the only country in the world that has been able to achieve this extermination of identities other than the French identity. For Castells, 'the French model became the most effective model in building the citizen identity, which is an identity which is abstracted from any other historical group except the state, the democratic state' (2000: 8).

9   This was particularly evident in the garment industry where, despite a boom in clothing and textile exports in 2001, the SA Clothing and Textile Workers' Union (Sactwu) reported the loss of an average of 1,400 formal jobs a month. Factory closures in the clothing sector, Cape Town's biggest employer, wreaked havoc for Manenberg women traditionally recruited into the garment industry. In the first ten months of 2001, 19 companies shut their doors, resulting in the loss of 2,249 jobs (*Cape Argus* 29 October 2001).

10   At a Mowbray community policing forum on 14 November 2001, then Provincial Minister of Safety and Security Hennie Bester spoke of the logistical headache the South African police have had to deal with in attempting to fight ordinary criminal activity while having to commit resources to ongoing problems of urban terror, taxi violence, gang drug trafficking and turf wars, criminal syndicates and so on.

11   Manenberg residents interviewed in 2000 by Christoph Haferburg and University of the Western Cape postgraduate students called upon the city to build more houses for residents who had been waiting on housing lists for 10–15 years.

Chapter 3: Remaking Modernism

1   This paper is based on research conducted for a National Research Foundation (NRF)-funded project based in the History Department at the University of the Western Cape, the Project on Public Pasts. The financial support of the NRF towards this research is hereby acknowledged. Opinions expressed in this paper and conclusions arrived at are those of the author and are not necessarily to be attributed to the NRF. Thanks also to Abby Loebenberg for sourcing the images contained in this paper.

2   This regionalism has also been understood in terms of architectural historian and critic Kenneth Frampton's theories of 'Critical Regionalism' which he produced in various forms proposing the idea of architecture that is 'universally aware' yet 'locally rooted'.

3   Lewcock, R. (1963) *Early Nineteenth Century Architecture in South Africa: A Study of the Interaction of Two Cultures 1795–1837*, Cape Town: A.A. Balkema; Fransen, H. and M.A. Cook (1980) *The Old Buildings of the Cape*, Cape Town: A.A. Balkema; Japha, D. and Japha, V. (1992) *The Landscape and Architecture of Montagu 1859–1915*, Occasional Publications Series, University of Cape Town: School of Architecture and Planning; Rennie, J. (1978) *The Buildings of Central Cape Town*, Cape Town: Cape Provincial Institute of Architects.

4   In the most recent project awards by the South African Institute of Architects, the project for La Motte Farm, near Franschhoek in the Cape, by Van der Merwe, Miszewski Architects received an award for 'convert[ing] the barn into the main living areas of a new residence and add[ing] two new wings of accommodation to form a large *werf* space, typical of Cape country estates of the eighteenth century' (Steenkamp *et al.* 2006: 42).

5   The VASSA (Vernacular Architecture Society of South Africa) Journal publishes the efforts made by the Vernacular Architecture Society in this regard.

6   There have been architectural competitions for Freedom Park, Robben Island, Red Location Apartheid Museum, the Constitutional Court and others.

7   The degree of integration of black architects into the professions of planning and architecture remains problematic, but since the 1990s many more students have enrolled and completed degrees in the spatial disciplines and entered practice. A few practitioners have also returned home from exile during apartheid.

8   For example, the Mew Way sports hall in Khayelitsha, near Cape Town, by architects Mike Smuts and Lucien le Grange.

9   See Watson, V. and Turok, I. (2001) 'Divergent Development in South African Cities: Strategic Challenges Facing Cape Town', *Urban Forum* 12 (2): 119–38. Dewar, D. (2001) 'Some Issues in Developing Settlement Policy Alternatives in South Africa', in C. de Wet and R. Fox (eds) *Transforming Settlement in Southern Africa*, Edinburgh: Edinburgh University Press; 208–24.

10   WISER Call for Papers, 'The Townships Now' (Wits) June 2004, H-Net List on South and Southern Africa, 22 April 2004 09:47:58–0400. In June 2004, the Wits Institute for Social and Economic Research (WISER) held a two-day interdisciplinary symposium entitled 'The Townships Now'.

11   The most high-profile example is the N2 Gateway project in Langa near Cape Town.
12   The Hostels to Homes project was managed by engineers Liebenberg and Stander, while the Langa Hostels projects have been converted by Architects Associated.

Chapter 4: Engaging with Difference

1   This extract is from Watson (2004).
2   A national, state-sponsored development programme introduced by the post-apartheid government.
3   Ministry for Provincial Affairs and Constitutional Development (1998: 20): 'the participatory process should not become an obstacle to development ....'
4   Consensus-seeking processes can have an added benefit in that the shared understanding, mutual trust and 'identity-creation' which are built up, linger on as new 'cultural resources' or 'cultural capital' (Healey 1999: 114).

Chapter 6: Memory, Nation Building and the Post-apartheid City

1   This argument is the basis of a semiotic approach to the built environment, for example, Agrest and Gandelsonas (1973), Jencks and Baird (1970).
2   The deaths in detention exhibit in the museum indicates that executions for political crimes against apartheid were at their highest in the 1960s, when apartheid was at its strongest.
3   I say this despite the fact that it is located on former mining land, and uses this to partially structure its narrative.
4   Anthony Appiah (1992) describes the fluid, ambiguous and obscure identities he negotiated growing up in independent Ghana with alternating adherence to Ghana, Asante, development, heritage, democracy and chieftancy. In the days of post-independence nationalism, many shared the meaning of what Ghana was, primarily because it was clear what they were against (British imperialism). However, the Ghana inherited from the British was a range of ecologies, cultures and languages, different religious traditions and notions of property. 'Once the moment of cohesion against the British was over', he argues (1992: 262), 'the symbolic register of national unity was faced with the reality of our differences.' Nkrumah negotiated this through a pan-Africanist vision, strangely disconnected from the Ghanaian state, but functioning as an idea to differentiate between a new us and a new them. This constituted his national appeal. Comparisons with Thabo Mbeki's revisioned pan-Africanism are worth making, but outside the scope of this discussion.
5   Freed apparently visited South Africa three times as advisor during the early stages of the museum's design.
6   This idea was supposed to have been extended, by the installation of a 'deposition studio' for ongoing recordings of museum-goers' testimony but, as far as I know, the studio has never been functional due to lack of funds.
7   In this context, in South Africa, the traditional idea of 'ubuntu' as an appropriate concept around which to mobilise post-apartheid consciousness is often rehearsed.
8   The museum's curatorial staff recently produced a comic, 'Timeliners: Soweto in Flames', to teach young people about the contribution of South African youth in its history. It is aimed at the schoolchildren who visit the museum.
9   Its marketing campaign précised this narrative into 15 neat, sequential, easily consumable parts.

Chapter 8: Memory and the Politics of History in the District Six Museum

1   Staff at the District Six Museum, Cape Town, where I serve as trustee, have provided useful suggestions for this paper.

2   See also Bundy (2000).

3   For a fuller account of the history of the development of 'native villages' and the tourist gaze on South Africa, see Rassool and Witz (1996).

4   See, for example, 'The Land Claim and Submission to the Minister of Land Affairs submitted by The Land Claim Committee, the Southern Kalahari Bushmen', many of whom presently reside at Kagga Kamma, 7 August 1995. See also Rassool (1998).

5   In pursuance of this project, a new tourist guide through Mandela's biography was published in 2000, written by one of the authors of the Legacy Project discussion document. See Callinicos (2000).

6   For an extensive examination of the creation and cultural politics of the District Six Museum, see Rassool and Prosalendis (2001). This discussion draws on and extends insights in this book.

Chapter 9: A Second Life

1   I would like to thank the following people who assisted in various ways and at various stages with this project: Irene Mafune, a former employee of the Robben Island Museum and formerly a masters student at the Centre for African Studies, University of Cape Town, for facilitating my initial contact with the tour guides and arranging my first interviews with them; Richard Whitening for conducting me through the material in the Robben Island Museum Library; Thotane Pecheke who arranged my last one-on-one interview with an ex-prisoner who works on the island and was at one point also a tour guide; Euclides Goncalves, my research assistant, who painstakingly transcribed the interviews/conversations, sometimes from barely audible recordings; Gaby Cherminais and the Robben Island Exhibition Unit for permission to quote from their training manual. Finally, but most importantly, my profound gratitude to all those ex-political prisoners who took time off to speak to me despite their reservations about journalists and researchers either appropriating their stories or distorting them.

2   Perhaps the most famous instance of a sufferer telling the story of his pain over and over again is recorded in Samuel T. Coleridge's poem 'The Rime of the Ancient Mariner'. In this poem, a mariner slays an innocent bird of good omen that had brought good luck and favourable winds to his ship. As a consequence of his act, the winds fail and the ship stalls and, one after the other, all the sailors die. He is the only one that survives; but he only survives because he is condemned to wander the earth and recount the story of his dastardly deed to every stranger that he meets as he journeys through the byways and thoroughfares of the world in an unending act of penance. Like the narratives of the tour guides of Robben Island, the goal is to memorialise the event as a cautionary tale with lessons for the future. The mariner is given a second life, so to speak, that is narratively imbued with meaning and significance only as display of a previous life. However, unlike the tourist-driven narratives of the guides, the ancient mariner in this extended ballad is the guilty party living out his curse in a tale where the lines of innocence and guilt are clearly drawn with no hope of expiation except in death.

3   In this regard, but on a slightly different note and for analogy and comparison, see Davison (1993) and Lindfors (1999).

4   This narrative is largely a condensed version of the 'Robben Island Timeline' compiled by Harriet Deacon, Nigel Penn, André Odendaal and Patricia Davison.

Chapter 10: Social Institutions as 'Places of Memory' and 'Places to Remember'

1 The term 'coloured' population is essentially understood as a classificatory category to describe a social group defined in particular ways under colonialism and apartheid. Over time, the meanings attached to this social category came to shape not only the everyday lives, actions and identities of its 'members' but also the discursive ways in which they reinforced, contested or re-imagined themselves and their place within South African society.

2 Such state institutions include children's homes, orphanages, hostels, schools of industries, places of safety, reformatories, prisons, old age homes and health and social clinics.

3 Anthony Platt noted in 1977 that child-saving in the US was motivated mostly by a middle-class desire to control the dangerous and perishing classes, and to halt the drain on the state imposed by the poor. For a discussion of the US experience, see Platt (1969) and Van Krieken (1986).

4 In his presentation to a committee set up by government in 1943 to investigate the 'skolly menace', a Major Goldby pointed to two articles that appeared in the *Cape Times* on 25 January 1944. He argued that the articles emphasised the nature and pervasiveness of the 'skolly phenomenon'. See Cape Archive (1944).

5 The worsening socio-economic conditions of the coloured population at the Cape in the 1930s attracted considerable attention from liberal white clergymen, university academics and other like-minded individuals. They coordinated their attempts to address social welfare and unemployment issues through bodies like the South African Institute of Race Relations (SAIRR) and the affiliated Joint Council Movement (JCM). Lewis (1987: 154, 171) notes that the Wilcocks Commission was 'in itself set up at the behest of the SAIRR'. In Johannesburg in 1938, members of a municipal investigation also highlighted the 'danger' presented by rural 'immigrants' at that time. Problems associated with rapid urbanisation were essentially linked to the absence of 'mechanisms of civilising'. Senator Rheinallt-Jones (SAIRR 1938: 15) noted in 1938 that 'crimes of violence are not those committed by your town-dwelling, intelligent urban native, but by the untutored, uneducated raw native from the rural areas'.

6 The Coloured Advisory Council was a statutory body established by the Union Government in 1943. The first eight members of the CAC were Dr Gow (President of the African Political Organisation), S. Dollie (pharmacist), M. de Vries, G. Golding, P. Heneke, David van der Ross, S.G. Maurice and F. Hendricks (all members of the Teachers League of South Africa). Many served in various capacities on the boards of school bodies, other state institutions (like the Ottery School of Industries), university administrations and provincial bodies in Cape Town in subsequent years. See Lewis (1987: 173).

7 The Department of Railways and Harbours established a camp at Kimberley in the 1930s for the training of selected coloured men from the better parts of the labouring class that were in the service of that department. This training was to be divided into physical training and vocational training (practical railway work) and lasted for a period of six to 12 months. The establishment of the Centre for Technical Training for coloured ex-soldiers after 1945 was premised on similar goals. See Wilcocks Commission (1938: 22).

8 In an interview with Dr F.A. Bester on 9 May 1996 at his home in Pinelands, he noted that his experience with coloured boys from impoverished surroundings in the period 1948 to 1968 was that they 'were just like that'. He recounted:

> Once, a few boys ran away and we sent a search-team out to find them. We found them deep in an uninhabitable field in Cook se Bos, in the middle of a storm, sheltering under large

cardboards, shivering and cold, and eating 'mif' (mouldy) bread and 'vrot' (rotten) meat. We couldn't figure out why they would give up their warm beds, education, daily and warm meals, and a secure place of shelter. We decided that that was just the way people of that group were.

Bester was principal of the Ottery School of Industries for 20 years in the period 1948 to 1968. For a more historical contextualisation of Bester's comments, see Chisholm (1989: 304–9). Chisholm describes the impact of the works of W.A. Willemse (an Afrikaner academic nationalist) on discussions about urbanity, poverty and race in the late 1930s and early 1940s. Willemse asserted in 1938 that it was not just the home or the family that explained delinquency, but rather the racialised home. In this discourse, crime was reduced to biology and blood. Crime was 'brought on' by mental defectiveness and illiteracy that was supposedly rife mainly among 'non-white' communities. Willemse argued that crime and poverty were caused by 'nationally and religiously mixed homes', mixed marriage homes and homes in which bad discipline was rampant. See Willemse (1932, 1938 and1940).

9 There is also a vast untapped literature in doctoral and masters theses in (mostly) Afrikaans-language universities under apartheid, written by academics and professional practitioners who readily used 'non-white' subjects to test 'scientific hypotheses'. See Badroodien (2001: 309) for a long list of doctoral theses, written predominantly at the University of Stellenbosch and Potchefstroom University, on the coloured population.

10 In a letter dated 14 June 1946 from the Secretary for Social Welfare to the Secretary of Education, it was noted that members of the CAC regularly visited the site to oversee and monitor the progress of social provisioning for coloured ex-soldiers at the Ack-Ack camp. See Pretoria Archives (1946b). See also Cape Archive (1945).

11 Vivian Bickford Smith notes that the urban segregation of race was a key aspect of the early twentieth-century town planning of Cape Town and was considered to be an important characteristic of a modernising society (cited in Salo 2004: 80).

12 An Afrikaner educationalist, W.K.H du Plessis, argued in his doctoral thesis on schools of industries in the 1950s that

> the inability of the coloured teachers to keep order and control made it necessary that white trade instructors sometimes guide them. The Cape *skollie* doesn't seem to want to follow instructions from fellow coloureds. The situation should improve once the coloured personnel gain some experience, once they start improving their qualifications, and once they learn how to control and discipline their own boys [*sic*].
>
> See Du Plessis (1958: 296)

13 An irony of the period after 1960 in Cape Town is that social institutions that predominantly served the needs of the 'submerged coloured' community were much better resourced and financed than institutions servicing the 'less dangerous' sections of the coloured population.

Chapter 11: Living in the Past

1 This paper has benefited from discussions with Geoff Blundell, Martin Hall, David Pearce, Nick Shepherd, Ben Smith and Lindsay Weiss. I would like to thank Jeremy Hollmann for photographing the displays at the Voortrekker Monument. I am also grateful to the National Research Foundation for funding the original visit and to the University of the Witwatersrand, University of Cape Town and University of the Western Cape for hosting my stay in South Africa in 2002. Other funding bodies that have supported this research include the Mellon Foundation, the National Science Foundation and the Institute for Social and Economic Research at Columbia University.

Chapter 12: On a Knife-edge or in the Fray

1   A letter was also faxed to the effect by the MJC, undated, signed by Yagyah Adams.

Chapter 13: Leaving the City

1   This chapter is based on research in the Mbhashe District of the Eastern Cape. The research was generously funded by the National Research Foundation's Project on Public Pasts in the UWC History Department and the Arts Faculty Research Committee at the University of the Western Cape. Neither is responsible for the conclusions of the chapter. Khayalethu Mdudumane, Maurits van Bever Donker and Shanaaz Galant contributed in no small measure to the formulations. As graduate students in my History after Apartheid course at the University of the Western Cape, they also accompanied me to the site of Sarhili's grave. Suren Pillay, Terri Barnes, Crain Soudien, Noëleen Murray, Maurits van Bever Donker, Jill Weintroub and Leslie Witz commented on earlier drafts. I am indebted to James Ferguson (1999) for the title. I am using the terms 'urban' and 'city' interchangeably in this chapter although I believe their overlaps may be subject to problematisation later.

2   Official responses to urban sex workers and the homeless, as two random examples among many, typify such relations.

3   Located along the eastern coast of South Africa, the Eastern Cape province is situated roughly between the Western Cape and KwaZulu-Natal, and encompasses the 'Wild Coast' tourist route.

4   Tyhali was the son of Ngqika, the Rharhabe chief.

5   For an extended commentary on Mqhayi's contribution to the memory of Hintsa and its relation to the discourse of segregation in the 1930s, see Lalu (2003).

6   I am using the notion of 'gesture' as proposed by Agamben (2000: 58), as *mediality* or means without end. Like interruption that figures in Gayatri Spivak's (1990) strategic use of essentialism, gesture places memory and its ends in suspension. Gesture, we might say, is endless.

Chapter 14: The World Below

1   It should be noted that each of these terms is contested and carries a specific history of usage and denotation. Our distaste for the practices of racial classification and our understanding that notions of race are bankrupt as social scientific designations, is weighed against the fact that history forces these terms on us as analytical categories in the present context.

2   Part of the story of Prestwich Street is the story of the dispersal and proliferation of sources. At the same time, the status of these sources is ambiguous, existing as they do in a semi-public domain, or in a public/private domain. We would like to place on record our appreciation of the role played by Antonia Malan, and by André van der Merwe, the Project Facilitator acting for the developer, in allowing substantial access to their personal archives on Prestwich Street. SAHRA, a publicly accountable body, only allowed us to copy material from their archive after protracted negotiations, and after we had signed a release form saying that we would not use the material to 'perjure' the organisation or its representatives.

Chapter 15: Transit Spaces

1   For example, Giorgio de Chirico, *Mystery and Melancholy of a Street*, 1914.

2   *Africity* propounded as a new urban paradigm was perhaps most significantly tabled by Mabogunje, A. (1991) 'A New Paradigm for Urban Development', proceedings of the World Bank Conference on Development Economics, but many have addressed

the question in similar terms, including the coterie of urbanists clustered around Kool-haas: see Belanger *et al.* (2000) 'Lagos' in Koolhaas, R. (ed.), *Mutations*, Barcelona and Bordeaux: ACTAR.

3   The Truth and Reconciliation Commission amounted to a programme of legal, political and psychological springcleaning at the scale of the nation, conceived of as a precursor to renewal. A rhetorical need for 'national transformation' to start with a blank slate drove the commission's hearings in which *apartheid*'s crimes were aired, remembered and sometimes forgiven, with amnesty awarded to confessors where appropriate.

4   This charge is not laid specifically at the feet of the profession, which would presumably defend itself with the counter-claim that 'planning' as a discipline was only 'invented' in Abercrombie's inter-war generation.

5   The two examples cited represent many researchers, artists and practitioners who address this issue.

6   Clearly HIV/AIDS plays a key role in effecting this change in attitudes to the future; to one's 'life chances'.

7   Approximately 25 per cent of South Africa's population live in townships.

Chapter 17: Museums on Cape Town's Township Tours

1   This chapter is based upon research conducted for a National Research Foundation (NRF)-funded project based in the History Department at the University of the Western Cape, the Project on Public Pasts. The financial support of the NRF towards this research is hereby acknowledged. Opinions expressed in this chapter and conclusions arrived at are those of the author and are not necessarily to be attributed to the NRF. I also wish to thank my colleagues, Ciraj Rassool and Gary Minkley, who have worked together with me closely over the years in this research on public history. In this chapter I draw a great deal upon their individual contributions as well as on our collaborative work. Thanks to Duke University Press for permission to republish parts of my paper 'Transforming Museums on Post-apartheid Tourist Routes', which appears in *Museum Frictions: Public Cultures/Global Transformations*, edited by Ivan Karp, Corinne A. Kratz, Lynn Szwaja and Tomás Ybarra-Frausto, with Gustavo Buntinx, Barbara Kirshenblatt-Gimblett and Ciraj Rassool, Durham, NC: Duke University Press, 2006.

2   Noel Solani (2000: 88) makes a very interesting point that, when Robben Island is described in tourist brochures, it is referred to as the 'home' of Nelson Mandela for 18 years, but when other political prisoners are concerned, the term used is incarceration, thus implying that, in effect, Mandela was not a prisoner but had merely moved home.

3   The description of the routes is based on 11 township tours which myself, colleagues and graduate students took between August 2000 and July 2001. In all but one instance, the tours were not specially arranged. We took the same tour as that offered to groups of tourists. We informed the guide that our intention was to find out what histories were being narrated on township tours. Audio-recordings were made of the tours and copies of the tapes are to be deposited at the History Department at UWC and at the District Six Museum.

4   The citation is from the paper by P. Mokaba (1994).

5   There is one exception which I will refer to later.

6   This discussion arises from the difficulties of establishing a community museum in Lwandle. See discussion below and the paper by Mgijima and Buthelezi (2001).

7   In one instance, a tour company has gone so far as to purchase a shebeen for tourists to visit.

8   One important aspect of further research would be to establish whether this is only a feature of Western Cape tours. In Soweto, for instance, the tourist package is presented as a visit to sites of repression and resistance: from the Hector Pieterson Memorial Square, to Vilakazi Street, where the homes of Mandela and Tutu stand, to Morris Isaacson School, where the events of 1976 broke out, and Kliptown, site of the Freedom Charter's adoption. Perhaps Soweto is able to present tours along these routes as it is able to capitalise on its media image as the centre of resistance in South Africa.

Chapter 19: A Renaissance on our Doorstep

1   Originally published in the *Mail & Guardian*, Johannesburg, 3–9 June 2005.

Illustration credits

Index

Figures are indicated by **bold** page numbers and tables by *italic*.